The Great Mental Calculators

THE GREAT
MENTAL CALCULATORS

The Psychology, Methods, and Lives
of Calculating Prodigies,
Past and Present

STEVEN B. SMITH

New York   Columbia University Press   *1983*

Library of Congress Cataloging in Publication Data

Smith, Steven Bradley.
The great mental calculators.

Bibliography: p.
Includes index.
1. Mental calculators.   2. Mathematical ability.
I. Title.
QA28.S65   1983   153   83-8734
ISBN 0-231-05640-0

Columbia University Press
New York   Guildford, Surrey

Clothbound editions of Columbia University Press books are Smyth-sewn and
printed on permanent and durable acid-free paper.

153
5

For my mother,
Martha Smith,
and her sisters:
Margaret Cottingham,
Mary Weaver,
Elizabeth Edghill,
and
Hester Pennington

Contents

FOREWORD

About fifty years ago when I still was a student, I wanted to find out what problems other calculating prodigies could handle. It took hours and hours going from one library to another to find a single article. It was very interesting for me then, Mr. A did a calculation I never did; Mr. B uses a method I never thought of; Mr. C also works with logarithms, etc.

So when on October 10, 1978 Dr. Smith contacted me via the *Guinness Book of Records,* I gave him all the information he wanted and I assured him that a complete book on the great mental calculators was absolutely necessary.

My enthusiasm grew strongly after our meetings and interviews in September 1979, at Brown University, Providence, Rhode Island. First he saw me at work as an afterdinner speaker, then we went out for a drink in a cozy little pub where we continued our interview. About a year later we met again at CERN (the European Organization for Nuclear Research in Geneva).

After a long break Steve sent me the manuscript asking for criticism, but I had no criticism. The book is not a dry story. It reads easily and is good fun. There is only one word for it—excellent. This book is, by far, the best and most complete on the subject that has ever appeared—the definitive work.

I would also like to add a message to the readers, and especially to the young readers. In the last thirty years mankind developed computers. Now, we are becoming the slave of the computer. Big computers are absolutely necessary for higher physics, traveling to the moon, etc. But what with pocket calculators, children are no longer able to multiply 4 × 12. Everybody is born with a memory for numbers, but without use this memory for numbers is lost. In my youth, and even twenty-five years ago, mental arithmetic was used in primary schools. Nowadays this is all finished, unhappily.

I hope that Steve's book will stimulate people, particularly youngsters, to try to improve their memory for numbers and their mental arithmetic. Perhaps then a new calculating prodigy will be discovered.

Wim Klein
The Dutch "living" computer

INTRODUCTORY COMMENT

Dear Reader:

You are about to embark on a journey during which you will view a succession of weird characters—idiots and geniuses, capering freaks and respected academics—who have two things in common: a consuming passion for numbers and the ability to handle them, fondle them, bring them to heel. In different ways all of them can perform miracles of the mind, do what you would never attempt, because you know that you would not succeed. (But perhaps you are mistaken. . . .)

What traits, if any, do they share? What is the common denominator between the country bumpkin Jedediah Buxton, numbly guzzling his free beer while answering dumb questions, and the dazzling, Leonardo da Vinci–like genius of Professor Alexander Aitken? One recurrent trait, childlike wonderment that sets both the moron and the thinker apart from the common run of humanity.

Perhaps this is because many calculating prodigies *were* children; perhaps because numbers, like puppy dogs, befriend those who want to play with them; probably because, as we shall see, numbers are ideal toys.

A key word can be found in the chapter on Zacharias Dase, the "strange calculating genius" (*sonderbare Rechengenie*). *Sonderbar* means "strange, weird, odd." Yes, we are an odd lot, often at odds with the society we were born into. We are out of context. Few, if any, of the people described in this book were socially adapted conformists. Some were slandered and ridiculed. Others, more fortunate, managed to carve out a position for themselves that permitted them to indulge their eccentricities. None of them tried to become one of the crowd, to belong.

For quite a few the early years were a desperate struggle to survive; some were disabled, some were ill-treated, some were persecuted, some were abysmally poor. In their misery, numbers were a warming light that brightened the darkness—a light they would have overlooked in the glaring radiance of high noon.

Mental calculation is a mind-enriching skill that takes some ingenuity to devise but is easy to apply.

A skill that is easy to apply. . . . How easy? Far more difficult than learning to shave or to tie your shoelaces; much easier than learning your mother tongue, a lengthy apprenticeship beset with setbacks and fraught with frustrations mercifully forgotten once you have acquired the basic elements. (Easier in fact than drafting and redrafting and rewriting this introductory note.) Any other calculator will confirm this, if he is honest enough—or ingenuous enough—to admit it. Easy to start with, and getting even easier as you go along. I would not call the green pastures of arithmetic an idiot's delight, but you need no towering IQ to discover the key to numeric bliss. It is ideal relaxation for lazy people. In fact, once you have passed a critical threshold you don't even have to do the work yourself: a little man in your brain—or a tiny Turing machine— takes over and processes the numbers, then lays out the results for your inspection and approval.

It is child's play. Child's play? Yes—numbers are ideal toys. They are far more fascinating than the dreary playthings we were blessed with in the good old days before the advent of electronics: balls of various shapes and sizes; cowboys-and-Indian outfits; dolls and furry animals that were cute and cuddly, but offered little intellectual stimulation. Besides they do not get lost, broken, or stolen. You can handle them at any time, even by night, without turning on the light. Parents cannot interrupt you. And as you go on splitting them, merging them, shaping them, you produce more and more and more of them, each with its own intriguing properties. You discover new relations between them. Each operation has its own charms. Factoring: the neat reduction of what seems like an intractable erratic block into its components, like carving a turkey. Remainder checks: from the simple, straightforward striptease of casting out nines through the slightly more sophisticated elevens test to the esoteric erudition of the thirty-sevens that seem so forbidding at first sight and turn out to be so simple and satisfying. The detective work of root extraction: sniffing around the long string of digits, viewing them from different angles, prying and trying out different remainder checks until the solution falls into your lap. It is like solving a cryptic crossword in a British paper. And oh for the powerful lure of powers with their intricate interlinkages! And the constantly renewed joy of recognizing old friends! No, I wouldn't go as far as some of my fellow calculators and indiscriminately welcome all numbers with open arms: not the horny-handed, rough-and-tough bully 8 or the sinister 64 or the arrogant, smug, self-satisfied 36. But I do admit to a very personal affection for the ingenious, adventurous 26, the magic, versatile 7, the helpful 37, the fatherly, reliable (if somewhat stodgy) 76. . . .

Quite apart from the obvious practical uses of mental arithmetic and the opportunities it offers for making friends, making money, showing off, and giving pleasure, there are far greater intrinsic rewards: mastery, dependability, transformation, insight.

Mastery: there are few areas of knowledge in which you can make faster progress. What was inconceivable yesterday is within your grasp today and an effortless achievement tomorrow. If ever you are plagued by doubts about your capacity to cope, here is a powerful boost to your ego and self-confidence.

Dependability: Life in this irrational world is chaotic, confusing, unfair. The response to love is contempt; backbreaking efforts go unrewarded; results seem to bear little relation to input. In the world of numbers all comes out right in the end. Figures never fail you. No matter which route you take, everything miraculously falls into place. If it doesn't it is your own fault, and alternative techniques will eventually show you where you went wrong and teach you to avoid similar mistakes. Errors are not stumbling blocks, but stepping stones to greater proficiency.

Transformation: Like Mandrake the Magician you wield your wand and your numbers evolve. What moves is more interesting than what is set, just as a kaleidoscope is more riveting than a fixed pattern. And change is particularly impressive if it is gradual and modifies only some of the features. Aaron's parlor trick of changing a bundle of sticks to writhing snakes would have been far less spine-chilling if he had turned the sticks into a polka-dotted hippopotamus. Similarly a plate of spaghetti transformed into a mess of squirming white worms is more graphically gruesome than if they changed into poison ivy or a snarling mountain-lion. Why do so many calculators proceed from left to right? Starting on the right has advantages: what you have once acquired stays put and is not affected by succeeding operations. But starting on the left is more entertaining, as the string of digits snakes forth like a stream of lava, expanding, meandering, twitching, changing shape, then slowly settling down as fresh digits are latched on and slowly congeal in turn.

Insight: Thousands of years ago Pythagoras discovered the poetry and intrinsic truth of figures. There are many different ways of coming closer to God. Lighting candles; fasting, chastity, and other forms of mortification; the Trappist mode of keeping your trap shut; mandalas, mantras, and tantras may work for some. But there are more congenial ways of making God's inscrutable ways easier to scrute. The study of nature is one; the analysis of words and how they grow is another; so are yoga and meditation. And one way of catching a glimpse of the harmony of the Universe and the glory of God is to delve into the mystery of numbers. . . .

But then, if figurework—or figureplay—is so easy, so profitable, so pleasure-giving, so enriching, why aren't there more people who go in for it? Why are prodigies so few and far between?

First, there is the brute power of sheer inertia. For centuries housewives suffered excruciating backaches sweeping floors with primitive handbrooms until one day someone had the brilliant idea of adding a handle.

Then there is the negative conditioning in schools where figurework is not fun but a "discipline." One of the basic pleasures of life is eating. I am sure you agree with this statement. You would not if you were one of the unfortunate geese that are force-fed around the clock to produce delicious pâté de foie gras.

Then again a prerequisite for enjoying numbers—or anything else—is discriminating perception. To a tidy housewife a fingerprint is an anonymous unsightly smudge on a polished surface. To a dactyloscopist each print is unique and tells a different story. To the average person numbers are very much alike: if you have seen one, you have seen them all. The death of 310 people in a disaster is not felt to be 5 times as tragic as a casualty toll of 62; 53 is perceived as very similar to 653 or 219. Before you can begin to enjoy figures you must appreciate their individuality, both in terms of quality (143 versus 144) and quantity (143 versus 1,430 or 14,300).

But even if you are ready to learn, who would teach you? Like driving instructors, calculating prodigies are impatient. If you can solve a problem in 30 seconds, it takes almost inhuman forbearance to spend half an hour to show how you did it. Imagine a chess champion trying to explain his strategy to a beginner who has just learned how chesspieces move. And then: why should a prodigy dissipate the awe-stricken admiration he inspires in his audience by trivializing his skill?

Furthermore many calculators evolved their techniques in early childhood. The methods became an intimate part of themselves. They could not adequately explain or transmit them, if only because there is no appropriate terminology. And so each of us goes about reinventing the wheel, and some of these wheels are mighty bumpy!

There is thus a conspiracy of noncommunication between the spectator who wants to gape and admire, but does not wish to know, and the performer who wants to impress, but does not wish to explain.

But if you were motivated enough to buy this book and if you know the multiplication tables I could teach you how to extract cube roots in less than a week and it would take me a month or two to train you in the fundamentals to become a calculating prodigy. (You can take me up on this offer!)

Let me warn you however: mental calculation is a heady brew and may lead to addiction. Many of the people described in this book became obsessed by figures. You may be doomed to spend sleepless nights squaring, cubing, factoring — not to while away insomnia, but because the numbers will keep such a tight grip on you that they will not allow you to sleep.

And now turn the page and feast your mind on the amazing freak show that is about to unfold before your eyes. If you wish to come and join us, the door is open. Feel free to enter — at your own risk and peril.

Hans Eberstark

ACKNOWLEDGMENTS

There are more people that I would like to thank than space permits, but here are some of the most important.

First of all, I must thank Jo Ann Smith of DJ Computer Services, Wenatchee, Washington, who, for the past two years plus has helped in the struggle to wrestle this monster to the ground. And thanks for the following to the following:

Suggestions: Bruce Chalmers, Amitava Gupta, Michael L. Hines, Barbara Hutmacher MacLean, Gary R. Martins, Garry J. Tee, and Lawrence Weaver.

Translations: Margaret Cottingham, Michael Smith, Yvonne Monsauret.[1]

Editing: Margaret Cottingham, Hester Pennington, Mary Weaver, and Holly Wells.

Calculations: Gary R. Martins and Darrin Smith.

Reference library services: Rita Keller and her colleagues at the Wenatchee Public Library.

Support, moral and other: The staff and management of the Wenatchee World.

Special thanks to Bradley and Elizabeth Smith of Gemini Smith for good advice.

I am much indebted to the calculators who have cooperated through interviews and/or correspondence: Arthur Benjamin, Maurice Dagbert, Shakuntala Devi, Hans Eberstark, R. H. Frost, Wim Klein, and Shyam Marathe.

And finally, deep appreciation to Jeanette Marantos for all sorts of assistance, particularly faith, hope, and charity.

---

[1] Many of the translations are my own and I am responsible in all cases for the final form in which they appear.

Grateful acknowledgment is made to the following for permission to quote excerpts from previously published material: Wim Aarts, "Wereldkampioen Worteltrekken op de NOT 1974," *Teachware*, The Hague, September 1974; A. C. Aitken, "The Art of Mental Calculation, with Demonstrations," *Transactions of the Society of Engineers*, London, 1954; A. C. Aitken, *Gallipoli to the Somme*, Oxford University Press, London, 1954; Fred Barlow, *Mental Prodigies*, Philosophical Library, New York, 1952; J. Bernstein, *The Analytical Engine*, Random House, Inc., New York, copyright © 1963 by J. Bernstein; W. L. Bryan and E. H. Lindley, *On the Psychology of Learning a Life Occupation*, Indiana University Press, Bloomington, 1941; " 'De Flesh' and 'De Steel'," *The Dallas Morning News*, February 6, 1977; A. Gradenwitz, "A Remarkable Arithmetician," *Scientific American*, New York, 1907; *Guinness Book of Records*, UK Edition, Enfield, Middlesex, England, 1982; I. M. L. Hunter, "An Exceptional Talent for Calculative Thinking," *British Journal of Psychology* 53, The British Psychological Society, Leicester, England, 1962; "Obituary of Alexander Craig Aitken," *Proceedings of the Edinburgh Mathematical Society*, vol. 16, ser. 2, p. 2, Edinburgh Mathematical Society, Edinburgh, Scotland, 1968; B. Rimland, "Inside the Mind of the Autistic Savant," reprinted from *Psychology Today*, no. 3, copyright © 1978 by Ziff-Davis Publishing Co., New York; Patricia Sethi, "The Human Computer," *Times of India*, Bombay, February 4, 1978; N. Smith, "Woman's Math Sets World Record," *The Dallas Morning News*, January 26, 1977; S. Ulam, "John von Neumann, 1903–1957," *Bulletin of the American Mathematical Society* (May 1968), vol. 64, no. 3, pt. 2, pp. 1, 38–39, American Mathematical Society, Providence, Rhode Island; J. D. Weinland, "Memory of Salo Finkelstein," *Journal of General Psychology* 39, Provincetown, Mass., 1948; Bayard Webster, "She Does Cube Roots in Her Head," *The New York Times*, November 19, 1976.

Jedediah Buxton

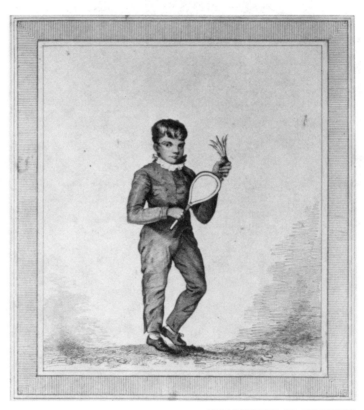

Zerah Colburn

George Parker Bidder

Truman Henry Safford

Jacques Inaudi

Périclès Diamandi

Alexander Craig Aitken

Arthur Griffith

Wim Klein

Shyam Marathe

Shakuntala Devi in 1952

STEVEN B. SMITH

Hans Eberstark

PART ONE

PSYCHOLOGY OF
MENTAL CALCULATION

Introduction

I'm more of a mathematical singer. I use words like most people use numbers.
> —Bob Dylan, in an early television interview

That men should wonder in contemplation of those things which exceed the common limits of experience and observation, is not strange. Such is the narrow compass of our faculties, even in their most perfect state, that it becomes difficult, while we see the outward effect produced, to trace the hidden energy which prompts and impels the inward cause.
> —Zerah Colburn (1833)—calculating prodigy

THIS book was originally intended to be the complete work on the much-neglected topic of calculating prodigies (as great mental calculators are traditionally called).[1] I have subsequently concluded that there will always be documents and calculators beyond my grasp or ken. The book thus falls short of my original goal, for which nothing less than an encyclopedia would ultimately suffice, but it is by far the most comprehensive work on the subject in existence. Further investigation may augment what is presented here, but I do not expect that substantive emendations will be required.

[1] There seems to be a widespread misconception that all calculating prodigies are "idiot savants," mentally retarded people with one outstanding talent seemingly out of keeping with their general abilities. Such people do exist, but most calculating prodigies are far from retarded. For discussion, see chapter 5.

The term "lightning calculator" is also sometimes encountered, but it is not always apt. Some calculating prodigies are characterized by the astonishing size of their mental calculations and not by the speed at which these are conducted.

There are a variety of abilities, including speech and arithmetic, which can be described as typically human. While such "higher-level" mental abilities are arguably not confined to human beings, they are certainly not widely shared by other species (and none approach us in extent and versatility). It is reasonable to suspect, therefore, that there may be a psychological connection between them.

From time to time children appear (and more rarely adults) who have developed an astonishing ability for mental calculation. The thesis of this book is that this ability is based upon the same faculty as that for speech. A corollary is that any child capable of language is a potential calculating prodigy.

If the potential for such calculation is part of the equipment supplied normal children, why is it manifested so infrequently? The answer lies in the area of opportunity and inclination. As children we learn to speak on the basis of myriads of examples, which, except in the most peculiarly deprived of childhoods, we could hardly avoid.

Children, even at play, are typically surrounded by language, but in the case of mental calculation most juvenile activities simply serve as distractions. Thus a condition favoring its development is an isolation, and an absence of other diversion, not often found in the lives of children, particularly today, when mass communication is ubiquitous.

Frank D. Mitchell (himself a calculating prodigy, though curiously limited; see chapter 40) described the typical youthful isolation of mental calculators (1907:98–99):

> Several of the calculators—Mondeux, Mangiamele, Pierini, Inaudi—were shepherd-boys, an occupation which, since it requires an ability to count and affords ample leisure, is peculiarly favorable for practicing calculation; several, again,—Grandmange (born without arms or legs), Safford, Pierini, the present writer,—were sick or otherwise incapacitated for active play to a greater or less extent, and thus enjoyed an equally good opportunity to practice calculation. Fuller and Buxton, on the other hand, whether precocious or not, were men of such limited intelligence that they could comprehend scarcely anything, either theoretical or practical, more complex than counting; and their purely manual occupations left their minds free to carry on almost without limit their slow and laborious calculations.

Alexander Craig Aitken, a distinguished twentieth-century mathematician, and one of the greatest mental calculators in history, said of his youth in New Zealand (1954:301): "I grew up in a remote part of the

Empire, before the days of radio, when even the telephone, that modern necessity but chief among the interrupters of thought, was a rarity."

Of course, physical or psychological isolation alone is not sufficient to produce a calculating prodigy; the child's interest must for some reason be attracted to calculation, and it is rare for a child to pursue interests not shared by his peers. If mental calculation were even as popular as, say, surfing, we would have calculating prodigies in abundance.

Children need friends for amusement and companionship. They often devise imaginary friends to keep them company when flesh and blood friends are absent. Calculating prodigies have made numbers their friends.

George Parker Bidder, a great mental calculator and one of the finest civil engineers of the nineteenth century, wrote of learning to count, first by ones, then by tens (1856:258): "This may appear to you a simple process, but I attach the utmost importance to it, because it made me perfectly familiar with numbers up to 100; they became as it were my friends, and I knew all their relations and acquaintances."

Gradenwitz (1907:93) wrote of Gottfried Rückle, a German mathematician and calculating prodigy: "Numbers, in his own words, are his passion, figures are his best friends."

Wim Klein, a Dutchman and perhaps the world's greatest living mental calculator, told me:[2] "Numbers are friends for me, more or less. It doesn't mean the same for you, does it, 3,844? For you it's just a three and an eight and a four and a four. But I say, 'Hi, 62 squared.' "

Shyam Marathe, a contemporary calculator from India, says: "When I say that numbers are my friends, I mean that I have some time in the past dealt with that particular number in a variety of ways, and on many occasions I have found new and fascinating qualities hidden in that number. In this way I remember numbers, and my repertoire of such numbers is very large. So, if in a calculation I come across a known number I immediately look to him as a friend."

Calculating prodigies themselves remark that their abilities derive from interest and not from some special faculty. Bidder, for example, writes (1856:252): "I have, for many years, entertained a strong conviction, that mental arithmetic can be taught, as easily, if not even with greater facility, than ordinary arithmetic. . . ." Or, as Mitchell says (1907:99): "Mathematical precocity, then, stands in a class by itself, as a natural result of the simplicity and isolation of mental arithmetic. There is noth-

[2] Quotations not otherwise attributed are based on personal interviews.

ing wonderful or incredible about it." In a paraphrase of Aitken's remarks following his presentation to the London Society of Engineers we find (Aitken 1954:307): "He understood the question to be whether the ability was different in degree or kind. He thought it was different only in degree. He had heard of calculators and had got to know them. . . . They were not so very remarkable."

Juggling is an activity having some similarities. Any sufficiently diligent nonhandicapped person can learn to juggle, but the skill is actually acquired by only a handful of highly motivated individuals. If the analogy were more exact, juggling would be learned only by children who, though never exposed to it, discovered it on their own.[3] Under such negative circumstances, that calculating prodigies exist at all is testimony to the native human affinity for calculation.

---

[3] I am also ignoring the fact that juggling does not represent a higher-order mental ability.

Chapter One

Imagining Numbers

THERE are two sorts of calculating prodigies—those who mentally "see" numbers and those who "hear" them. The former are called "visual," and the latter "auditory," or "auditory-motor" (from the movement of the lips that frequently accompanies calculation).

Until Alfred Binet's (1894) study of Jacques Inaudi and Périclès Diamandi (the former an auditory calculator and the latter a visual one), it was assumed that all calculating prodigies were of the visual type. Because of this belief Binet questioned Inaudi carefully about the possible presence of visual images in his calculations, to which Inaudi responded (Binet 1894:64): "I hear numbers . . . and it is the ear that retains them; I hear them resound in my ear, in the way I pronounce them, with the sound of my own voice, and this interior audition stays with me a good part of the day."

Some time later, in answer to a question by Binet's collaborator, Charcot, Inaudi said (Binet 1894:64): "Sight doesn't help me at all; I don't see numbers. I will even say that I have much more difficulty recalling numbers which are given to me in writing than those which are spoken to me. I feel very ill at ease in the first case. I don't like to write numbers myself at all; writing would not help me remember them. I much prefer to hear them."

To Binet's persistent inquiries, Inaudi finally said in exasperation (Binet 1894:65): "I am asked . . . if I see numbers: how could I see them, since it was barely four years ago that I learned them and I calculated mentally long before that time?"[1]

Only in one minor way did Inaudi's visual memory come into play in

---

[1] Inaudi did not learn to read and write numbers until he was 20.

connection with his calculations. He said that he could recall fairly well the location of a spectator who had given him a particular number.

In the case of past calculators we often have no direct statements about how they imagined numbers, but there are tendencies typical of visual and auditory prodigies which, if sufficient data are available, usually make classification easy.

The characteristics typical of auditory calculators are:

1. Some sort of verbalizing while calculating—speaking aloud, muttering, or moving the lips. This is often accompanied by other motor activities—exaggerated gestures, head-wagging, pacing, and the like.

2. Self-taught left-to-right methods of calculation (see chapter 10).

3. Precocity (most began to calculate before learning to read and write numbers).

Auditory Calculators

Inaudi was a typical auditory calculator. Binet noticed that his lips moved while calculating, and that he sometimes muttered numbers loudly enough to be heard for several meters. Where Binet had Inaudi calculate while singing a vowel, which inhibited his articulation, the time required to do calculations increased two- or threefold (Binet 1894:68).

Inaudi also displayed some of the nervous mannerisms common to auditory calculators (Binet 1894:37): "During the calculations, he makes various gestures, tics without importance and, moreover, very variable. . . ."

All Inaudi's calculations were carried out from left to right, including subtraction, at which he was particularly expert.

E. W. Scripture, in his 1891 paper "Arithmetical Prodigies," the first general work on calculating prodigies, mistakenly represents the great nineteenth-century child calculators, Zerah Colburn and George Parker Bidder, as visualizing their calculations, and he assumed that such was the case with other calculating prodigies. Binet, although he was the first to uncover an auditory calculator, did not challenge Scripture's conclusion that earlier calculators were visual.

Frank D. Mitchell, in his 1907 paper "Mathematical Prodigies," questions Scripture's assumptions and concludes that Colburn and Bidder were auditory calculators.

Scripture pronounced Colburn a visual calculator on the basis of a statement in the *New-York Medical and Philosophical Journal and Review* by Professor MacNeven (1811:22): "He has never been at school, and neither reads nor writes. It cannot be said of him that his talents are merely premature, they are altogether extraordinary, and would be no less surprising at the age of five and twenty than at seven.[2] On inquiring how he performed those calculations, he said he saw them quite plain before him."

Apparently it did not occur to Scripture to reflect on what a statement like this might mean in the case of a 6-year-old child who knew nothing of written arithmetic. The "seeing" to which Colburn referred has no more visual content than the phrase, "I see what you mean."

Colburn had all the characteristics of auditory calculators. His calculating ability became evident shortly before he was 6, but it must have been some time developing before that. Of his method of multiplication, he wrote in his *Memoir* (1833:189): "This method was made known at Birmingham, in the Spring of 1816; its peculiarity consists in beginning at the left hand, disposing first of the higher numerals, then the next highest; and so on to the end."

The account of Colburn in the *Annual Register* (1812:309) alludes to his moving his lips while calculating. Furthermore, he was very particular about the verbal form of questions posed to him (MacNeven 1811:20): "When the questions were propounded with the thousands and hundreds by themselves; as, two thousand four hundred and one, or five thousand three hundred and twenty nine, the boy would impatiently cry out, put them in hundreds, that is, what number multiplied by itself will produce *fifty three hundred* and twenty-nine, &c."

Colburn also sometimes spoke while calculating (MacNeven 1811:20):

"*Ques.* What will 6 multiplied by itself 6 times produce?

"This sum he worked aloud . . . , as fast as he could repeat the words: 6 times 6 is 36; 6 times 36 is 216; 6 times 216 is 1296; 6 times 1296 is 7776; 6 times 7776 is 46656; and 6 times 46656 is 279936."

Colburn also seems to have been given to nervous gesturing, at least early in his calculating career (MacNeven 1811:22): "His movements are precipitate, and he is incessantly active." Colburn (1833:173) remarked in his *Memoir:*

Since the author commenced writing this book, he has met with some gentlemen who saw him when quite a child, who have mentioned a circumstance, of which, if it ever existed, he has no collection. It was in relation to

[2] Colburn was still 6 when MacNeven saw him.

his personal appearance, when engaged in studying out the answer to a question; — that his body immediately assumed certain contortions, as if he were affected with what is called St. Vitus's dance, which continued until he obtained the result. As he does not recollect that this circumstance has ever been mentioned to him by others, during the period in question, he is not prepared to give any account of the cause of such apparent nervous affection. That it was the case, he is not prepared to deny; he is not conscious of ever feeling such mental fatigue as should produce such corporeal distortion. Perhaps it might have been owing to nothing more than mere childish motions. He is at a loss to account for the silence of others in relation to this, if it actually proceeded from the nerves.

In the case of George Parker Bidder, Scripture wrongly attributes to him a statement by his son (of the same name), who was an able mental calculator, though not in the same class as his father. Bidder, Jr. wrote to the *Spectator* (December 28, 1878): "If I perform a sum mentally, it always proceeds in a visible form in my mind; indeed, I can conceive no other way possible of doing mental arithmetic."

Even so, we must conclude either that Bidder, Sr. was a visual calculator, or that the younger Bidder was not familiar with his father's methods of calculations. In fact, the latter is the case. In the same letter, Bidder, Jr. writes of his father: "In multiplication his process was simply cross multiplication, so as to get the answer figure by figure." Though he refers to his father's talk before the Society of Engineers, he does not seem to be familiar with its contents, in which Bidder (Sr.) wrote (1856:260): "in mental arithmetic you begin at the left hand extremity, and you conclude at the unit. . . ." This is not cross multiplication.

We may reasonably presume that cross multiplication was the technique employed by the younger Bidder. This technique is characteristic of visual prodigies; his father's left-to-right method is, as already noted, typical of auditory prodigies. (For details of these calculating methods, see chapter 10).

Furthermore, Bidder, Sr. learned to calculate before learning to read and write numbers, a fact on which he placed great stress in his talk before the Society of Engineers (Bidder 1856:256–57): "The reason for my obtaining the peculiar power of dealing with numbers may be attributed to the fact, that I understood the value of numbers before I knew the symbolical figures. I learned to calculate before I could read, and therefore long before I knew one figure from another. In consequence of this, the numbers have always had a significance and a meaning to me very different to that which figures convey to children in general."

In his rather full account, he makes no mention of visual imaging, as one would expect were this his method.

Richard A. Proctor suggested, on the basis of personal experience, that calculating prodigies achieve their results by visualizing numbers as patterns of dots (1875:162–63):

> the writer used formerly to possess, though in a slight degree only, a power of finding divisors, products, and so on, which—*unlike ordinary skill in calculation*—required only to be expanded to effect what Colburn effected. It was, in point of fact, simply the power of picturing a number (not the written number, but so many 'things'), and changes in the number, corresponding to division or multiplication as the case might be. Thus the number 24 would be presented as two columns of dots each containing ten, and one column containing four on the right of the columns of ten. If this number were to be multiplied by three, all that was necessary was to picture three sets of dots like that just described; then to conceive the imperfect columns brought together on the right, giving six columns of ten and three columns each of four dots; and these three gave at once (by heaping them up properly) another column of ten with two over: in all seven columns of ten and one column of two,—that is, seven-two. This takes long in writing, but, as pictured in the mind's eye, the three sets representing 24 formed themselves into the single set representing 72 in the twinkling of an eye (if the mind's eye can be imagined twinkling).

A similar technique was used in dividing.

If any of the prodigies calculated in this way one would expect it to be Bidder, who taught himself the multiplication tables by arranging shot in rectangles, and proposed that as the best method of introducing all children to multiplication (chapter 9). But Proctor was forced to admit in a subsequent paper, on the basis of statements by Bidder's son (Proctor 1879:460), "that in Bidder's case that theory cannot possibly be maintained."[3] He continued to account for Colburn's feats by his "dot" theory, unaware that Colburn's methods for basic arithmetic operations were identical to Bidder's. No mental calculators of note have acknowledged the dot method, and it seems unlikely that it could be extended to calculations involving large numbers.

Neither Jedediah Buxton, an eighteenth-century mentally retarded farm laborer, nor Thomas Fuller, a Virginia slave, ever learned written numbers. Buxton multiplied from left to right, though in a peculiarly primi-

---

[3] As previously noted, Bidder's son erred in his description of his father's method of multiplication, but the actual method is no less inconsistent with Proctor's "dot" theory.

tive way. Instead of multiplying by a hundred directly, for example, he would multiply first by 5 and then by 20. Buxton also devised new names for large numbers. He called 10^{18} "tribes" and 10^{39} "cramps." Nothing is known of Fuller's methods.

Henri Mondeux, a nineteenth-century calculator who was mentally disturbed if not retarded, began to calculate long before learning to read and write numbers. (It is not clear that he ever learned to deal effectively with written numbers or words.) He too was a left-to-right calculator.

Truman Harry Safford, a well-known nineteenth-century astronomer, spoke and went through a great many nervous contortions while calculating, according to observations made when he was 10 (*Chambers's Edinburgh Journal* 1847:266): "He flew around the room like a top, pulled his pantaloons over the top of his boots, bit his hand, rolled his eyes in their sockets, sometimes smiling and talking, and then seeming to be in agony. . . ."

Whether he preferred a verbal presentation of problems is not known, but he was not disturbed by it: "And here I will remark, that I had only to read the sum to him once. He did not care to see it, but only to hear it announced once no matter how long." He also multiplied from left to right: "And what was still more wonderful, he began to multiply at the left hand, and to bring out the answer from left to right. . . ."

Frank D. Mitchell, of the Psychological Seminary of Cornell University, was the author of "Mathematical Prodigies" (1907), to my mind the best work on calculating prodigies (despite the title—calculating prodigies do not necessarily have any talent for true mathematics). He was also a calculating prodigy of sorts, though quite limited, since he confined his attention almost exclusively to the last two digits of numbers, particularly powers and roots (e.g., What are the last two digits of the 17th power of 76?).

Mitchell described his numerical imagination (1907:94–95):

> Before closing this part of the paper, the writer may say a few words about his memory type. He learned to count orally, and his calculations began at once, without further aid; he cannot remember ever counting on his fingers, using pebbles, or the like; and even when he learned to make written figures later on, they never came to be associated with his mental calculations, which remained strictly auditory (auditory-motor) throughout. Ordinarily, the motor element is almost entirely absent; when the calculations remain in the familiar fields already described, they are accompanied by no perceptible innervation of the muscles of speech. When he attempts unpracticed feats, however, such as complete 3-figure multiplications, the tendency to pronounce some or all of the figures is marked.

But while the writer's type is unquestionably auditory in calculation, the presence of written figures is not a hindrance to him, as it is to Inaudi. On the contrary, if the numbers involved are at all large, — say a 9-figure number whose cube root is to be found, — the presence of the number on a sheet of paper before him is a distinct aid, saving a considerable effort of memory, and greatly facilitating such tests as casting out the 9's.

Ugo Zaneboni was a visual calculator, although Mitchell (1907:122) noted: "It is not at all clear, however, to just what extent he used visual images in his mental calculation proper, as distinguished from figure-memory proper; and in the experiments of Guicciardi and Ferrari there are some indications which clearly show a leaning in the auditory-motor direction."

The contemporary Dutch calculator Wim Klein says, "I'm an audible. I hear numbers in my own voice—also in my own language." Klein mutters constantly while calculating; he paces and gestures, shaking his hand as though trying to get rid of a piece of flypaper stuck to it.[4]

But Klein is not a typical auditory calculator in certain respects. Perhaps this stems from the fact that he took up mental calculation at 8 or 9, after learning written numbers. Like visual prodigies he cross-multiplies, rather than calculating from left to right. (He multiplies two digits at a time, the only calculator known to have done so.) And unlike Inaudi, the classic example of an auditory calculator, Klein finds it advantageous to work with the problem in view. Unless one is confused by written numbers, it is an advantage to the memory to see a problem while solving it. Cross multiplication is also particularly advantageous if the calculator writes out the answer from right to left as it is obtained, as does Klein, since, once a digit of the answer is obtained, it need not be remembered (see chapter 10).

The American calculator and magician, Arthur Benjamin, is auditory. He multiplies left to right and was hyperactive as a child. Although his movements are relatively subdued in performing, he says, "I certainly couldn't just stand still completely."

Visual Calculators

Visual calculators fall into two categories—those who "see" numbers in their own handwriting (just as Inaudi always "heard" numbers in his

[4] A Dutch friend of Klein's says that when Klein is engaged in a long and difficult calculation, such as extracting the 13th root of a hundred-digit number, a good part of his muttering consists of swearing.

own voice), and those who conjure up a more or less accurate mental image of the figures as they were written when presented to the calculator. In the first group are Périclès Diamandi and Salo Finkelstein, and in the second group are Gottfried Rückle, Maurice Dagbert, Shyam Marathe, and Mlle Osaka. (Nothing is known of the way in which Bidder, Jr. visualized numbers.)

Binet (1894) reported that Diamandi visualized numbers and other objects (e.g., horses, dogs) in an empty space surrounded by grayish masses (apparently something like clouds). Though the numbers always appeared to him in his own handwriting, the form of presentation was not without effect. When numbers were presented to him on a blackboard, he recalled them as white against a black background. Numbers shown in various colors could be recalled with the appropriate color, though the process of memorization took longer. Diamandi also volunteered the information that it was easiest for him to first memorize the numbers without bothering about the colors and then to associate the colors with the numbers.

When they first met, Diamandi gave Binet a large sheet of paper on which were written 2,000 digits in rows and columns (Binet 1894:119). Diamandi was asked whether he could visualize the whole table at once. He replied that the numbers were in a grayish fog until he concentrated on some particular place in the table—then the numbers around that place became clear. Diamandi's visual imagining of numbers was not "photographic," in that he altered the presented image in the process of memorizing it, but the question of whether his created image was qualitatively comparable to a photograph remained.

Binet was able to show that it was not, since Diamandi did not have equally direct access to all parts of the image. If one can recall a square of digits as though it were a photograph, then there should be no more difficulty in calling out the digits in columns than there is in calling off the rows. But this was not the case with Diamandi. When called upon to recite a table in columns from right to left, he made many errors and it took him three times as long as it took him to correctly recite the numbers in rows.

Binet (1894:142) asked him to memorize a somewhat asymmetric table (table 1.1) which contains a total of 92 digits. The blanks were left to make vertical recall more difficult. He was given the table on Thursday and returned to recite it on Saturday. He first recited it in left-to-right rows, from top to bottom (the order in which he had learned it), which required 64 seconds. Then he was asked to give the table in descending columns from right to left. He made numerous errors and was forced to

TABLE 1.1
Table Memorized by Diamandi

	325	824	632	859
	462		385	629
45	647	625	863	331
	589	817	730	012
		638	849	237
539	826	666	534	129
	394		318	
694	332	499	001	836

Source: Binet 1894:142.

begin over several times. The time required to go all the way through without serious error was 168 seconds—the time nearly tripled.

Mitchell (1907:120) suggests that visual calculators should have an intrinsic advantage in reciting numbers backward. In spite of the plausibility of this idea, it does not seem to be so. Several auditory calculators, including Buxton, Inaudi, and Klein, are known to have been adept at repeating numbers backwards. Nevertheless, visualizing is helpful in calling off numbers in more unusual orders (that is, other than forward or backward). Table 1.2 compares the times of Diamandi and Inaudi for reciting a square of 25 digits (Binet 1894:147–48). As can be seen, apart from recitation in rows as numbers,[5] Diamandi was much faster.

It is evident that though Inaudi was quicker at memorizing a square of 25 digits than Diamandi, he was markedy slower at reciting them in any order other than left to right as numbers. To some extent, at least, this inferiority must be attributed to the auditory nature of his memory. For example, to repeat the numbers in ascending columns, right to left, he was guided by the positional value of the digits—he would take first the units digit of each number top to bottom, then the tens, and so on.

Binet duplicated the experiment with himself as subject, and found that, while he was slower in recitation than Diamandi, he was faster than Inaudi.

Gradenwitz (1907:93) wrote of the mathematician Rückle:

A remarkable fact is that the capacity of *visual* and *auditive* perception is alike developed in Dr. Rückle; that is to say, he is able to retain both the figures he sees and those he hears. However, the most important base of his achievements is the power of visual perception, acoustical perception being

[5] This means reciting each row as a number, rather than digit by digit; e.g., fifty-three thousand, nine hundred fourteen.

TABLE 1.2

Times Required to Repeat 25 Memorized Digits in Various Orders

	Diamandi	Inaudi
Time necessary to learn 25 digits	180 sec.	45 sec.
Time necessary to repeat these digits, left to right	9 sec.	19 sec.
Time necessary to repeat these as five-digit numbers, left to right	9 sec.	7 sec.
Time necessary to repeat a square table of 25 digits by descending columns	35 sec.	60 sec.
Time necessary to repeat a square table of 25 digits by ascending columns, right to left	36 sec.	96 sec.
Time necessary to repeat a square table following a spiral line (see below left)	36 sec.	80 sec.
Time necessary to repeat a square following parallel line, across the table diagonally (below right)	53 sec.	168 sec.

```
→  5—3—9—1—4
               |
   2—7—3—9  8
   |      |   |
   4  2—6 5  9  ↓
   |  |   |   |
   3  5—2—8  1
   |
   8—3—4—7—2
```

```
  \  \  \  \  \
  5  3  9  1  4
  \  \  \  \  \   ↗
  2  7  3  9  8
  \  \  \  \  \
  4  2  6  5  9
  \  \  \  \  \
  3  5  2  8  1
  \  \  \  \  \
  8  3  4  7  2
```

Source: Binet 1894:147–48.

only a transitory phase to the optical fixing of the material. Whenever he hears a number spoken, he immediately visualizes it and so to say photographs it on his brain.

Rückle memorized numbers just as they were presented to him, including the color, if colored chalk was used. When memorizing dictated numbers, however, he saw them in his own handwriting (Müller 1911).

Mlle Osaka, the stage name of an apparently retarded French calculator, said that she saw numbers as though written "in white upon a blackboard," and that they were "more legible than the real ones" (Tocquet n.d.:29). Whether she saw numbers in her own handwriting is not discussed in Tocquet's *The Magic of Numbers,* the only account of her I have seen. In her performances, however, she accepted numbers dictated to her, never looking at the blackboard, so she could hardly have seen them as written there.

Salo Finkelstein, a Polish calculator of the 1930s, also saw numbers in his own handwriting regardless of how they were presented to him (Bousfield and Barry 1933:355). The numbers appeared to him as though written on a freshly washed blackboard, 5 to 7 cm. in height, and 35 to 40 cm. from his eyes. Only about six digits at a time were clear, and Finkelstein, like Diamandi, had a definite preference for horizontal arrangement. He could, however, memorize a square of 25 digits at a rate of about 2 seconds per digit and call off the numbers in the square in any order desired. This is about the same as Inaudi's learning time and three times as fast as Diamandi's. Generally the color of the digits presented to Finkelstein was immaterial; he visualized the numbers achromatically in his own handwriting. But in the case of yellow, he reported that the numbers were tinged with yellow and resembled the original digits. This he found distinctly unpleasant.

If the projection ground was moved away from him the numbers appeared to grow smaller, just as they would if actually written on that surface.[6] He preferred a homogeneous gray projection ground, corresponding to retinal gray in brightness. He could also obtain images with his eyes closed, but he preferred to work with his eyes wide open as it helped him concentrate (Weinland 1948:255).

The East Indian calculator Shyam Marathe visualizes numbers from a blackboard more or less as they are written, though in performances, at least, the writing is his own. He told me that at a demonstration he gave at the Rand Corporation, he ran into trouble because, running out of space at the bottom of the board, he wrote the numbers quite small and later he had difficulty "seeing" them. Marathe also finds it difficult to calculate unless his eyes are open. He said: "I am a visual calculator. How can I see numbers with my eyes closed?"

In the process of calculating, numbers not previously viewed must be imagined. In this case Marathe reported, the digits were imagined in his own hand, "or as an ordinary person would write them."

[6]This is quite startling, and reminiscent of the results of Binet's experiments in hypnotic hallucination, in which he reported (1894:64) that a subject hypnotized to see a tree with a bird on it will see tree and bird mysteriously much closer when opera glasses are suddenly placed before the eyes, but only if the glasses have been properly adjusted for the patient's vision. Many similar effects were obtained with hallucinations, such as causing the image to appear double by pressing upon one of the eyes.

Some visual calculators use auditory methods to retain numbers while they are forming visual images. (They do not, however, mutter while calculating or writing out memorized numbers.) In memorizing written numbers, Diamandi would glance at the paper and mutter some numbers, repeating the operations until all the numbers were memorized.

Müller observed that while Rückle's mental calculations were visual, if he was concerned about forgetting, he would repeat the numbers to himself. This is particularly remarkable in view of the fact that Rückle's number images were essentially duplicates of the originals.

Other visual calculators, like Finkelstein and Marathe, seem to have no verbal component in memorizing numbers.

Whether Zacharias Dase, a nineteenth-century compiler of numerical tables, was an auditory or visual calculator cannot be established with certainty, but the available evidence suggests that he was visual. Schumacher notes that on one occasion, when multiplying two six-digit numbers, Dase wrote down some intermediate results (Gauss and Schumacher 1861). This is not decisive evidence, however, since writing down intermediate results can be helpful, even to an auditory calculator.

A more telling piece of evidence is that Dase was able to glance at a number for about a second and then call it off forward and backward. Since auditory calculators usually repeat numbers to fix them in their minds, this suggests that Dase was visual.

Dase also had a genius for rapid counting. He liked to total the books in the library of a new acquaintance. He could count at a glance a handful of peas tossed on the table, the spots on a group of dominoes, or the letters in a line of print.

In 1945 Maurice Dagbert appeared before the French Academy of Sciences (Fayet et al. 1945; portions of the report are included in Tocquet n.d.:32–33 and Barlow 1952:58–59). The academy report on his performance revealed (Tocquet n.d.:32): "M. Dagbert can, with absolute accuracy, represent the figures to himself as if they were written in white on a blackboard. His mental pictures are less clear if the figures are red on a blue background, and even less clear with yellow figures on a green background."

It seems that when Dagbert can see the blackboard on which the figures are written, he recalls the numbers exactly as written there. Barlow (1952:62) quotes de Cressac:

All the calculations made by this performer are written in sequence on a blackboard. As soon as the board is full of figures, the subject repeats everything by heart and without error—but on one condition—the board thus prepared must always be perfectly clear and plain to his mental vision. If a figure is badly written: if a smudge of chalk has been incompletely rubbed out: if a sign has been added out of place, the whole marvellous mechanism of his memory falls to pieces. In fact, during the mnemonic process, the subject 'sees', so he tells us, the board with all its details and faults. If the figures have been well and clearly written, the recall is perfect but, otherwise, the contrary is the case.

Hans Eberstark, a simultaneous translator, visualizes numbers in his calculations, but uses an essentially auditory method to memorize numbers. Digits represent for him sounds, which he can then recite. By this means he has to date memorized something over 11,000 places of pi. He says: "This is like seeing Russian words in the Cyrillic script, or Greek words in the Greek script, or Japanese words in the syllabic katakana script. The only difference is that I memorize these words and the script is the numeric script.

"But I memorize numbers directly. To me, if I see 64,822, it is pronounced *pfoon*. I don't have to think of spellings like *p-f-u-n* or *p-f-o-o-n*. To me *pfoon* is spelled 64,822.

"I convert figures into words. These are like words in a new language. They sound like words in other languages that I know, so what I remember is something that is similar to this word—a concept—and I remember the divergence from the representation of this concept in another language.

"For example, for 64,822, *pfoon,* I would think of the German 'pfund,' meaning 'pound.' It's like memorizing a dialect version. Suppose there was a dialect in which the word 'clever' was pronounced *clay-vuh*. You think of 'clever'; on the other hand you think of the realization *clay-vuh* instead of 'clever.' You remember the two.

"This is the first part. What I actually deal with is syllables, words, even though these words do not make sense, primarily. I make them make sense by thinking of similar sound patterns.

"Secondly, there is motivation. What interests me in multiplying figures is seeing what sort of a sound comes out. If I multiply two five-digit numbers I get a nine- or ten-digit number that would have a certain pronunciation. This means that I would generate a word myself and then I could see what this word comes out as."

For details of Eberstark's mnemonic system, see chapter 6.

Other Types of Calculators

Sensory imagination in calculation is not limited to sight and sound. There is even a case of a "tactile" calculator. Tocquet (n.d.:25) wrote of Louis Fleury:

> He said that he "felt the outlines of imaginary cubarithms passing beneath his fingers," that is to say the embossed counting symbols used by blind people. "When he was carrying out an operation," wrote Dr. Desruelles, who studied Fleury at the asylum at Armentières, "his fingers moved with extreme rapidity. With the right hand he grasped the fingers of the left hand one after another; one represented hundreds, another tens, a third units. He moved his fingers feverishly over the lapel of his jacket and it was curious to watch him using these tactile images to obtain sensations corresponding to those he would have had in touching cubarithms."

The case of Alexander Craig Aitken, an outstanding twentieth-century mathematician, is also exceptional. He did not engage in mental calculation until he was thirteen, and it was mental algebra, rather than mental arithmetic, that excited his interest. Furthermore, his calculations seem to have been predominantly neither visual nor auditory (Aitken 1954:302):

> I myself can visualize if I wish, and at intervals in a calculation, and also at the end when all is done, the numbers come into focus; but mostly it is as if they were hidden under some medium, though being moved about with decisive exactness in regard to order and ranging; I am aware in particular that redundant zeros, at the beginning or at the end of numbers, never occur intermediately. But I think that it is neither seeing nor hearing; it is a compound faculty of which I have nowhere seen an adequate description; though for that matter neither musical memorization nor musical composition in the mental sense have been adequately described either.

But in memorizing numbers, as opposed to calculation, Aitken relied upon mental audition (1954:301):

> Memory in my own case is visual if I desire, though in the main auditory, but resting on a rhythmic foundation. I was interested to find Mr. Fred Barlow, in his book [1952:149], referring to the "appalling waste of time and energy" committed by Dagbert, a French calculator. Dagbert claimed to have memorized π to the 707 places of decimals to which it had been cal-

culated by W. Shanks in 1873. It amused me to think that I had done this myself some years before Dagbert, and had found it no trouble whatever. All that had been necessary was to range the digits in rows of fifty each, each fifty being divided into ten groups of five, and to read these off in a particular rhythm. It would have been a reprehensibly useless feat, had it not been so easy.

Chapter Two

Consciousness

Now, taking you back to your early infancy, endeavour to recall the first things to which your attention was invited. As infants you were first taught to speak;—you were then taught letters;—then the combination of letters into words; then of words into sentences; and after that you gradually acquired an extensive vocabulary of words and facts. We possess and store these words and facts in our minds, to be occasionally called forth as we need them. For instance, in reading the page of a book, it is clear to me, however rapidly you may read it, that every letter of that page passes in review through the mind. The mind first combines the letters upon the page into words, then the words into sentences, and from those sentences, it extracts the meaning.

Now, in mental calculation I have accumulated, not a very great number of facts, after all;—but I do possess them, and although at this moment I am unconscious of their being so stored up, yet the moment I have a question to solve I have them instantly at command. And it appears to me that, in both cases, the phenomena may be compared to that which we have all observed in Nature. If, on a dark night, there occurs a storm of lightning, during the instant of the flash, although immeasurable in point of time, every object is rendered clear, and out of that view, so placed before us, we can select some one object for our consideration. So I believe it is in the mind; whenever, as in calculation, I feel called upon to make use of the stores of my mind, they seem to rise with the rapidity of lightning. The reasoning faculty seizes upon a particular series of facts necessary for the purpose, deals with each fact according as the circumstances require, and transmits it to the memory for registration."

—George Parker Bidder (1856)

MENTAL processes may be either conscious or unconscious. For ordinary people arithmetic is a conscious process. We have committed to memory methods for addition, substraction, multiplication, division, extracting square roots, etc. When required we (hopefully) recall these methods and apply them to the problem at hand. We are fully aware of the methods used and exactly how they are applied.

Language, at least one's native language, is processed unconsciously. We have a desire to express something and an elaborate unconscious system is put into action; the result is a sequence of articulated sounds reflecting our original urge to speak.

Language and Consciousness

Speaking is accomplished so easily by normal people, even small children, and the study of grammar so notoriously difficult and dull, that it is often hard to convince those who have not spent years studying the inner workings of language that the ability to speak at all requires the unconscious mastery of an immensely complicated grammatical system — incomparably more complicated, in fact, than that required for arithmetic. Talking is almost as natural as breathing, and like breathing, it may be easy, but it is far from simple.

Any native speaker of English can tell you that "Fred is" can be contracted to "Fred's" in the second sentence below, but not in the first. Only a handful of linguists could provide a rationale for this.

> I wonder where Fred is in Europe.
> I wonder why Fred is in Europe.

Most of us feel woefully inadequate on those rare occasions when we come to grips with grammar on a conscious level — perhaps in trying to learn to recognize split infinitives, or to figure out whether to use *who* or *whom* in a sentence like "I wonder —— it was he saw." And despite the admonitions of grammar books, sentences such as "The committee proposed Rudolph and I as co-chairmen" are quite common, and hardly anyone notices anything amiss.

In spite of appearances, this sort of thing is very simple (in fact, if it were not, attempting to cope with it on a conscious level would be futile). The stuff that every native speaker of English (or any other language) must know in order to speak is so subtle and complex that it is hard to figure out how we ever manage to learn it at all.

While we English speakers struggle painfully over the nominative versus the objective case forms of a few pronouns, native speakers of Russian easily juggle a half-dozen grammatical cases, three genders, and a bewildering variety of declensions. Small Russian children know (unconsciously, of course) that, in the nonoblique cases, after the numbers two, three, and four, adjectives are in the genitive plural while nouns are in the genitive singular. For the numbers five through twenty, both adjectives and nouns are in the genitive plural. Obviously, Russians are not genetically better equipped to cope with grammatical cases than speakers of English. It is just that most of us failed to acquire, as children, the rules recommended for the use of the nominative and objective cases in English, and it is very difficult for adults to make even minor alterations in their unconscious grammatical knowledge.

Russian, on the other hand, lacks definite and indefinite articles (in English, *the* and *a*), the use of which seems utterly self-evident to speakers of English. Try explaining to a Russian (or anyone else) why in the first sentence below *the* is appropriate, while the second sentence, which means almost the same as the first, requires *a*. Also explain why substituting one article for the other in these sentences results in very peculiar sentences, which, if they make any sense at all, mean something very different from the sentences below:

> Have you noticed *the* funny way Rita Sue's been acting?
> Have you noticed Rita Sue's been acting in *a* funny way?

Even though talking is the overt manifestation of an enormously complex grammatical system, it requires little or no conscious effort — indeed, for most people it is often easier to talk than to remain silent. Similarly, calculating prodigies often remark on how little effort their calculations require.

Bidder (1856:256) wrote of mental multiplication: "This is done without labour to the mind; and I can do any quantity of the same sort of calculation without any labour; and can continue it for a long period; but when the number of figures increases, the strain of the mind is augmented in very rapid ratio." Gradenwitz (1907:93) wrote of Rückle: "Many observers have been surprised at the absence of any appreciable mental fatigue as a consequence of these experiments, which is in striking contrast to the case of ordinary professional arithmeticians; in fact, 3 to 4 hours of mathematical arithmetic are to Dr. Rückle a pleasure rather than a strain on his brain." Weinland and Schlauch (1937:386) wrote of Finkelstein: "He claimed that he did not get tired. He said there was no work to it." Marathe told me: "There is no fatigue of mind or body when I deal with numbers."

The difficulty most people have doing arithmetic (particularly mental arithmetic) may be compared to the conducting of a conversation in a language with which you are not familiar—concentrating to catch the words before falling behind and losing the thread, desperately dredging your mind for words and the appropriate grammatical structures to approximate something you might have wished to say. Of course, we do not face similar difficulties in conducting far more complex conversations in our native language.

It is often supposed that language is just a matter of memory—we hear some words, phrases, sentences, etc., memorize them, and put this memorized material to use.

To some extent this is obviously true. We are certainly not free to invent words in the midst of a conversation, for example; no one would understand us. But at the same time some process that goes beyond mere memorization is clearly at work in language. Even the most ordinary of everyday conversations involve more than just trotting out previously memorized sentences and grammatical patterns. Some sort of processing, akin to calculation, is involved.

It is very unlikely that anywhere in the entire *Encyclopaedia Britannica* is the same sentence repeated. In fact, apart from revisions of some work or quotations from other works (and perhaps some cases of plagiarism), probably no more than a handful of sentences in the entire Library of Congress occurs more than once. All these new sentences (including the one you are now reading) require some sort of "calculation."

One of the reasons for the superiority of prodigies at calculation is that they have tapped some of the same unconscious capacity that underlies speech.

Unconscious Calculation

The very rapidity of much of the calculation done by prodigies suggests that at least part of the process must be unconscious. Zerah Colburn wrote (1833:191; Colburn always wrote of himself in the third person): "he describes the steps that the rule involves; his own mind was enabled to take these steps, and hurry to the result, not indeed quicker than thought, but more rapidly than his eye could have glanced at the figures they contain." And George Parker Bidder said (1856:256):

> Now, for instance, suppose that I had to multiply 89 by 73, I should say instantly 6,497; if I read the figures written out before me I could not ex-

press a result more correctly, or more rapidly; this facility has, however, tended to deceive me, for I fancied that I possessed a multiplication table up to 100 times 100, and when in full practice, even beyond that; but I was in error; the fact is that I go through the entire operation of the computation in that short interval of time which it takes me to announce the result to you. I multiply 80 by 70; 80 by 3; 9 by 70; and 9 by 3; which will be the whole of the process as expressed algebraically, and then I add them up in what appears to be merely an instant of time.

Shyam Marathe told me: "The process by which my own mind calculates is so quick that I feel that someone in me, different from my usual self, is calculating and I also feel that he is dependable."

Frank D. Mitchell was, as a child, a calculating prodigy, but a peculiarly limited one, largely confining his attention to the last two digits of numbers in multiplication, raising to powers, and extracting roots. He gave the following description of his technique for raising to powers (Mitchell 1907:89):

> After discovering these and similar properties, the writer found it a simple matter to find the last two figures of any power of any number, by counting along the proper series. The process was always, however, of the counting type already indicated. Thus to find the 8th power of 3, the process would be 3, ^{6}, 9, ^{18}, 27, ^{54}, 81, ^{62}, 43, ^{86}, 29, ^{58}, 87, ^{74}, 61; *i.e.,* he would count up to a power of 3, then by this power to the next, and so on, but passing very lightly over the intervening multiples, and in time learning to omit them altogether. In fact, before long the process came to be simply, *3, 9, 81, 61,* *i.e.,* simply squaring each number to get the next, the intermediate countings taking place so rapidly and automatically as hardly to appear in consciousness at all, except as brief "flashes." And even these "flashes" may sometimes be almost absent, so that only the 3 and the 61 stand out, the rest remaining a mere blur.

His technique was not simple memorization, however, for as he says (Mitchell 1907:91):

> He never committed these products and powers to memory; it was not necessary; with practice he was soon able to count to any desired one with great rapidity, in fact, just as rapidly, in the simpler cases, as he could have recalled the answer if it had been previously memorized.

Gauss, himself a calculating prodigy (and one of the greatest mathematicians of history) on April 10, 1847 wrote a letter to Schumacher regarding the calculating prodigy Dase (Gauss and Schumacher 1861 5:297–98):

> That feat [the mental multiplication of two 100-digit numbers] is nevertheless quite unusual, but it could only become truly psychologically interesting if one could get an adequate picture of what goes on in his mind. It would be difficult for Herr Dase to give us the necessary explanations about that, for which I would scarcely reproach him, for in fact I have some experiences of my own that have remained quite mysterious to me. One of these is the following: from time to time as I am walking I begin to count my steps mentally (incidentally always when I am walking rhythmically).
> So I count up to 100 and then I begin from one again. I do all this, once it has started, unconsciously. I think of other things, observe whatever happens to catch my eye; the only thing I am not able to do is speak during that time. And then only after a certain amount of time do I become aware that I am continuing to count rhythmically . . . and always accurately, naturally however without knowing whether or how often I have reached 100.[1]

Aitken was explicit regarding the role of the unconscious in his calculations (Aitken 1954:302):

> I have noticed also at times that the mind has anticipated the will; I have had an answer before I even wished to do the calculation; I have checked it, and am always surprised that it is correct. This, I suppose (but the terminology may not be right), is the subconscious in action; I think it can be action at several levels; and I believe that each of these levels has its own velocity, different from that of our ordinary waking time, in which our processes of thought are rather tardy.

Hunter (1962:254), in his study of the psychology of Aitken's mental calculating, elaborated:

> Although Prof. Aitken cannot recall with certainty the details of his early calculative development, there was clearly that cumulative, hierarchically organized progression which so pervasively characterizes the acquisition of any comprehensive skill, e.g. learning to use a verbal language, to use telegraphic language, to typewrite, to play chess. "In the process of constantly extending my ability, during the period when I was doing that, I had to think very

---

[1] I have called the attention of a number of people to this passage and was surprised to discover that several of them were compulsive counters. They count the groceries as they put them away, their steps from the house to the car, etc., and as with Gauss, the whole thing could lapse into unconsciousness. One woman told me she found such counting distinctly unpleasant, since it suggested she did not have control over her own mind.

much of what I was doing. I found that the gains were cumulative and, so to speak, stratified, in the sense that they formed a deposit sinking deeper and deeper into the subconscious and forming a kind of potential upon which, in certain states, I made drafts at astonishing speed." . . . The gross developmental outcome of all this intellectual effort and synthesis was to carry the young Aitken outwith the normal range of mental calculators. Figuratively speaking, he built up an extensive organized library of calculative resources around which he could find his way with ingeniously methodical rapidity: he could, so to speak, skim round the appropriate sequence of files pulling out apposite calculative instructions of varying levels of generality while, at the same time, implementing these instructions as they come to hand and so progressively specifying the co-ordinates of what is required by way of a confidently correct answer—all this before most people have taken in what the problem is.

Hunter (1962:245) also remarks on the inadequacy of Aitken's introspective accounts of his methods of calculation: "An absolutely complete description was never possible: in part because much calculative activity was unavailable to self-observation, in part because much that was available could not be put readily into words."

Tocquet (n.d.:25–26), writing of the blind calculator, Louis Fleury, notes the difficulty of getting an adequate description of the psychological processes involved in mental calculation: "But let us emphasise at once (and this observation applies to a great number of operations performed by lightning calculators) that these processes, which are carried out practically instantaneously, are for the most part unconscious. It is thanks to analysis that it has been possible to reconstruct them."

Some calculators have alluded to an unconscious monitoring which alerts them when a calculation has gone awry. For example, Gradenwitz (1907:93) wrote: "In solving multiplication problems, Dr. Rückle readily avoids any gross mistakes by an arithmetical checking process, which is even made automatically." Wim Klein says: "Aitken made a very interesting remark—that he felt when a calculation went wrong. This happens to me also sometimes. A voice says—no, not a voice, you feel it. You are busy calculating and suddenly you feel, bloody hell, this is wrong. Stop it. And it is wrong."

Unconscious Learning

Methods for carrying out mental processes can also be learned either consciously or unconsciously.

For example, in learning to touch-type we are at first consciously aware of the letter we wish to type, the key to be struck, and the position the appropriate finger must adopt to strike that key. Later the mental mediation between the intent to produce some sequence of words and striking the appropriate keys in the appropriate order becomes unconscious. In fact, experienced typists frequently cannot say, right off, what will happen if you punch the key under your right index finger in the basic typing position. They will, however, hit *j* instantly and without reflection if called upon to type the word *just.*

Touch typing, then, is an example of a mental process which is initially conscious and subsequently becomes unconscious.

Much second language learning by adults is of this type. When we acquire a second language most of us initially go through a conscious process of manipulating our first language into an approximation of the foreign language. We feel we have attained something of a mastery of a foreign language when we are no longer consciously translating.

For the most part, calculating prodigies also begin with methods which they work out consciously, and which gradually become, in large measure, unconscious.

On the other hand, our native language is acquired and used quite unconsciously. We learn our first language not by deliberately committing to memory some set of rules but by hearing examples, on the basis of which we infer a complex system which underlies our ability to speak.

There is at least one case of calculating prodigies who learned to calculate in just this way. Horwitz, Kestenbaum, Person, and Jarvic (1965; see also Hamblin 1966) reported on identical twin calendar calculators. They were self-taught, and their I.Q.'s were at that time in the 60–70s. The twins could tell, given a date, the day of the week on which that date fell, or will fall. One of the twins, Charles, was completely accurate only for this century, but his brother George made correct day-date identifications in centuries ranging from 4,100 B.C. to 40,400 A.D.

But their method was not simple memorization (Hamblin 1966:107):

"The old explanations must again be questioned," says Dr. William A. Horwitz, assistant director of the Psychiatric Institute. "Previously, we thought the special skills developed were a hypertrophied repetition of a memory function [in laymen's terms, an exaggerated over-development, by repetitive use, of one particular form of memory].[2] . . . But the twins can reach far beyond any calendar which exists. And since they cannot have memorized a calendar which doesn't exist, they must do some sort of calculation in their heads."

[2] Brackets in the original.

In any case the twins did not have good memories for calendar facts they could not compute; they had on several occasions memorized the dates for Easter in this century, but retained the information for only a few weeks.

Nor could they have been taught how to do it. The twins could not manage to learn, consciously, even the rudiments of arithmetic; they could not even give, say, the product of 3 × 6. Since the twins were incapable of solving the simplest arithmetic problems, they could hardly consciously learn a method which involves arithmetic.

In any case the twins could answer questions for which standard methods for finding the day of the week for a given date (see chapter 19) would be no aid; for instance, the months of the year 2002 in which the first falls on a Friday, or the years in which April 21 falls on a Sunday (Hamblin 1966:106).

The twins' ability at calendar calculations was acquired from extensive examination of a perpetual calendar in the *World Almanac,* which George discovered at age 6. By poring over examples, the twins, in some mysterious way, inferred an unconscious algorithm for calendar calculations. Interestingly, they did not incorporate all the data found in the perpetual calendar in formulating their algorithm. The calendar covered the years 0 to 2400 and is correct for the Julian calendar in giving dates before September 14, 1752, when the change to the Gregorian calendar went into effect in the British possessions. The twins were unable to make the correction for the Julian calendar as given in the almanac, even though the Julian calendar is easier to compute.

The twins' method of learning differs from that of arithmetic prodigies such as Bidder and Colburn. The twins learned to do calendar calculation by poring over examples provided by an external source, an almanac. Bidder and Colburn began with a knowledge of counting and devised their own methods of doing arithmetic operations. The only examples available to them were the results of their own calculations. There is no reason to believe, in the case of the twins, that they ever had any awareness of their methods.

Something mysterious, though commonplace, is operating here—the mysterious human ability to form unconscious algorithms on the basis of examples. When asked how they did it, the twins' replies were about as informative as one might expect from a man on the street if pressed to explain how he talks (Hamblin 1966:107): "It's in my head and I do it."

Chapter Three

Brain Hemispheres and Linearity

Brain Hemispheres

THE cerebral cortex, or gray matter of the brain, is divided into two hemispheres, left and right, apparently very similar in construction but in humans governing different mental activities. For most people, the left hemisphere (or left brain, as it is also called) is primarily responsible for speech, rhythm, keeping track of time, and other activities which can be loosely characterized as "linear." The right hemisphere is largely responsible for processing visual patterns (e.g., paintings, geometry, jigsaw puzzles) and the creative aspects of music (excluding sight reading). In some left-handers (about a third) this pattern is reversed—they are dominant for speech in the right hemisphere and for spatial relations in the left.

It has been known since the nineteenth century that the left half of the brain has something to do with speech; this is why a stroke paralyzing the right side of the body (also controlled by the left hemisphere) is often accompanied by speech impairment. In 1861 Paul Broca, a French surgeon, announced that he had located in the brain the source of articulate speech. Now known as Broca's area, the third frontal convolution of the left hemisphere is associated with speech. Broca discovered that lesions in this area impaired the ability to speak or write. The ability to move the tongue, lips, etc. was not affected, but speech was seriously disturbed or eliminated.

Much insight into brain-hemisphere functioning has been obtained from persons who have undergone commissurotomy, the surgical separation of the brain hemispheres. The operation has been performed on a number of people whose lives were severely disrupted by epilepsy, as it was found to reduce drastically the frequency and severity of attacks.

For the most part, those who have undergone such surgery appear normal, but the lack of communication between the brain hemispheres is revealed in various subtle ways. Since the left hemisphere controls the right half of the body, differences appear in what the individual can do with the right or left hand. For example, a young man who previously demonstrated considerable artistic talent was no longer able to draw or paint well after the operation—he was right-handed, and his left hemisphere, which controls the right hand, had no concept of composition, while he lacked the necessary motor skills to draw or paint with his left hand. Split-brain subjects also find it impossible to put together simple children's jigsaw puzzles with the right hand, though they can easily do so with the left hand.

If a split-brain individual is asked to identify objects by placing a hand in a bag into which he cannot see, he can easily name the objects in the bag by proving with his right hand (controlled by the left, or speaking hemisphere).[1] But if he probes with his left hand (governed by the mute right hemisphere), he cannot name the objects, even though the right brain knows what they are. His left brain can guess, but the guesses are likely to be wrong. The right brain, though it normally cannot speak, has some limited comprehension of language. In such cases the person may make an inaccurate identification, followed by a violent shaking of the head—the left hemisphere has guessed, and the right hemisphere, recognizing the inaccuracy of this guess, reacts negatively.

Ordinary calculation is generally taken to be a left-hemisphere function, even though the evidence is somewhat ambiguous. Early split brain cases suggested that the right hemisphere had virtually no ability to calculate. Later Sperry (1968), using different methods, found that the right hemisphere was capable of simple addition, subtraction, and multiplication.

Evidence from brain damage also seems to support the left hemisphere as the seat of ordinary calculation. According to Critchley (1953) 86 percent of right-handed individuals who have lost the ability to calculate through brain damage had left-hemisphere lesions. On the other hand, experiments conducted by Dimond and Beaumont (1972), tend to support a right-hemisphere basis for calculation.

[1] Unless he is among the one-third of left-handers dominant for speech in the right hemisphere.

Linearity

Rimland (1978) reports on a graduate student, Benj Langdon, who attempted to learn to equal the calendar calculation of the identical-twin idiots savants discussed in chapter 2. Although he became adept at calendar calculations, for a long time he could not match their speed. Suddenly he found that the operation of the algorithm had become largely unconscious—he no longer had to concentrate on the individual operations. He also found that he could match the calculating speed of the twins.

Rimland (1978:74) suggests:

> My hunch is that when this dramatic, quantum change took place in Langdon's capacity, the site of the processing had migrated from the left hemisphere of the brain—which specializes in logical, sequential, step-at-a-time processes—to some other area, quite possibly in his right hemisphere—which grasps patterns of information all at once. Whether my hunch is correct or not, it does become clear that a very complex set of calculations can be automated if repeated often enough, and can be done in what is, apparently, a simultaneous rather than sequential fashion.

Rimland's conjecture—that unconscious mental calculation is a right-hemisphere function—is in conflict with the view expounded here—that language and mental calculation stem from the same faculty, since, as noted above, language is known to be housed in the left hemisphere (in right-handers and most left-handers).

Rimland's conjecture is based on two considerations:

1. The great increase in speed attained by Langdon suggests the process is no longer sequential, but simultaneous. The right hemisphere is responsible for such nonlinear functions as spatial relations and music.

2. Conscious calculation is sequential and probably a left-hemisphere function. If calculation becomes unconscious, it is plausible to suspect that it is no longer a left-hemisphere function.

The case of language illustrates that a left-hemisphere process can be extremely complex and rapid, while nevertheless unconscious. A common experience of people thrown into a foreign-language milieu is that for a long time they understand very little (during which time they are more or less consciously translating) and then suddenly they find they understand almost everything. The fact that mental calculation becomes unconscious is not a strong reason for supposing that it moves from the left to the right hemisphere.

Moreover, statements by calculating prodigies are emphatic on the sequential nature of mental calculation. Bidder said (1856:254):

> in the solution of any arithmetical question, however simple, or complicated, every mental process must be analogous to that which is indicated in working out algebraical formulae. No one step can be omitted; but all and every one must be taken up one after another, in such consecutive order, that if reduced to paper, the process might appear prolix, complicated, and inexpeditious, although it is actually arranged with a view of affording relief to the memory.

In the nineteenth century, Binet engaged in speculation similar to Rimland's, regarding Inaudi's calculating ability (1894:105–6):

> One could make, in this connection, a second hypothesis, which would be only an exaggeration of the preceding explanations. The unconscious which is within us, and which psychology has in recent years often succeeded in illuminating, is perhaps capable of foreseeing the solution to a problem or long arithmetic operation without carrying the details of the calculations; and one could suppose that M. Inaudi has an unconscious of this type, but much better developed and more intelligent than that of most people. It is in this way that a great many professionals operate, those, for example, who at a glance judge the area of a piece of land, and who estimate the number of steres represented by trees not yet felled; it is well-known that practice comes to give an extraordinary accuracy to the approximate calculations which are carried out in an instant. Similarly, one can hypothesize that, when M. Inaudi is given a multiplication problem, for example, $38,972 \times 6,385,346$, he has the impression that the product will be between such and such numbers. On what could this impression be based, of what precisely does it consist? I don't know and I have not taken the trouble to research it, since it concerns a hypothesis; I simply indicate the hypothesis, since it presents some likelihood.
>
> M. Inaudi rejects it emphatically; he assures me with a certain heat that he has no instinct for solutions before having found them, that he does not predict them, and he does not seek to predict them, and for a reason that seems extremely serious: If he sought to predict, he would arrive only at approximations, while he is always interested in giving absolutely accurate solutions; for the accurate solution, it is necessary to carry out all the calculations; there is no other means of proceeding.

Chapter Four

Age

Critical Age

IN general, children, if thrown into a foreign language environment, learn that language with far more facility than an adult. Of course, a normal child learns his or her first language perfectly, but young children typically learn other languages perfectly as well, if they find themselves in circumstances in which their peers speak another language.[1]

This ability to acquire languages with native or near-native fluency drops off substantially about the age of puberty (although there seems to be considerable individual variation). To account for such facts, linguists have hypothesized that there is a "critical age," during which a child's mind is prepared to acquire an unconscious knowledge of language based upon the examples of speech that he hears. It is thought that if a child should fail to acquire a language during this period, he will never speak normally.

If language and the ability for unconscious mental calculation derive from the same faculty, one would expect calculating prodigies typically

[1] By "perfectly" I mean that, apart from personal idiosyncracies, their speech will be indistinguishable from that of those who furnished the model for that speech. It does not mean that their speech will be free of what teachers of English have traditionally regarded as grammatical errors.

It might be thought that the "foreign" accent found in the speech of many minority children and adults (e.g., Chicano) is a counterexample here, but this is not so. Such children speak Chicano English (as well as, in most cases, Spanish) among themselves, and even learn English to a large extent from other speakers of Chicano English. Furthermore, the accent serves to affirm group identity. The English of children who speak Spanish in the home but who live in communities having no significant Spanish-speaking population does not differ from that of their English-speaking peers.

to manifest their talent at an early age, and this expectation is fully borne out (Mitchell 1907:96):

> There is nothing more striking about the mathematical prodigies, nothing which has been the subject of more uncritical amazement, than their almost uniform precocity. Gauss began his calculations before he was 3 years old; the present writer, at 4; Ampère, between 3 and 5; Colburn, at 5; Safford, at 6 or earlier; Mathieu le Coq, Mr. Van R., of Utica, Bidder, Prolongeau, and Inaudi, at 6; Mondeux, at 7; the Countess of Mansfield's daughter, at 8 or earlier; Ferrol, Mangiamele, Grandmange, and Pierini, at early ages not definitely stated. Buxton's mental free beer record began from the age of 12; Zaneboni's calculations began at the same age; Dase attended school at the age of 2½, and took to the stage at 15. In short, precocity is unmistakably the rule. . . .

In fact, it is only the auditory calculators who, as a group, are particularly precocious. Wim Klein, who began to calculate at 8 or 9, appears to have been the oldest, and, as previously noted, he is in some respects not typical of auditory calculators.

As we have already seen, Colburn, Safford, Bidder, Inaudi, Mondeux, and Buxton were auditory calculators. Zaneboni was visual, but he was not very precocious. Dase may have been visual, but it is not known whether he was precocious in this calculations.

Mitchell (1907:122) characterizes Ferrol as an auditory calculator, and notes that he "in ordinary life was an abnormally poor visualizer."

Little is known about the imaging of the calculators not discussed in chapter 1, but of the others mentioned by Mitchell, most are known to have begun calculating before they learned to read or write.

Richard Whately (later Archbishop of Dublin) was confused by written numbers when he began school and lost his ability for mental calculation (see below).

In the case of Gauss nothing is known of his number imagery, but the extremely early age that his talent came to light suggests that he was auditory.

Ampère (Scripture 1891:6) began to calculate before he knew either letters or figures. Mangiamele, at the age of 10, appeared before the French Academy of Sciences (*Comptes rendus* 1837 4:978). It is noted there that his father was a shepherd and unable to provide him with any sort of education.

Whether the others mentioned by Mitchell calculated before learning written numbers is not known.

On the other hand, several visual calculators began serious mental calculation rather late. Diamandi began at 16; Mlle Osaka, Finkelstein, and Eberstark in their twenties. Just when Dagbert began to calculate is not clear, but he did not perfect his methods until he was a prisoner of war, in his late twenties or early thirties.

Louis Fleury, the tactile calculator, began mental calculation at 15 (Tocquet n.d.:22–23), and Aitken (1954:297), who had no number imagery while calculating, was nearly 14.

Loss of Calculating Power

A number of calculating prodigies are known to have retained the ability for mental calculation into their sixties (and beyond), including Buxton, Fuller, Bidder, Inaudi, Aitken, Dagbert, and Klein.

There are, however, various accounts of prodigies who reportedly entirely lost their abilities for mental calculation. Scripture (1891:15) wrote of Zerah Colburn:

> He was introduced to and examined by the members of the French "Institute," among whom was La Place. "Three months had now elapsed that he had not been exhibited, but had given his attention to study; even in this short space it was observable that he had lost in the quickness of his computations." [Colburn 1833:76] Before long his calculating power left him entirely.

Tocquet (n.d.:10) wrote of Colburn: "He lost his faculty to calculate, without any apparent reason, at the age of twenty."

Several such accounts appear to derive from F. W. H. Myers (1913). Barlow (1952:42) notes: "F. W. H. Myers expressed the opinion that apparently Mangiamele lost his gift after childhood," and (1952:44): "According to F. W. H. Myers, Safford's gift lasted only for about six years. His loss of power was remarkable in that his whole bent was mathematical."

I find nothing in the original sources which suggests that Colburn ever completely lost his ability for mental calculation, and the secondary sources cite no references to support their allegations. The quotation from Colburn's *Memoir* given above suggests only that the ability deteriorated when not put to use. This is no more surprising than the fact that the ability to speak a language falls off with lack of practice. We do know that at the age of 18, he was hired to do astronomical calculations (Colburn 1833:141). In any case, if the talent had been entirely lost, the *Memoir*, published when Colburn was 29, would certainly have said so.

Myer's opinion that Mangiamele lost his ability to calculate after childhood seems to be based on the fact that, after presenting himself before the French Academy when he was 10, he attracted no further attention as a calculator, and what became of him is not known.

In the case of Safford, it is known with certainty that the ability to do mental calculation was not lost, Myer's opinion to the contrary. For example, Willis I. William, who was Safford's successor as Professor of Astronomy at Williams College said (Ashbrook 1976:346):

> I remember on one occasion in connection with some work of mine that there was a column of about 40 numbers with from two to four figures in each number. Professor Safford slowly moved his pencil down the column and in about five seconds wrote the sum of the squares of these numbers.

I have come across two cases where the ability for mental calculation was clearly lost. The first is that of a "Mr Van R." of Utica, New York who, according to Gall (recounted in Scripture 1891:32) had a remarkable talent for reckoning in his head, but at 8 lost it entirely, and in later years had no recollection of the methods he used in childhood to obtain his results.

The other is the case of Richard Whately, D.D., the Archbishop of Dublin. He astonished his family when, at the age of 6, he named the number of minutes a neighbor past 60 had lived.

Whately wrote in his Commonplace Book (1866:5):

> There certainly was something peculiar in my calculating faculty. It began to show itself between five and six, and lasted about three years. . . . I soon got to do the most difficult sums ["sums" here refers to arithmetic calculations in general] always in my head, for I knew nothing of figures beyond numeration, nor had I any names for the different processes I employed. But I believe my sums were chiefly in multiplication, division, and the rule of three. In this last point I believe I surpassed the famous American boy [Zerah Colburn], though I did not, like him, understand the extraction of roots. I did these sums much quicker than any one could on paper, and I never remember committing the smallest error. . . .
>
> My father tried often, but in vain, to transfer my powers to written figures; and when I went to school, at which time the passion was worn off, I was a perfect dunce at cyphering, and so have continued ever since.

In both cases the ability was lost at a very early age, with no subsequent recollection of how the results were obtained. This parallels many cases of language loss in children who may spend a year or two in a foreign country in childhood, but who as adults have no (conscious) recollection of the language, which they may have spoken with native fluency. Languages retained through puberty do not appear to be subject to such loss.

Chapter Five

Intelligence, Sex, and Heredity

IF prodigious prowess at mental calculation were dependent upon intelligence, sex, or heredity, then it would be a phenomenon of a different sort from speech, since boys and girls, stupid and intelligent,[1] of every sort of family history, learn to speak.

The available evidence suggests that such considerations are not factors in the development of calculating prodigies (except insofar as they affect environment—e.g., boys and girls are not treated alike).

Intelligence

There are many reported cases of retarded children ("idiots savants") with special abilities for calculation. On the other hand, a number of calculating prodigies have been brilliant men, in some cases men of genius (e.g., Euler, Gauss, Bidder, Ampère, Safford, and Aitken).

Perhaps the retarded and the gifted are overrepresented in the ranks of calculating prodigies, or perhaps it is only that they are more likely to attract general attention. Had not Gauss and Euler been major figures in the history of mathematics their ability as calculators would be unknown today. Furthermore, low intelligence has been attributed to several calculators simply because they failed to realize popular expectations that men with such talents should be geniuses. This was particularly true of Colburn (as discussed in the chapter regarding him), but Dase was the victim of similar abuse. Scripture (1891:18–19), for example, writes:

[1] Only the most drastically retarded are incapable of speech.

On one occasion Petersen tried in vain for six weeks to get the first elements of mathematics into his head. Schumacher credits him with extreme stupidity. . . . In 1850 Dase went to England to earn money by exhibitions of his talents. Much the same is related of his great powers as in Germany; his general obtuseness also occasioned remark. He could not be made to have the least idea of a proposition in Euclid. Of any language but his own he could never master a word.

And Mitchell (1907:75) says: "He seems to have been little more than a human calculating machine, able to carry on enormous calculations in his head, but nearly incapable of understanding the principles of mathematics, and of very limited ability outside his chosen field. In this respect he resembled Buxton. . . ."

It is true that Schumacher, in a letter to Gauss dated April 7, 1847 (Gauss and Schumacher 1861 5:295), wrote that Dase "cannot comprehend the first elements of mathematics. . . . " Part of the problem here is the unwarranted assumption that one blessed with a talent for calculation should have any genuine mathematical ability. Certainly we should not be ready to brand a person who was not a calculating prodigy as incompetent, simply because he was poor at attaining mathematical concepts by the standards of Petersen, Schumacher, and Gauss. No one doubted his calculating brilliance, however (Gauss and Schumacher 1861, 5:295): "his ability for numerical reckoning now astounds everyone." Scripture states that Dase knew no languages but German; I cannot find his source, but if true that is hardly evidence of impenetrable stupidity.

In fact, there appears to be nothing in the references regarding him that gives any indication of his general intelligence, beyond the fact that he was not good at mathematics. He seems to have had sufficient acumen to organize and profit from performances of his calculating ability, even to financing trips to England, and he managed to persuade Gauss, who had no desire even to meet him, to recommend him for a job completing a table of factors. Perhaps Dase was as stupid as Scripture and Mitchell suggest, but there is really no evidence of it.

In spite of the general tendency to notice only the brilliant and the backward, as well as a tendency to assign the mediocre to the latter category, it seems possible that both genius and retardation account for more than their fair share of calculating prodigies. There is a property, shared by those at either end of the mental spectrum, which would account for such an unequal distribution—a tolerance for what ordinary folk find intolerably dull. This is a common characteristic of the retarded, who often specialize in memorizing great quantities of data on some subject or other. If the interest is stimulated sufficiently early in life, and if the data are computable, the human unconscious constructs, by some unknown means, a method for computing the data. Hamblin (1966:106) writes of the retarded calendar prodigies discussed in chapter 2: "George and Charles, like other idiot savants, are walking encyclopedias of trivia. They remember everything that has happened each day in their narrow world for the past 10 years."

Unconscious processes are formed on the basis of prolonged exposure to appropriate data. In the case of a child's first language, much of the data (verbal sounds) is literally in the air about him.

In cases where the data are not so easy to come by, the child must have a strong interest in the subject in order to ferret out the necessary information. What children find interesting is partly a matter of current fashion. When I was growing up, a child who spent his or her time skateboarding or spinning a hula hoop would have been regarded as emotionally, if not intellectually, retarded. (On the other hand, baton twirling, for girls, was practically *de rigueur*.)

A child who spent much free time learning Latvian as an amusement would be regarded as at least as peculiar as a child who factored large numbers for fun. Memorizing baseball or football statistics is not regarded in American society as bizarre, but memorizing log tables is certainly seen as strange.

People on either end of the intelligence scale seem to be less limited in what they may find interesting. Perhaps this is because they are already regarded as so peculiar that peer support for their interests is not required, or perhaps it is because the brilliant and retarded are not required to shoulder the responsibility of nurturing and transmitting popular culture.

Intellectual Loss

It is sometimes proposed that an exaggerated concern with mental calculation leads to intellectual debility in other areas. This is apparently an attempt to explain why a number of calculating prodigies have otherwise been rather ordinary individuals, in some cases even mentally deficient. Since expertise in arithmetic is generally regarded as a sign of intellectual superiority, why should some intellectually mediocre (or even inferior) individuals be so specially gifted in this one area? Perhaps they expended too much of their intellectual resources on calculation. The overlooked

answer is that the ability to do complex (though not necessarily sophisticated) problems in mental arithmetic depends upon interest and practice, not intellectual superiority.

Gentleman's Magazine said of Jedediah Buxton ("Life" 1754:251): "His
memory would certainly be equally retentive, with respect to other objects, if he had attended to other objects with equal diligence; but his
perpetual application to figures has prevented the smallest acquisition of
any other knowledge, and his mind seems to have retained fewer ideas
than that of a boy of ten years old, in the same class of life."

In fact, Buxton was somewhat retarded, and the comparative simplicity
of mental arithmetic was as much as his intellect could handle.

Something similar is suggested of Zerah Colburn's calculating ability
in an article on "Calculating Boys" (1878:100) in the *Spectator:*

> But it is pretty apparent that—perhaps partly from premature, exhausting
> mental exertion—the faculty itself really declined; that it could not flourish
> along with other faculties, which unfolded themselves as the child grew; and
> that, as Colburn's general intelligence and knowledge increased, his capacity
> to answer arithmetical puzzles sensibly diminished. Whately's aptitude for
> mental calculations vanished as soon as he went to school and began his
> education, and it seems true of all precocious calculators that they were at
> their best only when they had nothing to distract them, and before their
> minds were disciplined and stored with knowledge.

In fact, a number of calculating prodigies grew to be eminent men,
without serious diminution of their ability to calculate, including Gauss,
Bidder, Safford, Aitken, and von Neumann.

Even comparatively recently such views have been propounded (Weinland 1948:256–57):

> In one respect the conclusions at N.Y.U. differ from those in Berlin.
> Bela Sandor concludes his study by saying in reference to Finkelstein: "The
> general working of the intelligence suffers under the lasting, one-sided
> preoccupation of its more rudimentary functions. The gift of deduction and
> logical contemplation gradually deteriorates when the memory ceases to be
> an instrument of creative activity and becomes an end in itself." We at New
> York University, looked in vain for signs of deterioration. Of course, we had
> not known Finkelstein for long. It must be remembered, however, that he
> was not a highly educated man. At the time he became interested in num-
> bers he was a clerk. Subsequently he had travelled a great deal, met a variety
> of people, giving public performances, and read considerably. He seemed
> well-balanced and alert, although of course, not completely oriented in the

American environment. The author believes that F's mind was quite sound and that if anything, he had been improved rather than weakened by the series of experiences that went with his demonstration of calculation and memory.

Sex

There are far fewer recorded cases of female calculating prodigies than male ones, but female calculators are not unknown. They include the contemporary Indian performer, Shakuntala Devi (chapter 36); the Countess of Mansfield's daughter (discussed below); the possibly retarded Frenchwoman Mlle Osaka (chapter 40); and two cases of retarded calculators (Wizel 1904, Jakobsson 1944).

The apparent discrepancy in the frequency of male and female calculating prodigies can probably be ascribed to underreporting, lack of opportunity to develop the talent, and lack of encouragement for continued development (perhaps outright discouragement).

For the most part the calculating prodigies of whom we have record are those who gave public demonstrations for pay, or who became well known for some other reason (usually mathematics, e.g., Euler, Gauss, Ampère, and von Neumann). One suspects that few fathers and mothers were willing to cart their daughters around the countryside to make professional appearances; and far fewer women have gained eminence than men, particularly in fields associated with calculation. In most places and times a girl having such talent would probably have been ignored or discouraged from displaying it.

Few girls would have had the isolation and leisure to develop any natural bent for mental calculation. For various social reasons women and girls have traditionally been discouraged from being alone (or even from displaying much independence of mind or body). They were not sent out on lonely vigils with sheep; their chores were apt to be carried out in the presence of others, and too much human interaction is inimical to the development of mental calculation.

Colburn gives evidence of the attitudes which militated against the development of calculating prowess in girls (1833:174–75):

> The Countess of Mansfield called upon Zerah Colburn, while he was first exhibited in London, and alluding to the singular gift he possessed, stating that she had a daughter, Lady Frederica Murray, who was about his age, and gave indications of superior skill in figures. He was afterwards invited

to call at her ladyship's residence, and found the young lady did possess a certain degree of mental quickness uncommon in her sex and years. But her elevated rank, and the necessary attention to those pursuits which were more in accordance with her station in life, probably prevented her attending to that endowment.

Heredity

If the ability for mental calculation were hereditary, rather like hemophilia in the royal families of Europe or the supernumerary digits in Colburn's family,[2] we should expect to find cases of calculating prodigies who were members of the same family but not members of the same household. Instead we find that in every case of a family with two outstanding mental calculators both were members of the same household. Moreover, in every case where details are known, one of the individuals was the instigator while the other was an inferior emulator. Thus the evidence points to an environmental, rather than a hereditary influence.

George Parker Bidder and his son of the same name were both mental calculators, but Bidder, Jr. was a visual calculator, used cross multiplication, and employed mnemonics to retain numbers—techniques typical of artificial rather than natural calculators. By his own admission, he was much inferior to his father as a calculator (Bidder 1878:1635): "I cannot pretend to approach even distantly to the rapidity or accuracy with which my father worked."

In the case of the Klein brothers, Wim, the younger, was the instigator: "As soon as I started multiplying four digits my brother said, 'Oh, forget it, man.' He was a little bit infected by me. Because I did it he had to do it." And as in the case of Bidder and his son, Wim was auditory, while his brother was visual.

Then there is the case of the identical-twin calendar prodigies, George and Charles. George became interested in the calendar at 6, but Charles showed no interest until later. Horwitz et al. reported (1965:1075): "Although Charles is completely accurate only for this century, George can project his calendar identifications to centuries before and centuries beyond our present perpetual calendars."

The fact that other members of the same family may have good memories for something other than calculation, or show some talent for com-

[2] Colburn had six fingers on each hand and six toes on each foot, a peculiarity known to have been in his family for several generations.

putation, is sometimes adduced as evidence for heredity as a significant ingredient in mental calculation. For instance, Bidder, Jr. (1878:1635) remarks:

> As to the other members of my father's family, his eldest brother (who was a Unitarian minister) was not remarkable as an arithmetician, but he had an extraordinary memory for Biblical texts, and could quote almost any text in the Bible, and give chapter and verse. Another brother was an excellent mathematician. He was actuary of the Royal Exchange Life Assurance Office. . . . My children show considerable, I may say certainly more than average, but not extraordinary powers of doing mental arithmetic.

A paraphrase of some comments by Aitken (1954:307) following a talk states:

> His father's elder brother, whom he himself had never seen because he went to Australia to make his career, the first in that generation, by family tradition, was very remarkable. He did all his calculations, as did Professor Aitken himself, mentally and without paper. He was a farmer's son and it fell to him to work out volumes of timber and barrels, and so on. He had perhaps found in a book on mensuration Simpson's formula or variants of it and did them in his head. His (Professor Aitken's) father used to say that his uncle was the best arithmetician he had ever known by far and by far, and this legend or tradition was preserved in the family. He supposed that was why when he became thirteen or fourteen he wanted to be something like Uncle Tom. His own daughter said quite frankly that one mathematician in a family was enough. She could work out square numbers as quickly as he could without trouble. If she thought it worth while, she could do some of the things he did, but she did not think it worth while.

In fact, in very many if not most families someone can be found with a good memory for something or other, or with a talent for arithmetic. (These are the people you ask to keep the bowling, bridge, or dart scores.) Such examples do nothing to advance the argument for a role for heredity in the development of calculating prodigies.

According to Binet (1894:112) among Diamandi's 14 siblings one brother and one sister shared his ability for calculation, but Binet gives no details of any kind regarding their abilities. Tocquet (n.d.:21) mentions only a sister, Uranie: "It was at the age of seven that she noticed her special aptitude. Her brother's first successes later encouraged her to cultivate this gift." In any case Diamandi was certainly not among the natural calculators—a visualizer, he was not precocious (he began mental calculation at 16 after going into the grain business), and calculated relatively slowly.

The assumption that the ability must be inherited led to suggestions in a less sophisticated age of prenatal influence.

Inaudi's mother was reputedly obsessed with calculating (to straighten out the family's desperate financial plight) when she was pregnant with him. Binet (1894:27), though plainly skeptical, does not reject outright the possibility of prenatal influence: "could the mental state of the mother really have an effect on the child?"

Chapter Six

—

Memory

IT is often assumed that the superiority of calculating prodigies to ordinary people in mental calculation is a result of some innate superiority of memory, particularly for numbers, a theory that confuses cause and effect. It is rather interest in figures which accounts for the ability to remember them.[1] Mitchell (1907:116–18) put the matter well:

> Now it can hardly be questioned that the mathematical prodigy's figure-memory is superior to the ordinary man's. Dealing constantly with figures, the mental calculator learns to assimilate them readily. A 20-figure number, which for the most of us is a meaningless string of figures devoid of interest, for him "makes sense," and so is easy to learn, just as a page of French is more easily learned by a Frenchman than by a foreigner who knows little or nothing of the language. . . .
>
> [Inaudi's] skill in memorizing long numbers was the result of practice, perhaps in the service of addition, perhaps for its own sake, but was not the secret of his calculation. That he remembered the 200 or 300 numbers used in one of his public exhibitions was due to his *interest* in the figures, on account of their connection with his calculations; where the interest was lacking he could only remember a third as many figures in the same period of time.

Just as there is wide variation in the general intelligence of calculating prodigies, there is considerable difference in their memory ability for things other than numbers. Aitken, a brilliant mathematician with a deep interest in music and literature, wrote (1954:301): "My memory is not

---

[1] Experiments by Chase and Ericsson (1982) leave no doubt that, with extensive practice, ordinary people can learn to memorize numbers with a facility equal if not superior to that of calculating prodigies.

as good as it was some twenty or twenty-five years ago. At that time I found it easy to remember not only numbers and formulae and mathematical proofs, but music and poetry and indeed most things. The one requisite was that a live interest in the subject should fix an undeviating attention."

On the other extreme lies Mondeux, who seems to have been able to retain scarcely anything unrelated to calculation. Mondeux's teacher, Émile Jacoby, wrote to Hugh Godfray, Professor of Mathematics and Hydrography at Jersey, in his dedication of *Caractères de divisibilité des nombres* (1853:iii–iv):

> You knew Henri Mondeux well enough, my dear Hugh, to be convinced that his memory is nothing, and therefore, his education difficult. . . . Since you have seen, heard, studied him, nothing about him has changed. I will not say that he has forgotten: he, who knows so much, has never learned anything. Facts, dates, places, pass before his brain as before a mirror without leaving a trace. It is enough to tell you, my friend, that he does not remember you, or David's Place, or Jersey. . . .
>
> Your name is attached to this first work on which Henri cooperated; it passes each day before his eyes, and will perhaps become engraved in his memory. I would love for him to know it.

Shyam Marathe gives performances in memory as well as calculation and magic. He is, naturally, quite interested in each, and it is this interest which fuels his skills. Although he can, for a performance, remember a large number of names by associating them with numbers, when visiting the United States he found it quite difficult to retain the names of people he met socially, and memorizing the sequence of operations for calling forth the various functions of a digital wristwatch (stopwatch/chronograph) proved well-high impossible. Marathe is a performer, and his memory in the service of his interest is excellent, but in everyday matters he is rather absentminded.

In the case of most prodigies, where anything definite is known, their memory for things unconnected with calculation is not remarkable. Bidder wrote (1856:253):

> As regards memory, I had in boyhood, at school and at college, many opportunities of comparing my powers of memory with those of others, and I am convinced that I do not possess that faculty in any remarkable degree.
>
> If, however, I have not any extraordinary amount of memory, I admit that my mind has received a degree of cultivation in dealing with figures, in

a particular manner, which has induced in it a peculiar power; I repeat, however, that this power is, I believe, capable of being attained by any one disposed to devote to it the necessary time and attention. In other respects than numbers I have not an extraordinary memory; indeed I have great difficulty in learning anything by rote.

According to his manager, Inaudi was very forgetful, unable to recall towns in which he had appeared, constantly leaving behind personal effects, and forgetting appointments (Binet 1894:32).

Binet (1894:43) found that Inaudi's nonnumerical memory was not very good. He could repeat only five or six letters of the alphabet read off to him; he was incapable of repeating two lines of prose or verse. His memory of shapes, places, events, and melodies was unreliable. He could not learn historical dates, he said, because they had no meaning for him.

In only one circumstance was he able to repeat exactly a series of words—that was when these words were part of a numerical problem presented to him. Once again, this suggests that it is interest, not some genetic peculiarity affecting only one type of memory, that explains the superior memory for numbers of calculating prodigies.

Binet (1894:44) concluded that the development of a specific memory, such as the one displayed by Inaudi for numbers, was not the result of some anatomical peculiarity, but rather "a combination of mental faculties, attention, will, perseverance, and above all a passionate taste for studies that are connected with this memory."

Wim and Leo Klein were tested by Stokvis (1949:80), who concluded:

> As regards their general memory, exhaustive tests made in series showed, that the two brothers' general memory did not surpass the average. These tests included the memorizing of letter-sequences, of meaningless syllables and of texts from belletristic works.
>
> Neither did I feel justified in assuming the presence of an exceptionally developed specific memory. I found, on the other hand, that, in memorizing numbers, the two brothers tried to utilize the peculiar properties of the figures and numbers. . . .

Number Memory

There are three sorts of memory involved in mental calculation: short-term memory, "medium-term" memory, and long-term memory. Though it is sometimes difficult to draw precise boundaries around these types, they are clearly distinct.

Short-term memory is involved in the intermediate stages of calculation; the methods of mental calculators are devised to minimize short-term memory load. Bidder (1856:260) wrote:

> On paper when you multiply any number of figures, you begin with the units' places and proceed successively to the left hand, and then you add them up. That process is impracticable in the mind; I could neither remember the figures, nor could I, unless by a great effort on a particular occasion, recollect a series of lines of figures; but in mental arithmetic you begin at the left-hand extremity, and you conclude at the unit, allowing only one fact to be impressed on the mind at a time. You modify that fact every instant as the process goes on; but still the object is to have one fact, and one fact only, stored away at any one time. . . . The last result in each operation being alone registered by the memory, all the previous results being consecutively obliterated until a total product is obtained.

Even though the techniques of mental calculation are obviously devised with the aim of reducing short-term memory load, it is not necessarily the case that calculating prodigies lose the intermediate steps in a calculation. The following is from a paraphrase of Aitken's reply to a question during the discussion period following his address to the Society of Engineers (Aitken 1954:305):

> Professor Aitken replied that he was able to put aside in storage for a future occasion a result that had already been obtained. He knew that he would be able to bring it out correctly. It would have been noticed in his demonstrations that if he was diffident—as he had been once or twice—he was not so good and might make an error.
>
> He thought this ability to put an answer in storage was what distinguished the calculator from what might be called the man in the atreet. The man in the street forgot the stages between. One of the most interesting things about Bidder was that he did his stages one at a time and each one obliterated the preceding stages. He went from A to B to C to D, and finally he arrived at the answer PQR. He himself did not work in that way: nothing was obliterated. He could pull everything out at any time in the course of the calculation.

In fact, another comment by Bidder makes it clear that this obliteration was not complete (1856:264):

By this means I have only one result to register; as I get rid of the first series of figures I have no necessity for keeping in view the numbers with which I have to deal. It does not follow that I do not recollect them; on the contrary, I invariably bear them in mind; but my object is always to relieve my mind from the feeling of oppression arising from the necessity of keeping an accurate record, and to seek for that relief by dealing with the other parts of the operation, in such a manner as to accomplish it; for the only strain I have experienced has been whenever the registering power is at all oppressed.

So, to some extent, short-term memory and what I have called medium-term memory may slide one into the other.

Medium-term memory accounts for the ability of calculators to memorize long numbers for their performances. Unless the numbers have some special significance for the calculator these numbers are typically retained only temporarily, say until the next performance, when they are replaced by new numbers.

At a demonstration before some academicians Inaudi memorized a series of 24 digits (Binet 1894:57–58). He was asked by Binet to repeat them four or five days later. Binet did not know whether the numbers were correct, since he was not at the original performance, but he transcribed the digits as recalled by Inaudi.

Forty days later they met again. In the meanwhile Inaudi had given daily performances. When he was asked to repeat the earlier series of digits (a request he did not expect) he was able, with considerable effort, to recall a little more than half.

When Inaudi was questioned on the subject, he said that he forgot the numbers in his performances more or less voluntarily, unless they were somehow of interest. On the other hand he retained numbers he learned under odd circumstances, or which were the object of a bet, or which were associated with a new problem.

Binet then asked Inaudi to recite all the numbers presently in his memory. He was able to recall the 230 digits of his last performance (16 to 18 hours earlier) and a few digits from some other recent performances (going back five or six days), but that was all. The rest was forgotten.

It also became apparent that memorizing a subsequent series tended to wipe out a previous series, even when that was not Inaudi's intent. Having determined that Inaudi could easily repeat the 230 digits involved in his last performance, Binet asked him if he would be willing to do so at his (Binet's) conference on calculating prodigies. Inaudi agreed. At the conference Inaudi gave a demonstration of calculation involving some

230 new digits, after which he found that he could not recall all the previously memorized digits.

Shyam Marathe told me much the same thing—that the numbers faded with time, particularly after subsequent performances, and that he deliberately "erased" figures to make room for new ones.

The final category is long-term memory. This includes the multiplication tables and whatever other specialized information a calculator may have stored away to use in the service of calculation.

Short-Term Memory Limits

Bidder was, so far as I know, the only calculating prodigy to theorize on the computational difficulty imposed by short-term memory limitations (1856:256):

> As compared with the operation on paper, in multiplying 3 figures by 3 figures, you have three lines of 4 figures each, or 12 figures in the process to be added up; in multiplying 6 figures into 6 figures, you have six lines of 7 figures, or 42 figures to be added up. The time, therefore, in registration on paper will be as 12 to 42. But the process in the mind is different. Not only have I that additional number of facts to create, but they must be imprinted on the mind. The impressions to be made are more in number, they are also more varied, and the impression required is so much deeper, that instead of being like 3 or 4 to 1, it is something like 16 to 1. Instead of increasing by the square, I believe it increases by the fourth power. I do not pretend to say that it can be expressed mathematically, but the ratio increases so rapidly that it soon limits the useful effect of mental calculation. As a great effort I have multiplied 12 places of figures by 12 places of figures; but that has required much time, and was a great strain upon the mind. Therefore, in stating my conviction that mental arithmetic could be taught, I would desire it to be understood, that the limits within which it may be usefully and properly applied, should be restricted to multiplying 3 figures by 3 figures. Up to that extent, I believe it may be taught with considerable facility, and will be received by young minds, so disposed, quite as easily as the ordinary rules of arithmetic.

As I understand Bidder's measure, in multiplying two n-digit numbers on paper, the difficulty is the ratio of $n^2 + n$ to $2n$.

This can be generalized to account for any n-digit by m-digit multiplication: $nm + n$ to $n + m$. The difficulty in mental calculation, as he sees it, is the square of this ratio: $(nm + n)^2$ to $(n + m)^2$, or $n^2m^2 + 2n^2m + n^2$

to $n^2 + 2nm + m^2$. For $n = m$ (as in the examples considered by Bidder), the ratio is $n^2 + 2n + 1$ to 4. In the case of a six-digit by six-digit multiplication, this gives a 3½ to 1 ratio for multiplication on paper as opposed to 12¼ to 1 for mental multiplication.

Of course, Bidder's ratio is not intended as a direct measure of short-term memory load, but only as a measure of the relative difficulty of mental versus written multiplication. Nor does it pretend to be exact. Let us take another approach and see whether, on the basis of information provided by Bidder and others, short-term memory load can be estimated directly.

Bidder (1856:263) explicitly states that, for him, a sequence of three digits represents a single item in memory; thus, a four-digit number represents two items in memory. The limit of the number of items that can be conveniently held in short-term memory is about seven. Furthermore, since Bidder suggests multiplication of three digits by three digits as a reasonable limit of expectation for an ordinary child, it is reasonable to believe that a correct measure of short-term memory would assign a load somewhat below seven for a three by three multiplication.

The three-digit by three-digit multiplication as Bidder would have done it is shown in table 6.1.

TABLE 6.1
Short-Term Memory Load in Mental Multiplication

358	
464	2
120,000	3
20,000	4
140,000	3
3,200	5
143,200	4
18,000	5
161,200	4
3,000	5
164,200	4
480	5
164,680	4
1,200	6
165,880	4
200	5
166,080	4
32	5
166,112	4

The numbers in the right-hand column represent short-term memory load, on the assumption that three digits represent a single item in memory. In this I have assumed that the original problem is retained in its entirety until the final product is obtained (though it need not be). I have given no weight to trailing zeros, though, presumably, they contribute in some way to memory load,[2] but it hardly seems likely that, say 20,000, counts as two items in memory, just as does 23,486. In fact, counting trailing zeros as separate memory items will not, in this case, result in a higher maximum load, though in many cases it will increase the maximum memory load by one.

By this method, the maximum memory load for an m-digit by n-digit multiplication is approximately equal to $m+n$, or $m+n+1$ if $m+n$ is not a multiple of three. A four-digit multiplication gives a maximum memory load of nine, which is consistent with Bidder's and Colburn's remarks to the effect that this is a problem of considerably greater difficulty than a three-digit by three-digit multiplication—in fact, the upper limit on normal short-term memory is attained.

Numbers and Words

Numbers, for calculating prodigies, have many of the properties of words. Multidigit numbers are not conceived simply as sequences of single digits, but are apprehended as a single notion, just as one apprehends words as a single notion, even though composed of sequences of sounds.

Hunter (1968:342) remarks of Aitken, for instance: "he is able to recognize, and to think of, quite large numbers as distinctive, unitary items; this is comparable to the ability of literate people[3] to deal with a word as a unit rather than an unwieldy collection of letters or sounds."

Bidder said (1856:263):

I believe that much of the facility of mental calculation, and also of mastery over numbers, depends on having the idea of numbers impressed upon the mind, without any reference to symbols. The number 763 is represented symbolically by three figures 7–6–3; but 763 is only one quantity,—one number—one idea, and it presents itself to my mind just as the word 'hip-

[2] Aitken (1954:302) remarks: "I am aware in particular that redundant zeros, at the beginning or at the end of numbers, never occur intermediately"; that is, in the intermediate stages of his mental calculations.

[3] This is equally true of illiterate people, insofar as sounds are concerned.

popotamus' presents the idea of one animal. Now if you were called upon to represent the animal 'hippopotamus' by the figures 174754, it would be far more difficult to remember, because those figures have no relation to one another—they do not guide to another sequence; and hence I feel—and it is an opinion, on which, the more I reflect, the more I am confirmed, that you should have numbers impressed on your mind as an idea connected, or identified, with themselves, and not through the 'dry-bones,' of figures. The word 'mind,' if recollected merely in connection with four symbols, or the four letters M-I-N-D, would create a much greater difficulty to the memory, than the word 'mind,' with which a signification is immediately associated.

Numbers are, for calculating prodigies, rich in associations, which resemble the meanings of words. Arthur Griffith told Bryan and Lindley (1941:35) that he memorized numbers "by their meanings." For the number 365,419,798,163,452 he gave the following "meanings":

$$365 = \text{the number of days in a year.}$$
$$419 = 1 \text{ less than } 6 \times 7 \times 10.$$
$$798 = 7 \times 6 \times 19.$$
$$163 = 1 \text{ greater than } 81 \times 2.$$
$$452 = 1 \text{ less than } 3 \times 151.$$

Hunter (1962:246–47) writes of Aitken:

A number is apprehended as a multiplicity of numerical attributes and, so to speak, as bristling with signalling properties. . . . This simultaneous, immediate apprehending of numerical attributes is often autonomous in that no specific preparation is necessary. For example, on one occasion the thinker heard the year 1961 mentioned, and apprehended this as 37 times 53, *and* 44 squared plus 5 squared, *and* 40 squared plus 19 squared. He does not have to set himself to apprehend numbers thus; rather be must set himself to prevent such apprehending. . . .

Such examples could easily be compounded manyfold. For instance, Weinland (1948:252) says of Finkelstein:

He continually uses the associations that he has learned. One day when asked what associations he had with 5584, a number picked at random, he hesitated a moment and then said, "37 squared is 1369, a permutation of 1396 which multiplied by four gives 5584; 349 multiplied by 2 raised to the fourth power also gives 5584; 349 is also the greatest prime number in 5584."

Although words have a variety of meanings, the appropriate meaning is determined by context. (My dictionary lists over 30 primary meanings for the English word *back*.) Much the same is true of numbers for calculating prodigies (Hunter 1962:247, regarding Aitken):

> Although numbers are cues for cognitive action which is often autonomous, it does not follow that apprehending is uninfluenced by context. The way a number leads on varies with the task and with the numbers presented alongside it. . . . When asked to decimalize 1/851, the immediately dominant attribute is the factorization 23 times 37. When asked to extract the square root of 851, the immediate lead on is that 851 is 29 squared plus 10. When asked to decimalize 17/851, the immediately dominant property is that this fraction is very nearly 0.02. . . .
>
> In short, almost any presented number is rich in meaning, immediately leads on to a constellation of numerical attributes. Some numbers have more attributes than others and the attributes which are apprehended vary with the context—just as, for most people, the same word is apprehended in different ways according to its verbal and situational context.

Numbers sometimes have for prodigies something akin to connotations. Finkelstein, for example, reacted emotionally to numbers, just as everyone does to words (Weinland 1948:253–54). He thought 214 a "beautiful" number, while 8337 he described as "very nice" (though not, I suppose, the sort of number you'd like your sister to marry).[4] Zero was his "pet aversion."

When Shyam Marathe visited the United States, he flew over the Grand Canyon, which was for him a very emotional experience. And while looking for the first time at that vast expanse, he found that it reminded him of the 20th power of 9, which consists of some 20 digits. He said, "I actually recollected that large number, though I do not know what relevance it has to the Grand Canyon, but it appeared before my eyes for some time while I was enjoying the view."

Extended Multiplication Tables

Several writers have suggested that calculating prodigies have far more extensive multiplication tables than the 10 by 10 or 12 by 12 tables known to most of us. Scripture, for instance, writes (1891:46):

---

[4] Fortunately, this problem could not arise, since numbers had no gender for Finkelstein (Bousfield and Barry 1933:355).

To get an idea of the wonderful ease and rapidity with which such examples can be done in this way make use of a table reaching to 100×100. . . .
Did any of the prodigies possess such a table? Considering their enormous
powers of memory it would be almost unexplainable if they did not. Although Bidder asserts that he really had no such table, yet Mondeux actually
possessed part of such a table, and I think we can pre-suppose it in the case
of Colburn, Buxton and even Dase.

And Proctor (1879:462) went so far as to speculate that calculators
such as Bidder probably knew the multiplication table to "1000 times a
1000, or even farther."

Consider first the possibility of a table of 1,000 by 1,000. Allowing
for commutativity (i.e., one need not memorize both 638 times 414 and
414 times 638), it is necessary, for an n by n multiplication table, to
memorize $(n^2 + n)/2$ entries, or in this instance, 500,500 entries. Even if
we eliminate multiplication by zero and one as immediate, there would
be $(n^2 - 3n + 2)/2$ or 498,501 entries to memorize. The total number of
digits in such a table exceeds 3,500,000. Inaudi required 12 minutes (8⅓
digits per minute) to memorize a number of 100 digits (Binet 1894:54).
Of course, the greater number of digits, the more time is required for
memorization, but let us take this as an average. Furthermore, suppose
that a child devotes 40 hours every week to memorizing such a table.
More than 3½ years would be required at this rate to acquire the essen-
tials of multiplication. Since many prodigies were giving public demonstrations by age 6, a multiplication table of a 1,000 by 1,000 is not
credible.

In fact, only one calculator, Wim Klein, is known to make use of a
multiplication table of 100 by 100; he batches the numbers in pairs and
cross-multiplies. In the case of other calculators the evidence, where
available, is against their having made use of extended multiplication tables.[5]

Bidder (1856:259), as Scripture notes, specifically denied knowing the
multiplication table to 100 by 100:

> Now, gentlemen, I wish to impress upon you, that in order to multiply 3
> places of figures by 3 places of figures, the number of facts I had to store in

[5] Arthur Griffith said that he knew the multiplication tables to 120 by 120 when 15 years
of age, and, at 19 years, to 130 by 130 (Bryan and Lindley 1941:36). Whether he put this
knowledge to use in multiplying larger numbers is not stated. Griffith later claimed to know
the multiplication tables to 1,000 by 1,000 (Bryan and Lindley 1941:51), surely an exag-
geration. It should also be noted that Griffith was not above a little fakery (chapter 32).

my mind was less, than what was requisite for the acquisition of the common multiplication table up to 12 times 12. For the latter it is necessary to retain 72 facts; whereas my multiplication, up to 10 times 10, required only 50 facts. Then I had to recollect, in addition, the permutations among the numbers up to a million, that is to say, I had to recollect that 100 times 100 were 10,000, 10 times 10,000 were 100,000, and that ten hundred thousand made a million. In order to do that, I had only the permutations on 6 facts, which amounted to only 18 in number, therefore all the machinery requisite to multiply up to 3 places of figures was restricted to 68 facts.

In the case of Colburn (1833:189–90) as well, the procedure described for multiplication involves only single-digit products.

It is particularly farfetched to suggest, as does Scripture, that Buxton employed an extended multiplication table, since, when called upon to explain his procedure in multiplying 456 by 378, he said that he multiplied 456 first by 5, then by 20, and finally by 3, in order to get the intermediate product of 456 times 300. Buxton was unable even to make use of the fact that multiplication by 5 and then 20 is equivalent to multiplication by 100 (*Gentleman's Magazine,* June 1754:252).

Inaudi also denied any knowledge of extended multiplication tables (Binet 1894:74): "he does not possess, as one might believe, a more extended multiplication table than ours, comprising, for example, the products of two-digit numbers; his procedure consists of decomposing a complex multiplication into a series of simpler multiplications."

In fact, in one example cited by Binet (1894:74–75), Inaudi treated 25 as a single item in multiplying 325 by 638, but one would hardly have to be a calculating prodigy to know that 25 times 8 is 200.

Experimental evidence supports Inaudi's claim that he did not employ an extended multiplication table. Binet (1894:90) made some limited tests on Inaudi and found that he required an average of 0.6 seconds to multiply one digit by one digit. To multiply two digits by two digits required an average of two seconds, or over three times as long. Furthermore, the two-digit by two-digit problems were particularly easy because the multiplier in each case was 42.[6]

Scripture also claims (1891:46) without citation, that Mondeux possessed part of a table of 100 by 100. Of course, everyone who can multiply at all possesses part of such a table, so the question must be the extent of Mondeux's knowledge. The only justification for Scripture's claim

---

[6]Of course, it is also true that some things take longer to remember than others. Though I know my phone number, it sometimes takes several moments to summon it to mind.

seems to be a remark in Cauchy's (1885:493) report to the Academy of Sciences, to the effect that Mondeux knew by heart the squares of all the natural numbers less than 100. Powers have a strong attraction for calculating prodigies, and the very fact that no mention is made of a general knowledge of products less than 100 is strong indication that Mondeux had no such knowledge, for Cauchy would hardly have failed to note it.

Examples of methods of multiplications by Mondeux suggest that typically he multiplied digit by digit (Jacoby 1860:220–21), but in a few cases he multiplied one digit by two (e.g., 5×24, 5×15).

Wim Klein, as I mentioned earlier, is the only calculator known to have used a multiplication table of 100 by 100. This table was not deliberately committed to memory but acquired from repeatedly encountering the same combinations.

Hans Eberstark, like Klein, uses cross multiplication, but unlike Klein, he multiplies only one digit at a time. This is not because he could not memorize all the two-digit combinations, since he specializes in memorizing numbers (pi in particular), but because he feels that the two-digit method becomes confusing as the numbers grow larger:

> I wouldn't be able to tell you as quickly as Wim can what, say, 85 times 32 is; I'd have to work it out—85 times 32 is 170 times 16, which is 256 plus 16, which is 272 and add a zero[7]—2,720. But he knows 85 times 32 off by heart. It does take me about one or two seconds to calculate the answer. His method is all right up to about six digits or so, but after six digits I think that his method is confusing. Because there are too many long figures to add up, there are too many sources of mistakes.

The reason for assuming extended multiplication tables in the absence of evidence supporting their use in general (in fact, despite evidence to the contrary) seems to be a belief that memorization is always significantly simpler than calculation. This is the case, of course, for those of us who do arithmetic consciously. It is natural to assume, therefore, that calculating prodigies could profit from a multiplication table of 100 by 100, rather than 10 by 10. But in the case of calculating prodigies this is an unreasonable assumption. Why memorize that which can be so easily computed?

[7] Eberstark is here multiplying 16×17, which is 16^2 ($= 256$) plus 16. He of course knows 16^2 (a power of two) without calculating it.

Mnemonics

Books on memory often give methods for memorizing numbers. Typically these involve associating digits with consonants and then divising words having the appropriate consonants to represent particular numbers. Since vowels can be freely added, the same sequence of digits can be represented by a variety of different words (or sequences of words).

Such techniques are advantageous only if the words are easier to retain than the numbers themselves. But for calculating prodigies, for whom numbers have many of the properties of words, the advantages of such a roundabout process of recollection may be nil. Aitken (1954:301) commented: "Mnemonics I have never used, and deeply distrust. They merely perturb with alien and irrelevant associations a faculty that should be pure and limpid."

An unpublished report by Fred Barlow of tests conducted on Wim Klein in 1953 imputed to him the use of mnemonics, since he reported associations such as $429 = 3 \times 11 \times 13$ and 429 B.C. was the death of Pericles.

When Klein commented on this, he said: "I didn't use the word 'mnemonics.' Mnemonics could only disturb me; 429 is, first of all, 3 times 11 times 13, and on top of that, it was the death of Pericles, but not the reverse."

Calculators do have a variety of associations with numbers, and these may serve as a memory aid in particular cases, but such associations are haphazard, and a calculator must be able to retain numbers even in the absence of familiar associations. Bousfield and Barry (1933:354–55) reported:

> Mr. Finkelstein's process of memorization of numbers is aided by associations. In the course of the experiments, the following varieties were repeatedly reported: (a) dates of historical events; (b) mathematical associations such as powers, roots, logarithms, and prime numbers; (c) permutations of significant numbers; (d) ascending and descending series; (e) telephone numbers; (f) numerical characteristics of literary works, such as the number of paragraphs contained. Because of the readiness of the occurrence of associations, if some type of association is not apparent, the numbers appear to be unusual and acquire memory value on account of this lack.[8]

[8] This is reminiscent of the induction "proof" that there are no uninteresting natural numbers. Assume the converse: then there is a smallest uninteresting natural number. But being the smallest uninteresting natural number *is* interesting, etc.

In any case Finkelstein retained numbers by visualizing them, so that these associations were no more than an aid in fixing the numerical images in his mind. His most frequent error in memorization was a transposition of adjacent digits—an error which should not occur if a successful association has been formed, but a common error of those called upon to copy out figures.

Weinland (1948:254) paraphrased a report in Polish by Jakob Segal: "Finkelstein does not use mnemonic methods, he visualizes. Even when numbers are given orally he transposes them into pictures. His subjective pictures are clear and lasting. A big factor in his memory is the help he obtains from perceived complexes and combinations of numbers. These are not artificial but natural combinations and 'nice numbers' which he sees."

Binet (1894:166) compared the ability of the Greek calculator Diamandi to memorize numbers with that of Arnould, a magician and "mnemotechnicien"—one skilled in memorizing numbers by translating them into words.

In the system used by Arnould the digits zero through nine were represented by the indicated (French) consonants:

0	1	2	3	4	5	6	7	8	9
s	d	n	m	r	l	j	k	v	b
z	t	gn				ch	qu	f	p
							gu		

The vowels are supplied according to the user's ingenuity to create words or phrases. For example:

1514	t	l	t	r
	d	l	d	r

Therefore, some possible words for 1,514 are (Binet 1894:166): *idolâtre; utilité au roi; un tel douaire; été ladre; tous les dons royaux.*

Table 6.2 gives the times required by each to memorize numbers of varying lengths (whether these times are average, best, or the result of only one trial is not indicated). The numbers were given to them on paper, and the time is that which elapsed until they announced that they had memorized the number and the paper was taken away.

Again the round numbers suggest the timekeeping was less than exact.

TABLE 6.2
Times Required by Diamandi and Arnould to Memorize Numbers of Various Lengths

	Diamandi	Arnould
10	17 sec.	20 sec.
15	1 m. 15 sec.	1 m. 45 sec.
20	2 m. 15 sec.	2 m. 30 sec.
25	3 m.	2 m. 30 sec.
30	4 m. 20 sec.	2 m. 45 sec.
50	7 m.	?
100	25 m.	15 m.
200	1 h. 15 m. 20 sec.	45 m.

Source: Binet 1894:166.

The question mark for Arnould's time to memorize 50 digits is because Binet has ditto marks in that position, but it does not appear likely that Arnould took the same time to memorize 50 digits as he did to memorize 30. Probably Binet meant that Arnould, like Diamandi, took seven minutes to memorize 50 digits.

Binet remarks (1894:173): "A peculiar thing, nothing in the external attitude of the two men revealed that the operations of their memory were done under such different conditions. Mr. Arnould, like Mr. Diamandi, had the attitude of a student learning a lesson, looking at the book, then turning his eyes to mutter in a low voice."

As can be seen, Diamandi was a little quicker at memorizing short numbers, but as the numbers grew longer the edge was all on the side of the mnemotechnicien. On the other hand, Diamandi was considerably quicker at reciting numbers, evidently owing to the time required for Arnould to translate from words to digits. The best Arnould could achieve in repeating 100 memorized digits was 72 seconds—Diamandi's best time was 46 seconds. Although he offers few details, Binet reports that a number of other experiments had a similar outcome—in every case Arnould was significantly slower in reciting memorized numbers.

At the outset Binet (1894:169–70) wished to establish how many numbers Arnould could memorize if he (Arnould) were allowed to select the numbers. Arnould immediately pointed out the folly of that. He could dictate many thousands of digits, even a million, and repeat them without error, if allowed to choose the digits he wished. He knew by heart a few hundred lines of poetry. The consonants in these lines could be converted into two or three thousand digits. He could then begin again augmenting each digit by one, then multiplying by two, and so forth. Arnould then gave Binet sufficient demonstration of this ability to make it clear that further investigation along this line would be both dreary and unrevealing.

A few calculators have used mnemonics. Bidder, Jr. used a system about which I have no details (Mitchell 1907:81). Arthur Benjamin uses a system like that used by Arnould, with English words and sounds.

Shyam Marathe translates numbers into characters of the Sanskrit alphabet which he can summon to his visual imagination. Since these characters are subject to a variety of modifications, Marathe can use a single symbol to represent a series of digits; he tells me that he has a symbol to represent integers from zero to something over 4,000. He does not use this system except for memorizing large numbers. For small numbers he simply visualizes the digits.

The most remarkable use of mnemonics is by Hans Eberstark, a calculator who is also a simultaneous translator.

After Eberstark discovered that his memory of numbers had improved considerably simply through extensive calculation, he considered the possibility of developing a system for retaining figures.

"The first time I thought of memorizing figures by using some sort of a system was on a rather unappetizing occasion. Our cat vomited and there was a live worm in the vomit and it turned one way and the other; and then I thought about how to represent figures by vectors going in different directions. I evolved a system, which is all right for telephone numbers or series of up to ten digits, of converting figures into configurations of geometrical figures. That was the first type of conversion I ever tried my hand at."

Eberstark later evolved a system for memorizing numbers that is a more sophisticated version of standard methods for translating numbers into sounds, but unlike other systems, vowels as well as consonants are used to represent numbers. The sounds are drawn from a variety of languages, and while sound sequences may resemble words in various languages known by Eberstark, there is no necessary correspondence.

Eberstark is a visualizer when he calculates, but his mnemonic system is quasi-verbal. The sound sequences are "spelled out" in numbers—the numbers are the orthographic representations of the sounds. The sounds conjure up in his mind their spelling—that is, their numerical representations.

Some of the basics of his system are:

0 = open *o* (like the vowel in "caught", for those who pronounce it differently from "cot"); or trilled *r*, as in the Spanish word for "dog" — "perro"

1 = short *i* (as in German "Fisch") or *y*, as in "yes"

2 = *t* or *d*

3 = like the *e* in "get"

4 = *f* between vowels, or like the high central vowel of Turkish between consonants

5 = *s*

6 = *b* or *p*

7 = light *l*, like the *l* of German or French, or as in the English word "leaf"

8 = short *u* as in German "Mutter"; similar to English "book," or *w* ("wet")

9 = *k* or *g*

Short *a* (as in Spanish "blanco"), which has no numerical value, can be inserted to make sequences of consonants easier to pronounce.

This is only the basic system. Sequences of numbers frequently have particular phonetic representations. For example, 77 is dark *l*, as "ball," 69 is English *r*, 456 is French *r*, 03 is like the first vowel of the French word "peuple," 96 is long *a*, as in the German word "Wagen," and 654 is the Arabic sound transliterated into the Roman alphabet as *ḥ*.

Eberstark's major memory feat is the memorization of pi, which he knows to more than 11,000 places. In Eberstark's system the first 10 decimal places of pi (3.1415926535) are pronounced·

ayfisktapses

The first two digits, 3.1, are pronounced *ay* (like "eye") rather than *ey* (just as in German); the short *a* is inserted in *sktps* to make it easier to pronounce—sktaps.

Eberstark relates these sounds with words in various languages. He explained:

I could go one step further and try to remember this as making sense: *fisk* is like the Scandinavian word for "fish" and *ay* is like the English word "eye," so this is like the eye of a fish.

Now this is something that is easier to remember for me, because it has an emotional charge. I love to eat fish eyes and my wife feels terribly unhappy when I eat everyone's fish eyes in the restaurant. So the fish eyes become a bone of contention. For *taps* I could think of "tops." They taste excellent, they're tops.

So here I have a story. But I have to remember that it's *fisk,* not "fish," *taps* and not "tops."

Words in human language are of varying lengths. In the case of some calculators, "numerical word length" (the number of digits that constitute a memory unit) seems to be invariant; for example, for George Parker Bidder, a numerical word consisted of three digits.

Moreover, the numerical words of most calculators are quite short. Chase and Ericsson (1982) suggest: "Without a single exception in the literature, expert mental calculators and other memory experts have digit groups of 3–5 digits. . . ."

In Eberstark's case, this seems not to be so, perhaps because of the purposes for which his system was developed.

If one is memorizing numbers as an adjunct to calculation, three digits is a natural grouping. Or if one is memorizing numbers where the emphasis is on speed of learning, as in the experiments of Chase and Ericsson (1982), the maximum number of digits in a group may never exceed four, for the reason they give (reliable capacity of short-term memory).

But if one is memorizing a long series of digits for permanent retention (as in the memorization of pi), longer groups can be a distinct advantage, since long words are often as easy to recall as short ones, but longer numerical words yield more digits.

In reply to a question as to what a numerical word was in his system of memorization, Eberstark wrote me:

> One preliminary question, of course, is: What is a "word"? In English *World Health Organization* is three words; in German *Weltgesundheitsorganisation* is one; Finnish and Hungarian have even longer words. Thanks to my multilingual background I have no trouble with six or seven syllable "words" or "memory units."
>
> The more phonemes you admit, the shorter you can make your words. I have not shied away from sounds that may appear exotic to monolinguals, such as Arabic *ḥ*—(654), Arabic *ghain*—(456), Albanian "dark 1"—(77), not to speak of French *j* (555) or French nasal vowels. The difficulty is not so much one of pronunciation, but of consistently keeping them apart. Thus, most people could, I suppose, pronounce the simple rolled *r* [r] (alternative

for **0**), the double rolled *r* [r:] as in Spanish "hierro" (alternative for **00**), and American *r* [R] in "right" (**69**) and French glottal *r* (more or less identical in pronunciation to Arabic *ghain* [γ] and thus **456**). But [pero]—(**6300**), [per:o]—(**63000**), [peRo]—(**63690**) and [peγo]—(**634560**) may easily be confused. It is for this reason that I have refrained from incorporating any further *r* variants, such as the Japanese *r* in "sayonara," and set up additional rules to differentiate between simple [l] (**7**) and "dark l" (**77**). Even so, this is admittedly a weak point in my system.

The two "words" or "memory units" I referred to on the phone were [tɛpatspitstipɛdo:patú] (**2362561252163208628**), a 19-digit combination at the end of the 92nd line [of the computer printout of the value of pi (i.e. digits 9182–9200) and the six-syllable (or 5½ syllable) word [nu:lkλ'o:kaiγR'-ɛpupḷ], which has 24 digits: (**228879710893145669136867**) (right in the middle of the 3rd 1000-digit block).

As a result of having multisyllable memory units I can link them by making two adjacent units overlap.

Incidentally, the nonmemorizer also has multisyllable memory units, e.g. "American Express Card" or "Sir Winston Churchill."

Chapter Seven

Formal Considerations

THAT language and arithmetic are related in some elusive fashion has been noted by philosophers since antiquity. In one respect, however, language and arithmetic differ dramatically—the mechanisms of speech are unconscious, and it is the goal of linguistics to elucidate them, while arithmetic, for most people, is carried out entirely consciously.

In "Of Knowledge, Apes, and Brains," Lenneberg (1971:1) maintains "that man's ability for mathematical thinking is a product of the same species-specific form of cerebration as language." If Lenneberg is correct, it follows that mental arithmetic, like speech, is potentially an unconscious process. The puzzle then becomes, not why some people can calculate unconsciously, but why most people cannot.[1]

Logic, the basis for mathematical proofs, is clearly rooted in human language. The operators of logic, *and, or, if . . . then, if and only if,* and *not* are all borrowed from language. Even though logicians have devised a single operator (not based on language) that can be used in the place of the operators mentioned above, no mathematician would present proofs using this operator. Such proofs could not be assimilated intuitively until translated into something more language-like. We have more logical operators than are logically necessary because human beings find them easier to understand.

Little progress was made in investigating the properties of logic between the time of Aristotle and the latter part of the nineteenth century. Mathematicians constructed their proofs in words and were satisfied. Even today most mathematicians have never taken a course in logic. In the

[1]Though I agree with Lenneberg that language and arithmetic are similar in form, I find the particulars he gives to justify his conclusion too general or too doubtful to be convincing.

twentieth century logic itself became the subject of formalization. The result is still recognizable as language—unambiguous, in some cases slightly nonintuitive, and restricted to what is required for mathematical formalisms—but clearly based on language.

Fortunately, the relationship between logic and arithmetic has already been elucidated, in Kurt Gödel's (1931) classic work. One step in "Gödel's proof," as the substance of this paper is popularly known, is a method for coding logic into arithmetic in such a way as to preserve all significant relationships. Of course, logic reflects only a portion of language, but Gödel shows that an interesting segment of language can be represented arithmetically.

Addition and "And"

Lenneberg (1971) identifies the plus of addition with the notion conveyed by the English word *and*. With this identification I concur, for the following reasons. The word *and* and its translations are used in various languages for the additive operator in reciting arithmetic expressions, as in "three and two are five." It would seem very strange to say "One or one is two," even though it is *or* (corresponding to set union), rather than *and,* that mathematicians identify with addition. Students attempting to garner an understanding of the foundations of mathematics often find this a stumbling block.

And is also connected with addition in the "word problems" posed to school children: "If there are four cats in the living room, three dogs in the bathroom, two armadillos in the bedroom, and an anteater in the kitchen, how many animals are there in the house?"

Furthermore, when properties are attributed to conjoined subjects of a sentence as a group, rather than to the individual noun phrases comprising the subject, it can represent the adding together of some common property of each noun phrase, as in: "Ernie and Rita Sue weigh more than Joe Don." The preceding sentence is ambiguous, but in one sense, we understand that Ernie's weight added to Rita Sue's is greater than that of Joe Don. (In the other sense each weighs more than Joe Don.)

Finally, in counting, in a variety of languages, words translating as *and* are used as equivalents to the additive operator. American children used to be (and perhaps still are) discouraged by grammar-school teachers from using such expressions as "six hundred *and* ninety-three." (But Lincoln's Gettysburg Address begins: "Four score and seven years ago . . .").

There are various other languages in which *and* is used to express addition as a normal part of the counting process. In German, for instance, *thirty-two* is *zweiunddreissig* ("two and thirty") and in Spanish *treinta y dos* ("thirty and two"). Thus it seems that, even in languages that form their number words in a somewhat different way, words translating as *and* are associated with addition. This psychological association between *and* and addition plays an important role in the following discussion.

Conjunction and Distribution

The distributive laws of arithmetic have a precise structural parallel in language—the relation called by linguists "conjunction reduction." The parallel is so exact that the possibility of chance similarity must be discounted.

Noam Chomsky's (1957) *Syntactic Structures,* a seminal work in modern linguistic theory, contained a rule of conjunction reduction which related pairs of sentences to paraphrases with conjoined constituents[2] smaller than clauses. In Chomsky's words (1957:35):

> One of the most productive processes for forming new sentences is the process of conjunction. If we have two sentences $Z + X + W$ and $Z + Y + W$, and if X and Y are actually constituents of these sentences, we can generally form a new sentence $Z - X + and + Y - W$. For example, from the sentences $(20a - b)$ we can form the new sentence (21).
>
> (20) (a) the scene — of the movie — was in Chicago
>   (b) the scene — of the play — was in Chicago
> (21) the scene — of the movie and of the play — was in Chicago.

In subsequent work (e.g., Chomsky 1965) the source of conjoined phrases was not taken to be two independent sentences, as Chomsky has it here, but two sentences joined by *and.* Thus the source of (21) would be one sentence of the form: "The scene of the movie was in Chicago

---

[2] Roughly speaking, a constituent is a group of words which "hang together" in a sentence. Each of the major components of a sentence as learned in high-school sentence diagramming (subject, predicate, prepositional phrase, etc.) is a constituent. One constituent may include another, as a noun phrase, which in turn may form part of the predicate. Constituents can be set off by parentheses, as: (Fernando (flew (to (her bedside)))).

and the scene of the play was in Chicago."[3] For our purposes the only change we need make in Chomsky's formulation is to italicize the first "and" in the second sentence quoted above, and change the word "sentence" to "clause," i.e.: If we have two clauses $Z + X + W$ *and* ...

Suppose we modify Chomsky's notation slightly to render it more in keeping with that of arithmetic. We shall omit his "+" (which represents concatenation—intuitively, the linear order of constituents), replace *and* with the addition sign "+", and finally, replace the dashes with parentheses, to which they seem to be equivalent.[4] In this representation of Chomsky's rule of conjunction reduction, (1) gives rise to (2):

$$(1) \quad ZXW + ZYW$$
$$(2) \quad Z(X + Y)W$$

In this form the rule of conjunction reduction seems to be a special case of the distributive laws of arithmetic. Nor is this all. For empirical adequacy we must allow either Z or W to be null (as in [3a] and [5a] below). If Z is null (3) gives rise to (4), and if W is null, (5) gives rise to (6).

$$(3) \quad XW + YW$$
$$(4) \quad (X + Y)W$$
$$(5) \quad ZX + ZY$$
$$(6) \quad Z(X + Y)$$

These are the left and right distributive laws of arithmetic. Corresponding to (3) through (6) are sentences such as (3a) through (6a).

(3a) Rita Sue eats fricasseed swamp grass and Ernie
        eats fricasseed swamp grass.
(4a) Rita Sue and Ernie eat fricasseed swamp grass.
(5a) Ernie is myopic and Ernie is monophobic.
(6a) Ernie is myopic and monophobic.

There has been considerable controversy in linguistics over conjunction reduction; in particular, whether all, or no, or only some conjoined

[3] I have, like Chomsky, used locutions here which suggest that, according to linguistic theory, certain sentences are derived from other sentences. That is not the case. Sentences such as Chomksy's (20) and (21) have been taken to be derived from the same abstract source—that source having essentially, though not precisely, the structure of (20).

[4] See footnote 2 of this chapter.

phrases are derived from conjoined clauses (see Stockwell et al. 1973). For my purposes it is sufficient that some nonarbitrary relationship exist between conjoined clauses (examples [3a] and [5a]) and corresponding conjoined phrases ([4a] and [6a]). I use the term "conjunction reduction" to describe this relationship.

Though the distributive laws and conjunction reduction are identical in form, their respective roles in the systems of which they are a part (arithmetic and human language) are quite different. In arithmetic, parenthesization indicates the order of performance of operations—that is, the order of concept synthesization. In the case of the distributive laws, arithmetically equivalent results will be obtained with different arrangements of terms and operations. Algebra is based upon such considerations.

Conjunction reduction, though it represents a kind of linguistic equivalence (paraphrase), is conceptually far from arithmetic equivalence, since conjunction reduction does not relate structures for which different arrangements of terms and operations result in equivalent conceptual synthesizations—and to this fact, as we shall see, can certain cases of ambiguity be attributed. In fact, for cases of conjunction reduction, in order to get the correct order of conceptual synthesis, it is necessary to translate conjoined phrases into a form similar to that of conjoined clauses.

The structuralist tradition in American linguistics, which derived largely from the work of Leonard Bloomfield (1933), analyzed language into "immediate constituents," pairing words into successively more inclusive structures until an entire sentence was encompassed. At least part of the intuitive purpose, though never an overt justification, was to bracket forms appropriately to represent conceptual syntheses. For example, consider the subject of sentence (7).

(7)   Three armed bandits held up the liquor store.

In the most likely sense the subject of (7) would be bracketed into immediate constituents as (three (armed bandits)). But there is another possible bracketing: ((*three armed*) *bandits*).[5] In the latter sense the bandits should not be difficult to identify.

[5] In both spoken and written English, such bracketing differences are distinguished—by intonation in the former case and hyphenation in the latter, as in "three-armed bandits" versus "three armed bandits." Sometimes even hyphenation does not help; I recently saw a newspaper article which referred to "Sunday-best-dressed students." The intended interpretation is, of course, ((Sunday best) dressed)—students dressed in their Sunday-best—rather than (Sunday (best dressed)), which would presumably be students who are best-dressed on Sunday.

When Katz and Fodor (1963) first attempted to incorporate semantics into grammar, they assumed (and this assumption has been tacitly accepted in most subsequent work in linguistics, even that otherwise in substantial disagreement with theirs), that the tree structure (a notational variant of labeled parentheses) determines the order of concept synthesization—but tree structure on a more abstract level; that is, before any rules such as conjunction reduction have applied.

Smith (1969) argued that not all cases of conjoined phrases can be plausibly regarded as derived from conjoined sentences (my examples).

(8) Dr. Snowflake was pummeled black and blue.

(9) My favorite cocktail is Scotch and Koolaid.

Neither of the above can be paraphrased by conjoined sentences. One cannot conclude from (8) that Dr. Snowflake was pummeled blue nor from (9) that my favorite cocktail is Koolaid.

There are also cases of ambiguous sentences, in which one interpretation can be paraphrased by conjoined clauses, while the other cannot.

(10) Rita Sue and Ernie weigh 463 pounds.

(11) Arnold and Sergio can lift that horse.

In (10) it might be that Rita Sue weighs 463 pounds and Ernie weighs 463 pounds, or that their combined weight is 463 pounds. Perhaps only one of the strong men of (11) is required to lift the horse, or perhaps both are necessary. On the basis of evidence like this Smith proposed two sources for conjoined phrases; "derived" (derived from conjoined clauses via conjunction reduction), and "phrasal," in which the phrases are generated as such—that is, they are not derived from clauses. Sentences (8) and (9) are thus examples of phrasal conjunction, while (10) and (11) have two possible sources each—one phrasal and the other derived. In the derived interpretation of (10) Rita Sue and Ernie each weigh 463 pounds; in the phrasal interpretation their combined weight is 463 pounds. In (11) Arnold and Sergio can lift the horse together in the phrasal sense, but in the derived interpretation each can do so.

In the case of phrasal conjunction the order of concept synthesization corresponds to the surface (final) structure; this is not the case for derived conjunction, and this provides a major motive for proposing to derive the latter (but not the former) from conjoined sentences. Thus, unlike the distributive laws of arithmetic, conjunction reduction derives semantic justification from the need to relate certain structures to others more in keeping with the appropriate order of concept syntheses.

What could account for the fact that a law of arithmetic has a precise structural parallel in language? Is it chance? Are the distributive laws and conjunction reduction independent and only accidently similar? Hardly. The similarities are too extensive to be coincidental. Both involve not merely the absence of duplicated material, but parallel structural modifications (i.e., re-parenthesization) as well. Furthermore, conjunction reduction distributes other linguistic structures over *and,* which is, as I noted earlier, psychologically connected to the notion of addition.

Can it be that the distributive laws of arithmetic are borrowed from natural language? This too is not credible. Arithmetic is not some arbitrary scheme whose rules can be adjusted *ad libitum*. It is true that mathematicians have expended much effort on the axiomatization of arithmetic, but arithmetic has been around far longer than any axiomatizations. Arithmetic is as it is for necessary and not at all arbitrary reasons.

Are both based upon some more general cognitive faculty—does something in the human cognitive apparatus favor the use of the distributive laws in diverse psychological circumstances? This is more likely, if only by default—other alternatives seem even less plausible.

But the conjunction reduction relation, though not a peripheral phenomenon in language, and so far as I know universal, does not have about it the same sort of necessity as do the distributive laws. Arithmetic is literally inconceivable without the distributive laws;[6] the only apparent advantage of conjunction reduction to communication is that it allows more economical speech, at the price of some additional ambiguity, which goes almost entirely unnoticed either because the circumstances render only one interpretation plausible or because the alternatives differ inconsequentially.

There is another reason to doubt that the distributive laws and conjunction reduction are coincidentally derived from a single cognitive faculty. It has been cogently argued that conjunction reduction must be regarded as two separate rules (or relations), "deletion" and "regrouping," either of which may be individually manifested, and the combined effects of which are equivalent to the distributive laws. In the case of

---

[6]There are algebras, investigated by mathematicians, for which the distributive laws do not hold, but they would be of little use in balancing a checkbook or totting up the grocery bill.

arithmetic, deletion and regrouping cannot be isolated as processes. None of the following is generally true in arithmetic:

$$(12) \quad XY + XZ = XY + Z$$
$$(13) \quad YX + ZX = Y + ZX$$
$$(14) \quad WX + YZ = (W + Y)(X + Z)$$

Examples (12) and (13) represent deletion without regrouping, while (14) is regrouping without deletion. Though these two operations are inseparable in arithmetic, in language it seems that they can be isolated; that is, there are cases in language when only one or the other obtains (Crockett 1972).[7]

(15)   ((That boy) and (that girl)) (are insatiable).
(16)   ((That boy) and girl) (are insatiable).

Sentence (16) differs from (15) only by the omission of *that* before *girl* in the latter, and the sense of (16) is that of (15). If both deletion and regrouping had taken place we should have a bracketing like (17) for (16).

(17)   (That (boy and girl)) (are insatiable).

But if this were the correct structure, with *that* modifying both *boy* and *girl,* the demonstrative pronoun should be plural (i.e., *these*), just as the verb is plural.

(18)   These boy and girl are insatiable.

Example (18) is, of course, ungrammatical. Thus there appear to be cases (as in (16)) of conjunction reduction in which deletions, but no regrouping, has taken place.

There also seem to be cases of regrouping without deletion. Sentences (19) and (20) display such a correspondence.

(19) John (plays tennis) and Mary (shoots pool).
$\quad\ \ W \quad\quad X \quad\ + \quad Y \quad\quad Z$
(20) (John and Mary) ((play tennis) and (shoot pool)), respectively.
$\quad\ \ (W \ + \ Y) \quad\quad (X \quad\ + \quad\ Z)$

---

[7] These examples are my own, not Crockett's.

This is just the relationship represented in (14) (which is impossible in arithmetic): regrouping without deletion. It is as if language had borrowed the form of an arithmetic law while ignoring its content, and could therefore, when convenient, divide it in two, and make use of each part separately, in a way totally impossible in arithmetic.

This leads to consideration of another alternative—that conjunction reduction was imported into language from arithmetic (as a means of compressing communication?). Most linguists would reject this alternative out of hand, on the assumption that we humans must have been speaking fully developed languages, complete with conjunction reduction, long before we knew anything of arithmetic. In fact, I know of no reason for supposing that conjunction reduction preceded a knowledge of arithmetic in human consciousness. There are cultures with no knowledge of counting (or at least without the knowledge to say or write numbers),[8] but they are quite rare, and we have no idea about the mathematical knowledge of their remote ancestors, or whether conjunction reduction could have been borrowed from the language of a more sophisticated culture. It is easy to forget that human beings have been around for hundreds of thousands of years, presumably talking, while our actual knowledge of language goes back only some six thousand years, and much of this is inferential. The proposition that conjunction reduction was borrowed from arithmetic fits the facts as well, indeed better, than the other alternatives, and I can see no reason why it could not be true.

Turing Machines and Grammar

An algorithm is an explicit procedure for calculating something. Computer programs are algorithms, as are the methods we learned as children for addition, subtraction, multiplication, extracting square roots, etc.

In 1936 A. M. Turing, a British mathematician, succeeded in capturing the intuitive notion of an algorithm. Any algorithm can be represented as a "Turing machine," a simple hypothetical device conceived by Turing.

Linguists have attempted to represent languages by "grammars"—algorithms for listing sentences, along with grammatical and other information. But the formalisms devised by linguists to represent grammars

[8] See, for example, Seidenberg (1960).

have frequently turned out to be equivalent to the theory of Turing machines[9] (though this was expressly contrary to the intent of the linguists involved). Turing machines are, insofar as is known, completely general devices—anything that can be formalized at all can be represented as a Turing machine. Since a model (in this case, a grammatical model of language) should be limited to what is required to account for the data, this seems an unfortunate result.

It is also known that any device that can add, multiply, and branch (i.e., decide what to calculate next on the basis of the outcome of earlier calculations) can calculate anything computable by a Turing machine. Calculating prodigies appear to be just such devices. If the calculating ability of prodigies is based upon the same faculty as that for speech, as argued in this book, then it is likely that any adequate model of language will be equivalent to the theory of Turing machines. Thus the difficulty encountered by linguists in attempting to devise models for language more limited than that of Turing machines is just what is to be expected.

A Turing machine consists of an infinite tape[10] divided into squares, each square containing either a symbol from a finite alphabet or a blank; a reading head, which can scan one square at a time; and a control unit, which can be in any one of a finite number of "states" (these can simply be numbered one through n). The actions of the machine are determined entirely by the state of the machine and the symbol being scanned on the tape. A Turing machine is limited to the following operations: it can erase the symbol being scanned, it can print a new symbol on a blank square, it can move one square to the right or left, and it can change its own internal state. The tape contains the input at the beginning of the computation and is used for storing intermediate results, as well as printing the resulting computation. A Turing machine instruction might be: if the machine is in state 41 scanning q on the tape, erase q and move one square to the right and switch to state 36. The machine halts when it comes to a situation for which it has no instruction (e.g., suppose the machine is in state 14 scanning j on the tape, and there is no instruction covering this circumstance).

Turing was able to show that there is a universal Turing machine— one which can compute in the manner of any given Turing machine

[9]That is, it is possible to mimic an arbitrary Turing machine using the formalisms posited for grammars.

[10]The tape is specified as infinite to ensure that the machine never runs out of tape in doing a calculation. We could make an equivalent stipulation that more tape is available as required.

when the instructions for that machine are included as part of the input to the universal Turing machine. Particular Turing machines can be regarded as programs for the universal Turing machine. A modern digital computer is equivalent to the universal Turing machine in what it can calculate, so long as additional memory can be added whenever needed to complete a calculation.

Turing argued that all actual calculations, however complex, could be reduced to the simple operations of a Turing machine. Alonzo Church, an American logician, had already hypothesized that a class of functions conceived by him and Kleene (termed "λ-definable") are the only ones which, in some intuitive sense, can be calculated at all. Turing showed that λ-definable and Turing (machine) computable are equivalent notions. More generally, this can be taken to mean that anything intuitively well-defined can be represented by a Turing machine. No counterexamples to what has come to be known as "Church's thesis" have yet come to light.

Since one of its components is an infinite tape, a Turing machine could never actually be constructed, nor would it be an efficient computing device. Its interest lies in the fact that, because of its conceptual simplicity, many problems can be shown to be solvable or unsolvable for Turing machines. If there is no Turing machine which can solve a particular problem (equivalently, if it cannot be solved by the universal Turing machine), it is, by Church's thesis, unsolvable by any means whatever.

Calculating Prodigies as Turing Machines

Do calculating prodigies have the unconscious potential of the universal Turing machine? That is to say, is a human being, on an unconscious level, potentially the equivalent of a universal calculating device (like a digital computer)?

It might initially seem far-fetched to compare a human being, a "device" with very restricted short-term memory, to a Turing machine, which has unbounded memory. But, in fact, all "real" devices, be they human beings, digital computers, or whatever, are limited by available storage. Even though computer programs and the algorithms of calculating prodigies would work equally well for devices with unlimited storage, no programmer or mental calculator can afford to adopt procedures which fail to take into account the finiteness of memory available to him.

A device that can add, multiply, and branch can mimic an arbitrary

Turing machine, if sufficient memory is available. On a conscious level all of us have this potential, which can be realized to varying degrees, depending upon the individual and the availability of external memory aids, such as pencil and paper.

Chapter 2 discussed the fact that much mental calculation, by prodigies, multiplication in particular, is unconscious. Addition is less favored by calculators, but there is little doubt that the operations of basic arithmetic can be unconscious. But what of branching? Can a human being carry out branching instructions unconsciously?

In order to branch a device must have the ability to compare, and base subsequent actions on the outcome of such comparisons. For example, a branching instruction might be: if the outcome of some calculation is greater than zero, do X; otherwise do Y.

Aitken's complex calculating strategies (see part 2), and their often unconscious implementation, suggest that unconscious branching must be part of the human intellectual potential. He said (Bowden 1953:315): "Though these processes take time to describe, they pass in the mind with prodigious speed, though with the ease and relaxation of a good violinist playing a scale passage.[11] Often the mind is so automatic that it anticipates the will."

Aitken, like Bidder (chapter 2), describes the indistinguishable intertwining of memory and calculation. Such intertwining can presumably arise only when calculations are partly or wholly unconscious[12] (Hunter 1962:249; quoting Aitken):

Problem 7. Decimalize 1/43. 'As you know, I seize at once on a useful property. In this case, that 43 by 93 is 3999, one less than 4000. At once I begin to divide 93 by 4000, entering the answer at the proper place and continuing with the division.[13] Therefore, I have got 0.0232558. . . . You will notice that, not bothering further with the position of the decimal point, I have divided 93 by 4, getting 2325; I am adding to this one 4000th of itself—strictly speaking one 3999th, but by the time the little increment has been tacked on, it is indeed one 4000th of what then has been set down. Now I said to you that, while this proceeds, I have flashes from the side, small extraneous checks, verifications, and even hints for telescoping or simplifying. One of these occurs almost immediately above. Note the 558. I instantly observe that it is 6 times 93. Excellent check on my accuracy so far.

[11] Aitken was a good violinist.
[12] In the case of speech, the relative roles of memory and invention (calculation) are equally unclear.
[13] See chapter 12.

And as I take leave of it, with a 'glance' (not visual), I am dividing by **4000** (that is, by **4** with proper safeguards as to position) and getting 13953488372. . . . But again I note in the same way the 837, 9 times 93, checking again as I fly along. Also the 372, 4 times 93, telling me that I am almost there because it is *four* times, and 4 is my divisor. And indeed . . . 8372093 concludes the period. I am back at my first dividend, *with no remainder,* and so everything will now recur.

'But in actual performance, the answer runs with absolute uniformity. The flashes of recognition and reassurance, indicated by asterisks, pass by like flashes of electric bulbs and cause no distraction whatever. 0.023255813953488372093. Well, of course, I could have memorized this decimal. And perhaps it is memory as much as calculation. But the calculation is just as fast as if it were pure memory, and the two intertwine indistinguishably.'

Aitken's checks are branching instructions. Should one fail he would return to an earlier point in the calculation, try a different strategy, or make a different check; otherwise he would continue along the path mapped out. (Rückle and Klein also acknowledge unconscious monitoring of their calculations; see chapter 2.)

Calculating prodigies thus appear to have the ability to multiply, add, and branch on an unconscious basis, and therefore to be potentially (ignoring memory limitations) the equivalent of the universal Turing machine. If human language and the computations of calculating prodigies derive from the same faculty, as argued herein, then we should expect that an adequate model for language would also be equivalent in calculating potential to the universal Turing machine. The actual experience of linguists in attempting to devise models for language tends to bear out this expectation.

Grammar

In 1957 Noam Chomsky's revolutionary work, *Syntactic Structures,* set as a goal for linguistic theory the specification of an algorithm (or grammar) which would list all and only the sentences of a given language.

For the sake of simplicity, we can confine ourselves for the moment to written English. A sentence of written English is some finite sequence of characters of the Roman alphabet (including blanks and marks of punctuation), augmented by various other symbols and characters (as, for example, Arabic numerals). But not all such sequences are English sentences. For example, "xalf fo eldnub a si ahdduB ehT" is not a sentence of English.

We could require that the sequences be composed of English words, but this comes far short of limiting the product to English: "flax of bundle a is Buddha The." If, however, we invert the words of the last example (or the letters of the first) we get: "The Buddha is a bundle of flax." A little puzzling, perhaps, but certainly English. We could then take (written) English to be the set of all such sequences that are English sentences. If we wish to consider spoken, rather than written English, we can require that the sentences be represented in some suitable phonetic transcription.

A grammar of English may be regarded, then, as a device for listing (or otherwise precisely specifying) all and only the sentences of English. Even though we are very far from the relatively modest goal of identifying the parameters of such a device, no linguist would be satisfied with this. After all, much more is involved in a person's linguistic ability than simply producing or recognizing random grammatical sentences. Similarly a grammar must be a great deal more than a procedure for listing sentences—it must assign a grammatical structure to those sentences, assign meanings (however these are to be represented), possibly assign some sort of context (psychological, cultural, physical) to each, deal with the structure of discourse, etc.

Such considerations led Chomsky to draw a distinction between weak and strong generative capacity. Weak generative capacity refers only to the sequences of characters (sentences) which can be generated by a device (grammar) of a particular kind; strong generative capacity includes the structures assigned by the grammar to the sentences.

Is there a Turing machine which can list all and only the sentences of English? We must presume so, or by Church's thesis, give up forever the goal of a formal account of English. But Turing machines are too unstructured to serve as a grammatical model for human language; in particular, there is no natural way of assigning structural descriptions to the sentences it lists. (One could program the universal Turing machine to mimic some more structured device, but the model would properly be that other device—not the Turing machine.)

Chomsky (1965:62) addressed the issue in the following terms:

> Thus one can construct hierarchies of grammatical theories in terms of weak and strong generative capacity, but it is important to bear in mind that these hierarchies do *not* necessarily correspond to what is probably the em-

pirically most significant dimension of increasing power of linguistic theory. This dimension is presumably to be defined in terms of the scattering in value of grammars compatible with fixed data. Along this empirically significant dimension, we should like to accept the least "powerful" theory that is empirically adequate. It might conceivably turn out that this theory is extremely powerful (perhaps even universal, that is, equivalent to the theory of Turing machines) along the dimension of weak generative capacity, and even along the dimension of strong generative capacity. It will not necessarily follow that it is very powerful (and hence to be discounted) in the dimension which is ultimately of real empirical significance.

In a footnote regarding the possibility that an empirically adequate theory of grammar might be as powerful as the theory of Turing machines in weak generative capacity, Chomsky (1965:208) writes: "This possibility cannot be ruled out a priori, but, in fact, it seems definitely not to be the case. In particular, it seems that, when the theory of transformational grammar is properly formulated, any such grammar must meet formal conditions that restrict it to the enumeration [listing] of recursive sets."[14]

Chomsky's optimism on this point proved unjustified, as Peters and Ritchie (1971) showed that grammars of the sort Chomsky proposed were equivalent to the theory of Turing machines.

A subsequent attempt by Peters and Ritchie (1973) to restrict grammars met with somewhat greater success, but nonrecursive sets could still be produced. Furthermore, it is not clear that the proposed restrictions are compatible with an empirically adequate account of language. When meaning and other matters are considered, as well as the generation of sentences with grammatical descriptions, it seems even less likely that a satisfactory theory weaker than that of Turing machines will prove possible.

At present we simply do not know what sorts of formal devices will ultimately be required to account for the grammatical properties of natural languages, much less their semantic and other properties. It seems quite likely, however, that any adequate formalization will permit the mimicking of an arbitrary Turing machine within the confines of linguistic theory.[15]

[14] A recursive (or decidable) set is one for which there exists a procedure (e.g., a Turing machine) which can infallibly determine within a finite time whether a putative member of the set is or is not, in fact, in the set.

[15] For an interesting presentation of a number of issues closely related to those discussed in this chapter see Hofstadter's (1979) *Gödel, Escher, Bach: An Eternal Golden Braid.*

Innateness

Innateness is a controversial issue in linguistics—the extent to which language is innate (or "hard-wired," to borrow a term from computing) and whether these innate mechanisms are specific to language.

It is obvious that language is not completely innate—if it were we should all speak the same language. An earlier generation of linguists tended to emphasize the distinctions between languages at the expense of their similarities. For the past twenty years this trend has been reversed. Linguists have sought out similarities between languages and explained them in terms of innateness—the brain is constructed in such a way that it is limited in what it can conceive as a natural language.

There is no question that languages are more similar than there is any a priori need for them to be. Linguists were fond, a few years ago, of listing properties not found in any known languages, and which we can be (fairly) confident will never be found in any. These properties were of the following sort: there are no languages which require for any given sentence that the number of nouns be the square of the number of verbs, or in which questions are formed by reversing all of the words in the corresponding statement, or in which the number of words in a sentence must be prime.

At the same time one can point to properties found in all languages (e.g., nouns, verbs, relative clauses); and other properties (such as definite articles), though not universal, are so widespread that their presence cannot be due to chance.

This presents something of a problem. It seems likely that any empirically adequate formulation of grammatical theory will allow for the formation of grammars which can mimic an arbitrary Turing machine; that is, the basic operations of grammars underlying human speech do not exclude the formation of algorithms for generating the elements of any set which can be specified at all. Why, then, are the sets that are actual languages so limited in form? Why, for example, do properties such as those listed above not appear in languages, since the basic operations of grammars appear to allow them?

That something can be done does not mean that it can be easily or naturally done. (Tigers have been trained to walk across a pair of tightly stretched wires, but they don't appear to care much for it.) Computer languages provide good examples of this. Different computer languages have been devised for different sorts of problems, but in fact most computer languages are sufficiently general to solve any problem solvable by computer. For example, it would be possible to do scientific calculations using COBOL, a computer language devised for business applications, but it would be extremely tedious. Presumably, in forming spoken languages, our unconscious algorithm-forming faculty prefers to create structures which follow easily from natural mental mechanisms, rather than construct languages from theoretically possible, but inordinately complex structures (from the point of view of human cognition).

There are reasons other than available mental structures for why languages bear such similarities to one another. Some are no doubt rooted in the fact that languages serve a communicative function.

There are many things which do not occur in languages, not because they could not be learned but because they would impede (or at least fail to contribute to) communication. Take rhyme, for instance. On the basis of certain pathological cases, it appears that people can learn to speak in rhyme. But certainly rhyme limits the ease and flexibility with which ideas may be expressed, and no known languages require that sentences rhyme. A restriction to the effect that the number of words in a sentence must be prime would extract a heavy price on expression, particularly as sentences grow longer. For example, a sentence greater than 19 words and less than 29 words in length would have to be exactly 23 words long. A restriction like this might be learnable, but it would certainly be inconvenient. Other numerical restrictions would be equally unhandy.

Certain aspects of the structure of languages are probably determined by perceptual considerations. For instance, we seem to divide the perceptual world into objects and events involving objects. This roughly corresponds to the fundamental linguistic distinction of nouns and verbs. While the tendency to perceive the world in this way is no doubt innate (and likely shared with other species) it does not directly determine what unconscious algorithms can be acquired, though it does determine the manner in which humans are likely to talk about things.

Lastly, it is quite possible that all existing human languages have a common origin, but one so far removed in the past that it is no longer possible to demonstrate this commonality with any certainty. If all languages share a common origin, then many of their similarities may simply be due to common heritage.

Chapter Eight

——

Calculating Times and Extent

Calculating Times

THERE is little reliable information on the times required for prodigies to do various calculations, and the little there is is generally insufficient to draw valid conclusions, even for the calculators for whom they were taken. Only if a calculator should do a large number of similar problems under controlled conditions and average times computed (taking the error rate into account) [1] could a reliable estimate of his ability for that type of problem be made. No judgment of a calculator's speed can be formed on the basis of one or two problems. The appearance of difficulty and difficulty are two different things, and there are often shortcuts by which a problem may be quickly solved, should the calculator notice them.

In many cases the times we have are approximations taken by observers at stage performances. In some cases the ultimate source of quoted times may be promotional material supplied by the calculator himself. Beyond this, calculators have techniques to make it appear that they work faster than they do, such as repeating the number or writing it down, when they have in fact already begun calculating. The calculator may have encountered the problem before, or it may even be supplied by a confederate in the audience (though I think few genuine calculating prodigies would stoop to this). Finally, there may be some peculiarity of the problem which the calculator is fortunate enough to grasp and which renders the calculation relatively simple.

———

[1] The case of Finkelstein, discussed below, shows that a calculator can sacrifice accuracy to attain a low average calculating time.

There are also difficulties in the matter of measuring calculating times. If the problem is presented orally, does the timing start when the first digit of the problem is spoken or the last? And does the timing end with the announcement of the first digit of the answer, or the last? Similar problems arise in measuring calculating times for problems presented visually.

In many cases calculating times are not comparable because the manner of presenting the problems differ. It is, for example, unfair to compare problems presented to a calculator orally with problems presented visually and which he can see while computing—in the latter case the memory strain is far less.

Nevertheless, a few tentative conclusions can be drawn. We can be fairly certain that informal timings are not likely to err in the direction of being too long; if a time seems rather long, the calculation proceeded, at least in this case, slowly.

Though Buxton's calculations are very impressive in their extent, he was not a rapid calculator. Computing the square yards in a field 423 by 383 yards required two minutes (Holliday 1751:347). Even as slow a multiplier as myself can do the problem on paper in a quarter of the time.

The case of Fuller, the Virginia slave, shows how difficult it is to evaluate the available data. Fuller correctly gave the number of seconds in a year and a half (47,304,000) in about two minutes (Rush 1789). He then gave the number of seconds in 70 years, 17 days, 12 hours in "a minute and a half." He even assumed 17 leap years in his answer (2,210,500,800). This second problem seems, certainly, of considerably greater difficulty than the first, yet Fuller is credited with answering it more quickly.

There are only a few cases in which times are indicated for problems solved by Colburn; they are rapid, but because of the nature of the problems, little significance can be attached to them. For example, he is credited with finding, in seven seconds, the number of hours in 38 years, 2 months, and 7 days (Colburn 1833:172). The answer, 334,488, ignores leap years and assumes a 30-day month. Since Colburn already knew the number of hours in a year, in a month, and in a week, the problem is reduced to $(8,760 \times 38) + (720 \times 2) + 168$. This is the maximum he would have to compute—he may have known more.

Bidder appears to have been a rapid calculator, though in some cases I have difficulty accepting as accurate the times of solution attributed to him. At age 12 he was asked the distance a clock pendulum, which moves

9¾ inches per second, will travel in 7 years, 14 days, 2 hours, 1 minute, 56 seconds, each year computed at 365 days, 5 hours, 48 minutes, 55 seconds. He is credited with finding the solution, 2,165,625,744¾, in less than a minute (*Spectator*, January 25, 1879:111).

This is a much more accurate figure for the length of a year than was customarily used by mental calculators. By current reckoning the figure is slightly too large; the tropical year is now computed at 365 days, 5 hours, 48 minutes, 46 seconds. Calculators generally took a year to be either simply 365 days or 365¼ days. Perhaps Bidder knew the number of seconds in a year as posed by the questioner—perhaps not. He certainly knew the number of seconds in 365 days (31,536,000); and the seconds in 5 hours, 48 minutes, and 55 seconds (20,935) would not have taken him more than a few seconds to calculate. The problem would essentially then be: $(31,556,935 \times 7 + 14 \times 24 \times 60^2 + 2 \times 60^2 + 60 + 56) \times 9¾$.

Schumacher gave Dase two eight-digit numbers to multiply on paper, which he did, in one minute seven seconds in the usual way of multiplying on paper (Gauss and Schumacher 1861 5:295). He complained, however, that the need to write down the numbers slowed him down, and that he could calculate faster in his head. Schumacher gave him two different eight-digit numbers, and Dase wrote down the answer in 54 seconds. Presumably Dase was given the problem on paper and had it in view while calculating.

Schumacher also credits Dase with mentally multiplying two 20-digit numbers in 6 minutes, two 40-digit numbers in 40 minutes, two 100-digit numbers in 8¾ hours (Gauss and Schumacher 1861 5:295). Whether Dase could see the problems in doing these multiplications is not indicated. Of the last feat Schumacher remarked that it must have made the performance rather boring. From this we can infer that Schumacher was not actually a witness to this series of multiplications.

Binet (1894) was the first to obtain fairly reliable timings of mental calculators. He wished to measure the speed of calculations presented both orally and visually.

In his measurements of problems presented and responded to orally, he ran into several difficulties. He wanted to measure the time from the moment at which the questioner spoke the last word of the problem until the subject started to say the answer.

The first method he tried, using an instrument devised by the psychologist Wilhelm Wundt, had to be abandoned. Another method, that of having the subject stop the timing manually when saying the first word of the answer, was found to be unsatisfactory, as subjects had a tendency to move their hands in anticipation of speaking, thus yielding average times which were too short.

The next technique tried was to measure the subjects' initial lip movement. A device was built in Binet's laboratory which fit over the lips of the subject, such that, when he opened his mouth, a circuit was closed which halted the chronometer. The experimenter would start the timer manually as he spoke the last word. (The experimenter practiced a bit so as to make these two acts almost simultaneous.) The subject would do the problem keeping his mouth shut. When the problem was solved he would open his lips to speak the answer, stopping the timing. This didn't work either. Subjects were found to open their mouths in anticipation of the answer. (In any case, Inaudi, one of the subjects, murmured while calculating.)

The method finally employed was to place a "pneumographe" (Binet 1894:83) on both the experimenter and the subject. These devices left a trace, representing respiration, on a revolving cylinder. An assistant watched the two traces. The experimenter and the subject were at pains to speak loudly. Usually there was enough difference in the pattern of respiration to determine just when the experimenter ceased talking and when the subject began.

The first tests conducted on Inaudi using this technique consisted of extracting square roots (Binet 1894:84):

Problem	Response	Time
$\sqrt{625}$	25	1.49 sec.
$\sqrt{324}$	18	1.22 sec.
$\sqrt{837}$	28 (remainder 53)	2.56 sec.
$\sqrt{640}$	25 (remainder 15)	1.68 sec.
$\sqrt{4,920}$	70 (remainder 20)	3.00 sec.

The problems are not of much interest. Obviously Inaudi knew that 25^2 is 625, just as I do. Since he no doubt knew the squares of most numbers less than 100, and since he only announced the remainder rather than continuing the calculation for several decimal places, these problems only tested his ability to apprehend the data and recall the next perfect square below the number given. Note that the problem that took the longest is so simple that anyone could do it; the square root of 49 is 7, therefore the square root of 4,900 is 70; therefore the square root of 4,920 is 70 with a remainder of 20.

Next a few simple division problems were given (Binet 1894:85). The experimenter would first give the dividend, then, abruptly, the divisor.

Problem	Response	Time
$25 \div 15$	1⅔	0.95 sec.
$83 \div 9$	9 (remainder 2)	1.99 sec.
$388 \div 23$	16 (remainder 20)	3.30 sec.
$340 \div 26$	13 (remainder 2)	4.56 sec.
$35 \div 8$	04 (remainder 3)	0.79 sec.

The only thing of interest here is that it took Inaudi substantially longer to divide three digits by two than it did to divide two digits by one digit, which tends to substantiate his claim that he did not use an extended multiplication table.

A similarly conducted test was done on multiplication (Binet 1894:85).

Problem	Time
25×9	0.57 sec.
46×12	0.79 sec.
15×7	1.29 sec.
35×12	1.32 sec.
58×15	1.36 sec.

Again the problems are too easy to reveal anything about Inaudi's calculating speed.

Another series of problems was timed by a different method. Inaudi was given a sheet of paper containing 20 numbers written in columns. The same number was to be added to each number in the column. Only the results were to be announced. To take Binet's (1894:86) example, suppose one of the columns was made up of the numbers 3, 9, 2, 3, 6, 3, 1, etc., and 4 was to be added. The subject should look at the numbers and say "7, 13, 6, 7, 10, 7, 5, etc." The timing began the moment the paper was uncovered before the subject and ended with the pronouncement of the last result. There were 12 columns, to which it was necessary to add successively "the numbers 1, 2, 3, 4, 5, 6, 7, 9, 12, 18, 22, etc."[2]

The average times in seconds obtained for adding various numbers to each of the numbers in the columns were as follows: for 1—0.58; 2—

[2] It is not at all clear how many and which numbers were added, and whether they were added to all columns or only some. As will be seen below, Binet gives times for numbers not included in this series and fails to give times for numbers which are included.

0.55; 3—0.6; 4—0.7; 5—0.68; 7—0.73; 9—0.7; 12—0.77; 15—
0.7; 23—0.7; 28—0.7; 47—0.75; 369—0.7; 2,435—0.85.

Similar tests were conducted of additions and other arithmetic operations. The problems were submitted to Inaudi on paper and the results
announced five at a time, the average time being taken. The results of
these tests are given in table 8.1.

Inaudi was at some disadvantage since he had to read the problems, a
technique to which he was not accustomed, but, as Binet points out, this
was somewhat compensated for by the fact that he could begin calculating the next problem while announcing the results of the last. Using the
same number again and again (in many cases, very easy numbers at that)
also simplifies the matter.

Binet also compared Inaudi's speed of calculation with that of four
experienced cashiers of the Bon Marché store in Paris and three students
from his own laboratory. On the average, the cashiers had fourteen years
of experience. All had learned to read before learning to calculate. All
were accustomed to doing considerable calculation as part of their jobs.

Three said without hesitation that they visualized numbers when they
calculated. One said that he saw numbers, but the sound was also important. Some of them did, however, murmur when attempting to recall
a series of numbers read to them, and while carrying out mental calculations. This suggests that visualizing and verbalizing may complement one
another in the case of some individuals.

Table 8.2 gives the result of an experiment with addition. In each case,
the subject was asked to carry out 20 additions, submitted on paper, of
the sort indicated in the table. For example, $n + 23$ means that 23 was to
be added to each of the 20 numbers. No information is given as to what
the numbers were.[3] It is interesting to note that for numbers less than
20 the cashiers were faster than Inaudi, but they had the advantage of
being accustomed to working with written numbers.

Mental multiplication was also compared, and the results are given in
table 8.3. These tests were done with the problems in view. It is not
clear from Binet whether the answers were written down or spoken aloud,
and whether the timing was halted with the enunciation or transcription
of the first digit or the last. (Using Inaudi's method of left-to-right multiplication, it is not generally possible to fix the higher-place digits with
any confidence before those of lesser value are established. On the other
hand, one can easily produce digits from right to left before completing
the calculation.)

[3] Why results are given for only two of the cashiers is not explained.

TABLE 8.1
Times Required by Inaudi for Various Calculations

Additions			Total Time in Secs.	Avg. Time (Single Operation)
22 +	43 =	65		
38 +	=	81		
47 +	=	90	4.0	0.8
52 +	=	95		
64 +	=	107		
75 +	43 =	118		
99 +	=	142		
27 +	=	70	5.0	1.0
29 +	=	72		
38 +	=	81		
325 +	825 =	1,150		
433 +	=	1,258		
767 +	=	1,592	11.0	2.20
625 +	=	1,450		
348 +	=	1,173		
822 +	825 =	1,647		
347 +	=	1,172		
525 +	=	1,350	7.0	1.4
328 +	=	1,153		
445 +	=	1,270		
522 +	825 =	1,347		
633 +	=	1,458		
288 +	=	1,113	6.5	1.2
827 +	=	1,652		
637 +	=	1,462		
7,429 + 3,635 =		11,064		
6,093 +	=	9,728		
8,025 +	=	11,660	11.0	2.2
7,346 +	=	10,981		
3,282 +	=	6,917		
4,829 + 8,725 =		13,554		
6,623 +	=	15,348		
3,248 +	=	11,973	17.0	3.4
8,273 +	=	16,998		
6,458 +	=	15,183		

Subtractions			Total Time in Secs.	Avg. Time Per Operation
9 −	7 =	+ 2		
5 −	=	− 2		
2 −	=	− 5	4.0	0.8
4 −	=	− 3		
8 −	=	+ 1		

TABLE 8.1 (continued)

Subtractions		Total Time in Secs.	Avg. Time Per Operation
22 −	43 = − 21		
38 −	= − 5		
47 −	= + 4	4.0	0.8
52 −	= + 9		
64 −	= + 21		
325 −	825 = − 500		
433 −	= − 392		
967 −	= + 142	8.0	1.6
625 −	= − 200		
348 −	= − 483		
4,829 − 8,725 = − 3,896			
6,623 −	= − 2,102		
3,248 −	= − 5,477	14.0	2.8
8,273 −	= − 452		
6,458 −	= − 2,267		
6,831 − 3,635 = + 3,196			
9,298 −	= + 5,663		
6,395 −	= + 2,760	22.0	4.4
8,238 −	= + 4,603		
7,254 −	= + 3,619		

Divisions		Total Time in Secs.	Avg. Time Per Operation
6 ÷	4 = 1½		
3 ÷	= ¾		
7 ÷	= 1 + 3	4.0	0.8
9 ÷	= 2¼		
2 ÷	= ½		
22 ÷	16 = 1 + 6		
38 ÷	= 2 + 6		
47 ÷	= 2 + 15	7.0	1.4
52 ÷	= 3 + 4		
64 ÷	= 4		
522 ÷	412 = 1 + 110		
633 ÷	= 1 + 221		
998 ÷	= 2 + 174	12.5	2.5
827 ÷	= 2 + 3		
637 ÷	= 1 + 225		
522 ÷	= 1 + 110		
829 ÷	= 2 + 1 (5)[a]		
778 ÷	= 1 + 5,366 (336)[a]		
847 ÷	= 2 + 23	9.0	1.8
625 ÷	= 1 + 213		
9,425 ÷ 3,635 = 2 + 2,155			
5,381 ÷	= 1 + 1,746		
6,241 ÷	= 1 + 2,606	21.0	4.2
3,958 ÷	= 1 + 323		
7,235 ÷	= 1 + 3,600		

Multiplications			Total Time in Secs.	Avg. Time Per Operation
6 ×	7 =	42		
3 ×	=	21		
0 ×	=	0	3.0	0.6
8 ×	=	56		
2 ×	=	14		
29 ×	43 =	1,247		
35 ×	=	1,505		
18 ×	=	774	10.0	2.0
26 ×	−	1,118		
95 ×	=	4,985 (9,085)[a]		
325 ×	825 = 268,125			
433 ×	= 357,225			
967 ×	= 797,775		32.0	6.4
625 ×	= 515,625			
348 ×	= 287,100			
6,241 × 3,635 = 22,686,035			21.0	21.0
32,978 × 62,834 = 2,072,139,652				40.0

[a]Wrong in the original; the correct figure is given in parentheses.
Source: Binet 1894:88–90.

TABLE 8.2
Times Required by Inaudi and Others for Various Additions
(times given in seconds)

Additions	Inaudi	Cashier	Cashier	Student	Student	Student
n + 1	11.5	8	7	14.5	13	16
n + 2	11	8	8	13.5	15	24
n + 3	12	11	9.5	17	27	20
n + 4	14	10.5	7.5	16	26	24
n + 5	13.5	11	8	20	25	24
n − 7	14.5	11.5	10	24	23.5	28
n + 9	14	12.5	10	24	33	——[a]
n + 12	15.5	12	12	23	34	35
n + 15	14	14	12.5	19.5	33	32
n + 23	14	12	12	27.5	41	36
n + 28	14	12	13	22	44	34
n + 47	15	12	12	30	43	45
n + 969	14	21	20	40	44	33
n + 2,477	17	21.5	19	40	50	48

[a]Blank in the original.
Source: Binet 1894:96.

TABLE 8.3
A Comparison of Times for Multiplications

	3 × 7	49 × 6	63 × 58	426 × 67	638 × 823	4,279 × 584	7,286 × 5,397	61,824 × 3,976	58,927 × 61,408	729,856 × 297,143
Inaudi	0.6"		2"		6.4"		21"		40"	4'
Diamandi		6"	17"	21"	56"	92"	2' 7"	3' 10"	4' 35"	
1st cashier					4"		13"			
2d cashier	0.7"		4"		12"					
3d cashier	0.7"		4"							

Source: Binet 1894:98.

As can be seen one of the cashiers, M. Lour, the best of those from Bon Marché, achieved better times than Inaudi for the problems he attempted, but he could not continue when the problems got larger.[4]

Diamandi was subject to some different tests of his ability to multiply, but again, the results are not comparable because the conditions of the experiment differ.

In this case he was given the problems on paper. As soon as he had memorized the numbers the problem was hidden. The time was measured from the moment he was shown the problem until the last digit was written.

TABLE 8.4
Multiplications by Diamandi

36 × 7	252	6 sec.
49 × 63	3,087	17 sec.
329 × 63	20,727	21 sec.
439 × 56	24,584	38 sec.
637 × 224	42,688	56 sec.
3,257 × 639	2,081,223	92 sec.
8,637 × 4,538	39,185,706[a]	2 m. 7 sec.
46,273 × 729	33,733,017	2 m. 30 sec.
65,879 × 2,537	167,135,023	3 m. 10 sec.

[a] Wrong in the original; should be 39,194,706.
Source: Binet 1894:127–28.

Naturally, if the calculator cannot see the numbers of the problem as he is calculating the time required for calculation will tend to be longer, as there is a substantial additional memory load. Furthermore, the procedure is not at all satisfactory, since it is impossible to know whether the calculator had begun calculating while supposedly memorizing the problem. The results, however (table 8.4), are of some interest.

Thus, while Binet conducted a variety of experiments on the calculating ability of the two calculators, he did not, except in one very limited instance, subject both to the same experiments. Not only were the problems different but the conditions of the experiments differed. This cannot be explained by the fact that one was a visual calculator and the other auditory, since both were given problems visually in some cases.

[4] The 13-second multiplication of two four-digit numbers is probably a mistake. Elsewhere Binet says (1894:95): "All four calculators [from Bon Marché] could do two-digit multiplications without difficulty; some could, with effort, do multiplications of three digits (each of the factors had three digits); none could go as far as four digits." Another example of how difficult it is to get reliable and comparable data on calculating times.

In spite of such discrepancies it is evident that Inaudi was much faster at multiplication than Diamandi. To multiply two four-digit numbers took Diamandi a little over two minutes—Inaudi accomplished the same feat in 21 seconds.

Müller (1911:225) tested Rückle on some of the same multiplication problems given to Inaudi. He remarks: "Rückle proved to be quite significantly weaker than Inaudi in the multiplication of multi-digit numbers. The product of 6,241 × 3,635 was correctly found by Inaudi in 21 seconds, but by Rückle in 70.5 seconds." Inaudi also gave the product of 7,286 × 5,397 in 21 seconds, while Rückle took 112 seconds. Müller says that similar results were obtained for other multiplications, but no further examples are given. Unfortunately, the conditions under which the tests were conducted are not given, so that we do not know whether the results are comparable.

Zaneboni (Guicciardi and Ferrari 1897:414–15) was also tested on some of the problems given to Inaudi, and in general proved to be slower than either Inaudi or Rückle. To multiply five two-digit numbers by 43 required a total of 17 seconds (compared to 10 seconds for Inaudi). Five examples of three-digit numbers multiplied by 825 took 4'11" (for Inaudi, 32 seconds). Zaneboni required either 5'52" or 3'52" (there is a discrepancy in the table) to multiply 6,241 by 3,635. This is much slower than Inaudi (21 seconds) or Rückle (70.5 seconds). The multiplication of 32,978 by 62,834 required 9'20", compared to only 40 seconds for Inaudi.

In the thirties, Salo Finkelstein was subjected to a series of tests of his calculating ability at the School of Commerce, New York University (Weinland and Schlauch 1937). The average times required for various sorts of multiplications were not bad, but his accuracy was deplorable. It took him an average of 4.03 seconds to multiply two digits by two digits (30 examples) and he achieved only 93.3 percent accuracy. The range of times required went all the way from 2 to 14 seconds. Surprisingly, to multiply three digits by three digits took only slightly longer (5.7 seconds average for 6 examples), but his accuracy went down to 83.3 percent. Ten examples of four digits by four digits required an average of 13.5 seconds with an accuracy of only 60 percent. Finkelstein failed to get even half of the five-digit by five-digit multiplications correct (44.4 percent) and his average time went up to 25.8 seconds. No doubt he could have attained much greater accuracy if he had worked more carefully, but there is no way to estimate how much longer his calculations would have taken.

Wim Klein was tested by Fred Barlow in 1953 (notes in Klein's possession). The circumstances of the tests are vague. Some of the problems were presented orally, some were not, with no indication of which are which, etc. The straight multiplications, however, were undoubtedly given to him on paper. Thus Klein could see the problems as he worked them and, as he practices cross multiplication, he could write the digits right to left as he obtained them. Thus conditions are comparable to those of the tests of Inaudi and the cashiers of the Bon Marché given previously. (It should be noted, however, that the advantages to Klein in being able to see the problem and write down the answer as it was obtained are probably much greater than they were for Inaudi. Inaudi had only learned to read numbers a few years before, found written numbers confusing, and always worked with his back to the blackboard. Klein prefers to work with the numbers in view. Inaudi worked from left to right, and thus could not give any of the answer until all his calculations were complete. Klein, because he uses cross multiplication, can write down the digits as they are obtained, and thus is relieved of the necessity of keeping the answer in mind until he has completed his calculations. Again, even experiments conducted under identical conditions may not really be comparable.) The results of these tests show Klein to be in a different class from Inaudi, Diamandi, and Rückle, for doing multiplications *under the conditions stated above.*[5]

Klein multiplied two nine-digit numbers in 48 seconds. He multiplied two ten-digit numbers together in an average time of 65⅔ seconds each (6 problems). In the first two ten-digit problems he gave the wrong answer on his first attempt (not counted in the average times) but was correct in a second trial. The first coincided with a commotion in the hallway which he found distracting.

The 1982 U. K. edition of the *Guinness Book of Records*[6] contains the following: "Mrs. Shakuntala Devi of India demonstrated the multiplication of two 13-digit numbers $7,686,369,774,870 \times 2,465,099,745,779$ picked at random by the Computer Department of Imperial College, London on 18 June 1980, in 28 sec. Her correct answer was 18,947,668,177,995,426,462,773,730." Such a time is so far superior to anything previously reported that it can only be described as unbelievable.

---

[5] Klein appears to be superior even to Dase (see above), at least for problems in the range of eight to ten digits, but in Dase's case we have only one example.

[6] The American version is called the *Guinness Book of World Records.*

Extent of Calculations

So far as I can determine, the largest reported mental multiplication was by Dase, who, according to the mathematician Schumacher multiplied two 100-digit numbers in 8¾ hours (Gauss and Schumacher 1861 5:295). Unfortunately, none of the particulars (time, place, witnesses, the problem and Dase's answer, whether or not the problem was in view, whether the answer was written down as it was obtained, etc.) are known. Gauss was unimpressed (5:297). He even wondered who checked the answers to such problems. In any case he thought it a waste of time since, in his opinion, the problem could be done in half the time on paper by a skilled calculator.

Buxton squared a 39-digit number in his head, a labor of some two and a half months. This is a very long time, but Buxton, who was probably somewhat retarded, was a very slow calculator. In this case we are fortunate in having both the problem and Buxton's solution: $725,958,238,096,074,907,868,531,656,993,638,851,106^2 = 527,-015,363,459,557,385,673,773,542,638,591,721,213,298,966,-079,307,524,904,381,389,499,251,637,423,236$. We may be sure that it was done entirely mentally, since Buxton could not even read or write numbers. At the time of its publication it was not known whether the solution was correct. It is not—the 22d digit from the right should be 5 rather than 4 (for further details, see chapter 20).

Nothing comparable to these feats has been recorded in the literature known to me. Bidder, who was one of the finest mental calculators on record, indicated, in his address to the Institution of Civil Engineers, far greater limits on his calculating ability (1856:256): "As a great effort I have multiplied 12 places of figures by 12 figures; but that has required much time, and was a great strain upon the mind." His son, also a mental calculator, wrote in a letter to the *Spectator* (Bidder, Jr. 1878:1635):

> I myself can perform pretty extensive arithmetical operations mentally, but I cannot pretend to approach even distantly to the rapidity or accuracy with which my father worked. I have occasionally multiplied 15 figures by 15 in my head, but it takes me a long time, and I am liable to occasional errors. Last week, after speaking to Professor Elliot, I tried the following sum to see if I could still do it, —
>
> $$378,201,969,513,825$$
> $$199,631,057,265,413$$

And I got in my head the answer, 75,576,299,427,512,145,197,597,-834,725, in which I think, if you take the trouble to work it out, you will find four figures out of the 29 are wrong.

In fact, 14 of the 29 digits are wrong (see chapter 40).

The multiplication feats of Dase and Buxton appear to be unparalleled, but no doubt many calculators given unlimited time and sufficient motivation could do very large calculations.

Chapter Nine

Implications

. . . I would suggest that this mode of proceeding [teaching children mental arithmetic] presents advantages of much greater importance than even the teaching of figures; for far beyond the mere facilities in computation, would be the advantages afforded by the opportunity of making this branch of education conducive to the highest objects to which education can be directed; that is, to the cultivation of the reasoning powers in general.

—George Parker Bidder (1856:278)

Somehow the number world has become my choice world in which I can live a different life. My other life is just normal. I'm not at all an "all-rounder." I cannot do very well in every field. But this number thing has given me a confidence or a belief, that not only myself, but anyone who concentrates so strong for such a long time can have proficiency in any field he wants. For me it is numbers; for others it can be art, because this ability to concentrate once it gets born in you develops automatically. You should identify that you're having that; once the identification is there, then the development will be common with anyone.

—Shyam Marathe (in an interview with the author)

IF the mental calculations of prodigies and human language are based on the same faculty, then any normal child is a potential calculating prodigy, just as every normal child learns to speak. But the existence of a potential does not mean that it can be easily realized. Any 6-year-old child is capable of acquiring a foreign language with native fluency if placed in circumstances in which this is the language of his peers. On the other hand, a few hours a week of Spanish lessons given to English-speaking grammar-school children typically lead only to the acquisition of some garbled mispronounced phrases—the children do not in any sense become speakers of Spanish.

What then are the prospects for converting an ordinary child into a calculating prodigy? I think that it could be done, but the requirements are such that I doubt that it will be. A large number of examples would have to be processed by the child and interest in the properties of numbers stimulated. How many examples must be processed is unknown, but we may be sure that the number is considerable—prodigies invariably refer to the many hours they spent amusing themselves with numbers. We have very little idea even in the case of language how much data must be processed to acquire native fluency. An hour's practice a day at mental arithmetic by children in a classroom situation would probably be no more likely to produce calculating prodigies than an hour a day of Spanish in grammar school is likely to result in native fluency in Spanish. If the same children should move to Mexico, however, they would all master the language.

Calculating prodigies cannot be easily created for the same reason they appear so infrequently in the population—motivation. Children are not surrounded by people doing mental calculation as they are surrounded by people talking. Therefore, a strong interest in numbers is required of the child, and a willingness to isolate himself from the typical amusements of his peers. Calculating prodigies remark again and again that numbers are their friends. One suspects that a child with many human friends is less likely to find solace among numerical acquaintances.

For most children to develop a high-level skill in mental calculation would probably require an environment in which mental calculation was practiced and valued by those around them. To achieve such an environment today would be no mean feat. Perhaps a parent with a fascination for numbers and a strong commitment to such an endeavor could succeed, but such parents may be as rare in the population as children with the motivation to become calculating prodigies without outside stimulation.

Granting that the percentage of calculating prodigies in the population is not due for a drastic increase in the near future, we may consider a related issue: is there any benefit to be gained by systematically introducing a child to mental calculation? While instruction in mental calculation might lead in only a few exceptional cases to the development of a calculating prodigy, it would contribute to the development of an appreciation for properties of numbers and mathematical relations in general.

The benefits go beyond the ability to make quick calculations in concrete situations—such a program would instill in the child an appreciation of arithmetic properties, and engender an interest in abstract thought. As Bidder (1856:252) remarked over a hundred years ago:

> I have, for many years, entertained a strong conviction, that mental arithmetic can be taught, as easily, if not even with greater facility, than ordinary arithmetic, and that it may be rendered conducive to more useful purposes, than that of teaching by rule; that it may be taught in such a way as to strengthen the reasoning powers of the youthful mind; so as to enlarge it, as to ennoble it and to render it capable of embracing all knowledge, particularly that appertaining to the exact sciences.

Bidder also offers some excellent advice as to how such a program could be carried out (1856:278):

> I think it most essential that numbers should be taught before figures— that is to say—before their symbols and probably even before the letters of the alphabet are learnt. The first step should be to teach the child to count up to 10 and then to 100. He should then be instructed to form his own multiplication table, by connecting rectangular pieces of wood, shot, or marbles, or any symmetrical figures: probably marbles may be the best, as they are the very early associates of the child, and may be considered in some degree as his playmates, and therefore be likely to form the most agreeable associations in his mind.[1] Having formed these rectangles, he will be enabled by his previous experience in counting, to reckon the number of pieces in any rectangle, and thus to demonstrate to himself all the facts of the multiplication table, up to 10 times 10. Having thus acquired the multiplication table up to 100, he should then be taught to count up to 1000 by 10's and 100's. It would not then be difficult to teach him to enlarge his own multiplication table. In the first place he would have no difficulty in multiplying 10 by 17, because he will be quite familiar with the fact that 10 times 10 are 100, and 10 times 7 are 70, and adding them together will give the result, represented by 170. It will then be easy to follow this by multiplying 17 by 13. He knows already that 10×17 is 170 and 3 times 10 are 30, which added gives 200, and 3 times 7 are 21, which added gives 221, the result required. By patience and constant practice in this way, he would gradually be taught to multiply 2 figures by 2, and eventually 3 figures by 3. After this he will be led upon the same principles to the application of his faculties to the other rules of arithmetic.

[1] This assumes, of course, that only boys are to be taught mental calculation and that marbles are more commonplace childhood companions than they have since become. Bidder learned to multiply by arranging shot, and Mondeux and Ampère by arranging pebbles.

To the above I would add a few suggestions of my own.

The factors of numbers have a powerful attraction for mental calculators. Wim Klein, for instance, attributes his calculating development to a fascination with factoring, devoting the hours other children dedicated to sports and other amusements to factoring numbers up to 10,000. Aitken compulsively factored integers he happened to come upon (Hunter 1962:247):

> If I go for a walk and if a motor car passes and it has the registration number 731, I cannot but observe that it is 17 times 43. But as far as possible, I shut that off because it interferes with thought about other matters. And after one or two numbers like that have been factorized, I am conditioned against it for the rest of my walk.

A number which is not prime can be represented as a rectangular arrangement of tokens (marbles, beans, etc.); the tokens representing a prime cannot be so arranged (except the "rectangle" that can be formed by arranging the tokens in a single row or column). Two of the factors of a composite (nonprime) number are represented by the number of rows and by the number of columns in the rectangle. The prime factors can be found by taking the number of tokens in a row or column and forming (if possible) a rectangle of them. This procedure can be repeated for the rows and columns of rectangles until no further rectangles can be created. For example, 84, since it has a number of composite factors, can be arranged into a variety of rectangles: 42 by 2, 28 by 3, 21 by 4, 14 by 6, and 12 by 7. Suppose we take 14 by 6; 14 can be arranged into only one rectangle, 2 by 7, 6 can also be arranged into but one rectangle, 2 by 3. Thus, the prime factors of 84 are 7, 3, and 2.

Another advantage to the use of physical tokens for numbers is that the origin of the terms *square* and *cube* become immediately apparent (although in the case of a cube one has to imagine a multilayered model). The notion of a triangular number—one which can be represented by tokens laid out in the form of an equilateral triangle (like bowling pins) — can be introduced naturally. These numbers (e.g., 1, 3, 6, 10, 15 . . .) have some interesting properties. For example, the sum of any two successive triangular numbers form a square, as can be seen simply by pushing the tokens together.

Squaring numbers can also be a useful exercise, since a variety of methods may be applied to the numbers at hand, providing some practical insights into principles of algebra. For example, $49^2 = 50 \times 48 + 1^2 =$

$(4,800/2) + 1 = 2,401$; or $49 \times 7 \times 7 = (50 \times 7 - 7) \times 7 = 343 \times 7$; or 25 (hundred) less one (hundred) plus one squared; or $50 \times 49 - 49$; or $40^2 + 2 \times 40 \times 9 + 9^2 = 1,600 + 720 + 81$, etc. The preferred method will depend upon the problem and the predilections of the calculator. (It is probably best to gain proficiency in one method before facing a welter of others.)

There have been attempts at teaching mental arithmetic. Hunter (1962:253) reported on his experience in teaching mental multiplication by the left-to-right method used by many prodigies: "The students found mental multiplication easier to do by this plan than by the mental use of the methods they habitually used when calculating with the aid of an ongoing written record. Yet even after an hour of self-paced practice, the students reported that difficulty or total failure could occur at any of many stages in the calculative sequence."

Hunter's disappointment at the students' continuing problems in acquiring a relatively difficult mental algorithm seems to me misplaced— that they were to any extent successful after so brief a time is remarkable. Children spend a great many hours learning to multiply on paper with results that are often less than satisfying. (I know otherwise intelligent adults who have difficulty giving, offhand, the product of 7×9.) To learn to play tennis even poorly requires many hours of weekly practice over months of time. Why should one expect that an hour's practice at mental multiplication will achieve results superior to an hour devoted to learning to serve a tennis ball?

If it is necessary to reflect consciously on the next step to be taken, then it will be very easy to get lost in the process. So much time may elapse that the current partial product has faded, and the calculator will have to begin again. Hunter's students encountered such difficulties (1962:253): "They found difficulty in coordinating the subjectively distinct activities of: multiplying two numbers; adding two partial products; retrieving an already attained partial product; and recalling the stage now reached in the overall calculative plan."

What is most remarkable is that some students, even with this minimal experience in mental calculation, found parts of the procedure becoming unconscious (Hunter 1962:253–54):

> As practice continued, some students reported the development of occasional 'leaps'; that is, an enlargement of the onleading correctly accomplished in a subjectively unitary 'step', e.g., proceeding from one partial product to the next without any awareness of the normally intermediate steps of specifying two numbers, multiplying them, and adding their prod-

uct to the preceding partial product. However, even this economy raised difficulties for, lacking confidence in the correctness of the 'leap', the student might then undertake its verification and, thereby, disrupt the precarious continuity of the total thinking sequence.

Quite possibly further practice would have led to unconscious processes in which the students had justifiable confidence.

When missionaries introduced the study of arithmetic to Polynesia[2] the results were startling. Briffault (quoted in Seidenberg 1960:279)[3] observed:

> When schools were first established by missionaries in Hawaii, the children's progress in all elementary subjects was surprisingly rapid. Young Hawaiians soon learnt to perform mentally multiplications of four figures by four with such rapidity and accuracy that the teachers themselves were frequently placed in an embarrassing situation by being unable to equal the mental alertness and precision of their pupils. In Samoa, when elementary schools were first established, the natives developed an absolute craze for arithmetical calculations. They laid aside their weapons and were to be seen going about armed with slate and pencil, setting sums and problems to one another and to European visitors. The Honorable Frederick Walpole declares that his visit to that beautiful island was positively embittered by ceaseless multiplication and division. In order to curb the arithmetical importunity of his native friends he set them a problem in algebra. But after long meditation and consultation over it, and after declaring that "it couldn't be done," the Samoans would not rest until they had been initiated into the mysteries of the new science.

In keeping with Bidder's suggestion, Richard Salley, a former student of mine, undertook to teach three children—Mike, 11, Pam, 8, and Carole, 8—to do mental multiplication. Unfortunately, from Bidder's point of view, all the children had some knowledge of written arithmetic, though Pam and Carole had not been previously exposed to multiplication.

Salley used pinto beans arranged in rectangles to introduce multiplication up to nine by nine. After nine hours of exposure over a three-week period the girls became as fast and accurate at single-digit multiplication as was Mike.

[2]The Polynesians had a history of interest in numbers predating European contact. The French explorer Labillardière elicited from the Tongans names for numbers up to 100,000. When he pressed them for more they named numbers to 10^{12}, and these were subsequently published. The higher series turned out, however, to be composed of nonsense words and obscenities (Seidenberg 1960:280).

[3]I have been unable to consult Seidenberg's source: "R. Briffault, *The Mothers* (New York, 1927), 1:52–53."

The next step was to teach the children to multiply one digit by two digits. This was accomplished by "buying" ten beans for one cent. Through such purchases it was possible to construct rectangles up to 99 times 9.

After seven weeks and 20 contact hours (the children were encouraged to practice on their own) they were able to multiply mentally up to 99 times 19 with 90 percent accuracy. The project was abandoned at that time because of other demands on the children's time.

Bidder suggests extending his approach to geometry and algebra as well (1856:278–79):

> I would therefore introduce a boy, through this means, to natural geometry and algebra. By placing shots, or any small symmetrical objects on the circumference and the diameter of a circle, he would be able, by actual observation, to satisfy himself of their relative proportions. He might simultaneously be taught the relation of the area of the circle to the area of the square. He might also be taught the beautiful problem, that the square of the hypothenuse equals the squares on the other sides of a right-angled triangle—that the areas of all triangles on the same, or equal bases, and between two parallel lines, are equal. Of these, and many other useful facts, he would satisfy himself, long before he could appreciate the methods by which they are demonstrated in the elementary works on mathematics. Advantage may also be taken of this mode to develop many other ideas connected with geometry, as, for instance, that all the angles subtended from the same chord in the circle are equal. This might be shown by having a small angle cut in pasteboard, and fitted to every possible position in which two lines could be drawn within the circle upon the same chord. He might also be taught that the rectangles of the portions of any two lines intersecting a circle are equal. On this point I need not enlarge, because to all of you it will be apparent, that many other useful properties might be thus imprinted on the youthful mind. So again, as regards the series I have mentioned—the stones in the basket,[4] for instance, and also the summation of the series $1 + 3 + 5 + 7 + 9$: the summation of this series is equal to the square of the number of terms required to be summed up. If the learner once acquired a feeling for the beauty of the properties of figures—surmising that he had any natural taste for arithmetic—the discovery of these facts by his own efforts might incite him to farther investigations, and enable him to trace out his own path in the science.

[4] See the appendix.

PART TWO

—

CALCULATING METHODS

Chapter Ten

Basic Arithmetic

Multiplication

ACCORDING to Bidder (1856:257) multiplication is the "basis of all calculations." Binet (1894:74) wrote of Inaudi: "The basis of his calculations is multiplication." Mitchell (1907:103) elaborates on this theme, arguing:

> It has been suggested above that in the earlier stages the "natural" calculator who begins with counting—as distinguished from the "artificial" calculator who begins relatively late in life, using book-methods from the start—is interested mainly in *properties* of numbers and of simple series. Now these properties are revealed not by addition, but by multiplication, or the forms of counting which are equivalent to multiplication. . . . The differences between odd and even numbers, the properties of prime and composite numbers, as well as of squares, cubes, and other powers, series of all sorts, 2-figure endings, casting the 9's, and the like, all grow directly out of multiplication.

Left-to-Right Multiplication

With the exception of Wim Klein, all auditory calculators whose methods are known multiply from left to right. The form of multiplication described below (discovered independently by such calculators as Colburn, Bidder, Mondeux, and Inaudi) we will take to be the natural one.[1]

---

[1]"Natural" should not be interpreted here (or elsewhere) as superior. Natural methods are those typically discovered by untutored (and often unlettered) children. Natural methods are good ones, but not the only good ones. The best method in any given instance depends upon a variety of factors, not the least of which are the proclivities of the calculator.

The general form for left-to-right multiplication is: $(a_1 + a_2 + \cdots + a_n)$ $(b_1 + b_2 + \cdots + b_m) = (a_1 b_1 + a_1 b_2 + \cdots + a_1 b_m + a_2 b_1 + a_2 b_2 + \cdots + a_2 b_m + \cdots + a_n b_1 + a_n b_2 + \cdots + a_n b_m)$. For example, 348 times 461 would be computed as follows:

$$
\begin{array}{rr}
300 \times 400 = & 120{,}000 \\
300 \times 60 = & 18{,}000 \\
\text{sum} & 138{,}000 \\
300 \times 1 = & 300 \\
\text{sum} & 138{,}300 \\
40 \times 400 = & 16{,}000 \\
\text{sum} & 154{,}300 \\
40 \times 60 = & 2{,}400 \\
\text{sum} & 156{,}700 \\
40 \times 1 = & 40 \\
\text{sum} & 156{,}740 \\
8 \times 400 = & 3{,}200 \\
\text{sum} & 159{,}940 \\
8 \times 60 = & 480 \\
\text{sum} & 160{,}420 \\
8 \times 1 = & 8 \\
& 160{,}428
\end{array}
$$

The disadvantages of this system for written arithmetic are obvious, but as Zerah Colburn (1833:191) said: "True, the method here exhibited requires a much larger number of figures than the common Rule, but it will be remembered that pen, ink and paper, cost Zerah very little, when engaged in a sum."

Multiplication, as taught in grammar school, is designed to minimize the amount of writing required to solve a problem. We begin at the right so that there is no need to backtrack to account for carries, and trailing zeros are omitted. This is a sensible economy, especially in the days when all bookkeeping was done by hand. Other methods would have been wasteful of ink, paper, and time.

In mental calculation, on the other hand, the goal is to minimize short-term memory load. Beginning from the left allows you to approach the solution successively from below, and as Colburn (1833:191) points out: "The large numbers found first are easily retained, because consisting of so many ciphers," and by modifying the subtotal as you proceed you allow (Bidder 1856:260) "only one fact to be impressed on the mind at a time. You modify that fact every instant as the process goes on; but still the object is to have one fact, and one fact only, stored away at any one time."

Cross Multiplication

A number of visual calculating prodigies, including the younger Bidder, Diamandi, Finkelstein, and Eberstark, used (in Eberstark's case, uses) cross multiplication. It is a particularly advantageous method if the calculator has the problem in view while solving it and writes down the digits as they are worked out, since the answer is obtained from right to left, and once a digit is determined, it may be written down and thenceforth ignored. Wim Klein is the only auditory calculator known to use cross multiplication (two digits at a time), but unlike other auditory calculators he did not begin to calculate until after learning to read and write, and prefers to work with the problem before him.

Perhaps the best way to approach cross multiplication is from the point of view of the traditional method of multiplication taught in grammar school. The traditional method, as I mentioned before, resolutely economizes on the amount of writing required, but it is a poor method to use mentally because so much memory is needed. On paper this is no problem, since the paper serves as a memory aid.

Take as an example the multiplication of two four-digit numbers (whose product Finkelstein found in 17.5 seconds using cross multiplication; Weinland and Schlauch 1937:388):

$$
\begin{array}{r}
6,943 \\
7,859 \\
\hline
62,487 \\
34,715 \\
55,544 \\
48,601 \\
\hline
54,565,037
\end{array}
$$

In ordinary multiplication, the order in which partial products are obtained is given by the rows, starting from the right and going from the top to the bottom. In cross multiplication the order in which the partial products are obtained is from right to left, but in the order of the columns of ordinary written arithmetic.

Cross multiplication involves multiplying and adding up numbers within complexes, each complex corresponding to a column in ordinary arithmetic. We can conveniently refer to the units, tens, hundreds, thousands, ten thousands complexes, etc. The units complex consists of the units digit of one number times the units digit of the other; the tens complex is the sum of the tens digit of each number times the units digit of the other plus the carry from the units complex; the hundreds complex is the sum of the tens digit times the tens digit, the hundreds digit times the units digit, and the carry from the tens complex, and so forth. The steps in obtaining the partial products can be represented graphically (table 10.1).

TABLE 10.1
Cross Multiplication

Units Complex	Tens Complex	Hundreds Complex	Thousands Complex
6943	6943	6943	6943
|	⤬	⤬	⤬
7859	7859	7859	7859

	Ten Thousands Complex	Hundred Thousands Complex	Millions Complex	
	6943	6943	6943	
	⤬	⤬	|	
	7859	7859	7859	

The order in which the multiplications are carried out within a complex does not affect the result. Of course, it is easier to keep track of where you are if you consistently use some simple procedure as to which multiplication to take up next. One method is to multiply in the top-to-bottom order of the columns of ordinary multiplication. Another is to begin at the outside edges of the complex and move to the middle. In table 10.2, the latter method is used.

Hans Eberstark described for me an interesting variant of cross multiplication which he uses when the problem is not in view. He imagines one of the numbers in reverse order with the leftmost digit of the reversed number below the rightmost digit of the other number. He then

TABLE 10.2
Steps in Cross Multiplying

		Current Partial Answer
1. $9 \times 3 =$ 27	Write 7, carry 2	7
2. Carry 2		
$5 \times 3 =$ 15		
$4 \times 9 =$ 36		
53	Write 3, carry 5	37
3. Carry 5		
$8 \times 3 =$ 24		
$9 \times 9 =$ 81		
$5 \times 4 =$ 20		
130	Write 0, carry 13	037
4. Carry 13		
$7 \times 3 =$ 21		
$6 \times 9 =$ 54		
$8 \times 4 =$ 32		
$9 \times 5 =$ 45		
165	Write 5, carry 16	5,037
5. Carry 16		
$7 \times 4 =$ 28		
$6 \times 5 =$ 30		
$8 \times 9 =$ 72		
146	Write 6, carry 14	65,037
6. Carry 14		
$7 \times 9 =$ 63		
$6 \times 8 =$ 48		
125	Write 5, carry 12	565,037
7. Carry 12		
$7 \times 6 =$ 42		
54	Final Answer	54,565,037

imagines the reversed number moving digit by digit to the left below the other number, and he multiplies in columns. (You can practice with two slips of paper.) For instance, in the previous problem Eberstark would proceed as in table 10.3.

When the problem is in view, however, there are advantages to varying the order of multiplications within a complex to simplify the calculations, as Eberstark pointed out to me. For example, if there are two 8s in the same complex, the numbers by which they are to be multiplied can be

TABLE 10.3
Eberstark's Method of Cross Multiplying

1. $9 \times 3 =$	27	Write 7, carry 2	6943	
				9587
2. Carry	2		6943	
$9 \times 4 =$	36			9587
$5 \times 3 =$	15			
	53	Write 3, carry 5		
3. Carry	5		6943	
$9 \times 9 =$	81			9587
$5 \times 4 =$	20			
$8 \times 3 =$	24			
	130	Write 0, carry 13		

And so forth.

added together and multiplied by 8; or, if there is a carry of 9, and 9 is to be multiplied by 9 somewhere in the complex, then one can immediately multiply 9 by 10 and forget the carry.

In the above problem one could take advantage of such techniques in several instances. (These simplifications are of my own devising, but are of the sort suggested by Eberstark.) For example, in the thousands complex (item 4 of table 10.2), there are both 6×9 and 9×5 to be multiplied. One can immediately multiply 9×11 and simplify matters considerably. In the ten thousands complex (item 5) there is a carry of 16, as well as 8×9 to be multiplied. Since $16 = 8 \times 2$ and $8 \times 9 + 8 \times 2 = 8 \times (9 + 2)$, one can immediately multiply $8 \times 11 = 88$, eliminating concern about the carry.

Adding and Subtracting

Addition and subtraction are not operations favored by most calculators, no doubt because they do not lend themselves to shortcuts, and because, as Mitchell pointed out, not much in the way of numerical properties is revealed therein.

Inaudi was one of the few mental calculators to include addition and subtraction in his performances. He would add together five numbers of six digits each, and subtract one twenty-one-digit number from another. Just as in multiplication he began both these operations at the left. In adding he summed the first two numbers, obtained a total, and added it to the third number, etc., rather than proceeding a column at a time, as is done on paper. (Bear in mind that Inaudi never saw the figures at all in calculating, but memorized them by having them repeated to him several times.)

Binet (1894:74) gives the following example of Inaudi's method: "In subtraction, he operates in groups of three digits, beginning from the left. Thus, when he must subtract

$$426 \quad 384 \quad 631$$
$$227 \quad 529 \quad 472,$$

he works in the following way: he says (and this word *says* is particularly just) 227 from 426 leaves 199; but as there is a carry from the following number, the remainder is only 198; 529 from 1384 leaves 895,[2] etc." Thus, whenever possible, Inaudi would look ahead for carries and reduce his total accordingly.

Bidder proceeded similarly (1856:264): "With respect to Addition and Subtraction I have little to observe, because I follow the same system as in Multiplication; beginning with the left-hand figures and proceeding consecutively to the right. By this means I have only one result to register; as I get rid of the first series of figures I have no necessity for keeping in view [i.e., in mind] the numbers with which I have to deal."

One modern calculator, R. H. Frost (chapter 40), specializes in addition. He has been recognized by the *Guinness Book of World Records* (1978 edition) as the world's fastest at adding a column of 100 digits.

This is not at all comparable to Inaudi's additions, however, since the figures are in view and the sum is in the area of 500, there is relatively little problem of memory. It is more of a test of the absolute speed at which digits can be added.

Division

In the literature on calculating prodigies there is little discussion of division except in connection with factoring or decimalizing fractions. Bidder has one of the few (1856:264):

Division is, as in ordinary arithmetic, much more difficult than Multiplication, as it must be a tentative process, and is only carried out by a series,

[2] This is clearly a misprint—the number should be 855.

more or less, of guesses; but no doubt in this respect, the training arrived at by mental arithmetic gives the power of guessing, to a greater extent than is usually attained, and affords a corresponding facility in the process. Supposing, for instance, that it be necessary to divide 25,696 by 176, the following is the process: —100 must be the first figure of the factor; 100 times 176 are known at once to be 17,600; subtracting that from 25,696 there remains 8,096; it is perceived that 40 is the next number in the factor; 40 times 176 $=7,040$, there then remains 1,056—that, it is immediately perceived, gives a remaining factor of 6, making in all 146; thus only one result is retained in the mind at a time; but as contrasted with Multiplication it is necessary to keep registered in the mind two results which are always changing, viz.: the remainder of the number to be divided, and the numbers of the factors, as they are determined.

Bidder goes on to point out that if it is known that the divisor is a factor of the number divided (as in the above case), the process can be abbreviated by a knowledge of two-figure endings. The first digit of the answer is obviously 1, and there are only four two-digit endings which when multiplied by 76 give a result ending in 96; they are 21, 46, 71, and 96. Bidder immediately infers that it must be 46, as 121 is clearly (to him) too little, and 171 too much. He concludes (1856:265): "Thus, as before observed, the only facility afforded by mental calculation is the greater power of guessing at every step towards the result."

Binet (1894:74) gives a similar description of Inaudi's method of division:

in both dividing and extracting roots he multiplies; he makes a series of approximating multiplications; in a division, for example, it is by guessing that he finds the quotient, looking for and testing the number which, multiplied by the divisor, produces the dividend. These successive guesses are compared, with great ingenuity, by [Paul] Broca to looking up a word in a dictionary.

Aitken used a method of dividing by certain multidigit numbers, using short division (see chapter 12).

Chapter Eleven

Multiplication Shortcuts

C ALCULATING prodigies take advantage of various algebraic equivalences in order to simplify multiplications.[1] A common simplification, used by both prodigies and ordinary people, is to substitute a simpler number for the actual multiplier, and then to make the appropriate correction; that is, to make use of the algebraic equivalences:

$$ab = (a + c)b - cb$$
or
$$ab = (a - c)b + cb$$

where c is relatively small and $a + c$ or $a - c$ are easy numbers by which to multiply.

For example, Bidder (1856:260), in multiplying 173 by 397, said that he would multiply 173 by 400 and subtract 3×173.

Jacoby (1860:221) gave this as Mondeux's method for multiplying 384 by 22: $400 \times 22 = 8,800$; $16 \times 20 = 320$; $8,800 - 320 = 8,480$; $16 \times 2 = 32$; $8,480 - 32 = 8,448$.

And Darboux (quoted in Binet 1894:202) said that Inaudi, in multiplying 729 by 27 (to get the cube of 27) would multiply 730 by 27 and subtract 27.

An extreme example of this method is given in a report about Arumogam in the *Ceylon Morning Leader* of September 7, 1912 (quoted in Barlow 1952:56):

[1] I have not attempted (in this chapter or elsewhere in part 2) to compile a general list of shortcut procedures for mental arithmetic but only to describe those procedures known to have been used by calculating prodigies. For a brilliant collection of methods for mental calculation, see Menninger's (1964) *Calculator's Cunning*.

Thus to take a simple sum of multiplication, say, of 2555 by 3437. Of course, he deals with figures in millions and billions, but I take this for simplicity of illustration. He would take the first number as 2500 (2½ thousand), the remainder being 55. The other number he would take as 3500 (3½ thousand), the difference being 63. He would multiply 2½ thousand by 3½ thousand, and then make the necessary addition for the remainder 55 and the necessary subtraction for the difference 63, and declare the result in the twinkling of an eye.

Arumogam's exact procedure is not clear from this description. To get the product of a times b he begins in this case by multiplying $a + c$ times $b - d$, which gives $ab + bc - ad - dc$; this can be simplified to $ab + bc - d(a + c)$, so that adding $d(a + c) - bc$ to this total yields ab. Perhaps, then, Arumogam multiplied 3,500 by 2,500 to which he added 55 times 3,500 and subtracted 2,555 times 63.

In favorable cases, calculators may also take advantage of the fact that $(a + b)(a - b) = a^2 - b^2$. *Teachware* (Aarts 1974:9) gives the following examples of Klein's methods:

$$283 \times 657 = (470 - 187) \times (470 + 187) = 220,900 - 34,969 = 185,931$$
$$283 \times 542 = 283 \times 271 \times 2 = (277 + 6) \times (277 - 6) \times 2 = 153,386$$

Rückle, according to Gradenwitz (1907:93), if called upon to multiply 10,027 by 9,973 would seize upon the fact that 10,027 is $10,000 + 27$ and 9,973 is $10,000 - 27$. Gradenwitz admits that opportunities of applying this formula are "not always as favorable as in the present instance."

This method reduces multiplication to the difference of two squares, and can be used (without employing fractions) whenever the numbers to be multiplied are both odd or both even. Since there are a variety of effective shortcuts in squaring numbers, this can be a distinct advantage. The general formula is:

$$ab = \left(a - \frac{a - b}{2}\right)^2 - \left(\frac{a - b}{2}\right)^2.$$

Calulators sometimes use division to simplify multiplying. Darboux reported (Binet 1894:202) that Inaudi squared 27 by dividing 2,700 by 4 and adding 2 times 27. (Perhaps Inaudi offered this as an example of a technique he would use under some circumstances — it seems likely that he would know the square of 27 without having to calculate it.)

Aitken made use of the fact that

$$ab = \frac{(ac)b}{c}$$

in multiplying 987,654,321 by 123,456,789 (a problem posed to him by his children). He remarked (Hunter 1962:251): "I saw in a flash that 987,654,321 by 81 equals 80,000,000,001; and so I multiplied 123,456,789 by this, a simple matter, and divided the answer by 81. Answer: 121,932,631,112,635,269. The whole thing could hardly have taken more than half a minute." This is certainly easier than carrying out the entire multiplication, but what led Aitken to 81?

Calculators who are adept at factoring often make use of this facility to simplify problems. *Teachware* (Aarts 1974:9) gives the following example of how Wim Klein would multiply 3,658 by 153:

$$3,658 = 62 \times 59$$
$$153 = 9 \times 17$$
$$3,658 \times 153 = (62 \times 9) \times (59 \times 17) = 558 \times 1,003 = 559,674$$

Colburn also factored numbers whenever convenient in order to simplify his multiplications. As he did not like to multiply four digits by four digits, when called upon to square 4,395, he squared 293 and multiplied the result twice by 15. And when asked by the Duke of Gloucester to multiply 21,734 by 543 he did so by multiplying 65,202 by 181 (*Annual Register* 1812:509–10).

Colburn clearly knew nothing of algebra, and he plugged away using his technique of factoring even when a much simpler method lay at hand. When asked to square 999,999 he said that he could not, but finally succeeded by squaring 37,037 and multiplying the product twice by 27. For anyone with a grasp of algebra this is a very simple problem (see chapter 14). But Colburn was able to go further—he multiplied the result twice by 49 and then by 25.

Chapter Twelve

Decimalization of Fractions

A COMMON fraction is a ratio of integers (e.g., 11/16). Decimalizing a common fraction involves dividing the numerator by the denominator. The resulting decimal fraction either repeats the same sequence of digits endlessly after some point or it divides through with no remainder.

Converting common fractions to decimal fractions was a specialty of Aitken's. With his great calculating skill and mathematical knowledge he could bring a wide variety of techniques to the task—the plan adopted in any given case was always directed toward economy of effort. Hunter (1962:249) makes the following point with regard to the strategies Aitken employed in decimalizing:

> It is noteworthy that the number of feasible, as opposed to theoretically possible, plans is greatest with problems of intermediate complexity, more specifically, when the divisor is a two-digit number. With a one-digit divisor, plans other than straight division would introduce unnecessary calculative complexity. With many three-digit and almost all four-digit divisors, plans other than straight division would be too complex to carry through readily as a unit: indeed straight division itself may become laborious to the point of being not worth while attempting mentally.

When asked to comment upon how he went about decimalizing 1/851, Aitken wrote (Hunter 1962:245):

> The instant observation was that 851 is 23 times 37. I use this fact as follows. 1/37 is 0.027027027027 . . . and so on repeated. This I divide mentally by 23. [23 into 0.027 is 0.001 with remainder 4.][1] In a flash I can see that 23 into 4027 is 175 with remainder 2, and into 2027 is 88 with remainder 3, and into 3027 is 131 with remainder 14, and even into 14,027

[1] The parenthetical comments in this and the following quotation are Hunter's.

is 609 with remainder 20. And so on like that. Also before I ever start this, I know how far it is necessary to go in this manner before reaching the end of the recurring period: for 1/37 recurs at three places, 1/23 recurs at twenty-two places, the lowest common multiple of 3 and 22 is 66, whence I know that there is a recurring period of 66 places.

This illustrates one of the techniques commonly used by Aitken for solving such problems—to factor the fraction (in this case 1/23 × 1/37), to decimalize the factor with the shortest period of repetition, and then to multiply the decimalized fraction by the remaining common fraction (0.027027 . . . times 1/23; which is simply division by 23).

Some weeks later Aitken wrote some further reflections on 851 as a divisor (Hunter 1962:245):

> Certainly 15/851 and 17/851 would produce different reactions. For the first, I should have started at once to divide 0.405405405 . . . by 23, three digits at a time. [This is the same basic procedure as before. 15/37 is 0.405405 repeating.] The wiser course with 17/851 would be to do the corresponding thing upon 0.459459459459 . . . [this is 17/37]; but the fact that 17 into 851 is so very nearly 50 would make me want to correct 0.02 by subtracting 1/851 of it, in my own way of rapid compensation. In fact I should have 0.0199765 in a flash; but could not continue so easily, since dividing by 851 and adjusting is not so easy as dividing straight on by 23. I spoke before about not changing horses in midstream. Here is a case where the choice would be made at once; I should in fact go ahead with division of 0.459459459 . . . by 23, perhaps deciding to divide two digits at a time instead of three.

Aitken (1954:300) explained his "method of rapid compensation" referred to above in his address before the Society of Engineers:

> To begin with a very elementary example, it is not generally known that one can divide by a number like 59, or 79, or 109, or 599, and so on, by *short* division. Take for example 1/59, which is nearly 1/60. Set out division thus:[2]
>
> $$\frac{0.0169491525 \ . \ . \ .}{6 \ / \ 1.016949152 \ . \ . \ .}$$
>
> Here we have the decimal for 1/59, obtained by dividing 1 by 60; as we obtain each digit we merely enter it in the dividend, *one place later,* and continue with the division.

[2] I have changed the notation for division to conform to that commonly used in the United States.

As another example consider 5/23. Write it as 15/69. Then proceed:

$$0.217391304 \ldots$$
$$7 \overline{)15.21739130 \ldots}$$

In fact $5/23 = 0.2173913043478260869565$, a recurring decimal with a period of 22 digits. One could equally well have written it as 65/299, then carrying out division by 3, two digits at a time, and entering in the dividend *two places* further along . . .

There are other possibilities. For example the mental calculator is, or should be, very familiar with the factorization of numbers; he should know not merely that 23 times 13 is 299, but that 23 times 87 is 2,001. For example 5/13 [a misprint in the original—this should be 5/23] is equal to 435/2,001; and if we note that 435 is the same as 434.999999999 . . . , we have another method, in which, as we obtain the digits, we *subtract* them from the dividend, so many places later. Thus in the present case:

$$217 \quad 391 \quad 304 \quad 347 \ldots$$
$$2 \overline{)434 \quad 782 \quad 608 \quad 695 \quad 652 \ldots}$$

For example 217 from 999 gives 782, which we then divide by 2, obtaining 391; this subtracted from 999, gives 608; and so on.

Chapter Thirteen

Roots

Integer Roots

EXTRACTING roots[1] of perfect powers (traditionally termed evolution) is one of the most common calculations undertaken by prodigies (Aitken 1954:297):

> Or again—this was asked of another calculator—"What is the cube root of 327,082,769?"
>
> (*Answer:* 689, since by inspection it must be a little less than 700, for 7 cubed is 343; also it must end in 9, and cannot be 699.)
>
> Such cube-rooting (and there is a good deal of it in the records) is almost trivial, since the important digits yield by inspection the first digit, and mere inspection of the last digit of the proposed number gives the last digit of the answer (for example 7 would give 3, while 3 would give 7); the rest is commonsense [*sic*], having no reference at all to the other digits.

Calculators have always preferred extracting cube roots to square roots, the reason being that cube roots are more impressive because a higher power is involved, and cube roots are easier to do, since the last digit of the power unambiguously determines the last digit of the root (not true of squares), according to the following table:

Root	*Cube*
0	0
1	1
2	8

[1] Throughout this discussion, unless otherwise indicated, roots will be assumed to be integers.

Root	Cube
3	7
4	4
5	5
6	6
7	3
8	2
9	9

For instance, the cube root of 551,368 must end in 2 (assuming, correctly, that it is a perfect cube).

The table is quite easy to remember—for zero, one, four, five, six, and nine the final digit of the cube and the root are identical; in the other cases the final digit of the root and the final digit of the cube add up to ten.

The first digit of the root is almost equally easy to determine. It requires that one memorize the cubes of the integers from one to nine (1, 8, 27, 64, 125, 216, 343, 512, 729, respectively). Compare these to the digits to the left of the leftmost comma in the cube;[2] the cube root of the number next below that of the power is the first digit of the root. For example, 512 is the cube next below 551; therefore, 8 (the cube root of 512) is the first digit of the cube root of 551,368. Since the cube roots of numbers less than a million contain at most two digits, the cube root of 551,368 must be 82.

As can be seen, no great sophistication or computing skill is required to find cube roots of perfect cubes less than a million. Three-digit roots will cover perfect cubes up to a billion, and the first and last digits of the root can be easily found by the above methods.

An extension of the method for finding the units digit can be used to fix the last two digits of roots of perfect powers.[3] The method is described by Colburn (1833:180–82), Bidder (1856:266–67), and Mitchell (1907:93–94), all of whom discovered it independently, and it has probably been used by all calculators who were adept at evolution.

This method of "two-figure endings" (Mitchell's term) consists in memorizing all the terminating pairs of digits which when cubed (or squared, etc.) will produce a power ending in a particular pair of digits. The last two digits (tens and units) of perfect cubes determine, with

[2] That is, group the digits in threes starting from the right and consider the leftmost such group (which may contain less than three digits).
[3] It is also used to find factors (see chapter 15).

Roots 125

TABLE 13.1
Colburn's Table For Cube Roots

Cube	Root	Cube	Root	Cube	Root	Cube	Root	Cube	Root
01	01	24	24	41	81	64	04	79	59
03	87	—	74	43	07	—	54	81	61
04	34	25	05	44	14	67	23	83	27
—	84	—	25	—	64	68	32	84	44
07	43	—	45	47	63	—	82	—	94
08	02	—	65	48	22	69	89	87	83
—	52	—	85	—	72	71	91	88	42
09	69	27	03	49	49	72	38	—	92
11	71	28	12	51	51	—	88	89	29
12	08	29	09	52	28	73	97	91	31
—	58	31	11	—	78	75	15	92	48
13	17	32	18	53	37	—	35	—	98
16	06	—	68	56	36	—	55	93	57
—	56	33	77	—	86	—	75	96	16
17	73	36	46	57	93	—	95	—	66
19	39	—	96	59	19	76	26	97	13
21	41	37	33	61	21	—	76	99	99
23	47	39	79	63	67	77	53		

Source: Colburn 1833:182.

some ambiguity, the last two digits of the cube root, in accordance with table 13.1.

Colburn gives the following example of the use of his table:

Take for instance, 28,094,464. First, seek what number cubed, will end in 64. Ans. 04: then what number cubed, comes nearest under 28. Ans. 3. Combine them, 304, the root required . . . there is not the same latitude for mistaking in the root of a cube number, that there is in extracting the square root. Some difficulty, however, exists; for instance, if the given cube ends in 08, it will be a question whether 02 or 52 will be correct; and so of all similar cases.

As mentioned at the outset of this chapter, square roots have found less favor among calculators, because of the considerably greater uncertainty regarding the correct terminating digits. Nevertheless, calculators of the past, such as Bidder and Colburn, were frequently called upon to say "What number multiplied by itself will give ——?" The method used again was that of two-figure endings, in accord with Colburn's table given here as 13.2.

TABLE 13.2
Colburn's Table For Square Roots

Square	Root	Square	Root	Square	Root	Square	Root	Square	Root
01	01	24	18	41	21	64	08	89	17
—	51	—	68	—	71	—	58	—	67
—	49	—	32	—	29	—	42	—	33
—	99	—	82	—	79	—	92	—	83
04	02	25	05	44	12	69	13	96	14
—	52	—	15	—	62	—	63	—	64
—	48	—	25	—	38	—	37	—	36
—	98	—	35	—	88	—	87	—	86
		—	45						
09	03	—	55	49	07	76	24		
—	53	—	65	—	57	—	74		
—	47	—	75	—	43	—	26		
—	97	—	85	—	93	—	76		
		—	95						
16	04			56	16	81	09		
—	54	29	27	—	66	—	59		
—	46	—	77	—	34	—	41		
—	96	—	23	—	84	—	91		
		—	73						
21	11			61	19	84	22		
—	61	36	06	—	69	—	72		
—	39	—	56	—	31	—	28		
—	89	—	44	—	81	—	78		
		—	94						

Source: Colburn 1833:181.

As can be seen there is much more ambiguity in finding the final two digits of a square root than there is in finding the final two digits of a cube root. Bidder (1856:266–67) describes how he proceeded in difficult cases:

In reference to square numbers terminating in 25; although all numbers ending in 5, when squared, give 25 as terminals, I noticed that the squares of numbers ending in 5, 45, 55, and 95, ended in 025, and that those of the numbers terminating in 15, 35, 65, and 85, ended in 225; whereas the squares of those ending in 25 and 75, ended in 625. Hence in extracting the square root of 442,225, I perceived, as before, that 600 must be the first factor, and that the last one must lie between 15, 35, 65, and 85, and judging from the position of 442,225 between 360,000 and 490,000, the squares of 600 and 700 respectively, I saw that 65 was the factor required, and root was therefore 665.

Colburn (1833:181) also discusses the difficulties attendant to finding square roots:

> It is thought that there is little difficulty, according to the rule presented, in determining the two last figures of the root; it is obvious, however, that it requires a good share of quickness and discernment, in a large sum, to see which of the *four* roots in ordinary numbers, or which of the *ten*, where 25 is the termination, is the right one to be employed. Such discernment, however, the writer cannot impart.

A traditional method of testing the answers of arithmetic problems, known as the rule of eleven, or the elevens test, can be adapted to find one digit of a root, when the other digits are known.[4]

Any number can be represented as a multiple of some constant plus a remainder. In this case eleven is taken as the constant; thus $a = 11b + R$, where R is the remainder upon dividing a by 11 (or, for those familiar with modular arithmetic, a is congruent to R, modulo 11). One can check any arithmetic calculation by carrying out the same calculation on the remainders in place of the numbers in the original calculation. The correct answer to the original problem will have the same remainder as the remainder of the answer obtained in this way; for example, $897 \times 764 = 685,308,897 = (81 \times 11) + 6$; and $764 = (69 \times 11) + 5$. Multiplying the remainders (6×5) gives 30, or $(2 \times 11) + 8$; and $685,308 = (62,300 \times 11) + 8$. The remainder is eight in both cases. The test checks. This does not mean that the answer is necessarily correct, but if the test does not hold, the answer is certainly wrong.

With a little practice, dividing even fairly large numbers by 11 is not so difficult as it might first appear. However, there is another method for finding the elevens remainder recommended by books on practical arithmetic. Subtract the sum of the digits in the even-place positions (counting from the right) from the sum of those in the odd-place positions. (That is, subtract the sum of the tens, thousands, hundred thousands, etc. digits from the units, hundreds, ten thousands, etc. digits.) If the answer is negative, add 11 to get the remainder; if the result exceeds 11, subtract 11 (one or more times).

---

[4]A better-known method, "casting out nines," is of limited usefulness in fixing a missing digit of a cube root, since it gives three possible choices.

Take, for example, the cube 640,503,928. Add together the odd-place digits: $8 + 9 + 0 + 0 + 6 = 23$. Subtract from this sum of the even-place digits: $2 + 3 + 5 + 4 = 14$ and $23 - 14 = 9$. Thus 9 is the remainder upon dividing 640,503,928 by 11.

Having established the first and last digits of the cube in the manner described above, the middle digit (or any digit when the others are known) can be deduced by a reversal of the elevens test. The cube remainder unambiguously determines the remainder of the root, according to the table below.

Cube Remainder	Root Remainder
0	0
1	1
2	7
3	9
4	5
5	3
6	8
7	6
8	2
9	4
10	10

(This table can be easily constructed by cubing the numbers from 0 through 10 and taking the elevens-remainder of the cubes.) After finding the cube remainder, it is only necessary to find the middle digit which will give the appropriate root remainder. In the case of 640,503,928, the first digit of the root must be 8, since 9 cubed is 729 and 8 cubed 512. The last digit will be 2. We now have 8__2. The cube remainder is 9, so the root remainder must be 4. Since $8 + 2 = 10$, the middle digit of the root must be 6 ($10 - 6 = 4$). Therefore, the cube root of 640,503,928 is 862.

Fifth roots have also been a traditional favorite among calculators, since the units digit of the power, as in the case of cube roots, unambiguously determines the units digit of the root. Schumacher wrote to Gauss concerning Dase's delight in fifth roots (Gauss and Schumacher 1861 1:382): "He was especially fond of extracting fifth roots in his head, since he had noticed that at the fifth power the units were the same as they were in the root. I saw that in our number system the $4n + 1$ power has the same units as the root, a principle of which his result is but a particular case (for $n = 1$)." This means that the units digit of the root and power are the same for 9th, 13th, 17th, etc. roots. There are also roots for which the units digit behaves like cube roots: these are any roots of the $4n + 3$ power, where n is a natural number; thus 3d, 7th, 11th powers, etc. These two types cover all the odd powers.

In recent years calculators have taken to extracting roots of very high powers, and their successes in this area have been reported in the *Guinness Book of World Records*. The eleventh edition (1972:43) reported that, on October 5, 1970, Herbert B. de Grote of Mexico City had mentally extracted the 13th root of a 100-digit number in 23 minutes.

Since then the extraction of roots of high powers has become increasingly popular, no doubt owing to the availability of computers, both for providing data from which calculators can create algorithms and for providing problems for performances.

By the sixteenth edition (1977), the record was claimed by Wim Klein of the Netherlands, who extracted the 23d root of a 200-digit number in 10½ minutes. The 1978 edition reported that Klein had extracted the 73d root of a 500-digit number in 2 minutes, 43 seconds.

The difficulty of extracting a root of a perfect power has little to do with the size of the power involved. Much more important are the number of digits in the root and the particular power selected (note that in none of the cases above were even powers employed). Mitchell (1907:94) observed: "in general, the higher the root the easier the problem, and square and cube roots are the only ones which often come up." In this regard, times have changed.

The *Guinness Book of World Records* now recognizes the 13th root of a 100-digit number as a standard for testing the ability to extract integer roots. Wim Klein is the current record holder with a time of less than two minutes. Klein comments: "The problem is harder the more digits there are in the result. The 23rd root of 200 digits has nine digits in the result, and the same also for the seventh root of 63 digits. The 13th root of 100 digits has eight digits, but the 19th root of 133 digits and the 73rd root of 500 digits have only seven digits. I don't find seven digits interesting any longer. It is just a game for me.

"With eight digits, one digit is not sure, so you have to put in special tests. With nine digits there are two unknown digits in the middle. That makes it much tougher. The cube root of 30 digits gives ten digits— it's a hell of a work."

Klein's methods for extracting 13th roots can be illustrated with the following number:

147624208393707607056659537720222178703189569306592723679623056306150776820333360935495721848039014 4.

The first five digits of the root are fixed through the use of logarithms. Klein has memorized to five places the logs of the integers up to 150; this, coupled with his ability to factor large numbers, allows him to approximate the log of the first five digits of the power, which is usually sufficient to determine the first five digits of the root, though, as he says, "the fifth digit is a bit chancy."

Klein began by factoring 1,476 into 36 times 41 and taking the (decimal) log of each: log 36 = 1.55630 and log 41 = 1.61278; adding the mantissas yields 0.16908, but this is, of course, too little. Through various interpolations Klein estimated the mantissa of the log of 147,624 as 0.16925 (it is more nearly 0.16916).

Klein now had an approximation of the log of the 100-digit number above— 99.16925. This must be divided by 13 to obtain the log of the 13th root. Since 99 = 13 × 7 with a remainder of 8, to obtain the mantissa of the antilog of the 13th root he divided 8.16925 by 13, which is approximately 0.62840. He estimated the antilog to be about halfway between 4.2 and 4.3 and decided to try 4.25. The result was exact, so the first five digits of the root should be 42500, as indeed they are.

It is now necessary to determine the last three digits of the root. This he does from an examination of the last three digits of the power. In the case of odd powers, these uniquely determine the last three digits of the root, but in the case of even roots, like this one, this method yields four possibilities; in the case of 144 they are 014, 264, 514, and 764. (The choices always differ by 250.) To select the correct one Klein divides the original number by 13 and retains the remainder. In the case of 13th roots, the root remainder and the power remainder must be the same. The power remainder is 7; only 764 as the final three digits of the root will yield 7 as the remainder. Thus the 13th root is determined to be 42,500,764.

As an example of an odd root take: 75185285487713563581947553291145079861723813162341539358615509972979918152990226623589763080659858 31. The first five digits of the power are 75185, which is nearly 7519, and 7519 is 73 times 103. The mantissa of the log of 73 is 0.86332 and that of 103 is 0.01284. Their sum is 0.87616. Dividing 8.87616 by 13 yields 0.68278. This falls between the mantissas of the logs of 48 and 49, but is much closer to 48. Since 481 is 13 (mantissa 0.11394) times 37 (mantissa 0.56820), the mantissa of its log will be 0.68214; close, but still a bit low; 4,816 can be factored into 16 (mantissa 0.20412) times 7 (mantissa 0.84510) times 43 (mantissa 0.63347). This gives a mantissa of 0.68269. Then 4,818 factors into 66 (mantissa 0.81954) times 73 (mantissa 0.86332), which yeilds a mantissa of 0.68286. Thus, in the interpolation we want 9/17 of 20, which is about 10 1/2. The first five digits of the root should be 48170 (48160 + 10). This, in fact, is correct.

When Klein actually did the calculation he made a minor error (he was looking for the antilog of 0.68277 instead of 0.68278) and first took 48169 for the first five digits of the root. In this case, however, since the root is odd, the last three digits are uniquely fixed—since the power ends in 831, the root must end in 311. Upon dividing the power by 13 Klein got a remainder of 7. But dividing 48,169,311 by 13 gives a remainder of 8. To make these two remainders come into line he changed his solution to 48,170,311, which is correct.

Noninteger Roots

If a root of an integer is not itself an integer, it will be irrational, so that only an approximation to some number of decimal places is possible. For example, the cube root of 9 is not an integer; it is approximately 2.0800838, but the calculation can be carried out forever without reaching a point at which the digits repeat.

Calculators, in the past, were rarely called upon to extract roots which were not integers. One reason is that most people do not know how to extract roots. (Today pocket calculators have made such questions more popular.) Bidder remarked (1856:266): "the numbers submitted to me were almost invariably perfect squares, or cubes, arising from the circumstance that, in order to save themselves trouble, those who questioned me, squared, or cubed a number, as the readiest mode of testing the accuracy of my reply, which being found correct, they were satisfied and so was I."

Extracting noninteger roots is naturally far more difficult than extracting roots of perfect powers. Aitken said (1954:297): "The real test of ability to do square, cube or any other root is, in my view, to have a number proposed that is *not* an exact power, and to be asked to give the answer to several decimals; but this type of question you will hardly find in the published records." Bidder (1856:267) indicates that he was occasionally confronted with such problems, but gives no specifics about how he went about solving them: "if I suspected that the number was not a perfect square, or cube, I tested it by 'casting out the nines'— a process familiar to arithmeticians; and in such cases, the results were approximated to by a tentative process. . . ."

Aitken begins his discussion of extracting noninteger square roots with the remark (1954:298): "The central idea here is Newton's; but, remarkable to state, the Babylonians have it in their cuneiform inscriptions, and so did the wonderful Archimedes, the Syracusan Greek."

Aitken took as an example the square root of 51. The answer is, of course, somewhat more than 7, so 7 can be taken as a first approximation. On the other hand, it is somewhat less than 51/7, so that taking the mean of the quotients (49 and 51) yields a much better approximation: $50/7 = 5.1428571$. . . . To get even closer divide 51 by 50/7, which gives 7.14, so that the mean of the divisor and the quotient is 7.1414285 . . . and the correct answer to eight decimal places is 7.1414284.

Algebraically the method is as follows: let x be the number whose square root is sought. Choose for the first approximation the integer (call this y) nearest the square root of x. Then x/y is another approximation. Take the mean of the two:

$$\frac{x + y^2}{2y} = z.$$

Now z becomes the new approximation and is substituted for y in the formula to get a still better approximation.

The better the value initially selected for y, the better the value for z will be, thus reducing the calculations required to obtain a satisfactory approximation.

Aitken (1954:298–99) continues:

But the resources of mental division are not exhausted even here. An expert would know very well that 7.14141414 . . . is 707/99, and dividing 51 by this we have 5049/707, easily accomplished by dividing by 101 first, yielding 49.990099009900 . . . and then by 7, so that we have 7.141442715700 . . . , and the mean of this and 7.14141414141414 . . . is 7.14142842857 to 12 digits, whereas the true value of the square root of 51 is 7.14142842854 to that degree of accuracy.

In other words, in this case the initial value for y was taken as 707/99, and since this is a better approximation of the square root of 51, we get a *very* good approximation in z.

Aitken pointed to other methods which might be employed by a skilled mental calculator (1954:299):

> To revert to 51. How near is 50/7 to the square root? It was got from a divisor 7 and quotient 51/7. These are in ratio 49:51. The halfway mark between them is 50; I will say therefore that both 7 and 51/7 "deviate" by 1 in 50. The square of this is 1 in 2,500. I double and say, 1 in 5,000. Now 50/7 reduced by 1 in 5,000 is
>
> $$4,999/700 = 7.1414285 \ldots,$$
>
> remarkably near the true value 7.1414284 . . . , and in fact identical with the second approximation given above. It is clear by this time that we have several methods to choose from. There is yet another. Looking again at the first pair, 7 and 51/7, we note once more their ratio 49:51. Quarter the distance between 49 and 51, and take the *first* and *third* quarter, namely 49½, 50½, their ratio being 99:101. I say then that
>
> $$7 \text{ by } 102/99 = 7.14141414 \ldots$$
>
> is a good approximation to the square root of 51. Alternatively that
>
> $$51/7 \text{ by } 99/101 = 7.141442715700 \ldots$$
>
> is equally good; but we have met both of these before, and have seen that their average is spectacularly good. There are even subtler and more powerful approximations still. There is one known to me, quite simple, which I may illustrate by saying that in our example here (rather hard worn by now) we could correct 50/7 by reducing it not by 1 in 5,000, but by 1 in 4,999½. The result is
>
> $$7.141428428557 \ldots, \text{ as against } 7.141428428543$$
>
> and so committing an error of 1 in 500,000,000,000. This is an extreme approximation for square root; and I have never gone beyond it in mental calculation.

Klein (Aarts 1974:10) gives an example of essentially the same method as the first one discussed above for extracting a noninteger square root, but applied in a somewhat different manner. He considers the square root of 38, which is somewhat more than 6. He first divides 38 by 6 and obtains 6.3333. . . . Midway between 6.3333 and 6 is 6.1666. This number squared is 38.02695556. He then takes the excess and divides it by twice 6.1666; that is, $0.02695556/(2 \times 6.1666)$, and takes the answer as 0.0022 (it is 0.0021856 . . .) [I suspect Klein does some rounding off before making the calculation. For example, $0.027/(2 \times 6.17)$ is 0.002188 . . . , which is sufficiently accurate for his purposes.] He then subtracts 0.0022 from 6.1666 to obtain 6.1644. This squared is

37.99982736, or 0.00017264 too little. Dividing by 2×6.1644 yields 0.000014, which added to 6.1644 gives 6.164414. This last squared is 37.99999996386, a very close approximation.

Klein's iterative formula is

$$\frac{x - y^2}{2y} + y = z$$

where, as before, x is the number whose square root is sought, y is initially the nearest integer to the square root (or some better approximation), and z is the approximation to the square root. In subsequent iterations z is substituted for y.

Noninteger cube roots can also be approximated. Klein makes use of his knowledge of logarithms in extracting noninteger roots. The following example is also from *Teachware* (Aarts 1974).

What is the cube root of 3,721? Klein knows the logs to five places of the integers up to 150, but since 3,721 considerably exceeds that, he must do some calculations to obtain a good value for the log. In this case it is quite simple, as 3,721 is 61^2; the log of 61 is 1.78533, and doubling this gives the log required— 3.57066. The log of the cube root will be one-third of 3.57066, or 1.19022.

The cube root lies between 15 and 16, so Klein tries 15.5 (since $15.5 = 5 \times 3.1$, and he knows the logs of 5 and 31, it is not difficult for him to calculate). This gives 1.19033, which is too much. He tries 15.48 (4.3×3.6), obtaining 1.18977; then 15.488, the log of which is 1.18999.

Now 1.19022 is about two-thirds of the way between 1.18999 and 1.19033. The interval between 15.488 and 15.500 is 0.012, two-thirds of which is 0.008; by interpolation he gets 15.496 as the cube root of 3,721.

Klein then checks by multiplication: 15.496^2 is a bit more than 240.126, and $240.126 \times 15.496 = 3,720.992496$. Thus 15.496 is a good approximation to the cube root of 3,721.

Aitken (1954:299) described his methods for extracting cube roots:

> I will take for illustration the cube root of 128. You can see that it must be near 5, since the cube of 5 is 125. Trisect the interval from 125 to 128. The "middle third" yields the ratio 126:127. I assert that
>
> 5 by $127/126 = 5.0396825 \ldots$
>
> is very close to the required cube root, which is in fact 5.0396842 [to] eight significant digits. This method of 'thirding' is here ever so slightly in defect;

it is the business of the algebraist to ascertain the formula for the small error committed. I will not go into these delicate refinements. Here of course a proposed number may prove rather intractable, being remote from any suitable cube of an integer, or of a fraction with small denominator. I may mention also a similar method which I call "sixthing." Here for example we have that 128 is 5 by 5 by 5.12. I divide that former interval, 125 to 128, into *six* parts, and taking the *first* and the *fifth* of these I form the ratio 251:255. We have then

$$5.12 \text{ by } 251/255 = 5.0396863,$$

an approximation almost as good as the other, this time slightly in excess. I am not aware that this approximation has ever received notice.

Chapter Fourteen

Powers

RAISING numbers to powers (or involution) is a much more difficult matter than extracting roots of perfect powers. In the latter the calculator depends upon the fact that the number presented him is a perfect power, and of the proper degree; if it were not—if, for example, some of the numbers in the middle were jumbled—he would in general have no way of knowing. In involution no such latitude is allowed. Therefore, no one would undertake to raise seven-digit numbers to the 73d power, even though seven-digit roots of perfect 73d powers can be extracted. For the most part calculators limit themselves to squaring or cubing three- or four-digit numbers, or raising small numbers (not above two digits) to high powers.

Neither Bidder nor Colburn alluded to any special technique for squaring, cubing, or raising numbers to high powers, and it appears that their methods did not differ from those used for other multiplications. In one instance, when Colburn was asked (MacNeven 1811:20) to multiply six by itself six times, he went through the entire succession of multiplications, aloud and very rapidly. He is also credited with raising eight to the 16th power (*Annual Register* 1812:508):

> He was then tried as to other numbers, consisting of one figure; all of which he raised (by actual multiplication and not by memory) as high as the tenth power, with so much facility and dispatch that the person appointed to take down the results, was obliged to enjoin him not to be so rapid! With respect to numbers consisting of two figures, he would raise some of them to the sixth, seventh, and eighth power; but not always with equal facility: for the larger the products became, the more difficult he found it to proceed.

On another occasion he was asked to square 999,999 and replied that he could not. Using the method described by Aitken (below) this is a very simple problem, since $999,999^2 = 999,998 \times 10^6 + 1^2 = 999,998,000,001$. When asked to try again Colburn was eventually successful, but only by factoring $999,999$ as $27 \times 37,037$, squaring the latter and multiplying twice by the former. The incident is related by Colburn (1833:38–39), who, even as an adult, was apparently unaware that there is a simpler way to do the problem.

Aitken gives the following method for squaring numbers (1954:298):

> All that I use, perhaps more than once in the course of a calculation, is the algebraic identity $a^2 = (a + b)(a - b) + b^2$, where $a + b$ or $a - b$ is conveniently chosen, one or the other of these numbers ending in one or more zeros, and b being relatively small. For example, when Dr. Taylor asked me to square 777, I took b as 23, mentally multiplied 754 by 800, and added the square of 23, namely 529. The same with the rest; some were especially easy.

Arthur Griffith (chapter 32), without any knowledge of algebra, evolved some remarkable methods for involution. According to Bryan and Lindley (1941:42) Griffith had worked out methods for solving: $(a \pm b)^2$; $(a \pm b)^3$; $(a \pm b)^4$ for $b = 1$ or 2; $(a + b)^5$ for $b = 1$; $(a - b)^n$ for $a = 10^k$, $1 \leq b \leq 15$ and $1 \leq n \leq 5$ (a, b, and n are of course integers). Some examples are:

$$a^3 = [a + 1] \, [a \, (a - 1) + 1] - 1$$
e.g., $39^3 = 40 \times (39 \times 38 + 1) - 1 = 59,319$

or

$$a^3 = [a - 1] \, [a \, (a + 1) + 1] + 1$$
e.g., $41^3 = 40 \times (41 \times 42 + 1) + 1 = 68,921$

$$(a + 2)^4 = ([a \, (a + 1) + 1] \, [a + 2] + a) \, 2^3 + a^4$$
e.g., $32^4 = ([30 \times 31 + 1] \times 32 + 30) \times 8 + 810,000 = 1,048,576$

$$(a + 1)^5 = [a \, (a + 1) + 1] \, [a \, (a + 1) \, 5] + 1 + a^5$$
e.g., $21^5 = (20 \times 21 + 1) \times 20 \times 21 \times 5 + 1 + 20^5 = 4,084,101$

For $(a - b)^5$ Griffith used the binomial theorem:

$$a^5 - 5a^4b + 10a^3b^2 - 10a^2b^3 + 5ab^4 - b^5$$

Since a is a power of 10 (see above), Griffith could ignore it in his calculations, though it served as an automatic place holder in his evolving

TABLE 14.1
Griffith's Method of Raising to the Fifth Power

		$(a-b)^5$ in the Case $(100-3)^5$		
A. G.s Method			**Binomial Formula**	
1. $\quad 3^5 \quad = 243$		1. $(-b^5)$	-3^5	$=$ $\quad -243$
$\quad 100-43=57$	57			
$\quad 2+1$ to carry				
2. $\quad 3^4 \times 5 \ =405$		2. $(5ab^4)$	$3^4 \times 5 \times 100$	$=$ $\quad 40500$
$\quad 05-3 \ = \ 02$	$02..$			
$\quad 4$ to carry				
3. $\quad 3^3 \times 10 = 270$		3. $(-10a^2b^3)$	$-3^3 \times 10 \times 100^2 =$	$\quad -2700000$
$\quad 270- \ 4=266$				
$\quad 100-66= \ 34$	$34....$			
$\quad 2+1$ to carry				
4. $\quad 3^2 \times 10 = 90$		4. $(10a^3b^2)$	$3^2 \times 10 \times 100^3$	$=$ $\quad 90000000$
$\quad 90 \ - \ 3=87$	$87......$			
$\quad 0$ to carry				
5. $\quad 3^1 \times \ 4=12$		5. $(-5a^4b)$	$-3 \times 5 \times 100^4$	$= -1500000000$
$\quad 97-12=85$	$85.......$			
		6. (a^5)	100^5	$= \ 10000000000$
	8587340257			8587340257

Source: Bryan and Lindley 1941.

answer. Griffith obtained his answer from right to left, as illustrated in table 14.1.

Shyam Marathe is adept at raising single-digit numbers to powers as high as 20. He says that he formerly undertook to raise two-digit numbers to such powers in performances, but that he was liable to occasional errors and therefore limits himself to single-digit numbers, with which he works very confidently.

Does Marathe actually calculate numbers such as 9^8, or has he simply memorized the results? Since zero and one can be ignored there are only eight single-digit numbers which need be considered—2 through 9. The total number of digits in all of these up to the 20th power is less than 1,500. It is certainly possible to memorize such a sequence of digits. (The current record for memorizing pi is over 20,000 digits.)

On the other hand, memorizing is not Marathe's stated method (of which more later), and there are other indications that the answers are obtained by actual calculation. First, he gives answers to smaller powers from left to right; possibly he has these memorized. As the powers grow larger, he gives the results from right to left. On one occasion when we were talking over the telephone, he raised 9^8 for me. When I tried to read the number back to him to see whether it had been correctly transcribed, he said that he could not verify the answer for me in this way, though he could recalculate it if I wished.

Marathe refuses to give a detailed account of his method for involution, but he does provide the following clues (if they are not false leads); the readers may make of them what they will.

Marathe says that he works in a different number system, based upon a very large prime (something over 4,000). Actually, he says that our "number world" ends in 9, which is not prime, but that there are advantages in a number world which *ends* in a prime. Presumably, this means that the number base within which he works, less one, is a prime. Just what these advantages are he does not say, but he suggests experimenting with 13 to get the idea. For each of the 4,000 "digits" in his system he has memorized a symbol, based upon modifications of characters in the Sanskrit writing system.

Marathe says that he uses the system for multiplying large numbers as well as for involution. He would not explain, however, how it is possible to multiply using a base in excess of 4,000 without learning the multiplication table for that base, which would have roughly eight million entries.

Wim Klein, in a test by Fred Barlow in 1952, raised 87 to the 16th power. Klein probably got this by successive squaring. The result contains 32 digits.

Chapter Fifteen

———

Factoring

THE factors of an integer are those integers by which it is divisible without remainder (e.g., the factors of 12 are ±12, ±6, ±4, ±3, ± 2, and ±1). A prime number is an integer which has no positive factors except itself and 1. (Since any integer has as factors 1 and itself these are usually excluded in reciting factors, as are negative factors.) Integers that are not prime are said to be composite.

In the third century B.C., Eratosthenes of Cyrene, a Greek geographer, astronomer, poet, and mathematician, devised a method (known as the "sieve of Eratosthenes") for finding all the primes less than or equal to a number n. The idea is to write down all the integrers from 2 to n, then to cross off all those that are multiples of 2, those that are multiples of 3, those that are multiples of 5, and so on, until all multiples of primes not greater than the square root of n have been canceled. The method is foolproof, but foolhardy when n is large.

There is still no simple formula by which it may be determined whether a number is prime or composite, even though many mathematicians in the past turned their attention to the problem. The only way to go about it is by trial and error, a procedure guaranteed to work eventually.

Calculating prodigies must therefore use trial-and-error methods to determine whether a number is prime or composite; the trick is to find ways to reduce the number of trials which must be made.

If a number is composite, then it has a prime factor less than or equal to its square root. One could, therefore, set about dividing the number in question by all such primes. (Of course, if it is not known whether a potential factor is prime, composite numbers may have to be tested.) If no prime factor turns up in this testing, then the number is prime.

This procedure will be laborious when a prime is involved, or when the smallest factor is fairly large. In order to shorten the process, calculators find methods of testing for factors without necessarily carrying out the entire division. In some cases such methods may indicate that one number definitely is divisible by another. More often they lead to the elimination of certain possibilities, while division by (or multiplication of) possible factors must be carried out to test other numbers.

The method of two-figure endings has been used by various calculators to determine a class of numbers which could be factors of a given number. Colburn was most celebrated as a child for his ability to find the factors, if any, of numbers up to a million or more. Since no one knew a means by which factors could be obtained so rapidly, he was frequently questioned as to how he was able to find factors, or to determine that a number was prime. For a long time he was unable to tell how he did it, and the persistent entreaties to which he was subjected sometimes reduced him to tears. Many people believed that he was dissembling when he said that he could not describe his methods. As Colburn, writing about himself as a child, explained (1833:183):

> Much interest to learn his method prevailed, but for upwards of three years he was unable to disclose it. It was on the night of December 17, 1813, while in the city of Edinburgh, that he waked up, and speaking to his father, said, "I can tell you how I find out the factors." His father rose, obtained a light, and beginning to write, took down a brief sketch, from which the rule was described, and the following tables formed.

The tables referred to by Colburn are reproduced in table 15.1. The method is that of two-figure endings, here applied to factors. Only numbers ending in certain pairs of final digits will result in a product having a certain pair of final digits.

Colburn gives the following examples of the application of the method (1833:183–84):

> Supposing the factors of 1401 are required; refer to the table headed 01; 01 is of course a common factor to all numbers: take 03; as 67 multiplied by 3 gives 01, increase it by prefixing hundreds, and multiplying, thus: 3 × 167 = 501; 3 × 267 = 801; 3 × 367 = 1101; 3 × 467 = 1401. Now if 467 be a prime number, these two are all the factors that will produce 1401. Consult the table for 67—will 3 × 89 make 467? No. Will 3 × 189? No. 7 × 81 exceeds it; 9 will not divide a number which is not divisible by 3. 11 × 97 exceeds it: so will 13 × 59. It will be found that 467 is a prime number; therefore 3 × 467 are the only two factors of 1401.

TABLE 15.1
Colburn's Table of Factors

01		03		07		09		11		13		17		19		21		23	
01	01	01	03	01	07	01	09	01	11	01	13	01	17	01	19	01	21	01	23
03	67	07	29	03	69	03	03	03	37	03	71	03	39	03	73	03	07	03	41
07	43	09	67	07	23	07	87	07	73	07	59	07	31	07	17	07	09	07	89
09	89	11	73	11	37	09	19	09	79	09	57	09	13	09	91	11	11	09	47
11	91	13	31	13	39	13	93	11	47	11	83	11	47	11	29	13	17	11	93
13	77	17	59	17	71	17	77	17	83	17	89	19	43	13	63	19	59	13	71
17	53	19	37	19	53	21	29	19	69	19	27	21	77	21	39	23	27	17	19
19	79	21	43	21	67	23	83	21	91	21	53	23	79	23	53	29	49	21	63
21	81	23	61	27	41	27	67	23	57	23	31	27	71	27	97	31	91	27	49
23	87	27	89	29	83	31	39	27	93	29	97	29	73	31	49	33	37	29	87
27	63	33	91	31	97	33	73	29	59	33	61	33	49	33	43	39	39	31	33
29	69	39	77	33	79	37	57	31	81	37	49	37	41	37	87	41	81	37	79
31	71	41	83	43	49	41	49	33	67	39	67	41	67	41	59	43	47	39	57
33	97	47	49	47	81	43	63	39	49	41	93	47	53	47	77	51	71	43	61
37	73	51	53	51	57	47	47	41	71	43	91	51	57	51	69	53	57	51	73
39	59	57	79	59	73	51	59	43	77	47	79	57	59	57	67	61	61	53	91
41	61	63	81	61	87	53	53	51	61	51	63	61	97	61	79	63	67	59	97
47	83	69	87	63	89	61	69	53	87	69	77	69	93	71	89	73	77	67	69
49	49	71	93	77	91	71	79	63	97	73	81	83	99	81	99	79	99	77	99
51	51	97	99	99	93	99	99	81	89	89	99	87	99	87	91	83	93	81	83
57	93					91	99	89	89							89	89		
99	99					97	97	99								93	97		

27		29		31		33		37		39		41		43		47		49	
01	27	01	29	01	31	01	33	01	37	01	39	01	41	01	43	01	47	01	49
03	09	03	43	03	77	03	11	03	79	03	13	03	47	03	81	03	49	03	83
07	61	07	47	07	33	07	19	07	91	07	77	07	63	07	49	07	21	07	07
11	57	09	81	09	59	09	37	09	93	09	71	09	49	09	27	09	83	09	61
13	79	11	39	11	21	11	41	11	67	11	49	11	31	11	13	11	77	11	59
17	31	13	33	13	87	13	49	13	49	13	67	13	57	13	79	13	19	13	73
19	33	17	37	17	43	17	73	17	61	17	81	17	73	17	97	17	91	17	97
21	87	19	91	19	49	19	71	19	23	19	59	19	39	19	83	19	89	19	71
23	49	21	49	23	97	21	79	21	97	21	57	21	21	23	41	21	61	21	69
29	63	23	23	27	53	29	77	27	31	27	57	23	67	29	67	29	43	23	63
37	71	27	27	29	39	31	43	29	53	29	91	27	83	31	53	31	37	27	87
39	93	31	59	37	63	39	47	33	89	31	69	29	29	33	71	33	59	29	81
41	47	41	69	41	91	51	83	39	83	33	83	33	77	37	39	39	73	31	79
43	89	51	79	47	73	53	61	41	57	37	47	37	93	47	69	41	67	33	53
51	77	53	93	51	81	57	69	43	59	41	79	43	87	51	93	51	97	37	77
53	59	57	97	57	83	59	87	47	71	43	73	51	91	57	99	53	99	39	91
67	81	61	89	61	71	63	91	51	87	51	89	57	97	59	77	57	71	41	89
69	83	63	83	67	93	67	99	63	99	53	63	59	53	61	63	63	69	43	43
73	99	67	87	69	99	81	93	69	73	61	99	61	81	73	91	79	93	47	67
91	97	71	71	79	89	89	97	77	81	87	97	69	69	89	87	81	87	51	99
		73	73	73	73							71	71					57	57
		77	77	77	77							79	79					93	93

	51		53		57		59		61		63		67		69		71		73
01	51	01	53	01	57	01	59	01	61	01	63	01	67	01	69	01	71	01	73
03	17	03	51	03	19	03	53	03	87	03	21	03	89	03	23	03	57	03	91
07	93	07	79	07	51	07	37	07	23	07	09	07	81	07	67	07	53	07	39
09	39	09	17	09	73	09	51	09	29	09	33	09	63	09	41	09	19	09	97
11	41	11	23	11	87	11	69	11	51	11	51	11	97	11	79	11	61	11	43
13	27	13	81	13	89	13	43	13	97	13	39	13	59	13	13	13	67	13	21
19	29	17	87	17	21	17	27	17	33	17	77	17	51	17	57	17	63	17	69
21	31	21	93	23	59	19	61	19	19	19	81	19	93	19	51	21	51	19	67
23	37	27	39	27	91	21	79	21	41	23	69	21	21	21	89	23	77	23	51
33	47	29	57	29	33	23	33	27	43	29	47	23	29	27	47	27	73	27	99
43	57	31	63	31	47	29	71	31	31	31	73	31	57	29	61	29	99	29	37
49	99	33	41	37	61	31	89	37	53	37	99	33	99	31	99	31	41	31	83
53	67	37	69	39	63	39	81	39	99	41	43	37	91	33	93	33	87	33	81
59	89	43	71	41	77	41	99	47	63	49	87	39	53	37	37	37	83	41	53
61	91	47	99	43	99	47	97	49	89	53	71	41	87	39	71	39	89	47	59
63	77	49	97	49	93	49	91	57	73	57	59	43	69	43	83	43	97	49	77
69	79	59	67	53	69	57	87	59	79	61	83	47	61	49	81	47	93	57	89
71	81	61	73	67	71	63	93	67	83	67	89	49	83	53	73	49	79	61	93
73	87	77	89	79	83	67	77	69	69	79	97	71	77	59	91	59	69	63	71
83	97	83	91	81	97	73	83	71	91	91	93	73	79	63	63	81	91	79	87
								77	93					77	77				
								81	81					87	87				

	77		79		81		83		87		89		91		93		97		99
01	77	01	79	01	81	01	83	01	87	01	89	01	91	01	93	01	97	01	99
03	59	03	93	03	27	03	61	03	29	03	63	03	97	03	31	03	99	03	33
07	11	07	97	07	83	07	69	07	41	07	27	07	13	07	99	07	71	07	57
09	53	09	31	09	09	09	87	09	43	09	21	09	99	09	77	09	33	09	11
13	29	11	89	11	71	11	53	11	17	11	99	11	81	11	63	11	27	13	23
17	81	13	83	13	37	13	91	13	99	13	53	17	23	13	61	13	69	17	47
19	83	17	87	17	93	17	99	17	73	17	17	19	89	17	29	17	41	19	21
21	37	19	41	19	99	19	57	21	47	19	31	21	71	19	47	19	63	27	37
23	99	21	99	21	61	21	23	23	69	23	43	27	43	21	33	21	57	29	31
27	51	23	73	23	47	27	29	27	81	29	41	29	79	23	91	23	39	39	41
31	67	27	77	29	89	31	93	31	77	33	33	31	61	27	59	29	93	43	93
33	69	29	51	31	51	33	51	33	39	37	97	37	43	37	89	31	87	49	51
39	43	33	63	33	57	37	59	37	51	39	51	39	69	39	87	37	81	53	83
41	97	37	67	39	79	39	97	49	63	47	87	41	51	41	73	43	79	59	61
47	91	39	61	41	41	41	63	53	79	49	61	47	53	43	51	47	51	63	73
49	73	43	53	43	67	43	81	57	91	57	77	49	49	49	57	53	83	67	97
57	61	47	57	49	69	47	89	59	93	59	59	57	71	53	63	59	69	71	71
63	79	49	71	53	77	49	67	61	67	67	67	67	73	61	79	61	77	77	87
71	87	59	81	59	59	71	73	71	97	69	81	77	83	69	97	67	91	79	81
89	93	69	91	63	87	77	79	83	89	73	93	87	93	71	83	73	89	89	91
				73	97					79	91								
				91	91					83	83								

Source: Colburn 1833:185–89.

Take another number,—17,563; 03 ×21, with the continual prefix of hundreds and thousands will bring you to 5821 × 3 = 17,463; the addition of another hundred will increase it too much. 07 × 09 = 63: by the addition of hundreds, &c. you increase 09 to 2509, which multiplied by 7 gives the proposed sum. Is 2,509 a prime number? consult the table for 09; after the previous examinations you come to 13, which multiplied by 93, gives 1209; increase it 13 × 193 = 2509; therefore 13 × 7 = 91, which multiplied by 193, will give another pair of factors. Is 193 a prime number? it will be found such; therefore 7 × 2509, and 91 × 193, are the only factors.

There are other methods, used in conjunction with that of two-figure endings, to expedite factoring further. Bidder (1856:272) observed that all odd composite numbers must be the product of two odd numbers, and can be expressed as $(a +b)$ $(a -b)$, which is $a^2 -b^2$. Thus any odd composite number can be expressed as the difference of two squares. Prime numbers cannot be so expressed unless $a -b = 1$ (for example, $4^2 - 3^2 = 7$).

Suppose we wish to find the factors, if any, of an odd number c. If c can be factored, then there exist integers a and b, such that $a^2 -b^2 =c$. Since $a^2 -c =b^2$, if a value for a can be found, such that $a^2 -c$ is a perfect square, then c can be factored as $(a +b)(a -b)$; if no such value exists, then c is prime (except, as noted, when $a -b = 1$).

Suppose $a^2 -c =d$ and d is not a perfect square. Then Bidder would go on to test $(a + 1)^2$. But $(a + 1)^2 =a^2 + 2a + 1$ and therefore, $(a + 1)^2 - c =d + 2a + 1$; so that it is only necessary to add $2a + 1$ to d and check whether this is a perfect square. The procedure is repeated until a remainder that is a perfect square is found or a^2 exceeds c^2; in the latter case c is prime.

To take an example of Bidder's (1856:272–73), let c equal 3,139. The nearest square exceeding this is $57^2 = 3,249$, but 3,249 less 3,139 is 110, not a square. Now add twice 57 plus 1 to 110. This gives 225, which is the square of 15. Therefore, $3,139 = (58 + 15)(58 - 15)$, or 73 × 43.

Bidder concludes (1856:273):

By this it will be seen, that the necessity is avoided of dividing by 53, 47, 43, the primes between the square root as above and the actual factor, and it is an easy process, because having begun with 110, the next square gives an addition of 115, the next 117, the next 119, and so on, the addition of 2 in each case corresponding with an additional unit in the square numbers 57, 58, 59, &c., but it will occur to you that there is a certain point where you get wide away from the square root, and you have to go through a great number of additions, before you obtain a similar amount in the divisor. When you arrive at that point, this process should be abandoned, and you must fall back on dividing by 7, 11, 13, &c., and so on till the quotients are ascertained.

Both Aitken (1954:301) and Klein made use of the fact that if a number of the form $4n + 1$ can be expressed as the sum of two squares in one way only, then it is prime; if it cannot be so expressed, then it is composite. The following is an example of how Klein (Aarts 1974:11) makes use of this information to determine whether a number is prime.

Is 3,461 prime? It is a number of the form $4n + 1$ ($4 \times 865 + 1$), so the object is to determine whether it is the sum of two squares in only one way. One could go about this in the cumbersome way of checking $3,461 - n^2 = z$, where n represents the integers from 1 to the square root of 3,461. If z is a square, then 3,461 is the sum of two squares. In this instance one would have to test n for all values from 1 to 58.

But Klein makes use of two-figure endings to reduce the number of tests which must be made in this case from 58 to 5. Of the 21 pairs of digits which can be the endings of perfect squares only $61 + 100$ and $36 + 25$ add up to 61. A number ending in 61 can be the square of numbers ending in 19, 31, 69, and 81; a number ending in 36 can be the square of a number ending in 6, 44, 56, and 94.

Both 81^2 and 69^2 exceed 3,461, and can be discarded.

$$3,461 - 19^2 = 3100 \text{ (not a square)}$$
$$3,461 - 31^2 = 2,500 = 50^2$$

So 3,161 is the sum of two squares in at least one way ($31^2 + 50^2$); if this is the only way it can be expressed as the sum of two squares, then 3,461 is prime.

$$3,461 - 6^2 = 3,425$$
$$3,461 - 44^2 = 1,525$$
$$3,461 - 56^2 = 325$$

None of these are squares; therefore, 3,461 is prime.

Klein (Aarts 1974:10) gave the following example of how he would test 114,043 for various possible factors.

1. $114 - 043 = 71$, which is prime; therefore, 7, 11, and 13 are not factors.

2. $114 + 043 = 157$, prime; it's not divisible by 37.
3. $114 - 2 \times 43 = 114 - 86 = 28 = 2^2 \times 7$; neither 23 nor 29 are factors.
4. $114 + 4 \times 43 = 114 + 172 = 286 = 2 \times 11 \times 13$; 31 and 43 are not factors.
5. $1140 + 4 \times 43 = 1140 + 172 = 1312 = 32 \times 41$; 19 is not a factor.
6. $1140 + 8 \times 43 = 1140 + 344 = 1484 = 28 \times 53$; neither 17 nor 47 are factors.
7. $1140 + 16 \times 43 = 1140 + 688 = 1828 = 4 \times 457$; 41 is not a factor.
8. $1140 - 2 \times 43 = 1140 - 86 = 1054 = 31 \times 34$; 67 is not a factor.
9. $1140 - 8 \times 43 = 1140 - 344 = 796 = 4 \times 199$; 89 is not a factor.
10. $1140 - 9 \times 43 = 1140 - 387 = 753 = 3 \times 251$; 53 is not a factor.

These operations may at first have a rather magical appearance, but they are based upon the fact that if a has a factor of c and b has a factor of c, then $a \pm b$ has a factor of c.

Consider Klein's first conclusion: $114 - 043 = 71$, which is prime; therefore, 7, 11, and 13 are not factors of 114,043. In reality what Klein has done is to subtract 43,043 from 114,043 to get 71,000. Now 43,043 is $43 \times 1,001 = 43 \times 7 \times 11 \times 13$. If any of these numbers are factors of 114,043, they must divide 71,000. But since 71,000 is 71×10^2, and since none of these numbers are factors of 10, then to be factors of 114,043 they must be factors of 71. As 71 is prime, 7, 11, 13 (and 43) are not factors of 114,043.

Suppose that $a10^m + b$ is a number to be tested for factors; then all these tests are of the form:[1]

$$a10^m + b - b \pm k10^m b = c$$

The values of a and b depend upon the number being tested for factors; a represents the higher value digits, b those of lower value. (Note that different values for a and b may be possible for the same number.) The values of m and k are fixed for any given test.

If $b \pm k10^m b$ has a factor of j, then $a10^m + b$ has a factor of j, only if j divides c (i.e., c/j is an integer).

But $b \pm k10^m b = (1 \pm k10^m)b$. Thus tests of this form can be constructed for any number that is a factor of a multiple of 10, plus or minus 1. This, in fact, includes all primes, except 2 and 5. (The units digit of

[1] I am indebted to Arthur Benjamin, Bruce Chalmers, and Michael L. Hines for useful discussions of these matters. See Menninger (1964:92–80) for a general treatment from a different point of view. For a consideration of some cases in terms of the theory of congruences, see Burton (1976:79–80).

all other primes will be 1, 3, 7, or 9. A number whose units digit is 1, 3, 7, or 9 has a multiple ending in any series of digits you care to choose.) From the equation above we can immediately derive:

$$a10^m \pm k10^m b = (a \pm kb)10^m$$

Since we are not interested in testing for factors of ten, we can simply ignore 10^m (but note that the possible values for a and b depend upon m).

There are then two cases:

$$a10^m + b + (k10^m - 1)b$$
$$a10^m + b - (k10^m + 1)b$$

One is therefore always adding a multiple of 10, less one, or subtracting a multiple of 10, plus one.

Though the value for m and k is fixed for any given test, the values of a and b are not, so that the same test can be applied to the same number in a variety of ways and reapplied to the outcome. The traditional tests of casting out nines and elevens (below) are special cases of this test (where k and m are set at 1 and a and b range over various values).

Suppose we wish to test 22,424,471 for a factor of 23. Let $a = 22,424$, $b = 471$, $m = 3$, and $k = 2$ (since $2,001 = 23 \times 87$); then (ignoring factors of 10^3):

$$22,424 - (2 \times 471) = 21,482 = 23 \times 934.$$

The test could then be repeated taking a as 21 and b as 482.

$$21 - (2 \times 482) = -943 = 23 \times -41.$$

Significant simplifications are possible, however. We could have taken:

$$22,000 + 424 - (2 \times 471) = 22,000 - 518.$$

Now take a as 22 and b as -518, then:

$$22 - (2 \times -518) = 1,058 = 23 \times 46.$$

We could even have:

$$22 - (2 \times 424) + 4 \times 471 = 1,058.$$

Tests of this type can easily be constructed for any primes (except 2 and 5, which are trivial anyway), though there is no guarantee that the tests will prove easier than straight division. For example, suppose we wish to construct a test for 61; $61 \times 41 = 2,501$. In the last equation above set $k = 25$ and $m = 2$. Does 1,219,451 have a factor of 61? Let $a = 12,194$ and $b = 51$. Then $12,194 - (25 \times 51) = 10,919 = 61 \times 179$. And the test can be repeated on 10,919: $109 - (19 \times 25) = -366 = 61 \times -6$. Also note that we could have taken 12,190 as the initial value for a; then $12,190 - (25 \times 451) = 915 = 61 \times 15$, etc.

Most people are familiar with the procedure of "casting out nines" to check solutions to arithmetic problems. It will also tell you whether a number has a factor of 9; if, and only if, the sum of the digits is divisible by 9, then the number in question is divisible by 9. But as 9 is not a prime number the technique is not especially useful for finding factors. The same method works, however, for determining whether a number has a factor of 3; a number is divisible by 3 if the sum of its digits is divisible by 3; otherwise it is not. There are other similar methods. As discussed in chapter 13, if the sum of the even-place digits (tens, thousands, hundred thousands, etc.) of a number subtracted from the sum of the odd-place digits (units, hundreds, ten thousands, etc.) is zero or a multiple of 11, then the number has a factor of 11; otherwise, it does not.

Émile Jacoby, Mondeux's teacher, promoter, and biographer, wrote a book on this subject—*Caractères de divisibilité des nombres par des valeurs données de 1 à 50 (Characteristics of the Divisibility of Numbers for Specified Values from 1 to 50)*. The book was based entirely on information supplied by Mondeux. Every number from 1 to 50 is considered as a divisor, though in the case of composite numbers Mondeux usually points out that these reduce to other cases (e.g., every number divisible by 2 and 6 or by 3 and 4 is divisible by 12).

The results, obtained by a boy with no formal acquaintance with algebra, represent an immense labor of trial and error. The methods often do not appear to be simpler than dividing through by the given number. It seems that this was more of an intellectual challenge for Mondeux than a matter of practical use in his performances.

For example, his method for determining whether a number was divisible by 13 was as follows: Partition the number into groups of three starting from the right after the units digit (to take an example of Mondeux's, 86,795,321 would be partitioned 8/679/532/1). Multiply the rightmost digit in each triple by 3 (ignore the single digit on the far right, but include any digits on the far left, even though they may make up only part of a triple). Next multiply the middle digit in each triple by 4, and finally the leftmost digit in each triple by 1. Then add together the sums of the products of the odd-position groups, counting from the right; the isolated digit on the far right is treated as the leftmost digit of the first odd-position group (that is, it is multiplied by 1 and added to the sums of the third, fifth, etc., groups), and add together the sums of the products of the even-position groups. Take the difference of these two totals. If the difference is zero or a multiple of 13, then the number is divisible by 13; if not, divide the difference by 13 and the remainder will be the remainder which would have been obtained by dividing the original number by 13.

Take Mondeux's example (Jacoby 1853:24): 8/679/532/1. Products of the odd-group digits are: $9 \times 3 = 27$, $7 \times 4 = 28$, $6 \times 1 = 6$; these summed with the 1 on the right give 62. Products of the even-group digits: $2 \times 3 = 6$, $3 \times 4 = 12$, $5 \times 1 = 5$, $8 \times 3 = 24$; these sum to 47. The difference between the two groups is 15, not a multiple of 13, so 86,795,321 is not divisible by 13; 15 divided by 13 leaves a remainder of 2, which is the remainder upon dividing 86,795,321 by 13.

Obviously, actual division by 13 is much simpler.

Chapter Sixteen

Logarithms

I N his address before the Institution of Civil Engineers, George Parker Bidder (1856:255) remarked: "were my powers of registration [short-term memory] at all equal to the powers of reasoning or execution, I should have no difficulty, in an inconceivably short space of time in composing a voluminous table of logarithms. . . ."

He subsequently devised a method for mentally calculating logarithms. This method is described by Pole (1890–91), to whom Bidder communicated it before his death.

To calculate logarithms directly by means of an infinite series, the usual practice in constructing logarithmic tables, is impractical in mental calculation. As Pole points out (1890–91:251): "In general terms, it may be stated that his [Bidder's] mode of calculation was not based on any of the formulas proper for calculating logarithms in the first instance; for probably no amount of genius and skill would suffice for reducing them to manageable form for mental calculation, when the given number was large."

If a calculator has memorized the logarithms of a number of primes, say, all those less than 100, and if he is adept at factoring large numbers, it will be no problem to compute the logarithms of any composite number whose largest prime factor does not exceed 100—he need only add together the logs of the factors. Wim Klein uses this method in extracting integer roots of large numbers. The only difficulty is the possible introduction of round-off error.

Finding the logarithm of a large prime, where the answer must be accurate to a considerable number of places, is a much more formidable task. The method used by Bidder is essentially that mentioned above, combined with a method for extrapolating from the logarithm of a number in the vicinity of the prime whose logarithm is sought.

The problem facing Bidder was to find log $(a + b)$, where log a is known and b is relatively small compared with a; preferably $b = 1$. Since log $(a + b) = $ log $a + $ log $(1 + b/a)$, what is required is a good approximation for log $(1 + b/a)$.

Bidder knew the logarithms to eight places of numbers less than 100, and some few above. Those that he knew by heart he had originally calculated mentally (presumably rather slowly); he had never written them down.

From Pole's examples and discussion, which leaves much to be desired from the point of view of clarity, it appears that Bidder's approximation was:

$$\log \left(1 + \frac{b}{a}\right) \approx \left[\log (1 + 10^{-m})\right] \frac{10^m b}{a}$$

where $10^m < \dfrac{a}{b} < 10^{m+1}$.

Bidder had memorized the logarithms of 1.01 (0.0043214), 1.001 (0.00043407), 1.0001 (0.0000434), and 1.00001 (0.0000043), which he put to use in applying the above formula. Pole (1890–91:252–53) gives the following example of how Bidder would go about finding the logarithm of 1,051:

> For example, being given the number 1051, he would easily find the logarithm of 1050 ($= 30 \times 7 \times 5$) to which he would then have to make an addition for the difference of 1. This addition would be very important (for the accuracy aimed at), as it would affect the last five figures of the logarithm. . . .
>
> Suppose therefore, as in the above case, there is to be added to the logarithm a sum corresponding to an addition to the number of $n/1000$ ($=1$). Mr. Bidder would take the proportion $1/1050$: $0.0004341::1/1050:0.0004134$. This calculation would pass through his mind instantaneously, and thus he would get, by mental addition—

$$
\begin{array}{llll}
\text{Log.} & 30 & . \ . \ . & = 1.4771213 \\
\text{''} & 5 & . \ . \ . & = 0.6989700 \\
\text{''} & 7 & . \ . \ . & = 0.8450980 \\
\text{Addition for the } 1 & & & = 0.0004134 \\
\hline
\text{Log. of } 1051 & & . \ . & = 3.0216027 \\
\hline
\end{array}
$$

What Bidder apparently did in this case was to divide log 1.001 (= 0.0004341) by 1.05 to obtain the necessary increment. Notice that Pole's examples use logarithms to only seven places, rather than the eight places used by Bidder.

To get a good approximation for log $(1 + b/a)$, b/a should be as small as possible, preferably less than 1/1000. In some cases, therefore, Bidder would multiply the number whose log was sought by some other number, for which a more accurate logarithm could be obtained. He would then deduct the logarithm of the multiple from the result.

For example, to obtain log 877, he would multiply 877 by 13, which gives 11,401, or $600 \times 19 + 1$. He would then add the logarithms of 600 (= 2.7781512), 19 (= 1.2787536). and the approximation of log (1 + 1/11,400). This last was obtained by dividing log 1.0001 (= 0.0000434) by 1.14, which yields 0.0000381, correct to seven places. Having obtained log 11,401 (= 4.0569429), he then subtracted log 13 (= 1.1139433) to get log 877 (= 2.9429996), correct to the number of places specified. Had Bidder used the same procedure directly on 877, he would have got 2.9429974—the last two digits would have been in error.

But there were also cases in which Bidder would have to use values for b greater than 1. For example, he treated 350,107 as $7 \times 50,000 + 107$. Pole (1890–91:255) remarks: "In these . . . cases the calculation of the excess was more complicated, thus—

$$\frac{1}{1000} :0004341:: \frac{1.07}{3501} ::0.0001328."$$

This suggests that Bidder's procedure in this case was to calculate the log of the excess by multiplying log 1.001 (= 0.0004341) by 1,070 and dividing the product by 3,501 (in other words to divide by $a + b$ in the above approximation, rather than by a). This does not, however, seem to give better results and increases the difficulty of the calculation. The correct value for the excess to seven places is 0.0001327. This is the value which will be obtained by the use of Bidder's approximation (whether one divides by a or $a + b$). I suspect the value given by Pole comes from working the problem backward. The log of 350,000 is 5.544068, but the log of 350,107 is 5.5442008. Their difference is 0.0001328. The discrepancy between this and the correct value for the log $(1 + 107/350,000)$ is the result of rounding error.

Regrettably, Pole's paper suggests that his understanding of the details of Bidder's methods for obtaining logarithms left something to be desired. For example, he makes the following all too unhelpful remark (Pole 1890–91:253):

> But it would sometimes be necessary to add a larger proportion than above mentioned, say between (n/100 and n/1000. For these he adopted mentally a kind of proportionate sliding scale. Thus, for the number 601, he would see that n/600 would require 0.0007232, so that

$$\text{Log. 600} \quad . \quad . \quad . = 2.7781513$$
$$\text{Addition for the } 1 = 0.0007232$$

$$\text{Log. of 601} \quad . \quad . \quad . = 2.7788745$$

But no hint of a method is forthcoming.

Pole tested Bidder on the following numbers, which were broken down by Bidder in the manner indicated: 71 (from memory); 97 = (3,200 + 1)/33; 659 = 3 × 2 × 11 × 10 − 1; 877 = (explained above); 1,297 = (400 × 107 + 1)/33; 6,719 = 64 × 105 − 1; 8,963 = 27 × 4 × 83 − 1; 9,973 = (9 × 41 × 1,000 + 1)/37; 11,524 = 25 × (23 × 20 +1) − 1; 175,349 = 25 × (7,000 + 14) − 1; 229,847 = 230,000 − 153; 290,011 = 29 × 10,000 + 11; 350,107 = (already explained); 369,353 = 9 × 41,000 + 369 − 16.

Pole (1890–91:251) described the results of these experiments:

> Each of these [the above numbers] was given, separately, to Mr. Bidder, and the logarithm in answer was returned very quickly. The time occupied on each varied from half a minute to four minutes, being generally about two minutes.
>
> The logarithms were given in eight places, but the Author had only Hutton's table of seven places to check them with. The majority were stated at first quite correctly; but in some cases errors occurred (generally of one figure only), which were discovered and corrected on simply announcing that the answer was not exact. The experiment was at any rate amply conclusive as to the real efficiency of the mental power to perform the calculations for any numbers.

Pole (1890–91:256) closes with some remarks by Bidder's son, also George Parker Bidder:

> I remember very well my father's fondness for calculating logarithms, and the facility with which he performed the operation. We often discussed the

subject, and in consequence my own attention was drawn to it, and I eventually became able to calculate them mentally without much trouble, though not at a speed comparable with his, nor with such accuracy. Moreover, I always contented myself with six places of decimals.

Of course the great desideratum is to devise a method which relieves the mind, as far as possible, of the burthen of performing and registering long calculations. The details of my father's method, as described in the Paper, are new to me, and I think it may be interesting to compare it with my own, which, although in its main lines very similar, yet differs somewhat in form; for having obtained from him an idea of the general principles he adopted, I arrived at my own details independently. My method for numbers not large was as follows: —

I know by heart the logarithms of 2, 3, 7, and 11, and also the modulus 0.4343. My rule then was to select some multiple of the prime of the form $m + n$, where m is a multiple of 2, 3, 7, and 11, and n was very small, usually $= 1$.

$$\text{then } \log_{10}(m+n) = \log_{10} m + \log_{10}\left(1 + \frac{n}{m}\right).$$

$$\text{But } \log_{10}\left(1 + \frac{n}{m}\right) = 0.4343 \log_e\left(1 + \frac{n}{m}\right),$$

$$\text{and } \log_e\left(1 + \frac{n}{m}\right) = \frac{n}{m} - \frac{1}{2}\left(\frac{n}{m}\right)^2 + \frac{1}{3}\left(\frac{n}{m}\right)^3, \&c.$$

This I found quite practicable mentally for primes not very large.

For very large numbers (not having my father's great power of seizing instantaneously upon component factors), I adopted another method, which I can best illustrate by an example, which recently I worked out mentally, namely, to find the logarithm of 724871.

The method depends on the use of the powers of 1.1, 1.01, 1.001, &c., of which the logarithms are assumed to be known. It is not difficult to make out that—

$$724871 = 72 \times (1.001)^6 \times (1.0001)^7 \times (1.00001)^{4.5}$$

Adding the logarithms together, the result is obtained, .860261. The mental strain is much less than would at first sight appear.

There are difficulties with the explanation for the last case. It is true that the mantissa of the logarithm of 724,871 is 0.860261, and that it can be obtained from the logarithms of the factors as shown (although Bidder, Jr. has omitted a factor of 10,000 on the right side of the equation). But how he manages to factor 724,871 in the manner indicated is a mystery to me. Possibly he divided 72.4871 by 72, divided that quotient by $(1.001)^6$, etc., but I see no easy way to carry out this division (and obtain the necessary accuracy). Furthermore, the product obtained by multiplying out the factors is much closer to 724,867 than 724,871.

Chapter Seventeen

Compound Interest

I CANNOT improve upon Bidder's (1856) description of the discovery of his method for computing compound interest, so I have incorporated it as an appendix. Here I limit my discussion to the substance of the method and its application. The general formula for compound interest (including the principal) is $P(1+r)^n$, where P is the principal, r the interest rate, and n the number of years (or whatever the compounding period is; if the investment is for 20 years at 8 percent per annum compounded quarterly, for example, then $r = 0.02$, and $n = 80$).

Such problems are usually solved using logarithms. The log of $1+r$ is obtained, multiplied by n, and the antilog of this taken and multiplied by P.

Solving such problems mentally using logarithms is possible, but it requires memorizing a log table. George Parker Bidder as a child devised the following method for computing compound interest long before he became familiar with the concept of logarithms.

The expansion of $P(1+r)^n$ by the binomial theorem yields:

$$P\left\{1 + nr + \frac{n(n-1)}{2!}r^2 + \frac{n(n-1)(n-2)}{3!}r^3 + \ldots + r^n\right\}$$

As this stands, it is mentally unmanageable, but things are not so bad as they seem, since each succeeding term can be obtained with relative ease from its predecessor. For example, having obtained

$$\frac{Pn(n-1)r^2}{1 \times 2} = y,$$

the following term will be

$$\frac{y(n-2)r}{3}.$$

The formula (for the interest only) used by Bidder (1856) is $Pnr/t = y$, where initially P = principal, n = number of compounding periods, r = rate of interest (per compounding period), and $t = 1$.

After computing the initial values for $Pnr/t = y$, set $P = y$, reduce n by 1, and augment t by 1. Add the new value obtained to the previous value for y. Repeat this process until the value for y becomes inconsequential at the next step.

Bidder's method is easy to apply to the low interest rates compounded annually in his day (the example he gives is £100 at 2 percent for 35 years; see the appendix). It involves a great many more calculations at the high interest rates and frequent compounding periods found today.

As an example of the application of the method consider $2,000 compounded annually for 20 years at 5 percent. The steps are: [1]

Current Total

1.	$2,000 \times 20 \times 0.05 = 2,000$		$2,000
2.	$\dfrac{2,000 \times 19 \times 0.05}{2} =$	950	2,950
3.	$\dfrac{950 \times 18 \times 0.05}{3} =$	285	3,235
4.	$\dfrac{285 \times 17 \times 0.05}{4} =$	60.56	3,295.56
5.	$\dfrac{60.56 \times 16 \times 0.05}{5} =$	9.69	3,305.25
6.	$\dfrac{9.69 \times 15 \times 0.05}{6} =$	1.21	3,306.46
7.	$\dfrac{1.21 \times 14 \times 0.05}{7} =$	0.12	3,306.58
8.	$\dfrac{0.12 \times 13 \times 0.05}{8} =$	0.01	3,306.59

The total, using this method ($3,306.59), is within a cent of the correct amount.

---

[1] These calculations can be considerably simplified in some cases by canceling factors, and by dividing rather than multiplying. For example: $(2,000 \times 19 \times .05)/20 = (2,000 \times 19)/(2 \times 20) = 100 \times 9\frac{1}{2} = 950$.

The answers from item 4 onward are rounded off at two decimal places.

Chapter Eighteen

The Sum of Four Squares

S EVERAL calculators have shown an ability to reduce numbers to the sum of four squares. The psychologist Binet (1894:77–78) was told by Laurent, an examiner at the École polytechnique, that Vinckler, a calculator he knew, could decompose a five-digit number into the sum of four squares and give several solutions within 4 minutes.

Binet asked Inaudi to attempt the same thing, even though the problem was unfamiliar to him. The first number tried by Inaudi was 13,411. Within 3 minutes he came up with $115^2 + 13^2 + 4^2 + 1^2$, and, a minute later, $113^2 + 25^2 + 4^2 + 1^1$. Sometime later he added a third solution, $113^2 + 23^2 + 8^2 + 7^2$.

On a second trial Inaudi was given 15,663. This proved far more difficult, and it was about 15 minutes before he came up with the solution $62^2 + 57^2 + 83^2 + 41^2$. A few minutes later he found $62^2 + 41^2 + 97^2 + 27^2$.

Müller (1911:224–25) put the same problem to Rückle, who found a solution much more quickly. Given 15,663 Rückle found the solution $125^2 + 6^2 + 1^2 + 1^2$ in 8 seconds, and immediately added $125^2 + 5^2 + 3^2 + 2^2$. Rückle also found the following solutions:

$$11,339 = 105^2 + 15^2 + 8^2 + 5^2 \text{ (56 sec.)}$$
$$18,111 = 134^2 + 11^2 + 5^2 + 3^2 \text{ (26.5 sec.)}$$
$$= 134^2 + 9^2 + 7^2 + 5^2 \text{ (63.5 sec.)}$$
$$53,116 = 230^2 + 14^2 + 4^2 + 2^2 \text{ (51 sec.)}$$
$$= 230^2 + 12^2 + 6^2 + 6^2 \text{ (immed. after)}$$

It is evident that this sort of problem was not new to Rückle, as it had been to Inaudi.

The only method for solving such problems is trial and error, but the trials can be arranged in more, or less, productive ways. Inaudi did not go about it in a very productive way. An efficient approach is to begin with the largest square below the given number. The problem is then to represent a relatively small number as the sum of three squares. This may or may not be possible, but the task of finding a solution or determining that there is none is much simpler than it would be if one started from some arbitrary square and then tried to find a representation of a fairly large number as the sum of three squares.

The next step is to try the next largest square below the residue, etc., backtracking whenever necessary. This method has the advantage that the calculator becomes familiar with the ways in which commonly occurring residues can be reduced to the sum of two or three squares.

This is evidently the method used by Rückle. In the case of 15,663 he started with $125^2 = 15,625$ ($126^2 = 15,876$ and so exceeds the given number); 15,663 less 15,625 is 38. The problem is then to express 38 as the sum of three squares. Take the largest square below 38: $6^2 (= 36)$, and the remainder, 2, is $1^2 + 1^2$.

Rückle's solutions do not in every case begin with the largest square below the given number, but a solution from that starting point is not always possible—for example, there are no solutions for 11,339 starting with 106^2. But his solutions do not always use the largest possible value of the largest square. For example, in the case of 81,926 there is no solution starting with $286^2 = 81,796$, but there exist solutions starting with 285^2: $285^2 + 26^2 + 4^2 + 3^2$. He may have started with 280 simply because it is easier to square, or perhaps he looked for residues with which he was familiar. In any case, it is clearly an advantage to keep the residue of the largest square relatively small.

In one case Inaudi seems to have followed this procedure; in the other he did not. For number 13,411 his first solution starts with 115^2, the largest square possible (the other two solutions begin with 113^2). The time required for the first solution was about 3 minutes.

In reducing 15,663 to the sum of four squares he began with 62^2 (both of his solutions start with this number). This leaves a remainder of 11,819 to be expressed as the sum of three squares—not an easy task. To find the first solution took about 15 minutes.

The difficulty in finding a particular solution is in part reflected by the magnitude of the smallest square—the larger it is, the more difficult the solution, other things being equal. The smallest square of Inaudi's first solution for 15,663 was 41^2; for the second solution 27^2. The largest value for the smallest square of any solutions worked by Rückle was 6^2.

According to Binet (1894:78) Lebesgue, author of *l'Introduction à la théorie des nombres,* said that it took him 15 days to obtain several solutions in reducing a five-digit number to the sum of four squares. This is ridiculous. Anyone with pencil, paper, and a little patience should be able, following the procedure outlined above, to find several solutions in half an hour. Perhaps Lebesgue was trying to find all the solutions.

Finkelstein also specialized in this problem. According to Bousfield and Barry (1933:354) he claimed that he could reduce any four-digit number to the sum of four squares (no doubt true). "Our observations show that he succeeds in this task usually within one minute and is never over two minutes." Limiting the problem to four-digit, rather than five-digit numbers, makes things simpler. The largest square in any solution cannot exceed 99^2 (e.g., $9,999 = 99^2 + 14^4 + 1^2 + 1^2$), and calculators are often familiar with squares of numbers less than 100. He was also adept at reducing three-digit numbers to the sum of three squares—not always possible, but a necessary adjunct to representing four-digit numbers as the sum of four squares.

Table 18.1 gives the results obtained by Weinland and Schlauch in testing Finkelstein's ability to reduce three- and four-digit numbers to the sum of four squares.

It's evident that Finkelstein followed more or less the procedure outlined above, though in some cases he probably looked for remainders he

TABLE 18.1

Finkelstein's Times to Reduce Numbers to the Sum of
Four Squares

Number	Squares	Time (secs.)
863	$27^2 + 11^2 + 3^2 + 2^2$	60
1,486	$38^2 + 5^2 + 4^2 + 1^2$	12
9,625	$95^2 + 22^2 + 10^2 + 4^2$	6
1,100	$24^2 + 22^2 + 6^2 + 2^2$	25
4,444	$62^2 + 22^2 + 10^2 + 4^2$	15
6,777[a]	$76^2 + 31^2 + 6^2 + 4^2$	15
366	$16^2 + 10^2 + 3^2 + 1^2$	3.5
8,123	$81^2 + 39^2 + 5^2 + 4^2$	50
4,567	$61^2 + 29^2 + 2^2 + 1^2$	25
7,889	$81^2 + 36^2 + 4^2 + 4^2$	30
753	$24^2 + 13^2 + 2^2 + 2^2$	26.5
6,328	$32^2 + 20^2 + 2^2 + 70^2$	10
9,413	$95^2 + 12^2 + 12^2 + 10^2$	10

[a] Error in the original; the last square should be 2^2 rather than 4^2.
Source: Weinland and Schlauch 1937:388.

was familiar with or squares known to him. Surprisingly, he did not know all the squares less than 100, as this quotation from Weinland and Schlauch (1937:388) shows: "Problem: reduce 6,328 to the sum of four squares. Thought that $71^2 = 5,041$. Thought of subtracting it; didn't like it, so didn't. Thought 72^2. Doesn't know it. $70^2 = 4,900$ subtracted from $6,328 = 1,428$. Has it. 1,428 into 3 squares equals $32^2 + 20^2 + 2^2$, $6,328 = 70^2 + 32^2 + 20^2 + 2^2$." The time required was 10 seconds.

In another case Finkelstein reported his reasoning as follows: (Weinland and Schlauch 1937:388–89):

> Problem: reduce 9,413 to 4 squares. Took 91^2, it is 8,281. Subtracted from 9,413, result is 1,132. Subtracted 30^2, result is 232, 232 into two; $144 = 12^2$; not good; $32^2 = 1,024$; subtract from $1,132 = 108$. Rejects this also since he can't reduce this to two squares. Threw 91 away; took $95^2 = 9,025$. Subtracted, 388. Thought of $324 = 18^2$; not good. Took $16^2 = 256$. $388 - 256 = 132$; not good. $388 = 2 \times 144 + 100$. Answer $95^2 + 12^2 + 12^2 + 10^2$.

Again the time required was 10 seconds.

Wim Klein, judging by a couple of tests I conducted under less than optimum conditions (a bar in Providence, Rhode Island) is the best at this problem of any recorded calculator. I gave him 5,359. In about a minute, he came up with the following 12 solutions:

$73^2 + 5^2 + 2^2 + 1^2$; $71^2 + 17^2 + 5^2 + 2^2$; $71^2 + 14^2 + 11^2 + 1^2$; $71^2 + 13^2 + 10^2 + 7^2$; $70^2 + 17^2 + 13^2 + 1^2$; $69^2 + 21^2 + 11^2 + 6^2$; $67^2 + 29^2 + 5^2 + 2^2$; $67^2 + 25^2 + 14^2 + 7^2$; $65^2 + 33^2 + 6^2 + 3^2$; $65^2 + 31^2 + 12^2 + 3^2$; $65^2 + 30^2 + 15^2 + 3^2$; $65^2 + 29^2 + 17^2 + 2^2$.

As can be seen from the order of the answers, Klein uses the method outlined above. When I remarked to him that the procedure resembled the way one would program a computer to solve the problem, he replied: "We wrote the program at CERN [the European Organization for Nuclear Research, where Klein had worked], but the computer doesn't know when to skip stuff."

In another test I gave him ten different numbers and he gave me one solution each in a total of 1 minute and 14 seconds (a time which he felt was much too slow):

$2,791 (51^2 + 10^2 + 9^2 + 3^2)$; $4,131 (64^2 + 5^2 + 3^2 + 1^2)$; $8,497 (90^2 + 18^2 + 8^2 + 3^2)$; $7,540 (85^2 + 17^2 + 5^2 + 1^2)$; $5,286 (71^2 + 15^2 + 4^2 + 2^2)$; $2,702 (59^2 + 14^2 + 4^2 + 3^2)$; $9,066 (94^2 + 14^2 + 5^2 + 3^2)$; $8,344 (90^2 + 12^2 + 8^2 + 6^2)$; $2,211 (45^2 + 13^2 + 4^2 + 1^2)$; $8,820 (93^2 + 11^2 + 7^2 + 1^2)$.

Klein says: "It looks so bloody easy, but it's damn difficult for normal people."

The average time for Klein to find a solution was 7.4 seconds—less than half of Finkelstein's, and this was considered by Klein to be off his normal pace.

Klein would like to establish a record by splitting up ten four- to five-digit numbers as the sum of four squares within one minute.

According to Klein, Dagbert has added a new wrinkle to this problem. Dagbert reduces a number to the sum of six squares where the square roots must add up to a predesignated number. How he does this is a mystery.

Chapter Nineteen

Day-Date Calculations

ONE of the commonest feats of professional calculators is to give the day of the week for a date supplied by a member of the audience. It is not difficult for a skilled calculator, particularly since dates for centuries far from our own are rarely called for.

A conceptually simple system (though difficult to carry out mentally) would be to memorize the day of the week for some key date, then to compute the number of days between the key date and the date in question, and divide that number by 7. The remainder can be used to determine the day of the week.

This method given here, used by both Wim Klein and Hans Eberstark (it is also essentially the same as that found in Martin Gardner's *Mathematical Carnival*), is a variation on this idea, except that not all the days need be counted up. For example, if April 1 falls on a Thursday this year, then April 1 will fall on a Friday next year (unless next year is a leap year, in which case it will fall on a Saturday), because 365 divided by 7 leaves a remainder of 1.

This method is for dates in the twentieth century. Dates in other centuries are obtained by modifying the outcome.

The key year in the system is 1900, which represents zero; the key month is January, which is again zero.

To use the method, four numbers must be added—for the year, the leap years, the month, and the day of the month.

The number for the year is the last two digits of the year in question (this gives the number of years which passed since the key year). The number for the leap years is the last two digits of the year divided by four, ignoring any remainder. (This gives the number of leap years since the key year). If the year is evenly divisible by four (i.e., is a leap year), subtract one for dates in January and February.

The number for the month is the number of days later in the week that the first falls than it does in January. For example, the first of February is three days later than the first of January, so that if January 1 is Monday, February 1 will be Thursday.

The numbers for the months are: January 0, February 3, March 3, April 6 (or −1), May 1, June 4, July 6 (−1), August 2, September 5 (−2), October 0, November 3, December 5 (−2).

The number for the day of the month is simply that; August 16 is represented by 16.

Sum these numbers and divide by seven. The remainder indicates the day of the week—0 for Sunday, 1 for Monday, 2 for Tuesday, etc.

As an example, take December 7, 1941, the date of the Japanese attack on Pearl Harbor.

Year	41
Leap Years	10
Month (December)	5
Day of month	7
	63

Since seven goes into 63 without remainder, December 7, 1941 was a Sunday.

Such calculations can be further simplified by "casting out" sevens whenever convenient; that is, by dividing the component numbers by seven and retaining only the remainders. Take the same date, December 7, 1941. Since seven is divisible by seven without remainder, it can be ignored. The number for December, five, can equivalently be taken as minus two. Thus, $41 + 10 = 51$ less two is 49, and 49 is divisible by seven; so December 7, 1941 is again identified as a Sunday.

One can also, instead of adding the remainder, subtract the difference between the remainder and seven. For example, one can add six or subtract one, add five or subtract two, etc.

In dividing it is sometimes more convenient to work with negative remainders. Take 1935. Seven into 35 leaves no remainder; four times nine is 36, so the remainder for the year plus the leap year is minus one.

It is often useful to combine the year and the leap years and obtain a sevens remainder. For example, for the year 1984 this number is zero (minus one for dates in January and February). Remembering this facilitates calculating days for dates in 1984.

For other centuries it is necessary to add or subtract to make the necessary compensation. For example, dates in the nineteenth century are two days later than corresponding dates in the twentieth century, so for the nineteenth century add two to the total before dividing by seven (or add two after dividing, but then subtract seven if this total exceeds seven).

Add four for the eighteenth and six (or subtract one) for the seventeenth century. For the twenty-first add six; four for the twenty-second, two for the twenty-third, and nothing for the twenty-fourth.

For dates in the Julian calendar, add one for every century before 1100, and subtract one for every century after 1100.

PART THREE

LIVES AND CALCULATING ACCOMPLISHMENTS

Chapter Twenty

Jedediah Buxton

. . . The life of laborious poverty is necessarily uniform and obscure: The history of one day would almost include the events of all. Time, with respect to *Buxton,* changed nothing but his age, nor did the seasons vary his employment, except that in winter he used a flail, and in summer a ling hook. . . .
— *Gentleman's Magazine* ("Life of Jedediah Buxton" 1754:251)

JEDEDIAH Buxton was born in Elmton, six miles from Chesterfield, Derbyshire, England in 1702, and died in that same village 70 years later. His grandfather, John Buxton, was the vicar of Elmton and his father, William Buxton, was the schoolmaster there. Nonetheless, he was completely illiterate, unable even to write his name.

It is likely that Buxton was somewhat retarded ("Life" 1754:251): "his perpetual application to figures has prevented the smallest acquisition of any other knowledge, and his mind seems to have retained fewer ideas than that of a boy of ten years old, in the same class of life." He was, however, able to support a family by his labors. A letter to *Gentleman's Magazine* from George Saxe of Sherwood Forest, dated February 8, 1751, closes with a reference to Buxton as "this surprizing genius now cloathed in rags and labouring hard with his spade for the support of himself and a large family" (Saxe 1751). A later correspondent, T. Holliday (1751) of Haughton Park, mentions only a wife and daughter. (Buxton was nearing 50 at that time.)

Saxe (1751:61) remarks that he met Buxton by accident the previous summer and "proposed to him the following random question: In a body whose 3 sides are 23145789 yards, 5642732 yards, and 54965 yards, how many cubical ⅛ths of an inch?" Saxe then went about some necessary business, leaving Buxton among 100 or so of his fellow laborers. Saxe returned 5 hours later, having computed the answer in the meanwhile. Buxton said he was ready and asked whether Saxe would have the number forward or backward. Saxe chose the "regular method" and "found that in a line of 28 figures, he made no hesitation nor the least mistake." Unfortunately, the answer to the problem as stated contains 27, not 28 digits. (Perhaps the last side should have six rather than five figures.)

Saxe (1751:61) also attributes to Buxton considerable surveying skill, being able to pace off a piece of land almost as accurately as could be accomplished with a chain. He had paced off the entire lordship of Elmton, and reported its extent to its owner, Sir John Rhodes, "not only in acres, roods, and perches, but even in square inches; after this, for his own amusement, he reduced them into square hairsbreadths, computing . . . 48 to one side of the inch, which produced an incomprehensible number, that instead of entertaining the mind with any sort of pleasure, serves more to amaze and distract it." If Buxton erred, he would, in his terms "overhaul," and search out the error for himself.

On a later but unspecified date, he was visited by T. Holliday of Haughton Park, at the request of the editor of *Gentleman's Magazine,* to gather more particulars about Buxton and his calculations. Holiday (1751:347) found him to be "a very illiterate man," though he had "a good notion of the square, oblong, triangle, and circle."

The first question posed by Holliday was to give the area of a field 423 by 383 yards (answer: 162,009 square yards, given in two minutes). Holliday then asked Buxton for the acreage of the foregoing field. After 11 minutes he replied (1751:347), "33 acres, 1 rood, 35 perches, 20 yards, and a quarter just."[1] The answer is correct.

Buxton was then asked the number of barleycorns required to reach eight miles. His answer, 1,520,640, assumes three barleycorns to the inch.

Holliday then asked the number of times a coachwheel 6 yards in circumference would revolve in traveling the 204 (presumed) miles from York to London. Buxton correctly replied 59,840 times, but the time required was 13 minutes, rather a long time, even for so ponderous a calculator as Buxton.

[1] A rood is a quarter acre, and there are 40 perches to the rood. By "a quarter just" Buxton means one-quarter square yard exactly.

The next problem is (Holliday 1751:347):

> a tub or bin 346 inches long, 256 inches wide, 94 inches deep, how many gallons liquid measure and what corn [grain] will it hold? Answer, 3,454,464 solid inches, or, 1,768,685,568 half quarters of solid inches, making 12,249.872 gallons liquid measure, or 12249 gallons, 3 quart, and 34½ inches; or it will hold 191 quarters, 3 bushels, 3 quarterns, a half quartern, and 34½ inches remainder.[2]

There are a number of oddities about this problem and its solution. As the problem is stated, the answer is wrong—the number of "solid" (cubic) inches should be 8,326,144. Ninety-four is not a factor of the 3,454.464 "solid inches" in Buxton's answer, but 346 and 256 are factors, leaving another factor of 39. If Buxton's value for the cubic inches is assumed, all the subsequent calculations are correct, though the latter are far more difficult. It hardly seems likely that Buxton would have made so gross an error in the easiest part of the problem. Since no time of solution is included and the problem is far more difficult than any other put to Buxton by Holliday, perhaps this is a problem previously solved by Buxton and dictated to Holliday, who misheard him, but did not check the solution before submitting it to *Gentleman's Magazine;* or perhaps there is a misprint. This is also the only case in which Buxton is credited with giving a decimal fraction in a reply—in all other cases he simply announced the remainder, if any. This, I suspect, must have been added by Holliday, particularly since the answer is not exact, but is rounded off after three places, and the decimal fraction was not used in calculating the quarts or the quarters, quarterns, etc.

Buxton told Holliday (1751:348) that he was "drunk with reckoning" from 10 A.M., May 17, 1725, until the 16th of June, at the end of which he slept soundly for seven hours—raising the question of how much he usually slept. He determined never again to undertake such demanding calculations. The problem which led to his "drunkenness" was determining the number of grains of barley, vetches, peas, wheat, oats, rye, beans, lentils, and hairs one inch long, respectively, required to fill a container 202,680,000,360 miles on a side. Unfortunately, Holliday does not give the outcome of this grand calculation. The number of barleycorns (grains), hairs, etc. in a cubic inch he determined by experiment to be: 200 bar-

[2]A half quarter of a solid inch is a cubic eighth of an inch. Buxton figures 282 cubic inches to the gallon and eight gallons to the bushel. A quarter equals eight bushels (64 gallons) and a quartern is 1/16 bushel.

leycorns, 300 wheat corns, 512 rye corns, 180 oats, 40 peas, 25 beans, 80 vetches, 100 lentils, and 2,304 hairs one inch long.

Holliday does, however, give us Buxton's calculations for the grain in a cubic mile ("14 thousand, 93 mill. 420 thou., 936 quarters, 1 bushel, 1 peck, 1 quartern, 3 pints, and 5 and a quarter solid inches"),[3] the cubic yards in a cubic mile ("5 thousand, 451 mill. 776 thousand yards"), the cubic inches in a cubic mile ("254 millions of millions, 358 thousand, 61 mill. and 56 thousand inches in a cubical mile"), the number of hairs one inch long in a cubic mile ("586 thousand, 40 millions of millions, 972 thousand, 673 millions, and 24 thousand"). "But, if a hair be no longer than it is broad [i.e., 48^3 hairs to the cubic inch], he then found that there would be 28 tribes,[4] 129 thousand, 966 millions of millions, 688 thousand, 305 millions, and 152 thousand hairs, to fill the space of a cubical mile." All these figures are correct.

Buxton was often drunk with more than reckoning. His apparent lack of wit did not prevent him from being a premier beer hustler. He kept a mental record, which I include (Table 20.1), of all the free beer and ale he had been given since the age of 12, and where it was consumed. The total, 5,116 pints, averages out to 5 or 6 ounces a day. Bear in mind that this was beer which he was given, and does not include any beer that he may have paid for, or made for himself. The most interesting item on the list is the 72 pints he consumed at a "gathering for his dead cow." The dead cow was presumably Jedediah's, though why anyone should have given him beer on this sad occasion I do not know. Buxton referred to pints of beer as "winds," because he never took more than one breath to a pint or two to a quart.

His calculating prowess was the source of all this free booze, and he did not forgo drink while calculating (Holliday 1753:557): "He never regarded our talking, but sat as one heedless of everything about him, except his pot of beer, which he took notice of." I like to imagine Buxton, at whatever ceremony one might have for a dead cow, chug-a-lugging *nine gallons* of beer, while computing such nonsense as the area required for 3,584 broccoli plants.

Most schoolchildren have heard the old chestnut about the farmer who balked at paying some small sum to have his horse shod. The blacksmith proposed an alternate mode of payment—one cent for the first nail, two for the second, four for the third; i.e., each succeeding nail to cost twice the last. The shoeing required only 32 nails, and the farmer was stunned

[3] There are four pecks to the bushel; for the other units, see the preceding footnote.
[4] A "tribe" is Buxton's term for 10^{18}.

TABLE 20.1
Free Beer and Ale Given to Jedediah Buxton

	Pints		Pints
D. of Kingston	2,130	Rev. Mr Pegge	10
D. of Norfolk	266	Mr Richardson	7
Duke of Leeds	232	Mr Raynes	30
D. of Devonshire	10	Mr Stevens	5
Lady Oxford	280	Mr Far	1
G. Heathcote, Esq.	160	Mr Greenwood	77
Sir G. Savile, Bt.	20	Mr Shaw	2
J. Thornhagh, Esq.	20	Mr Barker	15
Sir L. Pilkington, Bt.	2	Mr Sisson	12
John Bristowe, Esq.	92	Mr Major	3
W. Villareal, Esq.	8	Mr Brigs	3
Sir H. Hunlock, Bt.	2	Mr Pilkington	2
—— Burton, Esq.	4	Mr J. Brigs	4
—— White, Esq.	1	Mr Beestings	45
Dr Burne	5	Gathering for his dead cow	72
Mr Hocks	251	Rev. Mr Hewet	2
Mr West	201	Col. Chadwick	3
Mr Vesey	16	Mr Halfhead	15
Rev. Mr. Hartshorn	19	Mr Wright	40
Mr Flint	317	At Elmton Manor	300
—— Clarke, Esq.	20	Mr Sherwin	15
—— Hallows, Esq.	12	Mr Carteret	16
Sir J. Jenkinson, Bt	1	Mr Lane	20
Mr Hancock	54	Mr Whitehouse	3
Mr Hall	63	Mr R. Parkin	40
Mr E. Sharpe of Elkesly	5	Mr R. Greenwood	64
Mr Th. Sharpe	16	Mr Th. Clarke	40
Rev. Mr Boawre	17	Mr Bullivant	7
Mr Willets	17	Mr Padley	10
Mr Mayor of Chesterfield	2	At my own house	10

Source: Holliday 1753:557.

to discover that he was over 40 million dollars in debt (2^{32} cents minus one).

Buxton undertook a similar but much larger calculation (Holliday 1751:348)—to determine the value of the 140th nail doubled at a farthing per nail (2^{139} farthings). There were 4 farthings to a pence, 12 pence to a shilling, 20 shillings to the pound; the result required is thus 2^{139} divided by 960 (farthings per pound). Buxton's answer was: 725,958,238,096,074,907,868,531,656,993,638,851,106 pounds, 2 shillings, and 8 pence. Holliday remarks: "For the truth of which I leave [to] those gentlemen that have leisure and curiosity to try it."

Modern computing machinery has now made it possible for gentlemen of little leisure and small curiosity to test Buxton's accuracy. The answer is, in fact, wrong, although the first four, and the last eight digits are correct, as are the odd shillings and pence.[5] The correct answer is: 725,935,716,098,002,055,388,532,495,854,438,851,106, 2 shillings and 8 pence.[6]

Buxton attempted to square the result of his calculation for the 140th nail, a labor of $2\frac{1}{2}$ months. Naturally, the product is not the true square of 2^{139} farthings (expressed in pounds), since his initial calculation is flawed. Buxton's value for the square of the number he miscalculated (Holliday 1751 1:348) is, in his peculiar terminology (omitting, as did Buxton, the odd shillings and pence of the original):

527 Tribes of tribes of cramps
015 Thous. mill. of mill. tribes of cramps
363 Mill. of mill. tribes of cramps
459 Thous. mill. tribes of cramps
557 Mill. of tribes of cramps
385 Thousand tribes of cramps
673 Tribes of cramps
733 Thous. mill. of mill. of cramps
542 Million of millions of cramps
638 Thousand millions of cramps
591 Millions of cramps
721 Thousand cramps
213 Cramps
298 Tribes of tribes
966 Thous. mill. of mill. of tribes
079 Millions of mill. of tribes
307 Thousand millions of tribes
524 Millions of tribes
904 Thousand tribes
381 Tribes
389 Thousand millions of millions
499 Millions of millions
251 Thousands of millions

[5] The fact that the small digits are correct indicates that Buxton did not compute the total number of farthings and divide by 960 but converted farthings to pence, pence to shillings, and shillings to pounds as he went along.

[6] I am indebted to Gary R. Martins for this and the following calculation.

637 Millions
423 Thousands
236 Pounds

This result is correct in all digits but one—it should read 905 rather than 904 thousand tribes.

The terms "tribe" (10^{18}) and "cramp" (10^{39}) are Buxton's own. I must confess that I do not understand the theory which underlies his numerical terminology. Note that he does not use the term "billion" at all (in Great Britain a billion is a million million). It seems that he invented "tribes" to avoid "millions of millions of millions," but just why he introduced "cramps" in lieu of "thousand tribes of tribes" I do not know. Perhaps that is simply the point at which his mind began to cramp.

Holliday visited Buxton once more, during November of 1753, and put four questions to him (Holliday 1753:557). The first was the acreage of a field 351 by 261 yards. After 11 minutes, Buxton correctly answered, "18 acres, 3 roods, 28 perches, and 14 remain'd."

The second gives an insight into Buxton's modus operandi: *"Suppose sound moves 1142 feet in one second of time, how long then, after the firing of one of the cannons at Retford, may the same be heard at Haughton Park, taking the distance at five miles?* After about a quarter of an hour he told me—in 23 seconds, 7 thirds, and 46 remain'd."

There are 26,400 feet in 5 miles; dividing this by 1,142 feet per second yields 23 seconds, with a remainder of 134. A third is a sixtieth of a second, so 7 thirds is clearly correct, but the remainder of 46 bewildered me for some time, until I realized that Buxton, instead of dividing 1,142 by 60, had rather multiplied 134 by 60 and continued to divide by 1,142—this gives 7 with a remainder of 46.

The third question remains a mystery to me. As I interpret the problem, it allows many solutions, none of which conform to Buxton's reply: *"Admit I set 3584 brocoli [sic] plants in rows, 4 feet asunder, and the plants 7 feet apart, in a rectangular plot of ground, how much land will these plants take up?* In near half an hour he said—2 acres, 1 rood, 8 perches and half."

Though I puzzled long over many of Buxton's problems, I was in all other cases eventually able to uncover his reasoning; in this I could not. As I understand it, we have a total of 3,584 broccoli plants in a rectangular field. The plants are in rows, the rows four feet apart, and within rows the plants are seven feet apart. The number of rows is not specified. The question is the area required for such a distribution of plants.

Assuming this is a correct interpretation of the problem, the fact that the number of rows is unspecified constitutes a serious difficulty. The number of plants, 3,584, can be factored many different ways, and therefore, a variety of rectangular layouts is possible—and the narrower the rectangle the less the required area.

Let us assume the most nearly square rectangle possible (thus requiring the largest area) with 56 rows and 64 plants per row. The length of the field will be 441 feet $[(64 - 1) \times 7]$ and the width 220 feet $[(56 - 1) \times 4]$. The area of the field will be 97,020 square feet. While this gives the required 2 acres (87,120), it is less than 2 acres, 1 rood (98,010 square feet), and this furthermore is the *largest* rectangle that can be constructed under the conditions of the problem as interpreted.

Suppose that Buxton neglected the fact that the length of the field will be the distance between plants in a row less one (similarly for the width), and simply multiplied (64×7) times (56×4), which is equivalent to multiplying the total number of plants (3,584) by 7 and then 4; this gives 100,352 square feet. (Calculating it this way, the number of rows is immaterial.) This value is close to Buxton's, but a little too much, yielding 2 acres, 1 rood, 8 perches and 164 square feet—but ½ perch is 136⅛ square feet.

It is possible to come within ⅛ square foot of Buxton's answer by multiplying 3,583 (number of plants less one) by 7 and then by 4, which gives 100,324 square feet, being 2 acres, 1 rood, 8 perches, 136 square feet, this last only ⅛ square foot shy of ½ perch. But the only field for which this would be appropriate is one with 2 rows of broccoli plants, each row containing 3,584 plants, which does not meet the conditions set forth in the problem.

I hesitate to pronounce Buxton wrong here, especially since, in every case, except that involving the immense figures obtained in connection with doubling the value of the horseshoe nails, he proved, despite my initial skepticism, exactly right. Furthermore, problems relating to the areas of land were most familiar to him.

The last problem posed by Holliday was to give the dimensions of a cubical bin which would hold exactly a quarter of malt, Winchester measure.[7] According to Holliday:

> This question exercised all his faculties, and he declared it was the hardest ever proposed; by this I perceived he had never engaged himself about the

[7] Winchester measure, often employed from the time of Henry VIII (though not normally used by Buxton), is still in use in Britain's former North American colonies; a bushel contains 2,150.42 cubic inches.

cube root: However, tho' so difficult it appear'd to him, he was very desirous to answer it, before it was too late in the evening, and after some time, he said to himself *there were nooks in it, but he would sift them about.*

After about an hour Buxton replied that the bin "would be a little more than 25¾ inches on a side, and 26 inches would be too much, all which is very true and very exact." As Holliday says, Buxton's answer was correct. Since there are eight bushels in a quarter, the amount required is the cube root of 17,200, which is approximately 25.813258. Buxton no doubt arrived at this answer through successive approximation by cubing various values.

According to *Gentleman's Magazine* ("Life" 1754:252) the only thing other than mental arithmetic that excited Buxton's curiosity was the king and the royal family. In the spring of 1754 he walked to London, a distance of 150 miles, in the hope of seeing the king, but the latter, as is so often the case with the heads of state, was on vacation (in Kensington). While in London, Buxton was introduced to the Royal Society, the members of which he called the *"volk of the Siety Court."*

During his stay in London, Buxton was taken to see *Richard III* at the Drury Lane Playhouse. As *Gentleman's Magazine* described it ("Life" 1754:252)

it was expected either that the novelty and the splendour of the show would have fixed him in astonishment, or kept his imagination in a continual hurry; or that his passions would, in some degree have been touched by the power of action, if he had not perfectly understood the dialogue; but *Jedediah's* mind was employed in the playhouse just as it was employed at church. During the dance he fixed his attention upon the number of steps; he declared after a fine piece of musick, that the innumerable sounds produced by the instruments had perplexed him beyond measure, and he attended even to Mr *Garrick* only to count the words that he uttered, in which, he says, he perfectly succeeded.

Gentleman's Magazine concludes:

Jedediah is now safely returned to the place of his birth, where, if his enjoyments are few, his wishes do not seem to be more: He applies to his labour, by which he subsists with cheerfulness; he regrets nothing that he left behind him in *London,* and it is still his opinion, that a slice of rusty bacon affords the most delicious repast.

Ah, for the life of a bucolic alcoholic calculator.

Chapter Twenty-one

———

Thomas Fuller

"No Massa—it is best I got no learning: for many learned men be great fools."

—Thomas Fuller (Rush 1789:63)

THOMAS Fuller was born in Africa about 1710. When he was 14, he was brought to Virginia as a slave. He was, according to the *Columbian Centinal* (1790), "a very black man."

In or about 1788 he was interviewed by two Pennsylvanians, William Hartshorne and Samuel Coates. An account of this encounter is contained in a letter by Dr. Rush (1789), read before the Pennsylvania Society for the Abolition of Slavery.

At the time of the interview Fuller was the property of Mrs. Elizabeth Cox and was living about four miles from Alexandria. He felt particularly indebted to his mistress, for even though she had been offered considerable sums, she had steadfastly refused to sell him.

Fuller was nearly 80 and "exhibited several other marks of the weakness of old age" (Rush 1789:63). He felt that his memory was beginning to fail him. He had spent his life working in the fields, "but had never been intemperate in the use of spiritous liquors."

Hartshorne and Coates put three questions to Fuller. They first asked him how many seconds there are in a year and a half, to which he replied in about two minutes—47,304,000. This is correct, assuming a 365-day year.

The next problem (Rush 1789:62) was to give the number of seconds a man has lived, who is seventy years, seventeen days and twelve hours old; he answered in a minute and a half, 2,210,500,800.

One of the gentlemen, who employed himself with his pen in making these calculations, told him he was wrong, and that the sum was not so great as he had said—upon which the old man hastily replied, "top, massa, you forget de leap year." On adding the seconds of the leap years to the others, the amount of the whole in both their sums agreed exactly.

Fuller's reply assumes 17 leap years and is correct.

The last question posed was:

suppose a farmer has six sows, and each sow has six female pigs the first year, and they all increase in the same proportion, to the end of eight years, how many sows will the farmer then have? In ten minutes, he answered, 34,588,806. The difference of time between his answering this, and the two former questions, was occasioned by a trifling mistake he made from a mis-apprehension of the question.

Fuller's answer, $7^8 \times 6$, is correct, and not an easy mental calculation.

Thomas Wistar and Benjamin W. Morris, "two respectable citizens of Philadelphia," witnessed a nine-digit by nine-digit multiplication by Fuller, according to Rush (1789:62), but the problem is not given.

Fuller's interest in calculation, like Buxton's, arose from extensive counting. After learning to count to 100, he thought himself, in his own words (Rush 1789:62), "a very clever fellow," and undertook to count the number of hairs in a cow's tail, which he found to be 2,872. He next counted the grains in a bushel of wheat, and in a bushel of flax seed. Dr. Rush writes (1789:62–63):

From this he was led to calculate with the most perfect accuracy, how many shingles a house of certain demensions [sic] would require to cover it, and how many posts and rails were necessary to inclose, and how many grains of corn were necessary to sow a certain quantity of ground. From this application of his talents, his mistress has often derived considerable benefit.

His obituary adds (*Columbian Centinel* 1790):

The power of recollection and the strength of memory were so complete in him, that he could multiply seven into itself, that product by 7, and the product, so produced, by seven, for seven times. He could give the number of months, days, weeks, hours, minutes and seconds in any period of time that any person chose to mention, allowing in his calculation for all the leap years that happened in the time; and would give the number of poles, yards, feet, inches and barley-corns in any given distance, say the diameter of the earth's orbit; and in every calculation he would produce the true answer, in less time than ninety-nine men in an hundred would take with their pens.

Fuller died in 1790, some two years after he had spoken to Hartshorne and Coates.

Chapter Twenty-two

―――

Zerah Colburn

The human mind is a machine of gigantic powers, and we may well conclude that not all, if indeed more than a few of its energies are developed.

—Zerah Colburn (1833:176)

I T would be difficult today to find anyone who recognizes the name Zerah Colburn, but for a brief period in the early nineteenth century he was, at less than 10 years of age, among the most famous people of Europe and America. A widely reprinted article said of him (*Annual Register* 1812:507): "The attention of the philosophical world has been lately attracted by the most singular phaenomenon in the history of the human mind that perhaps ever existed." Faraday interviewed him, Samuel F. B. Morse painted his portrait, Laplace tested him, and Washington Irving assisted in arranging his education. Even Napoleon expressed a desire to meet him, but was prevented from doing so by the incident at Waterloo.

Zerah Colburn was the first great juvenile calculating prodigy on record. His life is also the best known, since he left a remarkable autobiography, *A Memoir of Zerah Colburn, Written by Himself* (Colburn 1833), which recounts his life to age 28 (he died at 35). As the title suggests, the book is written entirely in the third person, and Colburn, the man, seems to have regarded Zerah, the child, in just this way. In similar fashion I refer to the author of the *Memoir* as Colburn, and its subject as Zerah.

Zerah was born on September 1, 1804, in Cabot, Vermont, the fifth of seven children of Abia Colburn, a small farmer. The child had six fingers on each hand and six toes on each foot, but this peculiarity was not unusual in his family—it was shared by his father and two of his brothers, and was known to have been in the family for four generations. The supernumerary digits were attached to the little fingers and little toes, and had complete metacarpal and metatarsal bones. No doubt this bodily peculiarity served to enhance Zerah's status as a natural phenomenon. In a bemused fashion Colburn (p. 72)[1] speculated on "Whether this be a proof of direct lineal descent from Philistine blood or not (see 1 Chronicles xx. 6). . . . " In the King James version the passage reads: "And yet again there was war at Gath, where was a man of *great* stature, whose fingers and toes *were* four and twenty, six *on each hand* and six *on each foot*: and he also was the son of the giant."

In early August of 1810 Mr. Colburn was at home working at a joiner's bench and Zerah was playing among the chips. The boy was a month from his sixth birthday. Mr. Colburn's attention was attracted by the fact that Zerah was repeating the multiplication table to himself. This seemed to him surprising, since Zerah's only schooling consisted of six weeks' attendance that summer at the district school, and he knew neither how to read nor write numbers. Mr. Colburn began to test him on the multiplication table and found him to be perfect. He then asked the product of 13×97, to which Zerah immediately replied 1,261. Colburn described his father's reaction (pp. 11–12): "He now concluded that something unusual had actually taken place; indeed he has often said he should not have been more surprised, if some one had risen up out of the earth and stood before him."

Zerah's talent was soon tested by many of the townsfolk, and word of his ability spread. Mr. Colburn took him to Danville during a session of the court, where he was questioned by judges, lawyers, and others. Since the Vermont legislature was to meet in Montpelier in October, Mr. Colburn was advised to take his son there at that time. Here Zerah was seen and examined by a large number of people. The questions were not always strictly arithmetic in nature, but were devised with an eye to confusing him (pp. 12–13):

which is the most, twice twenty-five, or twice five and twenty (2×25 or $2 \times 5 + 20$)? Ans. twice twenty–five. Which is the most, 6 dozen dozen, or half a dozen dozen ($6 \times 12 \times 12$ or 6×12)? Ans. six dozen dozen. It is a fact too that somebody asked how many black beans would make five white

[1] Page numbers refer to the *Memoir* (Colburn 1833).

ones? Ans. 5, if you skin them. Thus it appeared that not only could he compute and combine numbers readily, but also he possessed a quickness of thought somewhat uncommon among children, in other things.[2]

After a few days they traveled on to Burlington, but Mr. Colburn soon decided (p. 13) that "the thinly inhabited State of Vermont did not appear likely to furnish that efficient patronage which such an unusual case seemed to demand. . . . " He therefore determined that they should visit the largest cities of the United States. Zerah and his father returned to Cabot, and after spending one night, departed. This was to be their last night under the family roof.

They proceeded from there to Hanover, where Dr. Wheelock, President of Dartmouth, offered to provide for and oversee Zerah's education. Mr. Colburn turned him down, for other proposals were being presented to him, the various factions each impugning the motives of the others.

For the next year and a half father and son crisscrossed the northeastern United States seeking advice and patronage for Zerah's education, and giving public exhibitions of his calculating prowess.

Zerah and his father arrived in Boston on November 25, 1810, just three months after the discovery of his arithmetic talents. Colburn described his powers at the time of their exhibition in Boston in the following terms (pp. 14–15):

Questions in multiplication of two or three places of figures, were answered with much greater rapidity than they could be solved on paper. Questions involving an application of this rule, as in Reduction, Rule of Three, and Practice, seemed to be perfectly adapted to his mind. The Extraction of the Roots of exact Squares and Cubes was done with very little effort; and what has been considered by the Mathematicians of Europe an operation for which no rule existed, viz. finding the factors of numbers, was performed by him, and in the course of time, he was able to point out his method of obtaining them. Questions in Addition, Subtraction, and Division were done with less facility, on account of the more complicated and continued effort of the memory. In regard to the higher branches of Arithmetic, he would observe that he had no rules peculiar to himself; but if the common process was pointed out as laid down in the books, he could carry on this process very readily in his head.

[2] Bear in mind that this is Colburn, speaking of himself as a child.

Colburn gives the following samples of problems solved at Boston (p. 171):

> The number of seconds in 2000 years was required.
>
> > 730,000 days.
> > 17,520,000 hours.
> > 1,051,200,000 minutes.
> > 63,072,000,000 seconds — Answer.
>
> Allowing that a clock strikes 156 times in 1 day, how many times will it strike in 2000 years? 113,880,000 times.
> What is the product of 12,225 multiplied by 1,223? 14,951,175.
> What is the square of 1,449? 2,099,601.
> Supposing I have a corn field, in which are 7 acres, having 17 rows to each acre; 64 hills to each row; 8 ears on a hill, and 150 kernels on an ear; how many kernels on the corn field? 9,139,200.

In Boston a definite offer regarding Zerah's education was made and negotiations proceeded to the point that a legal document was drawn up. Six of the "first gentlemen" of that city offered to oversee his education, but upon reflection Abia Colburn found the terms of the agreement unacceptable, and he and Zerah continued their travels. It was a decision for which Mr. Colburn was frequently castigated by those who believed him more motivated by greed than by an interest in the future welfare of his son. In defense of his father, Colburn reproduces the Indenture in its entirely. It stipulates, in part (p. 17):

> —Therefore it is agreed that the said contractors on the second part shall be, and hereby are appointed Trustees to superintend the education of said child on conditions hereinafter expressed; and that they will use their influence and exertions to raise a sum of money not exceeding five thousand dollars, by donations and honorable exhibitions of the child, at such times and places within the United States as the said Trustees may direct. . . .
> And as an indemnity to the said Abia for the loss of his time, and for his services, and to enable him to remove to Hanover aforesaid, and dwell near said child, who is to be there placed for the present, it is further agreed that the said Abia shall receive for his sole use and benefit, the sum of twenty-five hundred dollars. . . .

In short, the trustees would undertake to oversee Zerah's education if he and his father worked to raise the money to pay for it. Of this Colburn writes (pp. 18–19):

Simply to receive the patronage and sanction of their respectable names as a suitable equivalent for the desertion of family during a period long enough to travel through the States and collect so large a sum of money, and then for giving up one half that sum with the boy, during the most important season of youth, did not harmonize with his views of parental obligation.

After the Boston episode, the pair appeared in New York, in Philadelphia, where Rembrandt Peale made a portrait of Zerah, and in Washington. Their reception in these cities was favorable, "the inhabitants signifying their approbation of his talent by liberal attendance and donations" (p. 20).

Particularly in these early days, before the novelty had worn thin; before his approaching adolescence deprived him of the natural human sympathy for handsome, precocious children; before Bidder, his British contemporary, entered the calculating arena; and before it became obvious that Zerah had nothing to contribute to mathematical knowledge, the Colburns sometimes collected substantial sums of money. On leaving Washington they traveled to New York carrying five or six hundred dollars. The trustees of the Indenture had regarded five times this sum sufficient to pay for the support and education of the child through college.

Arriving on the ferry from the Jersey side they went to a tavern where they had previously found accommodations. The landlord assured them of a room, and they sat in the barroom until nine o'clock. When Mr. Colburn inquired about his room the landlord discovered that he had made an error and that he had no vacancy after all, but that he had a room in the far back of the house to which they were welcome. Rather than go into the streets at that late hour, Mr. Colburn agreed. They were led across a courtyard and up three flights of stairs to a small isolated room. Once there, Mr. Colburn began to reflect on the situation. He had seen few other guests in the tavern, not nearly enough to fill all the rooms, and he knew that it could be inferred from accounts in the press that he was carrying a large sum of money. He rose, went to the landlord, and told the man bluntly that he suspected that he intended to kill him for his money, and that unless he and Zerah could be provided with accommodations in the front of the house, they would leave. The landlord became agitated and agreed. When Mr. Colburn appeared the following morning to pay the bill, the landlord offered to let them stay as long as they liked at a reduced rate if Mr. Colburn would keep silent about the incident. Mr. Colburn was apparently a man of greater frugality than fear, for he agreed to the offer, and he and Zerah remained there while they were in New York.

From New York City the boy and his father traveled by steamboat to Albany, then to Utica, Boston, and up to Norwich, Vermont, where the family was temporarily residing. After a week there they departed, Mr. Colburn leaving $500 with his wife. He would never again see his other children.

From this period we have two accounts of calculations performed by Zerah. The *Memoir* gives the following description of problems solved in Portsmouth, New Hampshire in June 1811 (pp. 171–72):

> Admitting the distance between Concord and Boston to be 65 miles, how many steps must I take in going this distance, allowing that I go three feet at a step? The answer, 114,400 was given in ten seconds.
>
> How many days and hours since the Christian Era commenced, 1811 years? Answered in twenty seoonds.
>
> 661,015 days.
>
> 15,864,360 hours.
>
> How many seconds in eleven years? Answer in four seconds; 346,896,000.
>
> What sum multiplied by itself will produce 998,001? In less than four seconds, 999.
>
> How many hours in 38 years, 2 months, and 7 days? In six seconds; 334,488.[3]

Such time and distance problems were commonly asked of him, and he, of course, knew the number of seconds in a year, etc. The question about the days and hours elapsed since the beginning of the year 1, according to our current calendar, must have been frequently put to him — at a later time, in London, the Duke of York posed the same question.

The other account is among the most interesting we have of any calculating prodigy, since it is a firsthand account of an exhibition by an uninvolved party.

The report is by Professor MacNeven for *The New-York Medical and Philosophical Journal and Review* for 1811.[4]

Zerah was (MacNeven 1811:19) "not yet seven years old." The report does not indicate where the demonstration took place, but the work was printed and sold by T. & J. Swords, "Printer to the Faculty of Physic of

[3] Zerah, as here, usually assumed a 365-day year and a 30-day month.
[4] Professor MacNeven was a man of many parts, for he contributed to the same journal a paper entitled, "A CASE, *exhibiting the Consequences of* LUES *cured by the* ROB *of* LAF-FACTEUR: *Communicated by Professor* MACNEVEN."

Columbia College," so perhaps it was New York City. The time must have been the spring or summer of 1811.

The problems included the sum of 1,347, 1,953, and 2,091 (5,391); the square roots of 1,369 (37), 2,401 (49), and 5,329 (73); the product of 93 times 9,143 (850,299); 45,954 divided by 37 (1,242), and 9,999 divided by 57 (175 and 24 over); the number of hours in 7 years, 14 days, and 40 hours (61,696); the number of hours in 9,125 days (219,000); the number of minutes in 219,000 hours (13,140,000); and the number of seconds in 25 years (788,400,000).

He also factored numbers, a feat for which he had an uncommon facility even from his earliest years (p. 20):

Ques. What two numbers multiplied together produce 1242?

He gave the following answers as fast as he could speak them.

Ans. 54	and	23	3	and	414
9	—	138	6	—	207
27	—	46	2	—	621

Ques. What two numbers multiplied together produce 1044?

Ans. 18	and	58	3	and	348
6	—	174	2	—	522
36	—	29	4	—	261
9	—	116	12	—	87.

Surprisingly, Mr. Colburn balked at Zerah's being asked to perform a rather simple three-digit multiplication (MacNeven 1811.21).

Ques. What will be produced by multiplying 123 by 237?
Ans. 29151
The child's father objected to so difficult a question as three figures by three, but the boy himself said he could do it, and kept his word. In another instance he gave the product of 1234 multiplied by 1234, and did it with great promptness and accuracy.

Mr. Colburn's objection does seem odd in view of the fact that Zerah was, according to the *Memoir,* accustomed to such problems from the commencement of his calculating career, and many of the other calculations appear far more difficult. Perhaps this was merely a piece of showmanship, devised to make the calculation appear more impressive.

Of his appearance and demeanor MacNeven (1811:21–22) reports:

> Nevertheless, very difficult questions fatigue him, and he frequently asks you not to give him such hard sums. While he is making out the answer, you perceive, by his countenance, how much his mind labours. His eye glistens, and his features contract. His physiognomy is very expressive; his forehead is rather small but angular, the orbital arch projects considerably; his eye is grey, intelligent, and always in motion. The cranium is arched, and remarkably broad between the parietal protuberances; the occiput is small; his hair is sandy. He is remarkably stout and well grown for his age. His movements are precipitate, and he is incessantly active.

According to MacNeven, Zerah committed no errors on that evening, though in one instance his reply was challenged:

> *Ques.* How many hours in 25 years, 11 months and 3 days?
> *Ans.* 226992.
> The gentleman who prepared this question had committed a mistake in the product, so that when little Colburn gave the answer, he told him it was incorrect. The child, after an instant's reflection, insisted that it was the gentleman himself who was in error, and in going over the calculation again he found this to be the fact.

For the next year they traveled about the East, as far south as Richmond, where they arrived, fortuitously, a few days later than planned, for the Richmond theater burned to the ground, taking the lives of several people to whom they carried letters of introduction. Mr. Colburn had never attended the theater, though he wanted to do so, and had they arrived on schedule, they would likely have perished in the fire. Colburn described their depressing visit (p. 26):

> When they arrived in the city, they visited the spot on which the theatre had stood, and beheld a striking lesson of the uncertainty of life, and the feeble tenure by which all earthly good is held. The place was lone and still; so lately echoing with cries of mirth—still later with the frenzied shriek and wail of despairing, dying men, women, and children, all was silent, and except foundation wall, and ashes, nothing was left to tell what life had glowed, what hearts had throbbed with joy, and soon with wildest grief, a few short days before.

Because of the disaster no patronage in Norfolk could be found, and after several days (p. 26) "among the bereaved and the suffering," they

sailed for Charleston at noon, January 12, 1812, in a party that included
the now unemployed actors of the Richmond theater. Here again they
very nearly met with disaster (pp. 27–28):

> As evening came on, the passengers began to prepare for spending it in
> the most jovial manner; with cards, and songs, and merriment, they passed
> their time until nearly eleven. When they retired to rest, the snow was falling
> fast, and it was very dark. At midnight the vessel struck in shoal water.
> Instantly the sleepers were awake, and soon learned the cause of their dis-
> turbance. The exuberance of their gaiety, which prehaps had not been wholly
> calmed by their short slumber, now met with a check perhaps equal to the
> terror and confusion of the burning theatre. The wind was high, the storm
> was severe, and the darkness so thick that on deck no object could be dis-
> cerned, not even the hand held up before the eyes. The scene was truly
> terrific; the vessel striking every minute with an awful shock; no coast to be
> seen; the commander unable to give directions for safety; men vociferating;
> women in agony, praying; all combined exhibited a scene of sorrow better
> conceived than described. Indeed there seemed to be no human probability
> of escape or of assistance. Some, under apprehension of the worst, went to
> the Steward, and swallowed as much strong drink as would suffice to render
> them insensible to the pain of drowning. One, a Captain in the Navy, de-
> clared if he ever set foot on dry land again, he would there abide. Another,
> a Frenchman, when first waked by the shock, learning the cause, was so
> completely paralyzed by fear, that beginning to dress, he put on his specta-
> cles and sat down on the edge of his birth [sic], with nothing over him,
> seemingly unconscious of everything around. Some of the men proposed to
> cut away the mast, as a probable expedient for safety—to this the Captain
> objected with all his authority; to this objection they were eventually in-
> debted for their safety. Thus three or four hours passed heavily along, when
> by a providential shift of the wind, the vessel taking the advantage, filled her
> sails, and ran ashore, fast bedded in the sand about two roods below high
> water mark. In the morning they landed on the beach, and traveling about
> a mile through the woods, discovered a house. From the inmates they learned
> that they were about thirty miles below Norfolk: that the place on which
> their vessel was cast was called False Cape. A few days were spent on this
> lonely beach under tents constructed with sails; during which time the cargo
> was landed, and the shattered vessel abandoned.

A year and a half had passed since the discovery of Zerah's calculating
powers, and he had as yet no formal education (though he had learned
to read). In December of 1811 Mr. Colburn wrote to his wife that he
intended to take Zerah to London, and asked her to make some dispo-
sition of the farm and the other children so that she could come with

them. She refused, although she considered meeting them in Boston on February 20 in the hope of convincing her husband to change his mind. Lamentably, as Colburn observes, she did not do so (p. 31): "Happy if she had done it.—Much better for her children—even full as well for Zerah, as the result of his wanderings in other lands, and his return, fatherless, to his native home, seemed to show."

While it is true that patronage sufficient to satisfy Mr. Colburn eluded them in the United States, it is also true that Zerah's potential for exhibition in this country had been nearly exhausted. Though his calculating ability increased over the years, his marketability in places where he had been previously exhibited declined.

Zerah and his father arrived in Boston in the early spring of 1812, and sailed for Liverpool in the New Galen on April 3. The voyage took 38 days, and on arrival, they went immediately to London. After weighing the advice of various "friends of science," access to whom derived from their letters of introduction, they engaged rooms in Spring Garden, where Zerah could be exhibited. The price of admission was one shilling sterling, while the weekly rent was two pounds. Just to pay the rent required that 40 people a week pay to see Zerah; and the cost of fuel, clothes, provisions, and the printing of handbills had to be met. Though London's haut monde came, they rarely gave more than the admission charge. Gifts usually consisted of toys and books—of which Zerah had a surfeit—while a little cold cash would have helped pay the bills.

The first entry under "Miscellanies" in the *Annual Register* for 1812 concerns "Some Particulars respecting the arithmetical Powers of Zerah Colburn, a Child under Eight Years of Age." The account, dated August 20, 1812, was widely reprinted with minor modifications in wording. By this time Zerah and his father had been in London some three months. Included in the "Particulars" is the following unattributed quotation (*Annual Register* 1812:508–9):[5]

> It is correctly true, as stated of him, that—"He will not only determine, with the greatest facility and dispatch, the exact number of minutes or seconds in any given period of time; but will also solve any question of a similar kind. He will tell the exact product arising from the multiplication of any number, consisting of two, three, or four figures, by any other number consisting of the like number of figures. Or, any number, consisting of

[5] Part of this passage, which is not identified in the *Annual Register* as a quotation, is also included in the *Memoir* (pp. 37–38), there identified as part of a London prospectus, or advertisement, dated 1813.

six or seven places of figures, being proposed, he will determine, with equal expedition and ease, all the factors of which it is composed. This singular faculty consequently extends not only to the raising of powers, but also to the extraction of the square and cube roots of the number proposed; and likewise to the means of determining whether it be a prime number (or a number incapable of division by any other number); for which case there does not exist, at present, any general rule amongst mathematicians.". . .

At a meeting of his friends, which was held for the purpose of concerting the best methods of promoting the views of the father [in the *Memoir* (p. 37) this reads: "the best method of promoting the interest of the child by an education suited to his turn of mind . . ."], this child undertook, and completely succeeded in, raising the number 8 progressively up to the sixteenth power!!! and in naming the last result, viz. 281,474,976,710,656, he was right in every figure. He was then tried as to other numbers, consisting of one figure; all of which he raised (by actual multiplication and not by memory) as high as the tenth power, with so much facility and dispatch that the person appointed to take down the results, was obliged to enjoin him not to be so rapid! With respect to numbers consisting of two figures, he would raise some of them to the sixth, seventh, and eighth power; but not always with equal facility: for the larger the products became, the more difficult he found it to proceed. He was asked the square root of 106929, and before the number could be written down, he immediately answered 327. He was then required to name the cube root of 268,336,125, and with equal facility and promptness he replied, 645. Various other questions of a similar nature, respecting the roots and powers of very high numbers, were proposed by several of the gentlemen present, to all of which he answered in a similar manner. One of the party requested him to name the factors which produced the number 247483, which he immediately did by mentioning the two numbers 941 and 263; which indeed are the only two numbers that will produce it. Another of them proposed 171395, and he named the following factors as the only ones that would produce it, viz. 5 × 34279, 7 × 24485, 59 × 2905, 83 × 2065, 35 × 4897, 295 × 581, and 413 × 415. He was then asked to give the factors of 36083; but he immediately replied that it had none; which, in fact was the case, as 36083 is a prime number. Other numbers were indiscriminately proposed to him, and he always succeeded in giving the correct factors, except in the case of prime numbers, which he discovered almost as soon as proposed. One of the gentlemen asked him how many minutes there were in forty eight years; and before the question could be written down, he replied, 25,228,800; and instantly added, that the number of seconds in the same period was 1,513,728,000.

The London Prospectus quoted on p. 38 of the *Memoir* contains the following statement not found in the *Annual Register:* "It had been as-

serted and maintained by the French mathematicians that 4294967297
($= 2^{32} + 1$) was a prime number; but the celebrated Euler detected the
error by discovering that it was equal to $641 + 6{,}700{,}417$. The same
number was proposed to this child, who found out the factors by the
mere operation of his mind."

It was Fermat who in 1640 conjectured that numbers of the form 2^n
$+ 1$ are prime when n is a power of 2. Because the numbers increase so
rapidly, it was difficult to determine in those days before nonhuman
computers whether Fermat numbers for n greater than 2^4 (16) were prime.
Fermat's conjecture was disproved when the eighteenth-century mathematician Euler factored $2^{32} + 1$. No further Fermat primes have been
found, and it is conjectured that their number is finite.

At first blush the likelihood of an 8 or 9-year-old child solving a problem that lay unresolved for a hundred years seems remote, but Colburn
includes it in the *Memoir,* thereby indirectly vouching for its authenticity
(although he gives no indication of how it was solved or the time required). It is possible that Colburn did not recall the problem and simply
accepted it on the authority of the Prospectus, but this appears unlikely.
He had a good memory for problems which were in some way remarkable; this is hardly the sort of problem which, once solved, would be
easily forgotten. Perhaps it is worth considering just how difficult, given
Zerah's methods, this problem really is.

First, there is no indication of the time required to obtain the solution;
it could have been days, or even weeks. Zerah would have recognized
that in the worst case the least factor would be five digits—as it turns
out the worst case does not obtain. He could mentally multiply four
digits by four digits very rapidly, and, as the *Memoir* notes, (p. 39), "in
some instances five digits by five digits have been given." Testing even
the worst case with mnemonic aids (such as pencil and paper) would
have been simple. Only primes had to be tested, and Zerah could determine whether a number less than a million was prime in a few seconds.
He was familiar with the terminating two-digit combinations of numbers
which could be factors of a number ending in 97. Examine Colburn's
table of terminal digits (chapter 15) for factors of numbers ending in 97.
There are only two single-digit primes to be tested, 3 and 7. Now consider two-digit-prime possibilities; there are only 20. When we get to
possible three-digit factors we need at the most perform 360 divisions to
test all possibilities for a number ending in 97, but many of these can be
immediately eliminated since they are not prime (e.g., 111, 303). Going
through Colburn's table in order (left column first, then moving to

the right column), and ignoring the fact that many of these three-digit numbers would not have to be tested because they are not prime, we should hit upon 641 as a factor on our 240th test of three-digit numbers. For a calculating prodigy this should be no great feat, though we should be surprised were it to be accomplished on the spot.

If this is so, why did a hundred years pass before Fermat's conjecture was proved false? Probably because no competent calculator undertook a systematic investigation of the problem. Fermat's reputation was such that even his conjectures went unquestioned by the few familiar with them. Zerah would have had no appreciation of the significance of the number presented him. Very likely he supposed it was not prime, since such appears to have been the case whenever large numbers were presented to him for possible factoring. His interlocutors had no simple means of conjuring up large primes, but a nonobvious nonprime above 100,000 can easily be created by multiplying together two three-digit prime numbers. In this regard Zerah had a distinct advantage over his predecessors—he had every reason to suppose the number was not prime, while they had every reason to suppose that it was. In fact, he may well have thought that it was concocted by multiplying together two three-digit and one four-digit prime. That he solved it is thus startling, but not incredible.

Occasionally, questioning revealed something of his methods. The *Annual Register* (1812:509–10) reports:

It has been already observed, that it was evident, from some singular facts, that the child operated by certain rules known only to himself. This discovery was made in one or two instances, when he had been closely pressed upon that point. In one case he was asked to tell the square of 4395; he at first hesitated, fearful that he should not be able to answer it correctly; but when he applied himself to it, he said it was 19,316,025. On being questioned as to the cause of his hesitation, he replied that he did not like to multiply four figures by four figures: but, said he, "I found out another way; I multiplied 293 by 293, and then multiplied this product twice by the number 15, which produced the same result." On another occasion, his highness the Duke of Gloucester asked him the product of 21,734 multiplied by 543; he immediately replied, 11,801,562: but, upon some remark being made on the subject, the child said that he had, in his own mind, multiplied 65,202 by 181. Now, although, in the first instance it must be evident to every mathematician that 4395 is equal to 293×15, and consequently that $(4395)^2 = (293)^2 \times (15)^2$; and, further, that in the second case, 543 is equal to 181×3, and consequently that $21734 \times (181 \times 3) = (21734 \times 3) \times 181$;

yet, it is not the less remarkable, that this combination should be immediately perceived by the child, and we cannot the less admire his ingenuity in thus seizing instantly the easiest method of solving the question proposed to him.

The number of partial products does not seem to be the critical factor in determining the degree of difficulty for Zerah in multiplication. He found it easier to multiply small numbers by large ones than to multiply numbers of equal length, even when the number of partial products was the same. The *Memoir* (p. 38–39) relates:

> On another occasion, he was requested to give the square of 999,999; he said he could not do this, but he accomplished it by multiplying 37037 by itself, and that product twice by 27. Ans. 999,998,000,001. He then said he could multiply that by 49 which he did: Ans. 48,999,902,000,049. He again undertook to multiply this number by 49: Ans. 2,400,995,198,002,401. And lastly he multiplied this great sum by 25, giving as the final product, 60,024,879,950,060,025. Various efforts were made by the friends of the boy to elicit a disclosure of the methods by which he performed his calculations, but for nearly three years he was unable to satisfy their inquiries. There was, through practice, an increase in his power of computation; when first beginning, he went no farther in multiplying than three places of figures; it afterwards became a common thing with him to multiply four places by four; in some instances five figures by five have been given.

This problem is revealing in several respects. First, note that the demands on the memory, insofar as the original problem is concerned, are minimal, and the constantly recurring partial product renders the problem easier yet. The fact that Zerah was unable to calculate the product directly suggests that six digits by six digits was out of his range, regardless of the simplicity of the problem.

Second, the problem should present no difficulty for anyone with a little knowledge of algebra and a facility for figures; 999,999 is $10^6 - 1$. Since $(a - b)^2 = a^2 - 2ab + b^2$, we obtain $10^{12} - (2 \times 10^6) + 1$, and if you are good at keeping track of digits, you do not have to be a calculating prodigy to solve this. (For an even simpler solution, see chapter 14.)

Among those who came to see Zerah were many members of the gentry; various bishops; Princess Charlotte, later wife of the King of Belgium; the great chemist, Sir Humphry Davy; General Ross, who lost his life in the burning of Washington; and William Wilberforce, the evangelical politician whose efforts were partly responsible for the abolition of slavery in the British possessions.

Zerah was also invited to the residences of the great, and among these was that of the Duke of York. As it happened the duke was away on business, but Zerah was questioned at length by the duchess and a large party of guests. He was later interviewed by the duke, when it happened that they both attended Sunday service at the Female Orphan Asylum. Aptly, the duke asked the number of seconds that had elapsed since the beginning of the Christian era: 1813 years, 7 months, 27 days; to which Zerah replied 57,234,384,000 seconds.[6]

To raise money friends recommended that a portrait of Zerah be published and sold. Thomas Hull drew the portrait, which was engraved by Meyer, and a number of copies were sold at one guinea each. The success of this venture suggested another—the publication of a memoir, to include a description of his life and a long list of questions answered by him. The book was to be sold by subscription (the price was first set at two and a half guineas, but later reduced to one guinea and a half), and a committee to oversee the collecting of subscriptions was set up. Sir James Mackintosh, inventor of the war rocket, and Sir Humphry Davy, one of the great figures in the history of science, were members of the committee.

In July 1813 Zerah and his father left for Dublin by way of Liverpool. Their purpose was to raise money by exhibition and by finding more subscribers for the book. They stayed four or five weeks in Liverpool, attracting little interest, and left about September 1 for Dublin. Though they were welcomed in Dublin by "the first people of the place," only 32 subscribers could be found. The difficulty was the same as that faced in London. Those on the subscription committee were willing to allow use of their names, but were not willing to expend much effort in finding new subscribers.

Colburn gives us a depressing view of the competition in the exhibition business (p. 63):

> There were exhibiting in Dublin, at this same period, a person of such gigantic stature that Mr. Colburn, who measured six feet; could stand erect under his arm horizontally extended: Miss Honeywell, an American, who was there cutting out watch-papers and other curiosities by the use of her toes. Also, an English woman named Harvey, remarkable for a fair skin, red eyes, and hair glistening like polished metal, nearly white: she had a brother possessing similar peculiarities.

[6] This answer assumes 453 leap years and a 30-day month.

From Dublin they went on to Belfast and then on to Scotland, visiting Glasgow and Edinburgh, and returning to London in early March 1814. The duties of the London subscription committee had been to this point nominal, Mr. Colburn himself having collected all the names. In their absence not a single new name was collected.

Prospects for profitable exhibition in London were dim. Zerah's education, beyond reading and writing, had been neglected. So that his childhood might not be a complete educational loss, a tutor was hired, and the stury of Hutton's *Algebra* began.

After their return from Scotland, Zerah's extra fingers were removed by Dr. Carlisle, who was very anxious to remove his supernumerary toes as well, so that they would not cause him any difficulty in learning to dance. Colburn comments (p. 72) that "as yet there has been no difficulty on that account."

Their string having played out in London, the Colburns left for Paris in July 1814. Napoleon, defeated once and banished to Elba, had not yet returned, and the country, to the disgust of the French, crawled with English tourists. In Paris they found a few Americans, among them William H. Crawford, Minister at the Court of France, and Washington Irving, yet to gain renown as an author. Both subscribed to the book. The French, on the other hand, paid little attention to the young calculator, which was hardly surprising in a country so steeped in misery.

On the advice of American friends, they rented a large house and purchased a lot of furniture, even though their means were scanty and their prospects doubtful. Fortunately, the friends paid the rent, and eventually the furniture was returned. A French tutor was obtained for Zerah but was dismissed within a few months, since Zerah could by then converse freely (he was 10).

Dr. Franz Joseph Gall, physiologist and creator of "cranioscopy," or phrenology, as his followers called it, was then in Paris. Gall believed that the intelligence and personality of an individual could be determined from an examination of the skull. Zerah was introduced to Gall through his tutor, and Gall, supposedly having no inkling of his identity (p. 77), "readily discovered on the sides of the eyebrows certain protuberances and peculiarities which indicated the presence of a faculty for computation." Even if the tutor did not tip him off, it is hardly likely that Gall did not know that his acquaintance was the famed American boy's tutor.

Because of Washington Irving's efforts on his behalf, Zerah was finally to receive an education. The Minister of the Interior had approved a request to establish him as a student at the Royal College of Henri IV, and the request was forwarded to the king for final approval. Before the matter could be concluded Napoleon returned from exile. The petition was finally approved by the emperor, who, Zerah was informed, expressed a desire to meet him.

Zerah entered the school on May 30, 1815. In his opinion, it was possibly better than any in England or the United States at that time. Discipline was strict, military dress required (large cocked hat, etc.), and frivolity frowned upon. As Colburn described it (p. 80): "They rose and slept, studied and played, ate and refrained from eating, at beat of drum." The youthful scholars were generally locked in to discourage intercourse with the temptations of Paris.

This uniform, and whatever else constituted an "outfit," was no small matter. The cost of everything else, including instruction, books, room, board, and medical attention, if necessary, was 1,000 livres (at that time $200), while the outfit cost three-quarters of that amount. Unfortunately, the cost of the outfit was not exempted for Zerah, and so his admission was provisional, contingent on coming up with the price of the outfit.

Meanwhile, Mr. Colburn had returned to London in the summer of 1815 to check on the status of the subscriptions, and discovered that Thomas Biggs, the authorized agent, had collected about a third of the subscriptions and had spent the money. Unable to raise the price of the outfit, and on the advice of new English friends who were embarrassed by the Colburns' previous inability to find patronage in England, Mr. Colburn removed Zerah from the school, and in February 1816 they arrived in London.

Back in London, Mr. Colburn's new friends, in spite of promises, were disinclined to aid father and son in their plight, which was now extreme. They scuffled and scrounged until July 1816, when the Earl of Bristol took an interest in Zerah. The earl was atypical of the peerage, being a younger son and former naval captain who had inherited the title and estates when his brother died childless. He invited Zerah to his country estate at Putney, where he customarily spent the summer months. The earl was especially concerned with Zerah's religious beliefs, since in France particularly, and in England to a lesser degree, doubt was growing about the validity of revealed religion. The earl had Zerah memorize the fifty-third chapter of Isaiah, for which he was paid a pound.[7]

[7]This chapter describes how the "servant," though himself righteous, suffered and died for the sins of others, but ultimately triumphed. This is naturally taken by Christians to be a prophecy of Christ.

The earl was impressed with Zerah and decided to pay all his expenses in attending the Westminster School, and furnished him with various religious books.

Zerah entered the lower school, September 19, 1816. The curriculum was limited to the study of Latin and Greek (the latter in the upper school). Since he was unfamiliar with the books used, and pronounced Latin in the French manner, he was placed in the lowest class. At 12, he was older than the other boys, and was speedily advanced.

Zerah's English academic career almost ended as soon as it began. The ancient custom of fagging was in practice at Westminster, as in other British educational institutions. After three weeks to accustom himself to the place, Zerah was assigned as fag to the son of a baronet, Sir John L. Kaye. His duties included washing dishes, cleaning boots and shoes, and serving the teatime meal at five o'clock. One Friday night, a few weeks after beginning his services, having been dismissed by his regular master, he was called upon by one of the older boys to do some work. Zerah worked so reluctantly that his master became disgusted with him, and punished him by twisting his arm and beating his shoulder black and blue. Zerah was 12 and his master 18. Resistance was not only futile but would have much worsened his situation, since the rule among the students was that any member of the under school who lifted a hand against a member of the upper school would receive "wrath without mixture," that is, their combined vengeance.

Zerah went to his father the next day, related what had happened, and showed him his wounds. Mr. Colburn went to the school administrators, explained the situation, and told them that he had sent his son there to be a student, not a servant. Though some regret was expressed, it was pointed out that fagging had prevailed in British schools for over 100 years, and other fathers had attempted to have their sons exempted, without success, and that if Mr. Colburn found the practice unacceptable, he had best remove his son. Mr. Colburn replied that if they had the power to expel Zerah for refusing to fag they might do so, but that he would instruct his son not to serve.

He left Zerah at the school Monday, telling him that he would return on Tuesday. In the interim Zerah was to perform no services for boys of the upper school. He managed to contrive to avoid them during the day, but Monday night a number of the largest boys cornered him and demanded that he polish a pair of boots. When he refused, citing his father's prohibition, they beat him until he complied.

When Mr. Colburn returned he learned of what had happened and went to see the headmaster, Dr. Page, while the boys hooted at the "yan-kee" from the windows. Dr. Page was conciliatory, even offering to expel Kaye (a great disgrace). Mr. Colburn said that he did not want the boy expelled, but neither did he want his son to fag, and threatened to "de-fend him by the law of Nature." Dr. Page finally relented, and Zerah was allowed to return without being required to fag.

Zerah had been their meal ticket for a long time, and now that he was boarding at Westminster School, Mr. Colburn found himself without a means of support. Since the money for educational expenses was given directly to Mr. Colburn, it occurred to him that, if these could be re-duced, he could pocket the difference. Zerah, like many other students, became a part-time boarder, living with his father and taking breakfast and dinner at the school. Zerah suspected, but was not certain, that the earl discovered the ruse.

Beginning in 1817 the earl made arrangements for Zerah to pass his summer vacations in the country under the tutelage of the Reverend Henry St. James Bullen, his Lordship's chaplain and a Cambridge gradu-ate. There Zerah studied the classics and the first six books of Euclid.

After spending two vacations in this way, Zerah was informed by Mr. Bullen that the earl wished him to remain there rather than returning to Westminster. This was not much to Zerah's liking, and when he in-formed his father, Mr. Colburn decided that this was a plot on Bullen's part to augment his income. Mr. Colburn wrote to the earl, who was at Spa in Germany, in the midst of a five-year continental vacation. His Lordship confirmed that it was his wish that Zerah should remain with Bullen, but offered Mr. Colburn fifty pounds per year for his support. He would not accede to this, and so in May 1817 Zerah left Westminster School.

Zerah was not 15, and he and his father were back on the street again. Mr. Colburn gave much anxious thought as to how they might capital-ize on Zerah's talents. He finally concluded that, since his son had con-siderable experience in appearing before audiences and was known to the public, he should become an actor. The idea of impersonating great men appealed to Zerah, who readily agreed. The owner of the Covent Garden theater encouraged them, and gave Zerah free passes so that he could study the actors. An acting coach was retained, and a fencing tutor.

Zerah first appeared as "Narval in Howe's tragedy of Douglas" in Au-gust 1819, in Margate, a seaside resort 70 miles from London. The pro-duction was not a financial success, and Zerah received no compensation.

After a month they returned to London, and Mr. Colburn decided

that they should again visit Scotland and Ireland. They were now so poor
that they had to make the 450-mile sea voyage to Edinburgh in steerage.
Though a few former friends were willing to contribute to their current
needs, there were no theatrical prospects for Zerah, and they left for
Glasgow. Here they found their friends of six years earlier either gone or
estranged, and so they soon sailed for Belfast, Ireland. Here old friends
were more sympathetic and were willing to assist in promoting their new
endeavor.

The theatrical company was about to leave for Londonderry, and the
Colburns followed, but they were now reduced to traveling on foot. On
the fourth day out, after much walking through winter rain, they arrived
in Londonderry. Zerah appeared here only in comic roles, which were
not to his taste.

Back in Belfast, he appeared in the spring as Richard the Third, and
later as Lothais, in a tragedy called *Adelgithe*. Still, no profit followed,
and about April 1, 1820 Zerah and his father proceeded to Dublin, but
found no theatrical employment for Zerah. While there, however, he
undertook his first extensive literary effort, a tragedy based upon Hoole's
translation of "Jerusalem Delivered," but Colburn admits (p. 129) "it
never had any merit, or any success." In July they returned to London.
This ended Zerah's ten-month infatuation with acting, a period during
which he was usually poor and often lonely and depressed. It was also
the only period of his youth he was to recall as wasted.

They continued in poverty and misery until January 1822, when Zerah
established a small school. Though still partially dependent upon the
charity of others, he found satisfaction in his work and increasing independence (p. 133):

> It is with peculiar satisfaction that he reverts to his commencing in this
> employment. Never before, unless when exhibited, had he any opportunity
> of feeling that he contributed aught to his own support. When sometimes
> he hears people wishing that they had his privilege of seeing the world, to
> think of the price at which he purchased this privilege, would suggest the
> idea that they little knew what it was which they desired.
>
> To visit foreign lands may well be wished, both for the pleasure of con-
> templating human life in all its various forms, both rude and refined, as
> well as for the knowledge thus imparted beyond what books can communi-
> cate. But by him, this pleasure has been purchased at so dear a rate, that he
> hardly knows if he ought to consider his course the best. One serious truth,
> however, he has learnt by his experience in life: that it is better for a man to
> depend on his own resources and exertions, than to make any calculation of

being supported by the patronage of others. Let his calling be what it may, if honest, though mean and laborious, let him pursue it with all perserverance and industry—he shall be happier and better provided for, than while waiting upon the great, liberal in promises.

Mr. Colburn renewed his efforts to obtain a fund for Zerah's permanent support. A prospectus was drawn up and a few prominent signatures obtained. Zerah even again visited Scotland and Ireland, prospectus in hand, but nothing came of it, and he continued his school.

In December 1822, Mr.Colburn's health began to decline, apparently as much from psychological as from physical causes. He had gambled away his family and his freedom on the future greatness of his son, who as a child sat upon the knees of the great but as a young man had become a simple schoolteacher. Mr. Colburn's hopes had been raised often, but never fulfilled.

Matters continued thus until the summer of 1823, when Zerah met Thomas Young, M.D., Secretary to the Board of Longitude, who was to give him employment in making astronomical calculations. He received his first payment in January 1824, most welcome since his father's rapidly failing health had forced him to close his school. Dr. Young began to visit Mr. Colburn, but he continued to decline and died February 14, 1824. Colburn reports, with typical precision (p. 137), that his age was "54 years, 3 months, and 8 days."

After his father's death Zerah went to various friends and acquaintances, including the Earl of Bristol. They were kind enough to provide him with the funds necessary to return to the United States, which was what he wished to do. He continued with his astronomical calculations for Dr. Young, and paid his father's debts to some needy folk. On Tuesday, May 25, he sailed for America. His letters of introduction led him to the acquaintance of people who wished to find work for him in New York, possibly at the high school for which plans were in progress. Zerah was pleased, but anxious to visit his family, and so after five days left for Cabot, with the intention of returning.

About sunset, July 3, 1824, he reached Cabot, his native village. Not knowing the way, he asked an elderly woman standing in her doorway if she knew where the widow Colburn lived. As it happened, the woman was his mother. Neither knew the other, nor could Zerah recognize other members of his family. They were much worse off than he had anticipated. Zerah scrapped his plans to return to New York in order to help his family.

He again opened a small school and wrote to Lord Bristol, as the latter had requested, of his arrival and circumstances. The earl's reply came in October, informing him that if he was in need of money he might write requesting a small sum, and the earl would be disposed to grant it. The letter also warmly recommends several religious books, including Butler's *Analogy* ("should be read over and over again, until you have made his thoughts your own"); Paley's *Natural Theology,* his *Evidences,* and his *Horae Paulinae* ("which last is a work inferior to none"); and Doddridge's *Rise and Progress of Religion in the Soul* ("he who has fully imbibed it, and daily practices its contents, will have nothing left to wish for").

Zerah replied that he would be delighted to receive some aid. He closed his school and took a job as an assistant in an academy in Fairfield, New York connected with Hamilton College. He went there in December, but, disappointed with his prospects, left for Burlington, Vermont in March 1825. Shortly before he left, the earl's reply arrived, giving him leave to draw 25 pounds sterling on the earl's account.

In Burlington Zerah gave French lessons and returned to classical studies, hoping to obtain a degree. In April the money from the earl arrived, and since his circumstances were not too bad, he gave his mother the $85 or so this represented. In today's money this would be in excess of $1,000.

From his childhood Zerah reflected on religion. Although he received no instruction in religion as a child, the New Testament was among his earliest books. At this time, having some leisure, and fearing that he might unexpectedly die and find his fate sealed before he could arrive at any mature conclusions on the topic of religion, he began in earnest to pray and to read the Bible, and to study religious works such as those recommended by the earl.

After five or six weeks of study he began to despair and, having no transcendental experiences, feared that true religion had forever eluded him. In this frame of mind he visited Mr. Preston, the Congregationalist minister in Burlington, who assured him, to his surprise, that if his account was correct, he had indeed experienced religion. Upon this revelation Zerah decided to become a clergyman.

A few days later he was invited to become a member of the Congregationalist Church, but he had considerable difficulty with the articles of faith. He was particularly disturbed by the notion of unconditional election and reprobation—the doctrines that some people are predestined for heaven and others for eternal damnation. He could not deny, however, that there was biblical support for these views, such as the eighth and ninth chapters of Paul's Epistle to the Romans. In spite of the fact he found these views distasteful and difficult to reconcile with the doctrines of free grace and moral agency, he became a member of the Burlington Congregationalist Church in July.

Having determined his future profession, and anxious to start saving souls before his own might be called to its Maker, he abandoned all notion of proceeding with his education, either classical or theological.

Not surprisingly, the ministers of the order were unwilling to grant him a license to conduct any sort of meetings, and recommended that he go to school and study divinity. Zerah decided to return to Cabot (p. 185) and "wait the openings of Providence."

While in Cabot he became friendly with the Methodists, and under their influence he became increasingly dissatisfied with Congregationalist doctrine. After much soul searching he reluctantly decided to break with the Congregationalists, and he wrote them to that effect, requesting something like an honorable discharge. They never replied, and he joined the Cabot Methodists in December 1825.

Zerah had long harbored literary ambitions, having written an unsuccessful (and unperformed) play during his brief infatuation with the theater. He includes at the end of his book several poems, or as he entitled them, "A Few Pieces in Rhyme." His explanation runs (p. 192): "The following little pieces were written in the days of boyhood; they are not inserted to claim any merit on the score of poetical talent, but rather to give a more full idea of the subject of this memoir in other things than arithmetic.—If they are worthy of criticism, he is glad to be instructed, though since he engaged in ministerial duties, he has had no time or taste for composition of this kind."

It is difficult to accept this explanation without reservation. Colburn is ingenuous in acknowledging the poverty of his verse, but what retired and unpublished poet could resist inserting samples of youthful poetry in a book if he could get away with it?

Of his seven years as a minister before writing the *Memoir,* Colburn says very little. As part of the motive for writing the *Memoir* he mentions the need to find support beyond the contributions of his congregation for a wife and three little girls, but he does not give their names. He also remarks that during that period he had been assigned to seven different circuits, six in eastern Vermont, and one in New Hampshire. The service had not been easy (p. 162):

He cannot speak of painful impressions leading him to this undertaking, such as many of his dear brethren in the ministry have had. It rather seemed that the Lord was disposed in the gentlest and most persuasive way to lead him along by holding up the fair and pleasing side of the picture to his view. He well knew how to catch the heart of his weak disciple; had he began by pointing out all the trials, and crosses, and sorrows of an itinerant preacher's life, it is more than probable he would have discouraged him from it in the beginning.

On March 2, 1840, in Norwich, Vermont, the Reverend Zerah Colburn died. According to his obituary, he was "Professor of the 'Latin, Greek, French, and Spanish Languages, and English Classical Literature,' in the seminary styled the 'Norwich University.'" At the time of his death his age was 35 years, 5 months, and 2 days.

Colburn is the only prodigy to receive much critical abuse, and most of this can be traced ultimately to Scripture's "Arithmetical Prodigies," the first extensive general treatment of the topic of calculating prodigies. Scripture's assessment of Colburn was (1891:16):

> It is to be remarked that Colburn's calculating powers, such as they were, seemed to have absorbed all his mental energy; he was unable to learn much of anything, and incapable of the exercise of even ordinary intelligence or of any practical application. The only quality for which he was especially distinguished was self-appreciation.

This assessment is not simply unfair; it is ridiculous. Colburn managed careers as a child performer and a minister. He made astronomical calculations, taught modern and classical languages and literature. Finally he left a very remarkable document, his autobiography. While Coburn did not achieve all that he and others had unrealistically hoped, he hardly merits Scripture's scorn.

A large portion of Scripture's pique may be attributed to snobbery. Scripture, a Ph.D. and a professor at Leipzig, seems particularly incensed that a man of Colburn's educational background should undertake a literary effort (1891:11):

> Autobiographies do not always furnish the most trustworthy evidence in regard to the man himself; when moreover, the author is convinced that he is nothing less than a modern miracle; and, finally, when having had no scientific and little literary education, he at a later date writes the memoir of his youth, we are obliged to supply the lacking critical treatment of the narrative.

The charge of conceit is no less ill-founded than that of incompetence. Colburn was a painfully honest man, conscientiously recording his shortcomings along with his merits—he was without false modesty or false pride.

There are in the *Memoir* a few statements which might seem to support a charge of conceit, for instance (p. 176): "At different periods, Zerah Colburn has heard of a number of persons, whose uncommon aptness in figures rendered them subjects of astonishment to others. He thinks it is no vanity to consider himself first in the list in the order of time, and probably first in extent of intellectual power." I am not certain whether Colburn means by "first in the order of time" that his talent manifested itself at the earliest age or that he was the first such prodigy. If the latter then he is deliberately ignoring Jedidiah Buxton, whom he discusses, presumably on the plausible grounds that Buxton's talent differed not merely in degree but in kind.

As to being "first in extent of intellectual power," he was mistaken— Bidder was a better calculator. Colburn remarks of him (p. 175): "The person who in the writer's judgment approached the nearest to an equality with him in mental arithmetic, was a youth from Devonshire County, in England, named George Bidder." Bidder and Colburn met once, after the latter had ceased making public appearances and had lost much of his former quickness (p. 175):

> Some time in 1818, Zerah was invited to a certain place, where he found a number of persons questioning the Devonshire boy. He displayed great strength and power of mind in the higher branches of arithmetic; he could answer some questions that the American would not like to undertake; but he was unable to extract the roots, and find the factors of numbers.

We know that Bidder, at a later date, was able to factor numbers and extract roots, since in his talk to the Society of Engineers he describes methods identical to those of Colburn for solving such problems. It is possible that at this time he had not worked out these methods, or was not adept at applying them, for I find no account of problems solved by Bidder as a child which involved factoring or extracting roots. (For a different view of this incident, see the next chapter.)

Mitchell, one of Colburn's few defenders, points out (1907:137):

> Now Colburn was not much of a mathematician, but one thing he did know, from the mathematicians who had examined him: up to his own time, no one had discovered any general method of finding the factors of numbers. Colburn himself had a new and original method of performing this operation very rapidly for numbers up to 6 or 7 figures, and of finding almost instantly the roots, of exact squares and cubes. He could not be expected to

understand that this method (by 2-figures endings) was really trivial; he *did* know that he could solve these problems, by an original method, and that eminent mathematicians were more amazed at this feat than at any other in his repertoire. Shall we blame him, then, for considering himself superior as a calculator to any one who simply excelled him in straight arithmetical operations, and that, too, at a time when he had given up public exhibitions and lost not a little of his former skill? Colburn could appreciate his own feats, but could not adequately appreciate Bidder's compound interest method, for example; he gives Bidder full credit, however, for "great strength and power of mind in the higher branches of arithmetic," and for defeating him in the competitive test in other directions.

Other instances might be cited in which Colburn seems astounded by his gift, but why should he not have been? Many others were, and among those who took an interest were Samuel F. B. Morse, Michael Faraday, and Sir Humphry Davy—men who could hardly be considered gullible.

In any case, Colburn never takes personal credit for his calculating talent; it was a gift of God, and he is plainly dismayed by his inability to discern its purpose or put it to practical use, as several statements in the *Memoir* show, e.g. (p. 165):

> In relation to the faculty of computation which he possessed, he would observe that in every particular, from its first developement [*sic*] to the present day, it has been to him a matter of astonishment. He has felt, and still feels, that it was undoubtedly a gift from his Maker, and consequently designed to be productive to some valuable ends. What the specific object was is unknown. Was it to place the young man in a situation where he might be eminently useful in scientific labors? If so, by neglect, or ignorance somewhere, that object remains frustrated. Was it that by rendering the young man so celebrated in early life, he might thus be introduced to the notice of the public when he came to address them on the great salvation? If the notoriety of his youth was designed as an introduction to him in his ministerial capacity, it would be a natural expectation that his talents as a Preacher would be equal, if not superior, to the striking displays of his early precocity. This however is far from being the case.

Colburn is equally frank regarding his intellectual limitations (p. 104):

> It is, however, a truth which may as well be stated here as any where else, that the mind of Zerah was never apparently endowed with such a talent for close thinking on intricate subjects as many possess. He was not peculiarly fortunate in arriving at a result which did not readily present itself, or for

which the process leading thereto was not soon discovered. . . . While in school he generally sustained himself among the four at the head of the class; but was not remarkable either for quickness of mind or closeness of application.

Scripture (1891:11) is so obsessed with discrediting Colburn that he maintains that he "was considered a very backward child." This claim is based on nothing more than Colburn's statement that his parents considered him in his early years (before the emergence of his talent for calculation—that is, before his sixth birthday) "the most backward of any of their children" (Colburn 1833:10). He was certainly *not* regarded as backward by those who saw him as a child. Professor MacNeven, who observed him at age 6, wrote (1811:22):

> The general intelligence of Zerah Colburn distinguishes him advantageously from Jedediah Buxton, a person no less remarkable for his powers of calculation, but otherwise totally destitute of taste or talent. . . . Little Colburn is prompt at repartee, and sometimes sarcastic. Being asked, a few evenings since, by a lady who meant to be witty, how much was three naughts multiplied by three naughts—just as much as yourself, says he,—nothing at all.

And a friend of Samuel F. B. Morse (not identified by name in Morse's biography) remarked in a letter (Prime 1875:68): "Zerah Colburn, the little calculator, has called on us two or three times, as Morse is painting his portrait. He is a fine, lively, little fellow, and the most inquisitive child I ever saw."

Scripture's hatchet job is inexcusable, but it is at least based upon an acquaintance with Colburn's *Memoir*. Alfred Binet (of Stanford-Binet fame), an important figure in the history of psychology, particularly because of his investigations of intelligence, is also responsible for the first (and very nearly the only) experiments conducted on calculating prodigies (Binet 1894). Binet, who had read Scripture, gives no indication of any firsthand acquaintance with the *Memoir*; but he not only repeats Scripture's charges, he embroiders on them (1894:9):

> The history of Zerah Colburn would be extremely interesting if it rested on documents worthy of confidence; this is unfortunately not the case. The principal remaining document regarding him is his autobiography, and since he made an exhibition of himself in public performances, and he speaks of himself with an insupportable vanity, one may rightfully assume that this biography is an advertisement.

In what sense Binet intends the term "advertisement" (*réclame*) is unclear. Zerah had ceased giving public demonstrations nearly twenty years before the writing of the *Memoir,* and it could hardly have been written to promote his career as an itinerant Methodist minister in a remote section of New England. Perhaps he is referring only to Colburn's supposed penchant for self-glorification.

But Binet goes further still (1894:10–11): "This agitated existence is the mark of a somewhat strange mind; Colburn was looked upon as an individual of mediocre intelligence, and absurdly puffed up with pride; his biography gives a thousand naive proofs of it, and he asserts again and again that he should be considered the greatest intelligence on earth."

Frank D. Mitchell, in his brilliant "Mathematical Prodigies," refutes Scripture's calumnies, but even he fails to recognize the considerable literary merit of the *Memoir* (1907:66): "The literary style of his *Memoir,* though far from Addisonian, is always readable, the book is interesting throughout, and even the specimens of his poetry given in the appendix are not specially bad, all things considered." True, the style is not Addisonian, but then neither is Swift's, nor Milton's; and why should it be? In fact, considering Colburn's excellent and honest prose, the poetry is execrable, and can only be excused by the author's extreme youth (the poems were all written long before the *Memoir*). A sample, selected only for its brevity, follows (Colburn 1833:198):

Invitation
Deeds of praise are unavailing,
 All our idle works are dead,
His the glory of fulfilling
 That emprize for which he bled.
Songs of triumph, loudly ringing,
 Should his boundless love proclaim:
Hear the choirs of angels singing
 Loud hosannas to his name.
In the courts of love immortal,
 Harps celestial sound his praise;
Now, even now, heaven's highest portal
 Echoes back the hallowed lays.
Mortals come! with reverence bending
 Round the footsteps of his throne;
Now embrace the wide extending
 Full atonement of his Son.

Colburn seemed unable to escape the contempt of those who knew nothing about him. In his *Biographie de Henri Mondeux* (n.d.:9–10), Émile Jacoby manages to get both Colburn's first and last names wrong, calling him "Zerald Colborn," and condemns him in the following terms:

> Finally, in more recent times, there is Zerald Colborn, who lived in France and was placed in the imperial lycée. . . . Zerald, according to some engineers who were his fellow students, did nothing in college, except calculations from memory; he either did not want to, or could not, learn anything, and one of his compatriots assured me, very recently, that this same Zerald Colborn, this calculating prodigy, whose skull the phrenologists identified as a type characteristic of mathematicians, is today a simple pastor in a poor small town of the United States.

An anonymous author in *The Spectator* ("Calculating Boys" 1878:1208) castigates Colburn not for vanity but for humility: "Zerah Colburn's 'Memoir' is an inane production, which would be tedious in the extreme except for its absurd *naiveté* and the frankness with which the author admits his mediocrity."

Unreasonable attacks on Colburn have continued into recent times. Fred Barlow (1952:84) writes: "In an appendix to his *Memoir*, Colburn attempts to explain his methods of finding square and cube roots. His rule, first formulated two years after he began, was so clumsy and involved as to be of little help and he admitted that it was 'a drag of a method.' "[8] In fact, Colburn's description, though mathematically inelegant, is quite easy to understand. It is identical to that described by Bidder, and is, furthermore, a method used by several prodigies for finding roots and factors. Its usefulness is attested to by the fact that Colburn was one of the most adept of all calculating prodigies at factoring. Though this was the method Zerah used from the outset in factoring, he was not able to explain it until December 13, 1813, over three years after his calculating ability first became apparent (see the *Memoir*, p. 183).

Much of the invective hurled at Colburn is based upon a misconception, but a misconception shared to some extent by Colburn and his father. Calculating ability in no way implies mathematical insight—if it did computers would have long since sent all the mathematicians to re-

---

[8] Barlow takes this quotation from Scripture (1891:54), who in turn attributes it to a letter by Hamilton in "Graves' Life of Sir Wm. R. Hamilton, p. 78." I have not been able to consult this work, but nothing of the sort is suggested by Colburn himself in his *Memoir*.

tirement villages. For the most part other calculating prodigies had no more mathematical insight than Colburn; but then, they did not write autobiographies. Colburn suspected, but did not fully appreciate, where his true talents lay. Our misfortune is that he left us no other mature literary products.

Chapter Twenty-three

——

George Parker Bidder

You may think that I attach much more importance to the science of arithmetic than it is justly entitled to. If, however, that be so, you must at the same time admit that I have reason for this feeling. It is to that science that I am indebted for the friends who encouraged my early career, as well as for those who afforded me the benefits of the comparatively small amount of education I received,—it procured me the friends, who opened to me, in manhood, the paths in the profession to which it is my pride to belong;—more than all, it has secured me the inestimable friend who now presides over us, and giving me confidence and the power of analysis, it has materially aided in raising me to the position I now hold.

—George Parker Bidder (1856:279)

G EORGE Parker Bidder, the son of a Devonshire stonemason, was born June 14, 1806, in the village of Moreton Hampstead, England. Bidder's early talent for calculation ultimately led him to a university education, a career as one of the foremost engineers in a period of great engineering accomplishment, and to a considerable personal fortune.

At 6, Bidder entered the village school, but it was not much to his liking and he was truant whenever possible. About this time his elder brother, also a stonemason, taught the boy to count—first to ten, and then to one hundred. This was the end of his brother's training. At this time Bidder had no knowledge of written numbers, nor did he even know the word "multiply."

Despite this, the boy soon began counting fives and tens, and set about to learn the multiplication table by arranging peas, marbles, and finally shot, into rectangles. He writes of this procedure (1856:258):

> I used to arrange them into squares, of 8 on each side, and then on count-ing them throughout, I found that the whole number amounted to 64: by that process I satisfied my mind, not only as a matter of memory but as a matter of conviction, that 8 times 8 were 64; and that fact once established has remained there undisturbed until this day, and I dare say it will remain so to the end of my days. It was in this way that I acquired the whole multiplication table up to 10 times 10; beyond which I never went; it was all that I required.

During this period Bidder often played at the workshop of an elderly blacksmith, who lived across the road. Once while he was there (Bidder 1856:258–59),

> somebody by chance mentioned a sum, whether it was 9 times 9 or what it was I do not now recollect; but whatever it was, I gave the answer correctly. This occasioned some little astonishment; they then asked me other ques-tions, which I answered with equal facility. They then went on to ask me up to two places of figures; 13 times 17 for instance; that was rather beyond me, at the time, but I had been accustomed to reason on figures, and I said 13 times 17 means 10 times 10 plus 10 times 7, plus 10 times 3 and 3 times 7. I said 10 times 10 are 100, 10 times 7 are 70, 10 times 3 are 30, and 3 times 7 are 21; which added together give the result, 221; of course I did not do it then as rapidly as afterwards, but I gave the answer correctly, as was verified by the old gentleman's nephew, who began chalking it up to see if I was right. As a natural consequence, this increased my fame still more, and what was better, it eventually caused halfpence to flow into my pocket; which I need not say, had the effect of attaching me still more to the science of arithmetic, and thus by degrees I got on, until the multiple arrived at thousands. Then of course my powers of numeration had to be increased, and it was explained to me that 10 hundreds meant 1000. Nu-meration beyond that point is very simple in its features; 1000 rapidly gets up to 10,000 and 20,000, as it is simply 10, or 20 repeated over again, with thousands at the end, instead of nothing. So by degrees, I became familiar with the numeration table, up to a million. From 2 places of figures, I got to 3 places;—then to 4 places of figures, which took me up of course to tens of millions; then I ventured to 5 and 6 places of figures which I could eventually treat with great facility, and as already mentioned, on one occa-sion I went through the task of multiplying 12 places of figures by 12 fig-ures; but it was a great and distressing task.

Bidder's father soon saw the pecuniary possibilities in his son's talent and withdrew him from school to exhibit his gift. When he was not quite 9 years of age, in April 1815, he was presented to Queen Charlotte by the Bishop of Salisbury, and answered a variety of difficult questions. His father found this mode of life so pleasant and profitable that his son's education was entirely ignored.

In the fall of 1817, the Reverend Thomas Jephson, Fellow and Tutor of St. John's College, and Sir John Herschel made the trip to Moreton to see the "calculating boy." They came away most impressed not only with Bidder's ability to calculate but with his general intelligence. Jephson and others from Cambridge offered to pay for the boy's education. This pleased his mother very much, but his father, reluctant to lose the revenue gained from his son's performances, agreed very reluctantly. Bidder was placed with another Reverend Jephson (presumably a relation of the first), master of the grammar school at Camberwell. After about a year his father removed him from the school to continue his exhibitions.

During their travels, father and son went to Edinburgh, where Sir Henry Jardine, the King's Remembrancer for Scotland, took notice of him. Sir Henry raised a subscription sufficient to pay for Bidder's education. The Reverend A. Stewart became his private tutor, and in 1819, at the age of 15, Bidder began to attend classes at the University of Edinburgh. In the spring of 1822 he won the prize for the study of higher mathematics given by the magistrates of Edinburgh. It was here that he became friends with Robert Stephenson, destined to become one of the great engineers of the time. Bidder left Edinburgh in 1824 when Sir Henry arranged a post for him on the Ordinance Survey.

Bidder did not forget the generosity of his benefactor nor his own good fortune as a lad of no means in attending the university. In 1846, after he had established himself professionally, he founded a scholarship, the "Jardine Bursary," of £40 a year, to aid poor students. And in the early days of his career, when he could ill afford it, he undertook to provide for the education of his two younger brothers.

There is a record of a few of the problems Bidder solved as a child. A letter from Charles M. Osmond (1879) to the *Spectator* includes some excerpts about Bidder from an old pamphlet. The pamphlet was 34 pages in length and lacked a title page, but Osmond guessed its publication date to be about 1820. It contained problems solved by Bidder along with his answers. According to Osmond the time and place were usually given, as well as, in many instances, the persons posing the problems.

The time covered was from 1816 to 1819, during which Bidder was 9 to 13 years of age. All the problems excerpted by Osmond are given below, along with my comments:

"1816 (10 years of age). What is the interest of £4,444 for 4,444 days, at 4½% per annum?—Answer, in 2 minutes—£2,434 16s. 5¼d."

In calculating the answer Bidder did not compound the interest; that is, he assumes that there are £4,444 in the account each year. The answer is correct, except that the odd pence (abbreviated as "d." from the Latin "dinarius") are closer to 6 than 5¼.

"1817 (10 years of age). How long would a cistern 1 mile cube be filling, if receiving from a river 120 gallons per minute without intermission?—Answer, in 2 minutes,—years 14,300, days 285, hours 12, minutes 46."

In solving this problem, Bidder, like Buxton, used a value of 282 cubic inches to a gallon. On that assumption, and assuming a 365 day year, Bidder's answer is accurate to within a few seconds.

I do not know how Bidder solved this problem. It comes down to resolving:

$$\frac{5280^3 \times 12^3}{120 \times 282 \times 60 \times 24 \times 365}$$

These multiplications can be considerably simplified by canceling factors—for example, 120, 60, and 24 are all factors of $5,280^3$. In any case, it is certainly a remarkable mental feat.

"1818 (11 years of age). Divide 468,592,413,563 by 9,076.—Answer, within 1 minute,—51,629,838."

The answer is correct, though it ignores a substantial remainder.

"There are 7 numbers in geometrical progression, the first is 6, and the seventh 705,894; what are all the intermediate terms?—Answer, in 1 minute,—42; 294; 2,058; 14,406; 100,842."

Each term is seven times the last. Possibly Bidder divided 100,842 by 6, and recognized the result, 16,807, as the fifth power of seven.

"1818 (12 years of age). If the pendulum of a clock vibrates the distance of 9¾ inches in a second of time, how many inches will it vibrate in 7 years, 14 days, 2 hours, 1 minute, 56 seconds; each year being 365 days, 5 hours, 48 minutes, 55 seconds?—Answer, in less than a minute,—2,165,625,744¾ inches."

This is correct.

"1819 (13 years of age). What is the cube root of 897,339,273,974, 002,153? — Answer, in 2½ minutes, — 964,537."

This is correct.

"To find a number whose cube less 19 multiplied by its cube shall be equal to the cube of 6. — Answer, instantly, — 3."

The problem asks for a solution to the equation $(x^3 - 19)x^3 = 6^3$.

> The following question was put by Sir William Herschel, at Slough, near Windsor, to Master Bidder, and answered in one minute; — "Light travels from the sun to the earth in 8 minutes, and the sun being 98,000,000 of miles off, if light would take 6 years and 4 months travelling at the same rate from the nearest fixed star, how far is that star from the earth, reckoning 365 days and 6 hours to each year, and 28 days to each month?" — Answer, 40,633,740,000,000 miles.

This too is correct.

The letter also includes an excerpt from an unspecified London morning paper, describing the one meeting between Bidder and Colburn:

> A few days since, a meeting took place between the Devonshire youth, George Bidder, and the American youth, Zerah Colborne [sic], before a party of gentlemen, to ascertain their calculating comprehensions. The Devonshire boy having answered a variety of questions in a satisfactory way, a gentleman proposed one to Zerah Colborne, viz., — If the globe is 24,912 miles in circumference, and balloon travels 3,878 feet in a minute, how long would it be in travelling round the world? After nine minutes' consideration, he felt himself incompetent to give the answer. The same question being given to the Devonshire boy, the answer he returned in two minutes, viz., — 23 days, 13 hours, 18 min., was received with marks of great applause. Many other questions were proposed to the American boy, all of which he refused answering, while young Bidder readily replied to all. A handsome subscription was collected for the Devonshire youth.

Of course, if Bidder was present when the problem was presented to Colburn (not "Colborne," as the paper had it), then he had eleven minutes, not two, to calculate.

The period of Bidder's professional maturity was one of the greatest in the history of engineering, and he was one of the finest civil engineers of the day. Among Bidder's accomplishments were: construction, with Robert Stephenson, of the first railway in Norway; service as engineer-in-chief of the Royal Danish railway; adviser for the Metropolitan Board of London regarding the drainage and purification of the Thames; and a successful argument against a break in gauge in the completion of the Indian railway system.

Most of Bidder's career was devoted to railway engineering, but he had an astonishing array of interests (ICE 1878–79:306):

> Next to railway matters, hydraulic engineering seems to have had the greatest attraction for him; perhaps from the facility with which his mathematical powers enabled him to investigate the abstruse problems presented in the consideration of the laws governing the movement of fluids. Drainage, both agricultural and municipal, the electric telegraph, submarine telegraphy, the caloric engine, foundations, the combustion of fuel, the relative value of free and convict labour, dock gates, naval construction, piers, the cost and efficiency of various kinds of motive power, rivers and estuaries, the calculation of roofs, steam navigation, the preservation of timber, the removal of wrecks, are some of the subjects outside his chosen domain in which he drew on his great stores of knowledge for the benefit of his fellow members [of the Institution of Civil Engineers].

Bidder's most famous engineering feat was the construction of the Victoria docks. Many people scoffed at the idea of constructing docks so far from London in the midst of marshes, but Bidder's engineering and business genius proved correct.

Because of his farsightedness in selecting the site, and by brilliant engineering, Bidder was able, for a modest cost, to provide more docking and warehousing space than were elsewhere available, as well as nearly 100 acres of deep water. The locks and 80-foot iron lock gates were larger than any others in London at the time. Cast-iron piles and concrete were used in constructing the walls of the docks. These materials were not only less expensive; they obviated the need for an expensive cofferdam.

Bidder also took an interest in military (particularly naval) matters, and was frequently consulted by the government. He was a member of the Royal Commission on the Construction of Ships, and on the War Office Committee on Gun Cotton and other Explosives. He was the Lieutenant-Colonel Commandant of the Engineer and Railway Volunteer Staff Corps, and was active in resolving problems submitted by the War Office. He also had a great love for the sea, and particularly enjoyed sailing his schooner, the *Mayfly*.

Bidder's shrewd business sense was to make him wealthy. He was one of the original founders of the Electric Telegraph Company, sat on boards of various railway companies, and was chairman or director of various other businesses, including the Netherlands Land Company and the Rock Assurance Company. In his engineering work, Bidder had a keen eye for profit, in many instances for personal profit. For example, he was instrumental in introducing gas lighting in Denmark through an English company in which he held substantial interest. But it was not an age when individuals were embarrassed by profit. His contemporaries, including his son, placed as much importance on his commercial abilities as his engineering genius.

After his death an article in the *Spectator* on "Calculating Boys" (1878) raised the ire of one of his friends, James Elliot, a fellow student at Edinburgh and a former professor of mathematics at Queen's College, Liverpool. He stated in a letter excerpted in the *Spectator* (Elliot, 1878:1634):

> I was very much dissatisfied with the article in the *Spectator* of September 28. It seemed like an attempt to depreciate Mr. Bidder's abilities. Ignorance is not a sufficient excuse, as he was so well known in London. Besides being a "calculating boy," he was possessed of first-rate business ability, and of a rapid and clear insight into what would pay, especially in railway matters. He became a wealthy man, which is a good proof of his possessing that insight.

In the same issue a letter from his son (Bidder, Jr. 1878:1634) points out:

> It would take too long to enumerate all the undertakings initiated and carried through by him, but I may, as examples, refer to the Electric Telegraph Company, of which he was one of the original founders, and amongst the first to perceive the importance of the telegraph as a means of communication. The magnificent Victoria Docks at North Woolwich, and I may say the whole of that now populous district, were the creations of his mind. He was called mad for proposing to construct docks away from London, in what were then marshes and watermeadows, but he had formed a just estimate of the capabilities of the position, and not only succeeded in carrying out his ideas, by the construction of the docks (a work of great engineering skill), but had such confidence in their future, that he persuaded the dock company to buy at the time sufficient land for their extension to treble their original size, and this extension is now being carried out.

Bidder also played a prominent role in most of the parliamentary debates on railway controversies, and was considered the most dangerous of witnesses. Opposing counsel once unsuccessfully attempted to have him excused as a witness before the House of Lords (ICE 1878–79:303) on the grounds that "nature had endowed him with particular qualities that did not place his opponents on a fair footing."

Bidder (1856:275–76) himself gives the following account of how his calculating skills were put to use on the witness stand:

> The Northampton and Peterborough Railway Bill was violently opposed by a compact body of landowners. Among other objections to the Bill, the effect of the works on the floods, in that valley, was particularly insisted on. The great objection was, not so much that we should embay the flood waters, while they were in a state of motion, but that when the flood abated, the water would be retained upon the land, so long as to chill and injure the vegetation. As you well know, learned Counsel, when they think you cannot give them a definite answer adopt a particular style of cross-examination, somewhat to this effect; they ask, "Will you undertake to say that the flood water will not be retained for a week?" and when the witness replies, "I do not think so;" they will say, "Will you undertake to say it will not remain there for a fortnight, or three weeks?" and so they go on, till they make out that your opinion is worth nothing. Mr. Sergeant Kinglake asked me such a question, and I determined I would give him a *bonâ fide* answer. I took the Ordnance map, and measured the area of the land in question, taking care to obtain a full area, so that he could not trip up my reply in that direction. I forget the exact figures but assuming it be 200 acres, I said, "I will take 9 million of feet as the area of 200 acres (which is also an excess), I will assume, that the depth of the flood is 3 feet (which is also an outside quantity), that makes 27 millions of feet upheld on this land." The question was, "How rapidly will that pass through the bridge?" The bridge had, say 1,000 feet of water-way, the head I insisted on, which would be the maximum head occasioned by the retention by the piers of the bridge, was 3 inches; the theoretical velocity due to that was 4 feet, and the practical velocity was 2½ feet; this gave 2,500 cubic feet per second; I therefore immediately answered, that "the flood would be upheld for three hours!" Now I was perfectly well aware that the learned Counsel could not test the process, but at the same time I was determined not to leave anybody the means of picking a hole in my garment; so I gave a *bonâ fide* result, to the manifest discomfiture of my friend of the long robe: and another learned Counsel, with the usual amiable desire of helping "a lame dog over a stile," suggested, (when he saw how they were taken aback,) that, perhaps, his learned Brother might get an equally satisfactory answer if he asked me, how many fish went through in the same time?

Bidder explained his method of finding the result (1856:276):

> A fact to be registered in the mind is, that approximately 220 cubic feet of water will flow, per minute, through a pipe of 12 inches diameter, at an

inclination of 1 in 100. Now from this fact there is no difficulty in ascertaining, approximately, the quantity of water flowing through any sized pipe, at any inclination. Assuming the inclination of a pipe of 3 inches diameter to be 1 in 400, the general laws of hydraulics demonstrate that the velocity will be reduced one-half by the lesser inclination, and one-half by the lesser diameter, the two combined reducing it to one-fourth in velocity; and the diameter of 3 inches as compared to 12 inches, giving an area of one-sixteenth, the result would be that the flow would be reduced (approximately) to one-sixty-fourth, or be about 3½ feet per minute.

I cannot recommend, that the Engineer should rely implicitly upon this mode, for ascertaining the details of his plans, or designs, but it will enable him, in times of leisure, to arrive at the outline of his plan, in the same manner that the Artist prepares the rough sketch of his picture, and subsequently fills in the details.

On another occasion, Bidder was able to discredit the proponents of a rival line before a parliamentary committee. He asked to see the field books of the surveyors of the opposing line, which he glanced at with apparent indifference, as if he saw nothing of interest there. The North Staffordshire line, which Bidder was representing, had challenged the accuracy of the levels of one of their rivals. When the surveyors had completed their presentation, Bidder rose and, on the basis of the intermediate rises and falls, proceeded to demonstrate that if the levels were as represented at one point, they could not be as represented at another distant point. Bidder's testimony successfully blocked the competition.

Bidder seems to have been a generous and cheerful man, very fond of children and animals. He noted one character failing in his speech before the Institution of Civil Engineers (Bidder 1856:279–80), saying:

> probably in consequence of some infirmity of temper, and the habit of early independence of thought and of self-reliance, I have not at all times studied, with the care I ought to have done, the feelings of my Brethren in the Profession, and thus I have not attained with all of them, the popularity I could desire. I hope, however, that my career will not close, before a better feeling is established with all of them; and especially with those who are associated with me in this Institution, of which I have been a Member, for upwards of thirty years.

Bidder was to be associated with the Institution of Civil Engineers for more than 50 years. For nearly 25 years he was a Member of Council, and 1860 and 1861 he filled the presidential chair (ICE 1878–79:305): "In the latter capacity he made a striking figure at the meetings, his massive head, with its plentiful covering of white hair, conveying the impression of an intellectual Jupiter, which was further borne out by the power and dignity with which he presided over the debates."

Bidder retained his calculating ability even in his last years. In the summer of 1877 he retired to Dartmouth, in Devonshire, the region of his childhood. The following fall he was visited by the Reverend E. Johnson, a man of varied intellectual interests, including mathematics. Bidder remarked that one might gain some appreciation of the infinitely small and the infinitely large from a consideration of light. Some faint idea of the vastness of the visible universe is conveyed by the fact that light traveling at about 190,000 miles per second (the value assumed at that time) across space may take many years to reach the earth, while a suggestion of the infinitesimal may be discerned from the fact that 36,918 waves of light, occupying one inch in length, are required to give the impression of red and 64,631 waves are needed to produce violet.

The Reverend Johnson wondered how many light waves must strike the eyes in one second to convey the impression of red, and pulled out a pencil to do the calculation. Bidder immediately said (ICE 1878–79:309): "You need not work it; the number of vibrations will be 444,433,651,200,000."

He then carried out other calculations with equal rapidity. Two days later, on September 28, 1878, he died, and was buried in the churchyard at Stoke Fleming, a neighboring village.

His obituary for the Institution of Civil Engineers concluded (ICE 1878–79:309): "In all save himself his wonderful vitality and energy raised vain hopes, and only when without one pang the spirit parted from its worn-out frame, was it apparent how frail the link that united them had become."

Chapter Twenty-four

Johann Martin Zacharias Dase

"He [Dase] is probably the most outstanding mental calculator of all peoples and all times."

—Dase (1849)

INFORMATION regarding the life of Johann Dase comes largely from his haphazard appearances in the voluminous correspondence between the mathematicians C. F. Gauss and H. C. Schumacher (1861).

Dase was born in Hamburg, June 23, 1824, the son of a distiller. According to a brief biographical sketch Dase (1849) himself wrote, he "developed through his own hard work, his inborn calculating ability and it has, it seems to him, been influenced only very slightly by his early schooling."

By the time he was 15, Dase was making appearances as a professional mental calculator. A year later he met Schulz von Strasnicky, a Viennese mathematician, who showed him how to compute pi by the formula: [1]

$$\pi/4 = \tan^{-1} \tfrac{1}{2} + \tan^{-1} \tfrac{1}{5} + \tan^{-1} \tfrac{1}{8}$$

Dase worked on the problem for two months, and came up with a result to 205 places, which was published in 1844 in *Crelle; Journal für Mathematik* (27:198). Twenty years earlier, William Rutherford of En-

---

[1] Pi is the ratio of the circumference of a circle to its diameter, that is $\pi = c/d$. It is an irrational number, which means that no matter how many decimal places it is computed to, it will never repeat.

gland had calculated pi to 208 places, but his result disagreed with Dase's from the 153rd place on. Dase was correct to 200 decimal places.

Sometime near his twentieth birthday Dase came to Altona, where Schumacher lived. He gave an exhibition of his talents but occasionally miscalculated considerably. He was especially fond of extracting fifth roots because, Schumacher remarked (Gauss and Schumacher 1861 3:382): "He had noticed that at the fifth power the units were the same as they were in the root."

Dase knew almost nothing of mathematics, even though Petersen, a prominent mathematician, had wasted a lot of effort in an attempt to teach him. Dase was at this time traveling about making money from exhibitions of his mental calculations. Schumacher was mystified by this (ibid.):

> Now he has fallen in with an oboist or corporal in the Hamburg Militia, with whom he travels, and lives from his exhibitions, although I can scarcely understand why people would give money to see him solve problems in his head. If there are reliable witnesses, that he can do it, then one gets nothing new from the exhibitions. All you see is a young man with a rather simple-looking face pronounce the right answer after a little while.

A year later Schumacher had the opportunity to test Dase personally. Dase made errors in every problem. A man who accompanied Dase attributed his poor performance to a bad headache and said that the great concentration required in his calculations frequently resulted in such headaches. But Schumacher remained doubtful in a letter dated August 8, 1845 (ibid. 3:32): "He smelled then somewhat of rum, probably accidently, since he is not supposed to drink anything but water."

Schumacher's only remarks on the problems submitted to Dase were that he gave him two six-digit numbers to multiply, which were done only partly mentally:

> He divided, I think, each number into two parts, in which the first contained the highest number and three zeros, the second the three lowest numbers. He calculated the four partial products in his head and wrote down each one with a pencil, which he then added together in his head. Perhaps he has been doing better feats now, since later in Berlin he took one thaler entrance fee, which one would scarcely pay for the feats he did for me.

A year and a half later, Dase was again in Altona, and this time Schumacher (ibid. 5:277) was much more favorably impressed. Dase was able to count at a glance the number of peas thrown on a table, and instantly added the spots on a group of dominoes (117). Schumacher reports that he was able to multiply and divide large numbers in his head, though no specific examples are given. Dase also succeeded in extracting the square root of a 100-digit number in his head in 52 minutes.

Dase was in the process of calculating the natural logarithms to seven places of the numbers from 1 to 1,005,000, of which two-thirds had already been completed. He expected to finish by Easter and was casting about for a publisher, which, Schumacher added, he would have trouble in finding.

By April 1847, Schumacher was describing Dase (ibid. 5:295) as a "strange calculating genius" (*sonderbare Rechengenie*). Dase had mentally multiplied two 20-digit numbers in 6 minutes, two 48-digit numbers in 40 minutes, and two 100-digit numbers in 8¾ hours. Apparently Schumacher himself did not witness these calculations, for he remarks: "The feat [of multiplying two 100-digit numbers] must have made the production rather boring." But apparently he did see a demonstration of Dase's root extracting ability, for he says: "Square roots of a 60-digit number he extracts in an unbelievably short time, though I did not note the time, and I cannot recall just how long it took."

Schumacher also informed Gauss that Dase was anxious to visit him so that Gauss could witness, and presumably comment favorably upon, his abilities. "So that he may blend the useful with the agreeable, however, he doesn't want to come until the students have come back to the lectures, so that he may give what he calls his production there."

In his reply (ibid. 5:296) Gauss was not at all encouraging. He pointed out that the preceding winter a Dane, who gave a similar demonstration, failed even to cover his costs. "In fact, the cost of the trip, the cost of the stay, the cost of the police permit (if, in fact, they will give him one; another traveling performer, Holtey, who wanted to give an exhibition of oratory here was denied papers), the rent, heating, and lighting of a hall, etc., would probably cost more than the admission price would realize."

In any event Gauss was not much impressed with what he had heard of Dase's calculating prowess.

From what I have learned through letters or published papers that have come to my attention, there is little testimony for any outstanding ability for calculation. One must distinguish two things here; an extraordinary memory for numbers and true calculating ability. These are, in fact, two completely separate qualities that may be connected, but are not always. One person might have a very good memory for numbers without being able to calculate well. . . . On the other hand, one can have a superior ability to calculate without having an unusually strong memory for numbers. The latter, Herr Dase has without doubt to an eminent degree. I confess, however, that I can attribute but little worth to it. Calculating ability can only be assessed as to whether someone does as well or better on paper than another person. Whether this is the case with Herr Dase I don't know; only when he tries to multiply two numbers, each one of 100 digits together in his head and it takes him 8¾ hours, that is in the final analysis a crazy waste of time, since a somewhat experienced calculator can do the same on paper in a much shorter time; he could do it in less than half the time. . . . [in any case] has the correctness of his calculations been tested?

Certainly a pertinent question when such immense numbers are involved, but a question to which Schumacher made no direct reply.

By this time Schumacher seems to have become something of an apologist for Dase. In his April 12 reply to Gauss (ibid. 5:300) he reported that Dase also was excellent when computing on paper.

In another letter the following day (ibid. 5:301–2) Schumacher wrote that there was no dissuading Dase from his intention to go to Göttingen, for he wanted to learn from Gauss what really important calculations he should carry out. In this letter, Schumacher also gives some concrete examples of Dase's numerical memory and his calculacting skill. Schumacher first wrote down the number 713,592,853,746. Dase complained that the numbers were written too small; he wasn't sure whether the eighth digit was a five or an eight. Schumacher then wrote 935,173,853,927. This Dase glanced at "for about a second" and was then able to repeat it backward and forward. Dase then offered to multiply this number by a multiple of Schumacher's choice. He selected 7, which was, of course, child's play for Dase, who immediately replied 6,546,216,977,489. As he was leaving, Schumacher asked him whether he remembered these numbers and he promptly strung them together as one number of 25 places and repeated them forward and backward.

Schumacher also had Dase multiply 49,735,827 by 98,536,474. This he did in the ordinary way on paper in 1 minute and 7 seconds: 4,900,793,024,053,998. Dase complained, however, that the necessity to write the number down slowed him up and that he could calculate faster in his head. Schumacher then gave him the numbers 79,532,853 and 93,758,479, which Dase multiplied in his head in 54 seconds:

7,456,879,327,810,587. Dase also counted, at a glance, the number of letters in two different lines of print in books (47 and 63).

Gauss was plainly displeased by Dase's projected visit. In his letter of April 16 (ibid. 5:303), he again pointed out the likelihood of financial failure, and that, furthermore, Dase would probably also fail in his other goal. "I have thought about the problem, but I can't recommend any job that would be proportionate to his abilities. . . ."

Gauss did acknowledge, however, that he personally would like to see Burckhardt's table of factors, completed in published form up to 3,000,000, continued. The problems were that no great calculating ability was needed to do it, and the market for such a work was likely to be very small, so that Dase could expect little reward for his labor. In fact, there was a continuation up to 6,000,000 in manuscript in Berlin, but nobody was willing to bear the costs of publishing it. As far as Dase's being of any use to Gauss himself, he wrote: "I, in my own life, have carried out very large calculations, very many of them, and occasionally I have used outside help; but I fail to remember any case in which purely mechanical calculating help, no matter how high the sum or big the problem, was of any particular use to me."

Gauss could recall a couple of cases in which calculators had been hired (a Professor Petzval had hired 23, paying them very well—a "Kaiserly wage"—to draw up a table for optical lenses), but he knew of no such opportunities at the time.

In the end Dase did not go to Göttingen. Not until two years later, in a letter from Schumacher to Gauss in May (ibid. 6:28), does Dase reappear in their correspondence. Dase had written to Schumacher from Vienna of his intention to continue the factor and prime number table up to ten million. For this the support of the Austrian Academy was needed, but before making a decision, the academy required Gauss's judgment. Schumacher remarked: "It seems to me, if the work is in itself useful, to be a completely appropriate use of such a calculating machine. There is nothing more to it than that; there is no *divinae particula aurae* in him."

Another year passed and Dase again went to Altona (from Vienna). His table of natural logarithms had been printed. He had three copies out of a promised 500, but the rest were in Vienna and would remain there until he came up with the money to pay for the paper. Dase was on his way to England to earn enough by performing to get his books out of hock. Schumacher laments: "It seems to me that the Austrian regime should have offered the poor devil the 326 fl. he needed."

In September of 1850 Dase was still hoping to go to Göttingen to give a "production." Again Gauss (ibid. 6:112) was discouraging:

> . . . I can only repeat that exhibits of his calculating ability before this public, as far as I can judge of their taste, would find only very little success, and would barely pay the cost of the trip, and that here I can scarcely foresee any occasion where his other talents would be of any use to him as far as making money is concerned.

Gauss did, however, in December of 1850, send Dase a lengthy letter outlining the history of tables of factors—quoted in the foreword to Dase's (1862) factor tables—and suggested:

> in my opinion the most immediately desirable task would be the working out of the four million from 6,000,000 to 10,000,000, naturally not to the exclusion of an eventual even longer continuation, given the ability to carry it out. You, yourself, possess several of the needful qualities to do so in outstanding measure: an excellent proficiency and sure grasp of arithmetical operations and, as you have already shown in several cases, an indestructible determination and patience. Thus, should you find yourself in a position, through the sponsorship of the well-to-do, the scientific aspirations of the well-disposed citizens of your country, or by any other means, to undertake such a task, it would be well received by the friends of arithmetic.

As a result of Gauss's recommendation Dase was able to find support from "several promoters of science in Hamburg," somewhat less than a year later. He died ten years later in 1861, at the age of 37. He had, by that time, completed the entire seventh million and all but a small portion of the eighth; he had also finished a considerable part of the ninth and tenth millions. The seventh million was published posthumously, in the year of his death.

Dase was a man determined to leave some mark of his passing on the world, as his search for a really important calculation to carry out attests—a calculation that would be valued by a universally recognized genius like Gauss. Ironically, the tables over which he labored for so many years and which bore his name are a trivial exercise for a modern electronic computer.

Chapter Twenty-five

Henri Mondeux

. . . Certain heads of the establishment of public instruction who claim to know everything and run everything . . . prefer to present for the admiration of their students an ass or a dog savant rather than a child genius. . . . the government, which makes foolish expenditures to nourish orangutans, chimpanzees, and a multitude of other beasts, did an immense wrong in abandoning a child who could throw light on more than one obscure point of mathematical science and who ought to be one of the glories of France.

—Émile Jacoby (1853:16)

THE childhood of Henri Mondeux was very difficult, and he was, in turn, a very difficult child.

Henri was born June 22, 1826, to a woodcutter in Touraine, in the village of Neuvy-le-Roi. He was the third child "of a second bed," as the French say, and his father had two half-grown sons by his first wife. Henri was the youngest, and unwanted, come to trouble his father's old age.

As a small child he was largely left to grow up among the farm animals. His shoulders were broad, his hands thick, and his body athletic.

A little girl in the area took something of a perverse interest in him. According to Émile Jacoby (1853:2), later Henri's teacher and biographer, she was "a kind of vixen in embryo" and "accustomed as she was to being corrected by the whip, she was pleased to torture and whip little Henri every time it took her fancy, and above all when he wouldn't commit the little frolics she enforced on him."

On one occasion he was rescued from drowning by his mother, who, acting on a presentiment, came home early. Henri had fallen into a sewage ditch trying to salvage a sabot he was using as a boat. He came down with scarlet fever a few days later. Jacoby (1853:3) commented: "Almost never in the country is a doctor called until after his care has become useless, and it is painful to say so, [but] the beasts are very often, if not always, taken better care of than the children, nay even than the men. Nature, then, rather than medicine, recalled to life our unhappy navigator."

As soon as he was better he began playing again in the fields and suffered a relapse. His body swelled and remained bloated for more than three weeks. Though he eventually recovered, his health was apparently permanently affected.

He was by this time about 4, and was sent to the fields as a shepherd. It was there that he began to calculate, like Bidder, by arranging pebbles.

Word of his calculating ability spread and people came to ask him questions. Some wished to further his education and offered him lessons in reading and mathematics, but he would never appear at the appointed time. He remained illiterate and ignorant of written arithmetic.

Then his mother died (Jacoby 1853:4): "his mother, who had hardly noticed his entrance into life, but who threw the casual glance of a mother on the heart of a child."

After this the older children, and particularly the "little vixen," treated him brutally, and he reacted by becoming the consternation of the village, attacking those weaker than he and plotting revenge against those who were stronger.

Henri's father had already beaten the next youngest son, Baptiste, to the point where he had left home. Baptiste was one of the few who had shown Henri any kindness, and had played at calculation with him. When the reports of Henri's troublesome behavior came to his father's attention, his solution was to try to beat the boy into grace.

Henri's father wanted to remarry, and when his beatings had no effect, he sent Henri to live with an uncle. The boy left happily, believing any change must be for the better. He was wrong. After much abuse and petty acts of revenge, uncle and nephew gladly parted company.

Henri was then placed in domestic service in the home of a rich man in the area. He took an interest in Henri's education and asked in return for lessons in calculation for his son. The arrangement did not last long. Henri was caught several times stealing from the office, and was sent home to his father.

Henri's new stepmother was taken aback at his return, since his father had conveniently neglected to inform her of his son's existence. He went back to sheep herding, and regained his reputation as a calculator and troublemaker. He was beaten now not only by his father but by his stepmother and older brother Jacques, whom he especially hated.

To escape the beatings he left home and became a vagabond, begging bread. He slept out-of-doors or in barns, flattening himself against the ground to crawl under the doors.

There was a poor mad country woman who sometimes shared with him some black bread and the damp straw of her pallet. Their association convinced the local people that he was a sorcerer, able to bring sickness to their cattle and children. This also explained his preternatural calculating ability.

Henri saw the advantage of such a reputation and did much to enhance it. Once he was caught stealing fruit from an apricot tree. The owner had recently lost a prize cow. Henri said, "Don't harm me, and I will find your cow." Reluctantly the farmer followed him through the woods and the cow was found.

Whether from a genuine desire to reform or because he was weary of his vagabond existence, Henri at this time presented himself to the priest and the schoolmaster.

The priest was happy to welcome Henri back to the flock, and the schoolmaster was delighted by the prospect of teaching a student with such extraordinary calculating ability. This excess of good will was short-lived. The school became a battleground, and Henri was soon barred. The beadle, wielding a whalebone (I suppose because he couldn't find the jawbone of an ass), chased Henri from the church.

But the boy had his revenge. He planted pins in the chair and prayer stool of the beadle, then hid in the church and witnessed his tormentor's painful seating.

Henri was beaten again, and again—not only for the trick he had played on the beadle, but because he would not go to mass on Sundays. The villagers beat his head against stones, tied a rope around his neck, and led him through town, whipping him the while. Even so, the wealthier people would call him in to entertain guests with his calculations, and give him food and money before sending him on his way.

The mayor of Montlouis tried to help by giving Henri an education, but this met with the violent opposition of Henri's brother Jacques, who never having been to school, did not want his brother to go.

Baptiste, the brother who had already fled his father's rages, found

Henri a job tending three cows and a female donkey on the farm of M. Moreau near Tours. His yearly wage was three pairs of sabots, some garlic, and all the black bread he could eat.

One day some young women met him in the fields. He offered to calculate the number of seconds one of the women had lived if she would tell him her age. In the group was the sister of Émile Jacoby, a teacher at the École Néopédique in Tours. When his sister related the incident to him, Jacoby checked the calculation and found it correct.

Shortly thereafter, Jacoby went with some of his pupils in search of Henri. After some hours' wandering about the countryside, he encountered a boy leaning on a crook and staring into space. The boy asked, "What time is it?" Jacoby was convinced that this was the lad he was seeking, and so replied (1854:10): "It is, my friend, half of a third of three-quarters of twelve hours."

Mondeux, apparently accustomed to such puzzling forms of greeting, said: "Ah, one thirty." (the problem is really very easy to do mentally, since $\frac{1}{2} \times \frac{1}{3} = \frac{1}{6}$, $\frac{1}{6} \times \frac{3}{4} = \frac{1}{8}$, and 12 divided by 8 is $1\frac{1}{2}$.) Jacoby asked Henri other questions (lost to history), which, it is reported, were answered with equal accuracy and dispatch.

At last Jacoby asked Henri whether he would like to learn to read and write, so that he could make better use of his ability to calculate. Henri replied enthusiastically in the affirmative, and Jacoby gave him his name and address. Henri asked Jacoby to wait so he could report to his master and return to Tours with him. Jacoby agreed and then waited in vain for a long time for Henri's return. Finally losing patience, he returned to Tours with his students. Henri's memory, apart from numbers and calculating techniques, seems hardly to have existed at all. After leaving Jacoby, he apparently forgot the whole thing until reminded sometime later by a shepherd who had overheard the conversation. As Henri had forgotten the name and address of his future benefactor, it was two months before he was able to locate him.

When Henri arrived, still dressed as a shepherd, the students were so excited that they carried him in on their shoulders.

Jacoby soon had a visit from Henri's father, who recounted, in painful detail, the sins of his youngest son. Jocoby extracted a promise that M. Mondeux would leave his son in the care of the teacher for five years. He said: "Ferocious beasts have been tamed. We will tame your Henri."

"May God grant it," replied M. Mondeux. "I will pray for you and die content."

Jacoby soon learned that these tales of Henri's ferity were not exaggerated. He described him as "a true little savage."

Finally, with the help of some patient pupils, Jacoby succeeded in getting Henri to take his first communion, which seems to have had some beneficial effect. Henri came to the recognition that *something* had to be done about his character.

His studies, however, remained a total loss. Trying to concentrate on anything other than calculation for more than a quarter of an hour exhausted him, and made him ill.

Jacoby was forced to give up trying to educate Henri along with the other students and allowed him to follow his own inclinations.

Henri gave a local demonstration of his talents, and although he had lost much of his former quickness and sureness, the newspaper gave him favorable coverage. He immediately set to work to regain and improve his calculating skills.

Henri was now 14, and since he could not be educated with the other children, Jacoby took him to Paris to the Academy of Sciences in the hope that the government might "adopt" him. The academy members were impressed by his calculating ability and appointed a committee to examine him. Their report, widely reprinted in the newspapers, was written by the famous mathematician Augustin Cauchy (1885).

Unfortunately, the academy report does not provide nearly so detailed an account of Mondeux's methods as one would like. It remarks that, in multiplying, he factored the numbers whenever convenient, since he recognized that the operations become easier when one is dealing with equal factors; that is, they become questions of involution, or raising to powers.

According to the report his method for involution was identical to that given by Newton's binomial theorem. By this means he was able to give the squares and cubes of a great many numbers very quickly, such as $1,204^2$ or $1,006^3$.

I assume that what Henri did was the following:

Since $(a + b)^2 = a^2 + 2ab + b^2$, then
$(1,200 + 4)^2 = 1,200^2 + 2 \times 1,200 \times 4 + 4^2$, or
$1,440,000 + 9,600 + 16 = 1,449,616$

This does not differ substantially from the ordinary method of left-to-right multiplication used by many prodigies (see chapter 14). If, however, Mondeux cubed 1,006 in one step by the binomial theorem, rather than by squaring and then multiplying by 1,006, this would be quite remarkable; that is, if he reasoned:

Since $(a+b)^3 = a^3 + 3a^2b + 3ab^2 + b^3$, then
$(1,000+6)^3 = 1,000^3 + 3 \times 1,000^2 \times 6 + 3 \times 1,000 \times 6^2 + 6^3 =$
$1,000,000,000 + 18,000,000 + 108,000 + 216 =$
$1,018,108,216$

The Academy report does not give any details of how such problems were solved, nor does it say whether Jacoby's instruction played any role in Mondeux's methods. It does mention that he knew most of the squares of integers less than 100, and that he was therefore able, in the presence of the academy, to give the square of 756 (using the fact that he knew the square of 75).

The report credits him with discovering the method for summing an arithmetic progression, and for calculating the fourth and even fifth powers (binomial theorem again?) of some natural numbers.

Henri was asked to "find a number such that its cube augmented by 84 would yield a sum equal to the product of the number by 37."

In other words, he was asked for positive integer values for x in the equation $x^3 + 84 = 37x$. To solve the problem Mondeux transformed this into $(x^3 + 84)/x = 37$. Obviously x is less than six. Five is not a multiple of 84. Four and three can be quickly tested and found to work. Two and one fail, so the foregoing are the only possible positive integers which are solutions.

Mondeux was also asked for two squares whose difference is 133. He immediately replied 66^2 and 67^2. He was told that there was a solution with "simpler" numbers. After a moment he found 6^2 and 13^2.

The method he used is interesting. In general, one wants positive integer values for a and b such that $a^2 - b^2 = c$, where c is given. Let the difference between a and b equal d;

$$\text{then } a = b + d \text{ and } (b+d)^2 - b^2 = c;$$
$$\text{then } b^2 + 2bd + d^2 - b^2 = c;$$
$$\text{therefore, } b = \frac{c - d^2}{2d}.$$

The trick is to find d such that b is a positive integer. Then a is simply $b + d$.

In the case where c is odd, there is always a very simple solution. Let $d = 1$; then $b = (c-1)/2$ and $a = b + 1$. That is why Mondeux immediately found 66 and 67 as values for a and b when c was specified as 133. He simply took half of 132 as b.

Finding the other solution is a little more difficult. It is clear that d^2 must be less than c, and d must be odd. Then it is only a matter of testing odd integers of 11 or less to see whether any work. Most values can be discarded rather quickly, for one reason or another; for example, d cannot equal five, since in that case $c - d^2$ would have to be a multiple of five, and 133 less 25 would have to end in five or zero, which it obviously does not.

The committee was curious to learn how long it would take for Henri to memorize a 24-digit number, arranged in four groups of six digits each. The time required was five minutes. This seems rather a long time, but perhaps Henri saw little point in the exercise since it was not connected with any calculation.

The committee found that Henri had an amazing aptitude for learning and putting to use methods which they showed him for simplifying arithmetic operations. They found that he could, when calculating, shut out environmental distractions.

On the other hand, they found his memory for names of people and places to be quite poor. Nor would he take much interest in geometry. The construction of squares and cubes interested him less than the numbers by which he represented them.

The committee was quite satisfied with Mondeux's moral progress, finding him "a religious child, endearing and docile."

The report concluded with a consideration of Henri's future. They concurred with Jacoby's view that he was not suited to be educated with other pupils, and recommended that the French government furnish Jacoby with the means by which to advance Mondeux's calculating abilities in the hope that he might some day distinguish himself in a career in science.

The report of the academy marked the apex of Mondeux's fame. He and Jacoby traveled about, and Henri gave demonstrations (often at schools), but the public at large ceased to know of him. Jacoby gave up on the idea of teaching Henri anything, and concentrated instead on learning from him and encouraging him to investigate this or that area of calculation.

Jacoby wrote, with Mondeux's help, a book entitled *Caractères de divisibilité des nombres par des valeurs données de 1 à 50*. The book concerns Mondeux's methods for determining whether a number is a multiple of a given integer from 1 to 50.

The general question of the divisibility of numbers was no doubt suggested by the traditional methods of checking arithmetic problems by "casting out nines" and the "elevens test." To determine the remainder of a number upon division by nine, add up the digits in the number; if the result is more than one digit, repeat the process until only one digit remains (nines or combinations of digits totaling nine can be ignored, or "cast out"; thus the name). If the digits total to nine, the number is divisible by nine; any other total is the remainder upon division by nine.

Many cases resolve themselves into simpler ones. For example, to determine if a number is divisible by 21, Mondeux checked whether it was divisible by both 3 and 7.

An example of a complex case is his method for determining whether a number is divisible by 37.

Divide the number into groups of three digits starting from the right (that is, in the ordinary manner of inserting commas in large numbers). Add together the first digit of each group of three starting from the right (the units, thousands, millions, etc. digits) and multiply this sum by 4. Next add together the second digit of each group of three (tens, thousands, ten millions . . .) and multiply the result by 3. Now add the leftmost digits in each group of three and multiply the sum by 7. Add together the products obtained for the first two groups and subtract from this sum the product obtained for the third group. If this result is zero or a multiple of 37, the original number is divisible by 37.

For example, is 918,695,348 divisible by 37?

$$8 + 5 + 8 = 21 \qquad 21 \times 4 = 84 \qquad 84 + 42 = 126$$
$$4 + 9 + 1 = 14 \qquad 14 \times 3 = 42 \qquad 126 - 126 = 0$$
$$3 + 6 + 9 = 18 \qquad 18 \times 7 = 126$$

Therefore, 918,695,348 is divisible by 37.

The book very nearly never saw print. Jacoby lost some manuscripts at sea, and twice various books and manuscripts were stolen. Of the last theft, he wrote (1853:vii): "It is deplorable that the police, so active, so vigilant, so wise in certain given circumstances, should be so powerless when it is a question of finding certain thieves."

Furthermore the mathematician, Cauchy, was discouraging. He said that the principles underlying Mondeux's methods were already well known, and that it was difficult to see to whom the book would prove useful. But Jacoby, encouraged by friends, decided to go ahead.

Mondeux's intuitive knowledge of algebra is astonishing, particularly for a person whose intellectual accomplishments in other areas were nil. Mitchell (1907) suggests that Jacoby's teaching may have been responsible, but this is unlikely. No doubt Jacoby directed Mondeux's attention to certain problems, but the sophisticated solutions are beyond Jacoby's modest knowledge of algebra. In fact, it is evident that the renowned geometrician, Cauchy, was not familiar with certain facts of elementary number theory known to Mondeux, for example, that every odd natural number is the difference between the squares of two successive natural numbers.

The *Nouvelle biographie générale* (1865:30) stated: "it is not known today [1860] what has become of him." According to Scripture (1891:21), Mondeux died in 1861.

Chapter Twenty-six

Truman Henry Safford

What to do with this remarkable boy was the question. A neighbouring bank offered him a thousand dollars a year to enact the part of a machine for calculating interest. Another admirer of genius, equally disposed to turn the penny by it, advised his father to carry him about the country as a show; in the hope, no doubt, that his intellectual greatness might stand as well in the market as the physical littleness of General Tom Thumb. If this plan had been carried into effect, we should have had him in England no doubt; when, *of course,* her Majesty and her principal nobility would have treated him with at least the distinction they lavished, so honourably to themselves and to the character of the British court, upon the dwarf!
—*Chambers's Edinburgh Journal* (1847 8:267)

S AFFORD was born January 6, 1836, in Royalton, Vermont. He was, like Zerah Colburn, the son of a Vermont farmer, but was more fortunate in that both of his parents were former teachers and people of considerable intelligence.

He is described as a sickly, nervous child, likely to die before reaching manhood. *Chambers's Edinburgh Journal* (1847 8:265) said of him:

Truman Henry Safford . . . is the name of a boy now ten years of age, who, if he lives, and continues to enjoy mental and corporeal health, will in all probability be one of the most remarkable men America has ever produced. . . . In his first year he was so delicate, so fragile, that perhaps no other mother could have reared him; but from the wan unearthly lips of the infant there came questions that made the listeners start and thrill by their preternatural intelligence.

In fact, Stafford lived to the age of 65 and became a respected astronomer.

The boy seems to have first taken an interest in arithmetic at the age of 3, with the encouragment of his father, who seems to have had some talent and love for the subject. But it was not until he was 6 that his parents had an inkling of the proportions of his talent for mental calculation. One day he (ibid.) "remarked to his mother, that if he knew how many rods it was around his father's large meadow, he could tell the measure in barleycorns. When his father came in, she mentioned it to him; and he, knowing the dimensions of the field, made a calculation, and told the boy it was 1040 rods; the lad, after a few minutes, gave 617,760 as the distance in barleycorns, 'in his head,' as the phrase is."

A rod, though often a measure of area, may also be a measure of length, varying locally from 5½ TO 8 yards. Safford assumed 594 barleycorns to the rod. A barley corn is one-third inch, so Stafford took a rod to 5½ yards.

Over the next two years, Safford seems to have acquired a considerable knowledge of arithmetic, algebra, and geometry.

In his eighth year, he contracted typhoid fever and was slow to recover. During his recovery he asked his mother for *Day's Algebra* and his slate and immediately embarked on an extensive calculation; when he found himself too weak to continue it, he wept long and bitterly.

In the spring of 1845, Chester Dewey, a mathematician, wrote of him (ibid.):

> He is not one of the calculators by instinct, if I may use the language, but a real regular reasoner, on correct and established principles, taking the easiest and most direct course. As he had Hutton's Mathematics, and wanted some logarithms, his father told me he computed the logarithms from 1 to 60 by the formula given by Hutton, which were afterwards found to be the same in a table of logarithms for the same number of decimals. He is a wonderful boy. His mind seems bent on the study of mathematics, and he takes his books about with him, that he may study some every day. He was also much interested in three lectures on chemistry that he attended. He seems very able to make a practical application of his knowledge. His mind is too active; and when roused in the night, or made wakeful by his nervous temperament, it is often difficult to arrest the current of his thoughts on some interesting calculation. The study of mathematical relations seems to be amusement to him.

In the spring of 1845 he visited Hanover, home of Dartmouth College, where he met faculty members and was given some new books.

Upon his return home he decided to devise an almanac, which was published in the fall of 1845. Safford was 9.

The next year he produced four almanacs—for Cincinnati, Boston, Philadelphia, and Vermont. *Chambers's Edinburgh Journal* reported (ibid.):

> While getting up the Cincinnati one, he became much abstracted in his manner, wandered about with his head down, talking to himself, &c. as is his manner while originating new rules. His father approached him, and inquired what he was doing, and found that he had originated a new rule for getting moon risings and settings, accompanied with a table which saves a full one-fourth of the work in casting moon risings. This rule, with a number of others for calculating eclipses, is preserved with his manuscript almanacs in the library of Harvard University.

Two editions of his almanac sold out—one of 7,000 and the other of 17,000 copies. It also seems he discovered a means of reducing by a third the amount of calculating required to compute eclipses.

When Safford was ten he was tested by a Reverend Henry W. Adams of Middletown, Connecticut, who left an account of the problems posed and Safford's responses. The first of Adam's questions was (ibid.:266):[1] "Can you tell me how many seconds old I was last March, the 12th day, when I was twenty-seven years old?" Safford supposedly replied at once "85,255,200." Let us hope not, since this answer is off by a factor of ten; the answer Safford must have given him was 852,055,200, which is correct, figuring 365.25 days to a year.

Adams next said: "The hour and minute hands of a clock are exactly together at 12 o'clock: when are they next together?" This answer too was immediate, "one hour, five and five-eleventh minutes." This is something of an old saw, designed to encourage the answerer to waste his energies applying calculus when the problem can be solved more simply by common sense and ingenuity—for example, since the hands crossed exactly 11 times in 12 hours, the time required is 12/11 hours. Since Safford surely had a broad background in such problems, it is likely that he had encountered this one before.

Adams asked: "A man and his wife usually drank out a cask of beer in twelve days; but when the man was from home, it lasted the woman thirty days. How many days would the man alone be drinking it?"

Safford, as was his wont, went through some physical contortions, but

---

[1] Not all these problems were done entirely mentally—in some cases Safford was aided by a slate, but it is not always clear from Adams' account which were so solved.

quickly replied, "twenty days." This again is a fairly elementary problem for a skilled calculator.

Next Adams asked: "What number is that which, being divided by the product of its digits, the quotient is three; and if 18 be added, the digits will be inverted?"

This time Safford "flew out of his chair, whirled round, rolled up his wild flashing eyes, and said in about a minute, '24.' "

I do not know how Safford went about solving this, but it is fairly easy to do by trial and error. Obviously the number is a multiple of three. Furthermore, if adding 18 to it inverts the digits, then the units digit must exceed the tens digit by two. The only two-digit numbers for which this is true are 24 and 57, and only the former fits the other conditions.

Adams next posed: "Two persons, A and B, departed from different places at the same time, and travelled towards each other. On meeting, it appeared that A had travelled 18 miles more than B, and that A could have gone B's journey in 15¾ days, but B would have been 28 days in performing A's journey. How far did each travel?" This provoked even more agitated behavior by Safford: "He flew round the room, round the chairs, writhing his little body as if in agony, and in about a minute sprang up to me and said, 'A travelled 72 miles, and B 54 miles—didn't they?' "

The answer is correct. As an algebra problem this presents considerable difficulty.

Adams' next question is a good example of how a problem of considerable algebraic difficulty can sometimes be easily solved mentally by the use of a little ingenuity: "What two numbers are those whose sum, multiplied by the greater, is equal to 77, and whose difference, multiplied by the less, is equal to 12?" This brought on more eye rolling and scurrying around before Safford produced the answer, seven and four, in about a minute.

The problem calls for a solution to the two equations $x(x+y) = 77$ and $y(x-y) = 12$. Assuming, as the wording of the problem suggests, that the numbers called for are positive integers, it is evident that x in the first equation must equal 7, since 77 can be factored only into 7 times 11; y must therefore be 4. Substituting these numbers into the second equation verifies this answer.

Why then, did Safford take approximately a minute to find this answer? Possibly because he recognized that there is another pair of values for x and y satisfying these equations ($x = \sqrt{60.5}$ and $y = \sqrt{4.5}$), but that it would be difficult to compute these. He therefore offered the integer answer to see whether it would satisfy his questioner, and it did.

"Well," said Adams, "the sum of two numbers is 8, and the sum of their cubes 152. What are the numbers?" Safford immediately replied "3 and 5." This is also very easy assuming the numbers called for are integers.

Adams remarks: "Now, in regard to these sums, they are the hardest in *Davies's Algebra*." Two things should be noted: first, Adams lists *Davies's Algebra* as one of Safford's books, and Safford had a very retentive mind. Second, as we have seen, many of the problems are rather easy by common sense and trial and error, although the algebraic solutions may be onerous.

The next series of problems involve no difficulties in conception, but the mental arithmetic is certainly very difficult.

Adams continued (ibid):

I took him into the mensuration of solids, said I, "What is the entire surface of a regular pyramid, whose slant height is 17 feet, and the base a pentagon, of which each is 33.5 feet?" In about two minutes, after amplifying round the room, as his custom is, he replied, "3354.5558." "How did you do it?" said I. He answered, "Multiply 33.5 by 5, and that product by 8.5, and add this product to the product obtained by squaring 33.5, and multiplying the square by the tabular area taken from the table corresponding to a pentagon." On looking at this process, it is strictly scientific. Add to this the fact, that I was examining him on different branches of mathematics requiring the application of different rules, and that he went from one sum to another with rapidity, performing the work in his mind when asked, and the wonder is still greater.

Then I desired him to find the surface of a sphere. "Hence," said I, "required the area of the surface of the earth, its diameter being 7921 miles?" He replied as quick as thought, "197,111,024 square miles." To do it, he had to square 7921, and multiply the product by 3.1416. Then I wished him to give me the solidity of a sphere; therefore, said I, "What is the solidity of the earth, the mean diameter being 7918.7 miles?" He writhed about, flew rapidly about the room, flashed his eyes, and in about a minute said, "259,992,792,083." To do this, he multiplied the cube of 7918.7 by 5236. [This should be 0.5236.] I believe he used a few figures in doing this sum, but it was unnecessary, as he performed a much larger one in his mind, as I shall soon show.

I then asked him to give the cube root of 3,723,875. He replied quicker than I could write it, and that mentally, "155 — is it not? Yes." Then said I, "What is the cube root of 5,177,717?" Said he, "173." Of "7,880,599?" He instantly said, "199." These roots he gave, calculated wholly in his mind, as quick as you could count one.

I then asked his parents if I might give him a hard sum to perform *mentally*. They said they did not wish to tax his mind too much, nor often to its full capacity, but were quite willing to let me try him once. Then said I, "Multiply, *in your head,* 365,365,365,365,365 [This number should be identical to the second one.] by 365,365,365,365,365,365!" He flew round the room like a top, pulled his pantaloons over the top of his boots, bit his hand, rolled his eyes in their sockets, sometimes smiling and talking, and then seeming to be in agony, until, in not more than one minute, said he,

"133,491,850,208,566,925,016,658,299,941,583,225!"

The boy's father, Rev. C. N. Smith, and myself, had each a pencil and slate to take down the answer, and he gave it to us in periods of three figures each, as fast as it was possible for us to write them. And what was still more wonderful, he began to multiply at the left hand, and to bring out the answer from left to right, giving first "133,491," &c. Here, confounded above measure, I gave up the examination. The boy looked pale, and said he was tired. He said it was the largest sum he had ever done!

At 14, Safford calculated the elliptic elements of the first comet of 1849. He graduated from Harvard in 1854, at the age of 18, and remained there for several years working in the observatory. In 1865 he became Professor of Astronomy at the University of Chicago and Director of the Dearborn Observatory.

Safford discovered many new nebulas and worked on the preparation of star catalogs. In 1876 he became Professor of Astronomy at Williams College, where he remained until his death.

Chapter Twenty-seven

Jacques Inaudi

He [Inaudi] gets up very late and comes to breakfast at noon with his eyes swollen with sleep. The afternoon passes peacefully at cards or billiards; after dinner in the evening, he leaves for the theater or "café-concert," where he gives his performance; he does not return until deep in the night. Apart from some "séances" in town, every day repeats the same series of activities, which follow one another mechanically. Here we have a stereotype, with no desire to change an existence which flatters his self-esteem and serves all his needs.

—Alfred Binet (1894:34)

INAUDI, the son of a poor Italian family, was born in the Piedmont on October 13, 1867. His father was a ne'er-do-well, who squandered the family's meager resources. He was never able to hold down a job for long, and for some years attempted to live off his son's calculating ability.

None of the other children showed any ability for calculation (one was a cobbler, another a waiter, etc.), though they tried to learn when they saw the advantages this talent bestowed upon their brother. Alfred Binet, the famed nineteenth-century psychologist who studied Inaudi, remarks on the possibility of prenatal influence (1894:27), though with considerable reservations. Inaudi's manager, Thorcey, was told that Inaudi's mother developed a mania for calculation during her pregnancy with him. It seems she had been party to père Inaudi's reckless spending and sought economies to ward off the bill collectors.

As a small child Inaudi was a shepherd. At about age 6 he began to calculate to alleviate the tedium of guarding the flock. Unlike Mondeux and Bidder, even at the outset he did not use pebbles or other tokens to represent numbers—all his calculations were done mentally. Calculating was to him a matter of words taught him by his elder brother. Neither of the boys could read at that time; in fact, Inaudi did not learn to read or write until he was 20.

After learning the numbers to 100, he began to calculate with what he knew. Later, he asked his brother to teach him the numbers above 100. If his brother introduced him to the multiplication table, Inaudi could not recall it, but he was able, he said, by the age of 7 to multiply two five-digit numbers in his head.

Inaudi soon gave up the life of a Piedmontese shepherd to join his brother in a vagabond existence in Provence—his brother ground an organ while Jacques kept track of the marmot and the donations.

To increase the take, it was decided that Inaudi should do calculations. He helped the peasants with their computations, and gave demonstrations in the cafés. An impresario got hold of him and arranged for shows in large cities.

In 1880, at the age of 12, he came to Paris for the first time, where he was presented to the Société d'Anthropologie by Paul Broca (Binet 1891:29).[1] Broca reported that Inaudi's head was very large and irregular, and found some deformations. He found Inaudi to be intelligent, lively, and not at all shy.

In 1892 Inaudi, then 24, was examined by Binet and Charcot, the latter a professor at the Salpêtrière. In the 12 years since Broca had studied him, Inaudi had learned to read and write, and the scope of his arithmetic abilities had increased. He was quite small—one meter, 52 centimeters (a little below five feet) and rather thick-set with a head much too large for his body. (In his childhood, it was thought that he could not survive because of this disproportion.) Beyond this, Charcot's physiological examination revealed nothing of interest.

In private Inaudi was found to be mild, modest, calm, and very reserved. In public he displayed more aplomb—as a child he was known for mischief, as an adult he was rather more ironic. During his performance he would explain his methods and add that nothing could be simpler, and that anyone could do as much. He was the first to acknowl-

---

[1] Broca is an important figure in the history of medicine and anthropology. (*Broca's Brain*, the title of Carl Sagan's 1979 bestseller, refers to him.) Broca is best known today for his discovery that the third convolution of the left frontal lobe of the cerebral cortex (Broca's area) is largely responsible for articulate speech.

edge his errors, and rarely lost his temper. Like most performers who interact with the audience, he had a stock of ripostes.

Although modest, he was naturally very proud of his calculating ability, and discomfited by comparisons with other calculators.

Binet found that, because of his lack of education, Inaudi's conversation was limited, but that he had considerable natural intelligence. Binet and his colleagues were most impressed by the speed with which Inaudi mastered the use of the d'Arsonval chronometer (a timing device), since most people were quite slow to comprehend the appropriate responses.

Inaudi read the newspapers, took an interest in politics, and played cards and billiards. He ate and slept a lot, dreaming occasionally of numbers (the only dreams of which he had any distinct waking memory); he liked sex (Binet 1894:32: "Les besoins sexuels sont chez lui bien développés."). Sometimes, pondering a numerical problem, he was lost to his surroundings and heard no one.

Inaudi's forgetfulness with respect to everyday matters contrasted with his excellent memory for figures. His manager remarked that he could not remember towns in which he had previously appeared. He was always leaving behind his gloves or his cane, and forgetting appointments.

Inaudi's performances consisted of: a subtraction involving two 21-digit numbers; the addition of five numbers of six digits each; squaring a four-digit number; a division (the size of the numbers is not clear); the cube root of a nine-digit number and the fifth root of a 12-digit number.

During his performances, Inaudi would stand with his back to the blackboard, arms folded, facing the audience. He never looked at the board. Members of the audience would say the numbers, Inaudi would repeat them to make certain that he understood, and his manager would write out the numbers on the blackboard as Inaudi dictated them. After the figures had been chalked up, his manager read them off loudly, and carefully. Sometimes Inaudi would repeat the numbers along with his manager. After all the numbers had been written upon the blackboard, Inaudi would repeat them before beginning his calculations. In total Inaudi thus repeated the figures three times to engrave them on his mind.

While calculating, Inaudi would whisper numbers and make various gestures. He was not disturbed by any noise around him or objections from the crowd, and in order to keep the audience from losing patience, he would make comments now and again.

Like virtually all stage calculators, he would provide the day of the week for dates suggested by the audience; Binet says he replied with (1895:38) "une rapidité surprenante."

Inaudi's performances were quite short. To do his six calculations and day-date identifications required only ten or twelve minutes.

Inaudi's modus operandi, with his back to the blackboard, imposes a much greater strain on the memory than working with figures visible to the calculator, who can then write down results as they are obtained.

On the other hand, some of the problems tackled by Inaudi are not difficult if one can keep the figures in mind; for example, the subtraction of one 20-digit number from another is quite easy, as is the extraction of the integer roots.

How many digits had Inaudi to memorize in a single performance? Binet (1894:38) concluded that the number must exceed two hundred, including the numbers in the problems, the answers, and the partial results. (The last may represent only a short-term rather than a long-term memory load.)

The method of presentation seems to have encouraged the audience to exaggerate the number of digits written on the blackboard. Some members of the audience estimated the number to be at least 400; Thorcey said the number of digits was rarely less than 300. The illusion of such a large number of digits was created largely by Thorcey, who solved the problems in written form while Inaudi solved them mentally. In working the solution, Thorcey provoked comment by occasionally making accidental mistakes, and more often, committing purposeful errors. He also worked very slowly, which of course made Inaudi's calculations seem all the faster.

Inaudi's speed at calculation was frequently exaggerated by observers, since he often began calculating while the data of a problem were being repeated. By the time he announced "je commence," he had usually completed computing part of the problem.

At the Salpêtrière, Inaudi was able, at the end of a two-hour session during which he was given various problems to solve, to repeat all the digits correctly—a total of 230. (It is not clear from Binet's [1894:39] remarks whether this figure included only the problems, the problems and answers, or the problems, answers, and intermediate results. It was probably the first, but the wonder is that Inaudi was able to do this every weekday night and twice on Sunday.)

Binet set out to determine how many digits Inaudi could learn after hearing them only once. Previous experiments by Gaultier on ordinary persons obtained the following results (Binet 1894:46) for the average number of digits recalled:

1. Seven, when the numbers were pronounced in a monotonous voice.
2. Nine, when the numbers were pronounced rhythmically.
3. Ten, when the numbers were grouped in pairs.
4. Twelve, when the numbers were pronounced rhythmically in pairs.

Inaudi's usual method of memorization was to have his manager read off the digits in groups of three, announcing, after each group, its value (that is, thousands, millions, etc.). Inaudi would then repeat each group of three along with its value.

This method was used to test the limit of Inaudi's memory for digits on a single hearing. The numbers were read to Inaudi in groups of three, but without an indication of their value—Inaudi would repeat each group of three, adding the value. In this way he was able to memorize and repeat 36 digits, but with visible difficulty. He said it was easier for him to repeat 400 digits resulting from various problems posed to him at a performance, as the numbers acquired an interest from their connection with particular problems—as opposed to a monotonous series of 36 digits.

A few minutes later he was to try 51 digits, to which he agreed reluctantly, and with reason. According to Binet (1894:49): "He omitted some, transposed some, he made errors of about ten digits; 42 were repeated exactly." Binet took 42 digits as Inaudi's limit for memorizing numbers at a single hearing.

This experiment is far from satisfactory, for various reasons. First, when numbers are transposed or omitted, how does one decide which digits are to be considered correct? If two digits are transposed, for example, is this one error or two? What if Inaudi were capable of correctly identifying 50 of 70 digits? Only if all the digits are correctly recalled can a sensible judgment be made regarding an individual's ability to retain digits after one hearing. (Another alternative would be to accept the first n digits recited without an error.)

Second, a single trial is hardly a satisfactory procedure. Inaudi's abilities no doubt varied considerably from time to time. Binet could have made a number of trials and taken the maximum—although the average number of digits Inaudi could retain under such conditions would have been of more interest.

Binet also sought to determine how long it would take Inaudi to learn 100 digits. Inaudi's manager first read off 18 digits in groups of three.

Inaudi then repeated them, slowly and with some difficulty. In this manner Inaudi learned the first 36 digits in a minute and a half; the first 57 in 4 minutes (the third batch of numbers consisted of 21 digits); the first 75 digits in 5 minutes and 30 seconds, and 105 digits in 12 minutes. (It seems that, by mistake, they went beyond the intended 100 digits.) Binet found that the digits in the middle of the series gave Inaudi the most difficulty.

Again, this experiment is not satisfactory. The times, given in round numbers, suggest carelessness on the part of the experimenters. The test, undertaken at the end of the rigorous session, found Inaudi at less than his best. (He felt that under different circumstances he could lower the time to about 10 minutes.)

Binet found that, although Inaudi was able to repeat the 230 digits of a performance given 12 hours previously, his memory hardly extended beyond the latest performance. Like some other calculators (e.g., Marathe) he more or less voluntarily eradicated the memory of previous performances unless there was something of special interest.

On the other hand, he tended to remember numbers which were learned under peculiar circumstances, were the object of a bet, or were connected with some new problem.

After Inaudi had recited for him the 230 digits of his latest performance, Binet asked him if he could repeat these digits at Binet's conference on calculating prodigies at the Salpêtrière. Inaudi agreed. But, at the conference, after he had committed to memory an equal number of digits in a demonstration of calculation, he found that he could not accurately summon up all of the old series of digits.

Here are some samples of problems (Binet 1894:76) solved by Inaudi. To solve many of these problems formally would involve considerable algebraic unpleasantness, which can often be avoided by a combination of common sense and trial and error (particularly if it can be assumed that the answer is an integer).

1. Find the number whose square and cube roots differ by 18. Answer: 729, given in one minute, fifty-seven seconds.

Obviously, the answer must be both a perfect cube and a perfect square. The smallest such number is 64 (4^3 and 8^2), but the other condition is not met. The next such number is 729 (9^3 and 27^2). It is difficult to believe that Inaudi took so long to solve this problem.

2. Find a two-digit number such that the difference between four times the first digit and three times the second is seven; and that, when reversed is the number reduced by 18.

This problem has no solution, as Inaudi discovered in two minutes.

3. Find a four-digit number such that the sum of the digits is 25; the hundreds digit plus the thousands digit is equal to the tens digit; the sum of the tens digit and the thousands digit is equal to the units digit; and if the digits of the number are reversed, it is augmented by 8,082.

Inaudi (Binet 1894:76) explained his reasoning in solving this problem: "Since the number is augmented by 8082 when reversed, the thousands digit must therefore be 1 and the units digit 9; I therefore subtracted 9, which is the units digit, from 25; this left 16 for the other three digits. Since the thousands digit and the hundreds digit equal the tens, the tens digit must necessarily be half of 16, that is to say 8." To obtain the hundreds digit it was only necessary to subtract the sum of the three from 25. The number sought was 1,789.

The next series of problems were given to Binet by Thorcey, Inaudi's manager (Binet 1894:77):

1. The sum of two numbers is 18; multiplied together they equal 17. The numbers are, of course, 17 and 1.

2. The sum of two numbers is 1,254 and their product is 353,925. The numbers are 825 and 429.

This one is difficult unless one is good at factoring large numbers; according to Binet, Inaudi was not.

3. Find three numbers such that their sum is 43 and the sum of their cubes is 17,299. The numbers are 25, 11, and 7. Another difficult problem.

4. Find a four-digit number, such that the sum of the digits is 16; the tens digit is double the thousands; the units digits is equal to three times the thousands digit plus the tens digit. Reversing the digits increases the number by 3,456.

$$a + b + c + d = 16$$
$$c = 2a$$
$$d = 3a + c$$

Substituting for d and c:

$$8a + b = 16$$

Since a and b are positive integers less than 10, either $a = 1$ and $b = 8$, or $a = 2$ and $b = 0$. Assume the latter. Then $c = 4$ and $d = 10$. Impossible, so the number is 1,825, and this checks when the digits are reversed.

5. The sum of three numbers is 65; the sum of the cubes of these numbers multiplied by their squares equals 70,405,013. Find the numbers.

Algebraically, $a + b + c = 65$

$$(a^3 + b^3 + c^3)(a^2 + b^2 + c^2) = 70{,}405{,}013$$

The numbers are 32, 21, and 12.

6. It is 863 kilometers from Paris to Marseille. A train leaves Paris at 8:15 A.M. for Marseille traveling at a speed of 39 kilometers per hour. Another train leaves Marseille for Paris at 10:30 A.M. at a speed of 46 kilometers, 500 meters per hour. How far from these two cities will the trains be when they meet?

Inaudi answered that the trains would meet at 7 hours 31 minutes, 13⁴/₆ seconds in the evening; 419 kilometers 451 meters 80 centimeters from Marseille, and 443 kilometers 548 meters 20 centimeters from Paris.

The answer, though very exact, is not exactly right. In 2 hours and 15 minutes the train from Paris will travel 87¾ kilometers. Let x be the travel time after 10:30 until the trains meet; then

$39x + 87.75 + 46.5x = 863$
$85.5x = 775.25$
x is approximately 9 hours, 4 minutes, 2¹/₁₀ seconds.

Thus the trains will meet at a little past 7:34 P.M. At that time the train from Paris will have traveled (about) 441 kilometers, 372 meters, and 80.6 centimeters; the train from Marseille will have gone (about) 421 kilometers, 627 meters, 19.3 centimeters.

Just what went wrong with Inaudi's calculation I do not know. I can see nothing in the statement of the problem or the answer which suggests a misprint that could account for the discrepancy.

Books on calculation often recommend that one learn to suppress words such as "times," "plus," and "carry"; and thereby accelerate one's calculations.

When Inaudi's attention was called to such shortenings, he said, in a lukewarm fashion, that he sometimes suppressed these (Binet 1894:105) "parasite words." But the experimenters noticed that during his calculations, Inaudi would mutter distinctly enough to be understood (Binet 1894:105), "multiplié par, je retiens" ("multiplied by, I keep").

Inaudi had a long and successful career as a performer, appearing all over Europe and even in the United States. He retired in 1934 and died in 1950 at the age of 83, in relative poverty. But even in his old age he continued to amuse his neighbors with his calculations.

Fred Barlow, author of *Mental Prodigies* (1952:48), reports that he undertook a series of tests of Inaudi's calculating ability.

> Considerable time was spent in the preparation of the problems before these were placed before him for solution. They were all of the type given in this book, but what was most impressive—even uncanny—was the promptitude of the responses. No blackboard was employed on this occasion and the answers were correct every time. When Inaudi was asked if he could give any indication of his methods all that he could say was that he "heard the answers."

Barlow (1952:48) added: "It was exactly as if he had known beforehand just what questions would be asked and had carefully worked out all the solutions."

Regrettably, Barlow does not give the problems, but after so many years in the business, it may have been difficult to find something new to spring on Inaudi.

Chapter Twenty-eight

—

Périclès Diamandi

IN 1893, a Greek in his mid-twenties, Périclès Diamandi, presented himself to the French Academy of Sciences, where he wished to demonstrate his ability at mental calculation. A commission was appointed but no report was issued. Instead the case was turned over to Binet and Charcot to investigate. They issued a brief note in the *Revue philosophique* for June 1893; a much fuller account is given in Binet (1894).

Diamandi's family was in the grain business. He was born in 1868 on the Ionian island of Pylaros. He first attended school at the age of 7 and throughout his academic career remained at the head of his class. In 1884 he left school and went into the family business. It was then that he discovered his aptitude for mental calculation, which was quite useful in his business affairs.

Diamandi's family was large—he was one of 14 children, of which, at the time of Binet's study, only 5 were living. A sister and a younger brother appear also to have had an unusual ability for mental calculation, but no details are given by Binet. Tocquet (n.d.:21–22) briefly discusses his sister, Uranie. Diamandi believed he got his talent from his mother, who had a good memory for a variety of things.

By the time of Binet's investigation, Diamandi had left commerce, and there is no indication as to how he supported himself—possibly he was sufficiently well fixed so as not to have to work. He read a great deal, including everything available on mental calculation. He had also written some novels and poetry, apparently unpublished. He knew five languages: Greek, Rumanian, French, German, and English.

Diamandi and Inaudi, his fellow subject in Binet's investigation of mental calculation, were a study in contrast. Diamandi was a visual calculator—Inaudi was auditory. As a child Diamandi had not been interested in mental calculation—for Inaudi, it was a passion. Diamandi was large and strong—Inaudi quite small.

Diamandi happened one day upon a newspaper account of a performance by Inaudi, and determined to attempt something similar. He gave performances in Greece and Bucharest. Finally he went to Paris in order to measure himself against his model. He repeatedly asked Binet to set up a face-to-face competition between him and Inaudi, in order to establish who was the faster calculator and who could learn more digits. Binet never agreed, which was just as well for Diamandi's ego. Inaudi was much the better calculator.

When Diamandi visualized anything—a house, a friend, a series of numbers, etc., he saw the objects of his mental vision in a wide space surrounded by many grayish "masses" (presumably something like clouds).

Diamandi had colored audition for the days of the week, and for other words and names as well:

> Sunday: white and gray
> Monday: light maroon
> Wednesday: white and black
> Thursday: coffee red
> Friday: white and black
> Saturday: coffee red

Perhaps Tuesday, omitted in the original, was too dismal to merit a color.

Some other associations were: Inaudi—blue; Charcot—bright white; psychology—black.

Numbers appeared to Diamandi's mental vision as though written in his own hand, and not as they were written out by the experimenter— four and five, in particular, appeared in his peculiar representation of them.

But the method of presentation was not entirely without effect. If the numbers were presented on a blackboard, they appeared in his imagination as though written in white on a black background. If some of the digits were written in color, the color would be associated with the digit in his mental vision. In one experiment in which he was called upon to memorize a table of five rows of five digits each, he could, with no difficulty, identify the position and value of six digits written in red.

On meeting Binet, Diamandi presented him with a large piece of paper on which he had written two thousand digits in 40 lines of 25 digits each. He had memorized the table, and could identify any number desired. When asked how he could visualize an entire table of two thousand digits, he said that he did not distinctly see all the digits at one time. When he thought of his table he saw a gray cloud; it was only when he directed his attention to a particular point in the table that the digits at that point broke away from the cloud.

Diamandi could accept problems put to him verbally, but with difficulty. He would hesitate, make errors, and ask that the numbers be repeated several times. He attributed these difficulties to a couple of circumstances: the necessity of evoking a visual image from spoken figures, and problems in comprehending the French. When he was presented with a problem in French, he was forced to make a word by word translation before creating a visual image of the numbers.

Binet found it difficult to determine exactly the time required for Diamandi to memorize a given number of digits because his speed at memorization was very variable. To memorize 24 digits required on one occasion 3½ minutes. In another experiment he looked at 18 digits for only 9 seconds, then, after a mental repetition of about a minute, he was able to recite them exactly—but, according to Binet, he could not have recited them immediately after having seen them.

When Diamandi attempted to learn numbers read aloud, he made so many errors in repeating them that the times lost all significance. For example, in learning 25 digits, the numbers had to be repeated so many times that it took about three minutes, and even then Diamandi made eight or ten errors.

Binet undertook two sorts of experiments to investigate Diamandi's ability to memorize numbers. In both cases the numbers were presented to him on paper as the only practical way of proceeding.

In the first series of experiments Diamandi was given sequences of digits of various lengths, and the time for him to memorize them was measured. Since he believed that he would be called upon to perform calculations with these numbers, he was very careful to get them correct, sacrificing speed for accuracy.

The table below gives Diamandi's attempts for memorizing numbers of various lengths. These are not average times, but times for unique experiments. Moreover, the times are not really those required to memorize the numbers, but the time required to memorize them and write them down from memory—Binet began timing as soon as Diamandi was shown the numbers and ceased timing after Diamandi had written the last digit.

Number of digits learned	Time
10	17 sec.
15	1 m. 15 sec.
20	2 m. 15 sec.
25	3 m.
30	4 m. 20 sec.
50	7 m.
100	25 m.
200	2 h. 15 m.

All but the 200 digits were done in a single afternoon session. The tests were separated by about ten-minute intervals.

Diamandi objected to the manner in which the numbers were written. Up to a hundred they were written in a single line; the 100-digit number was written in two lines. (Binet does not say how the 200-digit number was written.) Diamandi would have preferred to have the numbers written in squares—he felt that he could fix on more numbers at one time that way. In spite of his care, Diamandi made mistakes, though Binet is unforgivably careless in reporting them. He says (1894:125): "The errors committed were insignificant, affecting only one or two digits."

The test of 200 digits took up an entire session. Diamandi wrote the entire number without error, but was quite fatigued from the effort.

Diamandi always wrote the digits from left to right and found it more difficult to proceed as he got farther to the right.

In the second series of experiments Diamandi's ability to memorize numbers within a limited span of time was tested. He was given a piece of paper with a long number on it and he memorized as many digits as he could within the time allotted. Binet notes that Diamandi had two different methods of memorizing: he could memorize more digits but not so that he could retain them for long, or he could memorize fewer digits and remember them longer.

In three seconds Diamandi could retain an average of 11 digits; in five seconds, 16 digits; in six seconds, an average of 17 digits. The times here differ considerably from the first experiment, if for no other reason because the time required to write down the digits is excluded. Also Binet says nothing about the error rate, though he indicates earlier that it was much higher in this series of tests.

Diamandi held the curious belief that he could determine the psychology of people by examining their faces. Because of his exceptional visual memory, he claimed to have a vast visual storehouse of faces. He said (Tocquet n.d.:21):

> During my ten years of travel throughout the world, I had opportunities of observing faces of all categories. In this way a sort of cinematographic museum was formed in my mind, extending over an immense variety of types. When I study a face its image evokes all the corresponding images, and these stand out as from a group and appear before me; I have only to compare. I know that this wrinkle, that fold of the lips, that expression of the eyes, that shape of nose are the mark of this or that psychological disposition, the stigmata of this or that way of thinking or feeling. It is true that I had to work by trial and error for a long time, and that for certain traits of character I still do. But on balance, if in face reading I have not succeeded in attaining the absolute precision of a mathematical operation, I have achieved a relative precision, which I shall try to improve more and more by new observations, but which already seems to me to be far from negligible.

Chapter Twenty-nine

Frank D. Mitchell

> While mental arithmetic has never absorbed a disproportionate share of his time, there is scarcely a day in which some of the old familiar series do not at some odd moment or other run through his head, usually quite automatically.
>
> —Frank D. Mitchell, writing of himself (1907:95)

I N a 1907 issue of the *American Journal of Psychology* Frank D. Mitchell published a brilliant work on calculating prodigies. Therein he chronicles his own case, which might be described as that of a potential calculating prodigy who suffered a case of arrested development.

In most cases the last *n* digits of the numbers in an arithmetic problem determine the last *n* digits of the answer independently of what the preceding digits may be. As a child Mitchell focused his attention on these digits (1907:87): "Now the writer's mental calculations take the form almost exclusively of tracing the last two figures through the different operations, ignoring all other figures. This evidently simplifies the work immensely." In particular he was adept at finding the last two digits of any power of any number. He preferred to work with even numbers, and had devised a method, to be discussed, for converting from odd to even numbers and back again.

Mitchell learned to count at the age of 4, possibly even 3—first to ten, then to 100, and beyond. He took up counting by twos, threes, etc. He regarded the powers in these series as "natural resting-places," and so came to try counting in the power series, e.g., 2, 4, 8, 16, 32, 64 . . . ; 3, 9, 27, 81. . . . At first he did not omit the intermediate multiples, but simply emphasized those that were part of the power series: *2, 4, 6, 8,* 10, 12, *16* . . . , but gradually he came to omit the intervening numbers.

When the numbers exceeded 100, he tended to emphasize the last two digits, and eventually came to ignore all the digits but these. Thus in counting along the power series of three, instead of 3, 9, 27, 81, 243, 729, 2,187 . . . , he would usually say 3, 9, 27, 81, 43, 29, 87. . . . He was, by this means, able to count along various power series, for considerable distances.

Mitchell also learned to multiply by counting in multiples. To get the product of 7×9 he would count 9, 18, 27, 36, 45, 54, 63. Even as an adult, up to 12×12 he multiplied by abbreviated counting, suppressing most intermediate links.

Mitchell devised a method by which he could determine the last two digits of the product of any pair of numbers. Since the last two digits of the product are uniquely determined by the last two digits of the multiplier and multiplicand we can, for this purpose, ignore the other digits.

One could simply memorize the last two digits of all the products of all the pairs of numbers less than one hundred (which, if you memorize the full product, as has Wim Klein, could be useful for calculation in general), but Mitchell worked out a method which only required him to memorize the last two digits of the products of numbers divisible by four. The following account is an elaboration based upon a few examples he describes and discusses.

Suppose we are given two integers and we wish to know the last two digits of their product. Let the last two digits of the multiplier be a, the last two digits of the multiplicand be b, and c represent the last two digits of their product (technically, these are the least positive residues, modulo 100). To use Mitchell's method it is necessary to convert a and b into multiples of four, find the last two digits of their product, and make appropriate conversions of that product to obtain c.

If a (or b) is a multiple of four, retain the last two digits of a (or b).

Suppose that a and/or b is not a multiple of four. Then if it is:

1. Even and an odd multiple of two (e.g., $94 = 2 \times 47$), add 50 and retain the last two digits of the sum ($94 + 50 = 144$, so 44).
2. Odd and of the form $4n - 1$ (one less than a multiple of four), then add 25 and retain the last two digits.
3. Odd and of the form $4n + 1$, subtract 25 (if the number is less than 25, add 100 before subtracting 25).

Let d be the last two digits of the product of the numbers correspond-ing to a and b. Then find c (the last two digits of the actual product of a and b) in the following way (ignore all but the last two digits; answers may be negative):

1. If a or b is a multiple of four, or if both are odd multiples of two, then $c = d$ (e.g., 96×39 becomes 96×64; the last two digits are 44).
2. If a is odd and b is even and not divisible by four, then $c = d + 50$ (e.g., 41×94 becomes 16×44; the last two digits are 04, plus 50 is 54).
3. If a and b are odd and both are of the form $4n + 1$ or $4n - 1$, then $c = d + 25$ (e.g., 97×21 becomes 72×96; the last two digits are 12, plus 25 is 37).
4. If a is of the form $4n + 1$ and b of the form $4n - 1$, then $c = d - 25$ (add 100 to d, if necessary to get a number exceeding 25; e.g., 97×39 becomes 72×64; the last two digits are 08; $108 - 25 = 83$).

Mitchell summed up the advantages of this method (1907:90–91):

Now these properties early attracted the writer's attention, and he soon got into the habit of transforming odd numbers into even numbers in prac-tically all his calculations. The result was that (if we leave out of account multiples of 5, which belong to a class by themselves and are very easy to multiply) the whole of multiplication, so far as the endings were concerned, was reduced to the 200 possible products of any two of the 20 numbers 04, 08, 12, 16, 24, 28, 32, 36, etc.; whereas in order to do the same work without this transformation, the 3200 combinations of the whole eighty 2-figure endings prime to 5 would have to be considered. In finding powers, again, he had to deal with only 20 different series, each of which repeated after 20 terms or less; so that the whole problem of finding the last two figures of any power of any number was reduced to less than 400 simple cases, instead of an indefinite number of cases. He never committed these products and powers to memory; it was not necessary; with practice he was soon able to count to any desired one with great rapidity, in fact, just as rapidly, in the simpler cases, as he could have recalled the answer if it had been previously memorized.

Mitchell's explorations of power series led him to a variety of interest-ing discoveries (1907:88–89):

In the course of these calculations or countings, a number of properties gradually attracted the writer's attention; such as that every power of a number ending with 0 or 5 ends with 0 or 5, that the 4th power of any other number ends with 1 or 6, according as it is odd or even, that the 5th power ends with the same figure as the 1st, the 6th with the same figure as the 2nd, etc.; and that if 76, or any number ending with 76, is multiplied by a multiple of 4, the last two figures of the product are the same as those of the multiplier (*e.g.*, $76 \times 12 = 912$). Then he [the author] noticed that the ending 76 occurs at various points in the power series of different numbers (the 5th power of 6, the 4th power of 32, the 2nd power of 24, the 10th power of 4, the 20th power of 2, etc.), and that from these points the series of endings repeats, except that in some cases the ending of the next power will differ by 50 from that of the original number. Thus the endings of the first 20 powers of 2 are 02, 04, 08, 16, 32, 64, 28, 56, 12, 24, 48, 96, 92, 84, 68, 36, 72, 44, 88, 76; the 21st is 52 instead of 02; but the 22nd is 04, like the 2nd, and thereafter the endings recur in regular order. Finally it turned out that the *20th* power of every even number (not ending with 0) had the ending 76, and that odd numbers had a similar property, the 20th power ending being, however, 01 instead of 76, and even the 21st power being always the same as the 1st, except for multiples of 5.

Mitchell summed up his calculating ability (1907:91):

The writer's mental calculations usually deal only with the 2-figure endings of numbers, rejecting all previous figures if there are any; by far the commonest problem is to find (the ending of) some given power of a given number, or to investigate some property of some power or group of powers of one or more numbers; and problems involving odd numbers (except, of course, odd exponents) are almost always solved by changing the odd numbers into multiples of 4 (by adding or subtracting 25), and changing back to an odd number in the same way, if necessary, after the work of calculation is over. He might go on and indicate many other properties of numbers, or rather of endings, which he discovered and used in calculating; but enough has already been said to give a fair idea of the general nature of the processes employed, the gradual development of the calculating power, and the advantages of the various specializations which came to be adopted.

Of course his calculations are not absolutely confined within these limits. Besides finding endings in the power series of even numbers, he can also multiply endings very readily, and add or subtract them (by counting forwards or backwards) somewhat less rapidly, or divide them where the division is known to be exact; and he *can* work, though very much more slowly, with odd numbers. But even in the power series of 3, the odd series with which he has worked oftenest, it is easier in most cases to change 3 into 28; and in any other odd series he can scarcely work at all, except with the greatest effort. The even series in these other cases are so much easier and more familiar that it is practically impossible to resist the temptation to work in them, even when he tries to work laboriously in the odd ones as such.

Mitchell's ability as a mental calculator was not remarkable when the entire answer, rather than the last two digits, was required. Even multiplying pairs of two-digit numbers, when the product exceeded 100, took longer mentally than on paper. In multiplying three-digit numbers, the partial products had to be repeated two or three times, but, even so, he easily lost track. On paper he was fairly adept at multiplying two digits by two digits as the sum of two partial products, rather than four (that is, he multiplied one digit by two as a single step), particularly when the two-digit number to be multiplied was even. The odd cases less than 100 would usually be done in one step but above 100 often resolved itself into counting (1907:92)—"rapid and automatic, but counting nevertheless. Thus up to $23 \times 5 = 115$ he [the writer] would probably count by 23 directly, or depend on his memory; but after that, to pass to $23 \times 6 = 138$, he would first count in the 3, then the 20, thus reaching 138 from 115 *via* 118 and 128."

For two sorts of problems, Mitchell was able to find complete products fairly readily. The first was in squaring numbers where he got the last two digits from memory and the rest by interpolating between known squares or by applying the formula $(a + b)^2 = a^2 + 2ab + b^2$.

The second case was in multiplying numbers both of which have no prime factors other than two and three. Mitchell (1907:92) explained:

Here his method is to count (multiply) by 2's or 3's to some convenient multiple of one of the numbers, then by that multiple to some other, and so on, until the required product is reached. Thus to find 48×64 he would count by 48 to 384 ($= 48 \times 8$), then by 384 to 1536, then to 3072 ($= 348 \times 8 = 48 \times 64$), the required answer. To square 162, again, the stages would be 486, 1458, 2916, 8748, 26244, *i.e.,* multiplying successively by 3, 3, 2, 3, 3. In these cases much of the work would be automatic and half conscious.

Mitchell could also extract the roots of perfect squares and cubes when the roots contained no more than three digits. (For the application of two-figure endings to such problems, see chapter 13.)

Mitchell's calculating ability was incidental to his life after childhood.

Chapter Thirty

Gottfried Rückle

F EW details of Rückle's life are to be found in the documents concerning him known to me—not even the dates of his birth and death.
He was a mathematician who wrote his doctoral dissertation on *Qua-
dratic Reciprocity in Algebraic Number Fields,* Göttingen, 1901. Müller
(1911) tested his memory for both numerical and nonnumerical data
and, to a lesser extent, his calculating ability.

Rückle was especially good at rapid memorization of numbers—much
faster than Inaudi, Diamandi, or Arnould (tested by Binet [1895]),
though he was not nearly so fast, at least for numbers of less than 40
digits, as Finkelstein (chapter 33).

Rückle's memory for digits was visual, but unlike the visual calculators
Diamandi and Finkelstein, he memorized digits in the form in which
they were presented to him, and not in his own handwriting. He even
retained the colors in which numbers were written, if colored chalk was
used. If numbers were presented to him orally, however, he visualized
them in his own hand. In recalling numbers he could focus on a span of
six digits at a time.

Rückle seems to have been at least moderately precocious, for Müller
(1911:215–16) remarks in a footnote that he had, by 12 years of age,
memorized all the prime numbers, and the factors of composite numbers,
up to 1,000.

Like other calculating prodigies, numbers had for Rückle a great many
associations, and these served to aid him in memorizing numbers. Odd
numbers were easier for him to memorize than even numbers, and in the
case of odd numbers he was always interested in whether or not they
were prime. Some associations reported by Rückle were (Müller
1911:215–17):

353—prime
673—prime
841—29^2
295—5 times 59
925—25 times 37
624—25^2-1
635—5 times 127; 127 is the first prime number after 113
543—3 times 181, the product of two primes
429—3 times 11 times 13, the product of three primes
50,928—928 is divisible by 29
528—Rückle had often squared this number
548,519—the first and second halves differ by the prime 29
471,463—the first and second halves differ by 8
231,634—the difference between the two halves is 403, which equals 13
          times 31, and 31 appears in the first half
70,128—$701+28=729=9^3$
26,169—$26=2\times13$ and $169=13^2$
451,697—$451=11\times41$ and $697=17\times41$
893,047—$893=19\times47$, and 47 appears in the second half
86,219—$219=3\times73$ and $\log 73=1.86\ldots$
484,573—the first half is composed only of even numbers, and the sec-
          ond only of odd numbers
718,982—18 and 82 equal 100

Müller remarks in a footnote (1911:217) that Rückle once gave 28 in place of 72 in recalling a number. He explained that for many calculating operations reciprocal numbers adding up to 100 were "equivalent" for him. If, for example, he was calculating the product of 472 and 537, he would first multiply 500 times 537 and subtract the product of 28 times 537.

766,932—relation between 66 and 32: $2\times66=132$
458,741—$58=2\times29$ and $741=29^2-100$
156,978—78 is half of 156
75,327 84,222—(two adjacent blocks of numbers) the two blocks of
                numbers contrast—the first is made up entirely of
                odd, and the second entirely of even numbers.
846,712 964,373—(the 4th and 7th 6-digit blocks of a sixty-digit
                number) in the first we find 46 and in the second
                in a corresponding position 64 is found.

446,250   445,966—(two immediately adjacent groups) 446 is almost
                        double 250 and 445 is nearly half of 966
559—the accession of Cyrus
919—accession of the Saxon kings
893,429—429 was the year of Plato's birth
283,881—283 and 881 are prime; the Feldberg is 881 meters high

Müller (1911:224–25) also posed to Rückle some of the problems put
by Binet to Inaudi. When asked to find a number whose square and cube
roots differ by 18, Rückle gave the answer, 729, in 2.5 seconds, while
Inaudi required one minute 57 seconds, according to Binet (1894:76).
As I noted in the chapter on Inaudi, this time is unreasonably long.
Calculating prodigies are fascinated by powers, and 729 is the second
smallest number which is both a perfect square and a perfect cube (729
$=9^3=27^2$; the smallest is 64). I suspect the time attributed to Inaudi by
Binet is in error.

Rückle reduced the following five-digit numbers to the sum of four
squares:

$$15,663 = 125^2 + 6^2 + 1^2 + 1^2 \text{ (8 sec.)}$$
$$125^2 + 5^2 + 3^2 + 2^2 \text{ (immediately after the first)}$$
$$18,111 = 134^2 + 11^2 + 5^2 + 3^2 \text{ (26.5 sec.)}$$
$$134^2 + 9^2 + 7^2 + 5^2 \text{ (63.5 sec.)}$$
$$53,116 = 230^2 + 14^2 + 4^2 + 2^2 \text{ (51 sec.)}$$
$$230^2 + 12^2 + 6^2 + 6^2 \text{ (immediately after the first)}$$

Inaudi was also given 15,663 to reduce to the sum of four squares
(Binet 1894:78). Fifteen minutes were required to find one solution (62^2
$+57^2+83^2+41^2$). A second solution ($62^2+41^2+97^2+27^2$) was ob-
tained "quelques minutes après," the exact time not being given.

At first glance Inaudi's time of 15 minutes seems overlong in comparison to 8 seconds for Rückle, but the problem of reducing a number to
four squares was new to Inaudi. He did not, as did Rückle, begin with
the largest square below 15,663 ($125^2 = 15,625$), which simplifies finding a solution, since the other squares are limited to small numbers.
Starting with 62^2, as he clearly did (both his solutions begin with 62^2),
and attempting to find other squares to obtain a solution is a vastly more
difficult problem.

In cases of simple addition, subtraction, and multiplication, Inaudi was the superior calculator. The additions in (a) below took Inaudi 11 seconds; Rückle required 15.5 seconds. Both completed (b) in 17 seconds.

$$
\begin{aligned}
\text{(a)} \quad 7{,}429 + 3{,}635 &= 11{,}064 \\
6{,}093 &= 9{,}728 \\
8{,}025 &= 11{,}660 \\
7{,}346 &= 10{,}981 \\
3{,}282 &= 6{,}917 \\
\text{(b)} \quad 4{,}829 + 8{,}725 &= 13{,}554 \\
6{,}623 &= 15{,}348 \\
3{,}248 &= 11{,}973 \\
8{,}273 &= 16{,}998 \\
6{,}458 &= 15{,}183
\end{aligned}
$$

Inaudi performed the subtractions in (c) in 14 seconds; Rückle took 25 seconds, and made two errors. Only in (d) was Rückle's performance superior to Inaudi's—13 seconds to 22 seconds. (It is curious that Inaudi took longer for (d) than (c), since (c) appears to be more difficult.)

$$
\begin{aligned}
\text{(c)} \quad 4{,}829 - 8{,}725 &= -3{,}896 \\
6{,}623 &= -2{,}102 \\
3{,}248 &= -5{,}477 \\
8{,}273 &= -452 \\
6{,}458 &= -2{,}267 \\
\text{(d)} \quad 6{,}831 - 3{,}635 &= 3{,}196 \\
9{,}298 &= 5{,}663 \\
6{,}395 &= 2{,}760 \\
8{,}238 &= 4{,}603 \\
7{,}254 &= 3{,}619
\end{aligned}
$$

It should be noted as well that these problems were presented on paper, a method preferred by Rückle but not at all congenial to Inaudi, who had only learned to read numbers a few years before.

Rückle was markedly inferior to Inaudi in multiplying. Inaudi calculated the product of 6,241 times 3,635 in 21 seconds. Rückle required 70.5 seconds. Inaudi multiplied 7,286 by 5,397 in 21 seconds, while the same problem took Rückle 112 seconds. Müller remarks that the results were similar for other cases.

Müller also makes the interesting observation that, while Rückle's mental calculations were essentially visual, if he was concerned about forgetting, he would repeat the numbers to himself.

Though Müller remarks that, whenever possible, Rückle brought his knowledge of mathematics to bear in solving problems, only in one instance does Müller give an example. In multiplying **6,241** by **3,635** Rückle made use of the fact that

$$ab = \left(\frac{a+b}{2}\right)^2 - \left(\frac{a-b}{2}\right)^2$$

While this is algebraically unimpeachable, it is difficult to see how it simplifies the calculations.

Chapter Thirty-one

Alexander Craig Aitken

Familiarity with numbers acquired by innate faculty sharpened by assid-
uous practice does give insight in profounder theorems of algebra and
analysis.

—Alexander Craig Aitken, as quoted in his obituary (*Proceedings* 1968)

His calculating powers were not, however, based on conscious memory alone; he was a mathematician as well—an unusual combination—
and interested in analysing his powers and in the way his mind worked.
He has told me that results "came up from the murk," and I have heard
him say of a number, that it "feels prime," as indeed it was.

—J. C. P. Miller (*Proceedings* 1968)

ALEXANDER Craig Aitken was a great many things. He was an
eminent methematician who made important contributions to algebra, numerical analysis, and statistics. He was a self-taught classical
violinist of considerable skill, a student of languages, an amateur com-
poser, and a poet. In his youth he had been a soldier and something of
an athlete. And he was one of the greatest mental calculators who ever
lived.

Aitken was born in Dunedin, New Zealand on April 1, 1895, the
eldest of seven children. His father, at that time an assistant in a grocer's
shop, was a profoundly religious man who loved flowers. "Aitken's Surprise," a chrysanthemum, is named for him.

Young "Alec" spent all his summer vacations at his grandfather's farm
on the Otago Peninsula. There he gained a love of hiking and the out-
of-doors which never left him. He liked to pack a lunch and wander all
day; if it rained, he stuffed hay under his clothes and pushed on. Once

he discovered a colony of the rare royal albatross[1] and rushed home to report it, but nobody in the family would believe him. Later, one of his uncles was appointed ranger in charge of the colony.

Each year he was first in his class and at 13 obtained a scholarship to Otago Boys' High School. To this point he had displayed none of his great future gift for arithmetic and mathematics. He remarked (Hunter 1962:252):

> Arithmetic in primary school, since I recall hardly anything about it, must simply have bored me. Possibly, I wasn't taught well. Maybe I simply accepted what the teacher said and did it. When I went up to secondary school, with a scholarship from primary school, I was disappointed at my arithmetic mark. I found that it was only 143 out of 200. I lost 57 marks and if I'd had these I'd have been very high up. As it was, I got a scholarship in spite of that.

The first two years at Otago he did not win the mathematics prize.

Aitken's interest in calculation was first stimulated by algebra, not arithmetic (Aitken 1954:297): "I regard mental algebra as on a much higher plane than mental arithmetic, and incomparably more rewarding." He later recalled the incident that got him started (Hunter 1962:252):

> The master chanced to say that you can use this factorization to square a number: $a^2 - b^2 = (a+b)(a-b)$. Suppose you had 47—that was his example—he said you could take b as 3. So $(a+b)$ is 50 and $(a-b)$ is 44, which you can multiply together to give 2200. Then the square of b is 9 and so, boys, he said, 47 squared is 2209. Well, from that moment, that was the light, and I never went back. I went straight home and practised and found that this reacted on every other branch of mathematics. I found such a freedom. I well remember the stage when I was able to square numbers up to 300 and thought—now that is something! But I was to go far beyond that in future years. And so from the age of what might be 13½ years, up to 17½ when I left that school, I underwent what can only be described as a mental Yoga. I tried harder and harder things until, in the end, I was so good at arithmetic that the master didn't allow me to do arithmetic.

But Aitken's interests were by no means limited to arithmetic (ibid.):

> I was interested in literature just as much, Latin, French, English. But this great freedom suddenly encouraged me to think I had a memory and a cal-

[1] Gary J. Tee (1979:14) identifies the colony he found as the royal albatross which "elsewhere breeds only on subantarctic islands." According to Kidson (1973:130) and Aitken's obituary (*Proceedings* 1968:158) the colony was one of penguins.

culative power capable not only of arithmetic but also capable of, for instance, literary memory. I suddenly moved away. And indeed, did very well at school except for one subject, chemistry, which bored me. The master's way of teaching was the driest dust boys were ever subjected to. Moreover, he once, noticing me to be so inattentive, gave me six of the cane, which didn't improve matters at all. So I just let chemistry go, and so I didn't get the science prize. But I got every other prize that was to be got.

On the eve of Aitken's fifteenth birthday, his mother died suddenly. He and his sister, Pearl, crawled under the house, where they remained throughout the day. After that, Pearl, who was 13, took a large role in raising the family.

Long after the event Aitken wrote (Kidson 1968):

> When grief was fresh we could not bear
>   The irony of heaven's blue;
>   Such mockery of our despair
> When grief was fresh, we could not bear.
>   A haggard sky, a bitter air,
> We might have borne, when loss was new,
> When grief was fresh; we could not bear
>   The irony of heaven's blue.

Aitken took first place in the university scholarship examinations and went to Otago University in 1913 on a scholarship. His intention was to become a teacher of languages and mathematics, but his studies were interrupted by the outbreak of war. It is this period of Aitken's life about which we know most, for he wrote a book describing his wartime experiences, *Gallipoli to the Somme—Recollections of a New Zealand Infantryman* (Aitken 1963). Although the initial draft of the book was made shortly after the events recounted, the final draft was not written until Aitken was in his sixties. The book, however, does not discuss his ability at mental calculation.

His violin, given to him on the crossing to Egypt, runs like a leitmotif throughout his book, refusing to be abandoned. He managed to retain it throughout the war, though at times it was left in the custody of others. It even followed him back to New Zealand from France, like a faithful dog in a sentimental novel.

Aitken was hardly 20 when he enlisted as a private in the New Zealand expeditionary force. He missed the worst of the fighting in the Dardanelles, but was present for the famous British withdrawal at Gallipoli, in which the Turks were cleverly deceived to believe that the enemy was still present in force, only to discover that the British had secretly escaped. After a brief stay in Egypt, Aitken was sent to France. Before the war's end virtually all his New Zealand comrades had been killed or wounded.

Ironically, Aitken achieved some measure of renown for what was to him a trivial incident in a terrible experience. During the raid at Armentières on July 13, the 4th company was nearly extinguished. The roll book of platoon 10, from which Aitken had been recently reassigned (though he took part in the raid with his old platoon), was lost. Battalion headquarters wished to know the casualties and the state of the platoon,[2] but only last names were available. Aitken was lying exhausted on some coconut matting at company headquarters and overheard a conversation (Aitken 1963:107–8):

> something was missing; a roll-book; the roll-book of Platoon 10, my old Platoon. Urgently required, it seemed; Battalion had rung up, requesting a list of the night's casualties and a full state of the Platoon. Apparently surnames were available, but the book was nowhere to be found. This being suddenly clear, I had no difficulty, having a well-trained memory now brought by stress into a condition almost of hypermnesia, in bringing the lost roll-book before me, almost, as it were, floating; I imagined it either taken away by Mr. Johnson or perhaps in the pocket of Sergeant Bree in no-man's-land. Speaking from the matting I offered to dictate the details; full name, regimental number, and the rest; they were taken down, by whom I do not know. To me the essential thing was to help Captain Hargest out of his quandary.

Aitken adds in a footnote: "In later years this incident, to which I attached no importance, was much exaggerated by legend; as late as 1933 I met it again, with the Platoon expanded to a battalion!"

Aitken was seriously wounded at the Somme on September 27, 1916, and returned to New Zealand. He described his final acts of the war (Aitken 1963:167–69):

> We were about half-way across when German high explosive mixed with shrapnel, of the greenish-black kind, began to fall thickly. Not ten yards ahead a group of the 8th Company vanished in the smoke of a shell-burst, some falling where they stood, the others walking on dreamlike. I passed

[2] The number in the platoon is not specified; Tee (1979:14) estimates it at 50 to 100 men.

through the smoke. In a dim way I wondered why I had not been hit by the flying pieces, but the mind would not trouble itself with problems at that moment, the overmastering impulse being to move on. On! On! In an attack such as this, under deadly fire, one is as powerless as a man gripping strongly charged electrodes, powerless to do anything but go mechanically on; the final shield from death removed, the will is fixed like the last thought taken into an anaesthetic, which is the first thought taken out of it. Only safety, or the shock of a wound, will destroy such autohypnosis. At the same time all normal emotion is numbed utterly. Close upon this road now, I heard a voice abusing the Germans; crossing the road, I realized that it had been my own.

As I took the bank I looked left and saw Private Nelson, one of my men, fall forward on his knees and elbows, his head between his hands. I mentally registered 23598, Nelson, W. P., and the terrific electromagnetic force pulled me on. He was dead.

Now from two directions, half-right, half-left, came the hissing of many bullets, the herring-bone weave of machine-gun cross-fire. I saw some cut long straight scores in the ground, sending up dust; some, as I found later, cut my tunic, frayed the equipment, and made rents in the cloth cover of my shrapnel helmet; many seemed to whizz past my ear, some to bury themselves under my feet as I walked. Again these things are remembered as sometimes a deeply submerged dream may be recaptured in waking moments; at the time I took account of them only dimly, and certainly did not think of death for a single moment—no merit in this, we are not responsible for what we do in a dream or hypnosis. Suddenly at my left side my platoon sergeant, Livingston, dropped on one knee and looked up at me in a curious doubtful gaze. "Come on, sergeant!" I said, stepping forward myself. He was killed, I think, the next instant; I never saw him again.

All this occurred within a few yards of crossing the road. I glanced right and left and saw the Platoon, thirty of them, crumple and fall, only two going on, widely apart, and no N.C.O. A few yards farther on I was nearly knocked down by a tremendous blow in the upper right arm and spun sideways; simultaneously the right hand unclenched and the Spandau rifle and bayonet fell to the ground. Even then no thought of death came, only some phrase like "sledge-hammer blow", from a serial read years before in a boys' magazine. Pain came the next moment; the spurious self-hypnotism vanished and gave way to an overwhelming desire to run, anywhere. Of three men—as I heard later—crouching wounded in a shell-hole that afternoon, one tried to keep the other two in safety, but they broke away and made a wild dash in no particular direction, both being killed by machine-gun fire within a few yards. I had the same wild wish, but it was crossed and quelled by the resurgent rhythm of the first impulse, so that I found myself walking on mechanically, yet wondering what I should do, disarmed now, if I reached Gird Trench. A second wound dismissed the question. As the right foot was coming to the ground a bullet passed through in front of the ankle and fractured the several tarsal bones. I crumpled and fell sideways to the right into a providential shell-hole, curling up like a hedgehog.

Aitken then crawled on his left elbow and his left knee for some four hours to safety. Here his boyhood love of astronomy saved his life, for he used the stars to keep himself headed in a southerly direction.

Only twelve men and one officer reached the objective, Gird Trench — it was empty. The official history mentions (Aitken 1963:173) "3 companies of I/Otago almost annihilated by shell-fire and streams of machine-gun bullets. . . ." These were all men from Aitken's part of New Zealand. Of the 32 men in his platoon, 5 were killed and 25 were wounded; only 2 men remained unscathed at the end of the day. Similar casualties were sustained by the other platoons engaged in the attack. All these casualties probably occurred in the first ten minutes of battle.

Aitken returned to his study of languages and mathematics at Otago University. His study of mathematics, however, was carried on under unfortunate circumstances. Since there was no professor of mathematics at the university, Aitken was forced to study under the mathematics master of the Otago Boys' High School; he also corresponded with Professor D. M. Y. Sommerville of Victoria College. When he sat for the Final Honours examination for his Master of Arts degree in 1919, the poverty of his mathematical preparation was revealed. The material was quite different from what he had studied, and, although he received first class honors in Latin and French, he received only second class honors in mathematics.

In 1920, at the age of 25, Aitken graduated, married, and became a master at Otago Boys' High School, where he taught languages. He continued his mathematical studies, played the violin and wrote music, and took up high jumping. In 1923 he won the Otago championship in both the high jump and pole vault, though in the latter case, he said the real champion would have won, had the ground not been so rough.

In the meanwhile, Professor R.J.T. Bell had been appointed to the chair of mathematics at Otago University, and Aitken worked under him as a part-time tutor.

Bell immediately recognized Aitken's ability and helped him arrange to go to Edinburgh to study mathematics under Professor E. T. (later Sir Edmund) Whittaker. For this purpose he obtained a postgraduate scholarship from the University of New Zealand.

At Edinburgh, Aitken was a candidate for the degree of Doctor of Philosophy, but when his thesis was presented two years later, in 1925, it was so highly regarded that he was awarded the higher degree of Doctor of Science.

In November 1965, Professor E. T. Copson wrote to Professor Erdelyi about Aitken (*Proceedings* 1968:155–56):

> At the time when he taught languages at Otago Boys' High School he was more interested in mathematics, though he knew very little about modern mathematics. He never met a real mathematician until he was 28 and came to work with Whittaker. He brought with him some unpublished work on the Theory of Numbers which appeared later in the "Edinburgh Mathematical Notes". The work of people like Fermat fascinated him. With his gift of computation, he could guess results in the Theory of Numbers from a consideration of particular cases. Like Ramanujan, the integers were his personal friends. His first piece of serious work was the solution of a sixth order difference equation which arose in Whittaker's theory of graduation. Eddy Whittaker and Richard Gwilt had tried to use E. T. Whittaker's original version of the theory. I had tried to solve the difference equation by analytical methods and got nowhere. But Alec got a solution as an infinite series expressing the inverse of a difference operator as a Laurent series in the operator E. It did not look at all promising; but Alec with his great arithmetical skill was able to calculate the numerical values of the coefficients. Actually the method was not very good. . . . But Alec got over that trouble too. . . . It was an exceptional effort to do this work and gain his D.Sc. two years after he came to Edinburgh. The problem was one which fascinated him; it made use of his great gifts in classical algebra and his skill in computation.
>
> Even then he knew very little about modern mathematics; but Edinburgh suited him. E. T. W.'s lectures on determinants and matrices were unique; nowhere else in Britain was matrix theory taught at that time, and Aitken took to it at once. It was fascinating to see how he was able to apply techniques of that sort of algebra to numerical analysis. He was not long a research student—he joined the Edinburgh staff in 1925 and never left. It was not from lack of offers. They tried on more than one occasion to persuade him to go to the London School of Economics. But it was no use. Edinburgh had everything he wanted—concerts, musical friends, the hills to walk, a congenial job. . . . He must have been a very rapid worker; he once told my wife that for 75 per cent of his time he was thinking of music. He must have employed the other 25 per cent to a very great purpose. Of course by staying in Edinburgh he avoided all the administrative burdens which beset many of us and which he found rather uncongenial when he was elected Professor.

Much of Aitken's time was taken up by his interest in music. In a sense, his musical expertise paralleled his mathematical, for in both he was largely self-taught. But his knowledge of music was not limited to that of a performer. He composed music, which he kept, in his words, "most rigorously suppressed." He was also deeply interested in music criticism and the history of music. He prepared, in an elegant hand, a critical version of Bach's suites for solo violin, even though he knew them all by heart.

In 1848 Chopin had given a recital at Edinburgh. Aitken wrote to a friend, Professor J. Stewart Deas, of his efforts to recreate for himself the circumstances of that concert (*Proceedings* 1968:154):

> Over a long space of years I endeavoured to catch the spirit of place and time by even visiting the West end of Queen Street (where Chopin's recital was given) by night, with coat collar turned up, and recalling every detail of the recital, with every collateral circumstance—the stay at Calder House, at the Lyszczynski's house in Warriston Crescent, Chopin's letter enshrining his opinion of musical appreciation in these islands, the state of his health, the programmes of his earlier recitals in June and July in London, in August in Manchester, etc. etc. You may say that this effort of mine *à la recherche du temps perdu* bore rather meagre fruit. Well, what of it? I enjoyed doing it; I caught something of Edinburgh's extremely varied past—and I learnt a lot about other matters in the process.

Aitken also had a deep interest in and a wide knowledge of world literature. He could, for example, quote from memory long passages from Milton or Virgil. He himself wrote some poetry, mostly sonnets and humorous verse, but, like his musical compositions, these he kept mostly to himself.

Aitken published some 80 papers and several books, mostly in statistics, numerical analysis, and algebra.

After obtaining his degree, Aitken obtained the first of his appointments at the University of Edinburgh, where he was to remain for the rest of his life. He held lectureships in actuarial mathematics, statistics, and mathematical economics. In 1936 he obtained a readership in statistics, and in 1946 he was appointed to the chair of mathematics, succeeding Sir Edmund Whittaker. He held this position until his retirement to professor emeritus in September 1965.

In 1936 he was elected a Fellow of the Royal Society of London, very unusual for anyone working in statistics or numerical analysis at the time. He received a variety of other honors and, for *Gallipoli to the Somme*, he was elected to the Fellowship of the Royal Society of Literature.

In 1954 Aitken addressed the Society of Engineers on the subject of mental calculation, just as Bidder had a hundred years before. As part of his address, he also did some demonstrations of mental calculation (Aitken 1954:298). He gave the squares of 251, 299, 413, 568, 596, 777, 983, 3,189, and 6,371. The squares of the three-digit numbers were given almost immediately; the four-digit numbers took about five seconds, and in the first case, Aitken made an error which he immediately corrected. He gave, in two or three seconds, the square roots to five significant digits of some of the previous numbers (251, 299, 413, 596, 777), noting that in the cases of 299 and 596, the last digit might be too large, as was the case. He then gave the square roots to five digits of 3,189 and 8,765. The time is not specified, but it is noted that the results were "quickly given." He then computed the 96 digits of the recurring period of 1/97.

He recognized the following numbers as prime or composite: 1,327 (prime), 871 (13 × 67), 989 (23 × 43), 401 (prime), 1,193 (prime), 1,157 (13 × 89), 1,447 (prime), 901 (17 × 53), 1,369 (37²).

Fred Barlow, in his book *Mental Prodigies* (1952), refers to the "appalling waste of time and energy" by the French calculator Dagbert in memorizing pi to the 707 places it had been computed by W. Shanks in 1873. Aitken had done the same thing many years before and agreed that (1954:302): "It would have been a reprehensibly useless feat, had it not been so easy."

Some twenty years later Aitken learned that Shanks erred at the 528th place, so the last 180 digits of his calculation were wrong. After the ENIAC electronic computer had calculated pi to more than 2,000 places, Aitken decided to try again (1954:302): "I amused myself again by learning the correct value as far as 1,000 places, and once again found it no trouble, except that I needed to 'fix' the join where Shank's error had occurred. The secret, to my mind, is relaxation, the complete antithesis of concentration as usually understood."

Aitken illustrated this knowledge by reciting the first 250 digits of pi. He then, upon request, picked up at the 301st place, beginning with 72,458. After reciting 150 digits, he was asked to pick it up at the 551st place, beginning with 60,943, which he did.

Aitken was also interested in the duodecimal system and even learned to do mental calculation using base 12. He found that it had a variety of advantages over the decimal system (for example, 1/3 and 1/6 are terminating duodecimals), but he gave it up because he saw no future for the system.

I. M. L. Hunter (1962) undertook a psychological study of Aitken's calculations, based upon the latter's introspective description of his mental processes. Results of this remarkable study are reported in portions of Parts 1 and 2.

Aitken's obituary in the *Proceedings of the Edinburgh Mathematical Society* (1968:155) concludes:

> In spite of his transcendent gifts, which might have set him apart from and above his fellows he was the most approachable of men, for he possessed simplicity of heart and true humility. . . . his wide erudition, carried so lightly, made him a fascinating talker, and his penetrating and witty commentary on men and affairs never held a trace of malice. He was beloved by all who knew him.

Aitken's last publication, though non-mathematical, deserves more than a passing mention. Endowed as he was with an exceptionally sensitive and perceptive nature, he had not been granted the healing gift of oblivion. At certain seasons he was oppressed by the memory of the atrocious fighting of the campaigns in Gallipoli and on the Somme in which he had taken part (the adjective, with its classical overtones, is his own). It is a testimony to the stature of his mind and personality that nearly 50 years after the events he could come to terms with that experience, the more terrible because constantly re-lived, and set down in his book *Gallipoli to the Somme—Recollections of a New Zealand Infantryman,* a narrative of his war service, compassionate, restrained, yet vivid and intensely moving. For this superb piece of writing, Aitken was elected to the Fellowship of the Royal Society of Literature. To those who knew him best it stands as a testament and a memorial. He died in Edinburgh on 3rd November, 1967, after some years of indifferent health, and is survived by his widow, a son and a daughter.

Chapter Thirty-two

———

Arthur Griffith

He [Arthur Griffith] would pursue numbers on sight as a hound follows a fox. Once when asked what he was doing he replied:

"Well, if I know the fourth power of a number, I know how to find the fourth power of the number that is one bigger and I am trying for the way to find the fourth power that is two bigger."

That is, he had a way of finding $(a + 1)^4$ and was trying for $(a + 2)^4$. He was unable to find $(a + b)^4$ for all values of b. To have made that discovery would have given him a triumph like the discovery of a new continent. It was something that lay beyond his power.

—Bryan and Lindley (1941:44)

IN the fall of 1899 William Lowe Bryan and Ernest Hiram Lindley undertook a study of the 19-year-old calculator, Arthur Griffith. The results were not published until 1941, after the death at sea of Dr. Lindley. The study appeared as part of the Indiana University science series under the unlikely title of *On the Psychology of Learning a Life Occupation* (Griffith shared the book with a treatise on learning telegraphic code). The title must surely have predated the decision to stuff it with 40-year-old research. Bryan concocted a postscript (incorporating a lengthy excerpt from Mark Twain on becoming a river pilot), which concluded that Griffith was motivated "By love of applause" and "By the desire for money" (p. 61).[1]

Arthur Griffith was born in 1880 at Milford, Kosciusko County, In-

---

[1] Unless otherwise indicated page numbers refer to Bryan and Lindley (1941).

diana. His father was a stonemason, and the family was "scarcely in moderate circumstances" (p. 24).

Like various other calculating prodigies his interest in calculation stemmed from counting. He began to count as soon as he could talk, and his mother, to keep him quiet, would give him various objects to count, such as pebbles, sticks, or potatoes.

Jedediah Buxton kept a mental record of the free beer and ale he had been given; Thomas Fuller counted the hairs in a cow's tail. Arthur Griffith mentally recorded the grains of corn fed the chickens. His three-year total came to 42,173. He could, he claimed, recall for weeks the number of grains fed them on any given day.

At the age of 7, after a severe illness, he developed epilepsy. As he grew older, the frequency of the seizures subsided, and by the age of 19, he suffered attacks only two or three times a year.

Griffith attended school for seven years, where he was brilliant at arithmetic and fair in other subjects. He said (p. 24), "I can study history or geography a little while, but soon my mind gets full of numbers."

When he was about 12 he started to work out his own methods for doing rapid mental calculations. Thereafter his interest in counting declined.

After leaving school at the age of 17, he did odd jobs for farmers, but he spent most of his time practicing calculation.

One of Griffith's former teachers introduced him to Professor Lindley at a teachers conference at Warsaw, Indiana, in September 1899. Lindley invited Griffith to Indiana University so that his case could be studied. The boy arrived at the university on November 3, 1899 and remained for five months, residing at Lindley's house where he "was under constant observation during all his waking hours" (pp. 24–25). According to Bryan's introduction (p. 13): "After five months Griffith grew tired of the experiments and upon appearance of a minor smallpox scare suddenly left us. . . ." Perhaps he was also growing tired of the constant observation.

Moreover, Lindley's benignant condescension toward him must have been hard to bear (p. 25):

> He enjoyed his new experiences very much and for a long time evinced a devotion to his host which suggested an almost juvenile dependence. . . . His lack of experience with linen collars and his initial inability to button one properly to his shirt might easily be interpreted as indicating feebleness of mind. But not so. He watched most narrowly the movements of the

TABLE 32.1
Arthur Griffith's Calculations

$$6 + 7$$
$$9 + 7$$
$$3 + 7$$
$$2 + 7$$
$$8 + 7$$
$$7 + 7$$
$$5 + 7$$
$$4 + 7$$
$$0 + 7$$
$$9 + 8$$

Time for the 10 additions—15 sec.

Addition of 10:

1-place numbers	15 secs.
2-place numbers	23
3-place numbers	27
4-place numbers	51

10 operations of subtraction:

1-place numbers	15 secs.
2-place numbers	25
3-place numbers	34
4-place numbers	53

10 operations of division:

1-place numbers	15 secs.
2-place numbers	22
3-place numbers	42
4-place numbers	78

Multiplication by usual method:

963
×

1269	E. H. L.	31.6 secs.
1431	W. L. B	19.0
2592	A. G.	13.8
2482	A. G.	14.2

A. G.'s multiplication by short methods:

963
×

		A	B	C
2376	Visual	3.9 secs.	6.3 secs.	8.9 secs.
1836	Visual	3.2	7.8	9.5
2268	Visual	1.4	3.25	4.4
1269	Visual	1.4	3.4	4.6
1242	Auditory	1.5	4.2	5.6
1134	Auditory	2.0	4.2	6.0

Factoring by A. G.:

	A	B	C
$987 = 7 \times 141$	3.0	——	5.2
$463 = $ prime	1.4	——	2.0
$784 = 28^2$	.7	——	2.2
$563 = $ prime	.9	——	1.1
$828 = 23 \times \quad 36$	1.0	2.6	3.4
$564 = \quad 4 \times \quad 141$	.8	——	2.6
$595 = \quad 5 \times \quad 119$	1.1	——	3.4
$645 = \quad 5 \times \quad 129$	.6	——	3.2
$889 = \quad 7 \times \quad 127$	1.0	——	2.8
$924 = 11 \times \quad 84$	.6	2.8	3.3
$6528 = \quad 8 \times \quad 816$	1.4	3.6	4.5
$5624 = \quad 4 \times 1406$	1.2	——	3.7
$6825 = 25 \times \quad 273$	1.6	——	4.0
$43564 = \quad 4 \times 10891$	——	——	5.1
$68256 = 16 \times 4526$[a]	1.4	——	7.9
$95432 = \quad 8 \times 11929$	1.4	——	4.8

Extraction of Cube Root by A.G.:

491,169,069	7 seconds
50,435,836	5
331,373,888	4
322,828,856	8
290,117,528	8
163,667,323	25
108,531,333	45
90,518,849	9
649,461,896	14
967,361,669	11

Average, 13.6 seconds.

Extraction of Square Root by A G.:

287,296	18 seconds
356,409	17
375,769	4
522,729	12
717,409	7
748,225	5
786,769	35
857,476	7
1,038,361	7
1,108,809	25

Average, 13.7 secs.

Source: Bryan and Lindley 1941:37–39.
[a] The original contains the following footnote: "Error by A.G., correct number: 4226." The correct number in fact is 4,266.

family and within a few days was in fairly good conformity with the manners of the household. His earlier lack of mastery of the simpler amenities was not due to weakness of intelligence nor to lack of example, but rather to absent-mindedness due to preoccupation with calculation. This was further demonstrated by his quickness in mastering the simpler details of golf which led him to suggest to his host many good plays [while carrying his host's golf clubs?].

The results of Bryan and Lindley's tests of Griffith's calculating ability are given in table 32.1. The timings are explained as follows (p. 37):

> *Auditory Procedure.* When the operator had finished reading, he pressed a key and the time regulation began. The record made by the subject with electric pencil showed:
>
> A—The time when he began to write.
> B—In multiplication and factoring, the subject sometimes obtained his result in two groups. In such cases B shows the time when he began writing the second group.
> C—The time when he finished writing.
>
> *Visual Procedure.* The same except that when the operator pressed the key the numbers to be operated upon appeared on a screen in front of the subject.
>
> A. G.'s rates in addition, subtraction, and division were much slower than in multiplication, for the reason, as it developed, that in the latter he could make much more use of his short-cut methods.
>
> In testing A. G.'s rate in addition, subtraction, it was judged sufficient to determine the total time for 10 successive operations.

Regarding Griffith's ability as a calculator, Bryan and Lindley concluded (p. 27):

> In rapidity of calculation, Griffith ranks high among recorded cases. Compared with Binet's subject, he falls slightly below Inaudi in rapidity, but far excells Diamandi.
>
> In factoring of composite numbers below 1,500, and in extracting square and cube root, his speed was phenomenal. . . . As the subjoined table shows . . . , he is more rapid in multiplication than in addition, subtraction, or division.

In fact, the table tells us very little about Griffith's ability as a calculator. The tests were quite limited, and it is evident in one case, at least, that Griffith must have dictated the form the problems were to take, much to his advantage.

All the examples of mental multiplication involve multiplying by 963. But all the numbers to be multiplied are divisible by 27, and 963 times 27 is 26,001! To multiply 2,376 by 963, therefore, Griffith simply multiplied 26,001 by 88, a relatively easy calculation.

The examples of factoring done by Griffith are also remarkably easy. He felt no need to reduce the numbers to prime factors and in every case gave only two factors. Since all the numbers had small easy-to-determine factors, Griffith had only to divide through by that factor.

For example, if a number is divisible by four, the last two digits are divisible by four; if a number is divisible by eight the last three digits are divisible by eight; any number ending in 25 is divisible by 25; a number is divisible by 11 if the sum of the even-place digits (see chapter 15) subtracted from the sum of the odd-place digits is divisible by 11. Also note that the process can be repeated—if a number has a factor of eight one can divide through, and if the dividend is even the original number is divisible by 16 (or one can divide the last four digits by 16). Except for the smaller numbers, with whose factors Griffith was already no doubt familiar, these facts are sufficient to explain all the examples of factoring.

In fact, Griffith never came up with any difficult factors, though some are hidden in the numbers given; for example, $95,432 = 2^3 \times 79 \times 151$ and $5,624 = 2^3 \times 19 \times 37$.

Nor are the examples of root extractions very difficult. None of the cube roots exceed three digits. Since the first and last digits are immediate, it is only necessary to figure out the middle digit, which can be got by the use of two-figure endings, by casting out elevens, or by casting out nines and extrapolating. The square roots are more problematic, as can be seen by the times, because of the greater uncertainty regarding the smaller digits, but none provide any great difficulty.

Griffith had devised a great many methods for performing calculations, but he was quite incapable of appreciating their algebraic bases, even when these were pointed out to him. He worked out the following method for squaring numbers less than but near 100 (a method independently discovered by various calculators). It is based on the general principle that $a^2 = (a + b)(a - b) + b^2$. Therefore, $96^2 = 100 \times 92 + 4^2$ or, since 96 is 4 less than 100, subtract 4 from 96, write 92, square 4 and write 16 after it; then $96^2 = 9,216$. Griffith used this method down to 85^2 (of course, as an adult, Griffith no doubt had all the two-digit squares memorized). To square 83, Griffith relied on the principle that $(a - b)^2 = a^2 -$

$2ab + b^2$. Thus $1,002 \times 17 = 66$ (hundred), $17^2 = 289$, and $6,600 + 289 = 6,889$.

Some months later Griffith returned to Indiana University, where he gave a demonstration before the student assembly. For his last feat he wrote the number 142,857,143 on the blackboard and had Lindley write another number of the same number of digits below it. As Lindley wrote his number from left to right, Griffith followed along, writing their product, also from left to right, finishing immediately after Lindley finished writing the multiplier. According to Bryan and Lindley (1941:51), "The student audience rose with a shout."

If you think that there is something suspicious about the number Griffith wrote on the board, you are of course right; 142,857,143 is 1,000,000,001 divided by 7 and a nine-digit number multiplied by 1,000,000,001 will yield the original series of nine digits twice repeated. Thus Griffith had only to divide the original multiplier through twice by seven.[2]

Griffith subsequently traveled about under the cognomen of "Marvellous" Griffith, appearing on the American vaudeville circuit. He died of a stroke in Springfield, Massachusetts on Christmas night, 1911.

[2] Any remainder must be carried around to the beginning and the final total must come out even or there is an error; for an interesting discussion, see Gardner (1975:78–80).

Chapter Thirty-three

Salo Finkelstein

214 is a "beautiful" number. Some numbers F[inkelstein] appeared to like and some to dislike. Zero was his pet aversion. 226 is equal to $15^2 + 1^2$, permutated to 622 is the date when Mohammed went from Mecca to Modena [Medina]. In 611 he started to convince people of his religion and this number reminds him of 2611 which is the logarithm of the mantissa of 41681.[1] This number in turn is $2^2 = 4$, $4^2 = 16$ and $9^2 = 81$. 416-81 is also the telephone number of Prof. Henning in Dansig.

— James D. Weinland (1948:253)

THE date of Salo Finkelstein's birth is not included in the studies I have of him, but he appears to have been born in 1896 or 1897 in Lodz, Russia, now Poland. In 1932 he came to the United States, where he gave performances and tried vainly to interest New York banks in having him come in for about an hour each week to check their arithmetic. During the 1932 presidential elections, he added the votes as they came in and supplied ongoing reports of the standings of the candidates. He also hoped to hire himself out as a human computer to a mathematician seeking new mathematical laws. Shortly after his arrival, Finkelstein presented himself for testing at the School of Commerce, Accounts and Finance of New York University.[2]

Finkelstein said (Weinland and Schlauch 1937:382) that though he was good at arithmetic at school, he was not at all a prodigy. When he

---

[1] 0.41681 is the mantissa (to five places) of the logarithm of 2,611.

[2] This account is based upon information contained in reports of tests by Weinland and Schlauch (1937), Weinland (1948), and Bousfield and Barry (1933).

was 23, a friend claimed he could mentally multiply two three-digit numbers. Finkelstein subsequently discovered that he could multiply two six-digit numbers together in his head. Finkelstein calculated by visualizing numbers as written in his own handwriting on a freshly washed blackboard (see chapter 2). He practiced repeating numbers presented both visually and verbally and was sufficiently successful to give public demonstrations.

After a while, Finkelstein lost interest and gave up performing until he was 27 and read in the newspaper of a man with an outstanding memory for numbers. Finkelstein attempted new (but unspecified) feats to which scientists, doctors, and newspaper reporters were invited. Shortly thereafter, he was employed by the State Statistical Office of the Polish government, where he was frequently assigned to the treasury to carry out budgetary calculations. In 11 years of working for the government, Finkelstein said, no errors were found in his work. He attributed this accuracy to the fact that he always did the problems in two different ways. In public performances he did the same, saying "Check, no error," and offered $100 to anyone who caught him in an error after he gave this indication.

Although the data are scanty, results of the tests at New York University (Weinland and Schlauch 1937:396) indicate that, by the standards of calculating prodigies, Finkelstein was poor at multiplication. It took him an average of 4.03 seconds to multiply two digits by two digits (based on 30 examples) and he achieved only 93.3 percent accuracy. The range of times required went all the way from 2 to 14 seconds. Surprisingly, to multiply three digits by three digits took only slightly longer (5.7 seconds average for six examples), but his accuracy sank to 83.3 percent. Ten examples of four digits by four digits required an average of 13.5 seconds with an accuracy of only 60 percent. Finkelstein failed to get even half of the five-digit by five-digit multiplications correct (44.4 percent right) and his average time went up to 25.8 seconds.

His reported reasoning in multiplying 58 by 43 in 7 seconds was as follows (Weinland and Schlauch 1937:386): "$50 = 1/2$ of 100. $1/2 \times 43 = 21.5$, $\therefore$ $50 \times 43 = 2{,}150$. $8 \times 43 = 344$. $2{,}150 + 344 = 2{,}494$." Clearly, Finkelstein, in spite of his prodigious memory for figures (of which more is to come), did not make use of an extended multiplication table.

In longer multiplications, Finkelstein made use of cross multiplication. Since he was given the problems in written form he did not have to memorize them, and, using cross multiplication, he could write down the answers from right to left as he calculated them.

Finkelstein displayed considerably more ability for mental addition. It was discovered that the time required for him to add numbers went up linearly with the number of digits to be added according to the following equation (Weinland and Schlauch 1937:393):

$$Y' = -3.35 + .31X,$$

where Y' represents the most probable time in seconds to add, and X the number of digits to be added. The coefficient of correlation was .968, indicating that the equation gives a very good estimate of the time required for Finkelstein to add a given number of digits. The predicted time to add 100 digits is 27.65; the actual time was 26.7. This is a rate of almost four digits a second, and is certainly very good for a problem of this size. No indication is given of Finkelstein's accuracy in solving these addition problems, so we must assume that they were "all correct." He was given addition problems starting with 27 digits and going up to 100 digits, and was tested for both vertical and horizontal addition. Surprisingly, the adding times for these two methods did not differ significantly. It is not clear whether any of these problems involved more than single-digit numbers.

Finkelstein's most remarkable talent was for rapid memorization of numbers. The results of Weinland's (1948:244) tests of Finkelstein's number memory are very startling, but suffer from some lack of clarity regarding the circumstances of the experiment. The emphasis in these tests was on speed in memorizing, since Finkelstein maintained that he could memorize numbers without difficulty, if they were presented to him at one second intervals.

He refused to be tested after a passage of time on numbers he had previously memorized on the grounds that if he reviewed the material mentally, he could remember anything forever, and it could not be objectively determined whether he reviewed. These sound, frankly, a bit like excuses, but perhaps they are simply the truth.

Weinland (1948:244) described the testing equipment and condition as follows:

> Three pieces of apparatus were used in the various tests. A pendulum chronoscope was connected with a baloptican, in such a way that time was measured as long as the figures were projected on a screen. Finkelstein threw the light on and snapped a switch in his hand, turning it off, as soon as he was satisfied that he knew the numbers. The Whipple tachistoscope was used for some exposures. This instrument operates like a focal plane shutter camera

except that one looks into the tachistoscope during the exposure period. Anything requiring more than four seconds was measured with a stop watch.

Now, it is clear that in memorizing numbers having a span of five to nine digits, Finkelstein could hardly have controlled the length of the presentation manually, since the longest time given is a sixth of a second, and in some cases he memorized numbers flashed to him at a thousandth of a second. Equally obviously, no one can actually "see" images presented for periods of time such as a thousandth of a second (or even a hundredth). It can only have been the afterimage on the retina that Finkelstein saw, and this is determined largely by the brightness of the image. In fact, Weinland makes the curious comment (1948:256): "In the rapid work the span was probably more accurately measured than the speed, due to the light factor. When the light was bright enough so that the figures could be seen in a very short exposure the visual function was probably aided by the brightness." One would certainly hope that the span was accurately measured, since in Weinland's tables *span* refers simply to the number of digits to be memorized in a particular case.

Another difficulty with the experiment is that we are not told how long after the presentation of a particular example Finkelstein was asked to repeat it. If he was asked to repeat numbers immediately after they were presented, this, for shorter numbers, could amount to a test of perception but hardly of memory, since almost anyone can repeat a five-digit number immediately after seeing it. It is perhaps safer then, in evaluating these results, to concentrate on cases in which the total number of digits is sufficient to be certain some significant memorization was involved.

After a one-second exposure each (Weinland 1948:248), Finkelstein was able to repeat numbers of 20 and 25 digits, two 26-digit numbers (the first was correctly reported forward and backward), and one of 28-digits. A second 28-digit number took two seconds, and three pairs of adjacent numbers were transposed. He then went on to numbers of 30 digits (correct in 3 seconds), 31 digits (correct in 3 seconds), 33 digits (correct in 2 seconds), another of 33 digits (3 seconds; 2 digits transposed), 34 digits (2 seconds, 2 digits transposed), 35 digits (correct in 4 seconds), 39 digits (3 digits transposed; 4 seconds), another of 39 digits (correct; 4 seconds). These results are simply astounding. It is hard even to imagine that in one second's time anyone could take in a number such as

4863574987398646481035925469,

much less manage to fix it in the memory sufficiently well to repeat it backward and forward.

When faced with numbers not arranged in a horizontal string, Finkelstein worked much more slowly (Weinland 1948:250). For example, to memorize four four-digit numbers arranged in columns required times on separate trials of 3.386, 2.950, 4.840, and 3.945 seconds, even though, in each case, there were only sixteen digits involved. Single digits placed in squares of five-by-five matrices (that is, 25 digits in all) proved even more difficult. Here he required times of 13, 14.5, 18.5, and 20.75 seconds, and, in the first instance, three of the digits were wrongly reported.

Finally, Finkelstein made two trials at memorizing four-digit numbers, one matrix of 17 rows and another of 18 rows (Weinland 1948:251). The first test required 5 minutes and 44 seconds, and the second, 5 minutes and 41 seconds. In each trial, two of the four-digit numbers were incorrectly identified. Most of Finkelstein's other errors involved transpositions, but in these cases the numbers reported seem to have little to do with the correct ones, suggesting he may have made some erroneous associations (2251 for 8366; 8858 for 8665; 5246 for 6872; and 7585 for 8282).

Finkelstein used a variety of arithmetic, historical, and other associations (e.g., phone numbers) to fix three- and four-digit sequences of larger numbers in his mind. In some cases, however, he retained long sequences without special associations. Weinland (1948:252–53) gave some examples of series memorized and Finkelstein's reported associations:

No. 1:   Memorized with a two-second exposure. 2(1)794586389142879. On the first repetition F left out the 1 in parenthesis [sic]. When this was pointed out to him he immediately repeated the whole series *backward*, including the 1 and without mistake. He said in regard to this series that he found no particular associations and learned it "automatically."

No. 2:   Memorized with a one-second exposure. 7543829564. 7543 was observed as a descending series, lacking only the six. The last 564 reminded F of 1564, the birth of Galileo and Shakespeare.

No. 3:   Memorized with a three-second exposure. 76354*2197*86382-9742805863*1789*20. 2197 is 13 to the third power; 1789 is the date of the French Revolution. The other numbers were held without special associations.

Although Finkelstein, like most calculators, had a wide variety of associations with numbers, typically only a few of these might be used in memorizing a particular number. In one case, Weinland (1948:253) asked him to report all the associations he could with the following number:

141592653589793238462643383279.

141 is the square root of two; 592 can be permuted to 259 or 925; 925 can be divided by 37; 592 with 10 in front, 10592 is the telephone number of the P & F Manufacturing Plant in Lodz, Poland; 2595 is the number of the paragraphs in Spinoza's ethics. With a two after it 2592 is two to the fifth power plus nine squared;[3] 2,592,000 is the number of seconds in a month; 65-35 and 89-79 have resemblances in their second numbers; 89-79 are both prime numbers; in 32-38 the tens are identical; 462 has three even numbers; 643 with 1 in front, 1643 is the birth date of Newton and the year when the barometer was invented; 383 is a "nice" symmetrical number; 279 reminds one that 2 plus 7 equals 9.

Finkelstein's ability to memorize or calculate varied considerably from day to day, and if he made a major error, he would not continue, since confidence was of prime importance.

Finkelstein disappeared from the American scene as mysteriously as he appeared on it. Unable to find suitable employment, he left New York City. Weinland (1948:251) suggests that he may have returned to Poland. I have no further information on his fate.

[3] As stated, this is obviously incorrect $(2^5 + 9^2 = 113)$. I do not know what Finkelstein had in mind.

Chapter Thirty-four

Wim Klein

In Marseille on a Sunday afternoon, there was a chap who was eating flames, there was a lady who told the future, there was a chap with a monkey, and I was extracting cube roots. Ho, ho. I'd like to go back and do it again. It was fun. But I did not need to do it. I just got so fascinated with this vagabond life.

— Wim Klein, reminiscing about the postwar period[1]

WIM Klein (also sometimes referred to as Willem or William Klein) was born in Amsterdam on December 4, 1912—a Wednesday, as he is quick to tell you.

Klein's interest in calculation began at age 8, when he discovered factoring. "At school we had to factor numbers up to 500. Then I continued on to 10,000, 15,000, 20,000, 25,000. As you got so often the same combinations, it is logical that if you know that 2,537 is 43 times 59, and you're doing a little show for the godmother of a neighbor celebrating her eighteenth birthday, and they ask you for 43 times 59, you recognize straightaway 2,537."

Although Klein never set about to learn the multiplication table up to 100 by 100, he gradually acquired it from repeatedly encountering the same combinations. He contrasts this sort of memory, which comes about unbidden simply as a matter of repeated exposure to certain material, to deliberately committing something to memory; the latter he calls "me-

---

[1] Unless otherwise attributed, information in this chapter is based on personal interviews with Wim Klein.

chanical memory." "The multiplication and the squares up to 1,000, I just took as a game. Learning the logarithm table by heart up to 150 is memorizing, but in terms of multiplication I never memorized. It came from the experience I got by factoring—I got often that 2,537 is 43 times 59, and 5,074 is the double, and 7,611 three times the number—so you recognize it."

By exposure he has learned the multiplication tables up to 100 by 100, the squares of integers up to 1,000, the cubes of numbers up to 100, and roughly all prime numbers below 10,000. He deliberately committed to memory the decimal logarithms to five places of the first 150 integers. He also knows "some other small things like the first 32 powers of 2, the first 20 powers of three and so on; some logarithms base e; a lot of history; and I also learned by heart the date of birth and death of about 150 composers."

Klein's older brother, Leo, was also an exceptional mental calculator, but Wim was the moving force behind the brothers' interest. "Leo was a little infected by me. Because I did it, he also had to do it."

The brothers were, however, altogether different in their methods—Leo's memory was visual, while Wim's is auditory. Leo did not share Wim's fascination for factoring, nor did he care to go beyond three digits by three digits in multiplication.

To illustrate the difference between his methods and Leo's, Klein asked me to call out two three-digit numbers. I chose 426 and 843. He muttered in Dutch and after a few seconds said: "359,118." He then took a piece of paper and wrote:

$$
\begin{array}{r}
4.26 \\
8.43 \\
\hline
12.78 \\
170.40 \\
3408.00 \\
\hline
3591.18
\end{array}
$$

"My brother would say: 'There's twelve dollars and seventy-eight cents plus a hundred and seventy dollars and forty cents plus three thousand four hundred and eight dollars—three thousand five hundred ninety-one dollars and eighteen cents, which he had to translate into normal pronunciation as three hundred fifty-nine thousand one hundred eighteen.

"But I say, hey, 426 divided by 6 is 71, and 843 times 6 is 5,058; 5 times 71 is 355 [in this case thousand] and 58 times 71, by experience, without calculating it, is 4,118. You see the difference? If you had taken 427 I should have done quite differently: I should have said '427 divided by 7 is 61 and 843 times 7 is 5,901; 61 times 5,901 is 359,961.' You see how it helps using factorization as much as possible? There is a key-hole in a hotel and I've got a key ring with 500 keys. What I have to do is to pick the right key for that slot. For every problem I have to think straightaway which is the best way—just like a flash."

The difference between the brothers' memory showed up in other areas as well. Leo would come into a town, buy a map, scan it briefly, and know his way about. Klein recalls: "He would say to a waiter in a pub, 'I have to go *there*.' The chap would say, 'Well, you go like this.' My brother says, 'And if you go like this, is it not shorter?' The waiter says, 'Yes, sir.'"

When the brothers were children and took the streetcar to school, each conductor wore an identification number on his collar. Years later they saw an elderly man selling tickets on the streetcar. Leo asked Wim, "Do you remember him?"

"No."

"In the old days his collar number was 683."

Leo started to talk to the man and after a while he asked: "How many years have you worked on the tramway?"

"Oh, since. . . ."

"Yes, and years ago you were on streetcar number 60."

"Yes."

"And your collar number was 683."

The old man looked at him: "You damn. . . . That is correct."

Klein says: "There were hundreds of examples like this. Funny, eh? This visualizing. I cannot do it at all."

Klein's father wanted a successor to his medical practice, so Wim very reluctantly undertook the study of medicine, even though he was already dreaming of show business. In spite of all the time he was forced to devote to studies, he managed to give little shows now and then. He finished his theoretical studies "after a hell of a lot of trouble," but before he could finish medical school his father died, and Wim abruptly halted his studies. "The old man died in 1937. He was always very strict on the penny with my brother and me. After he died, we got a little inheritance. So the brothers took full profit of life. Then the war came. It became very tough, of course, as you may guess. I lost my brother in the war, also killed like hundreds of thousands of others."

For two years Klein worked in a Jewish hospital, as other hospitals were forbidden to Jews. Then the Germans started to take people from the hospitals to camps and Klein was forced into hiding. Leo was not so fortunate; he was sent to a camp in Germany from which he never returned. It is not a period Klein cares to recall. "I had to hide. Some people took care of me. Just say it was like the case of Anne Frank. That is sufficient."

After the war Klein had to find some way to make a living, since the Germans had confiscated all his money. "Everybody needed show business at that moment, after those awful years."

Klein's first postwar role as a professional calculator was a nonspeaking one. He was decked out as a sort of Indian fakir with turban and a false beard. His partner did all the talking while Klein chalked up the answers.

But the theatrical agency was dissatisfied: "They told me, 'Listen, this act with the beard stinks. Your presentation is vulgar. We will get you in contact with one of the best announcers in the country, and you will travel about with a group of excellent artists.' And then it developed as a really nice act. But then, as Wim Klein was too cheap, they came up with 'Pascal.' In Holland they don't know Wim Klein, they know only Pascal. Why Pascal? It is a French name, but Pascal was the inventor of the calculating machine. When Pascal came to France, where nine out of ten people call themselves Pascal, and my French with my Dutch accent was not good enough, so there I became Wim Klein."[2]

In France and parts of Belgium, Klein had to do his act in his "poor, bad, school French." (He later learned to speak fluent, if somewhat confusing, French, German, and English.) "There was an expression, which in Dutch was a normal expression, so I thought in French it should be the same, so I translated it literally from Dutch into French and it meant something quite different. Nobody told me, but the audience burst out in laughter the whole bloody week. They did not want to tell me what was wrong with it, and only the last day, they told me it meant something like 'How often in the week do you do it?' or something like that. Silly."

During the postwar period he appeared in France and Belgium, and began doing radio broadcasts in Holland. While in Brussels in 1949, Klein was down on his luck. "I spent all my bloody money. Then I met some friends and one said: 'I play the guitar and he plays the accordion. You have a blackboard. We make some music and you do some sums.'

[2] Klein is also sometimes known as "Willie Wortel" (Wortel being the Dutch word for root) from his ability to extract roots of large numbers.

We went to nightclubs, little pubs. First they made the music, then I came on with my sums, and then the guitarist went around with the hat.

"After a while we decided to go to Paris. We went to the Champs Elysées where people sit outside, and started to perform, but the police came and said: 'Shut up, you bloody beggars.'

"My friends went back to Holland, and after that I joined a little circus. But we went broke. A chap said, 'Why don't you just set up your act at the subway entrance? Lots of people do it.' And yes, it worked perfectly, but there were two enemies—the rain and the police.

"Some cops would say 'We're here this week, but next week some bastards are coming, so next week go somewhere else.' Or a Dutchman would say, 'Hey, can you fix me up with a nice girl?' 'Yep.' 'Emmanuelle, I've got a guy for you.' 'Here, my dear, this is for you. A tip.' Oh, what a great time."

But as Klein had no work permit, the French authorities finally kicked him out of the country. At the train he met a Belgian who had seen him perform several times in the Place Pigalle. The man was living in Mons near the French border. He said that he had contacts in Belgium through which they could organize a lecture tour in the schools. "They put me up in a little pension, and they bought me some decent clothes. After three months time I was out of debt."

In 1952 Klein got a job at the Mathematisch Centrum in Amsterdam, where he did various sorts of numerical calculations. "Computers—they didn't exist, or nearly not. I sat in a room with these five heavy-reformist girls [members of the Netherlands Reformed Church], always talking about God and the clergy. I would say 'Good God' and 'God damn it,' so they went to the boss and said, 'Klein is swearing like a docker.' He told them, 'Don't quarrel, let him swear.' They said, 'Yes, but. . . .' So he called me in and said, 'Listen, Klein, quiet down. I know they are idiots, but try to do better.' 'I try, I try very hard, but you know. . . .' "

In 1952 Klein began seriously lecturing in schools; again it came about by accident. Whenever important people visited the Mathematisch Centrum, Klein was called upon to give a demonstration, "not as a human computer, but as a human attraction." A French professor from UNESCO saw him there and asked him if he would come to Paris and give a lecture to the Department of Mathematics at the Sorbonne. The planned fifty-minute appearance stretched to two hours. As a result of contacts made there, Klein was able to obtain permission to give lectures in grammar schools throughout France. "So I wrote to the Mathematisch Centrum and asked for leave of two months or so. They replied, 'Wim, I'm afraid that this means the end—that you will stay longer than two years. But I'm sure you will have tremendous success.' "

In 1954 Klein met the New Zealand mathematician and calculating prodigy, Alexander Craig Aitken, at a mathematical conference in Amsterdam. Later in that year they appeared together on a BBC program. Klein recalls: "He was a lovely man. When Britain had not yet the decimal system, I used to do problems like multiplying £3, 7 shillings, 8 pence, ha'penny by 29. When I asked Aitken about such problems, he said: 'Oh, I've got enough trouble when I have to fill out my income tax form.' "

In 1955 Klein toured for nine months as one of the attractions of the "MIRACLES OF THE MUSIC HALL, Starring Some of the Most Unusual People Ever Seen." He was billed as "the man with the £10,000 brain." The cast included "the Dare-Devil Denglaros on their Racing Motor Bikes; the Amazing Devero, Escape from a Real Guillotine; Ladd West, World's Fantastic Aerial Contortionist; Rondart, World's only Dart Blower; the Roller Skating Jeretz from Geneva; Reggie 'yer see' Dennis, Britain's new radio Comedian; the Incomparable Mime Star, Danny O'Dare; and Personal Appearance of The Man Who Was Buried Alive— already seen by 4,719,329 people in 8 years tour."

Klein reflected on some of his fellow performers: "This chap was a real pig. He always escaped, but we all hoped that he wouldn't. Danny O'Dare, the Indian Rubberman, was just a poor devil. With the Moto-devils, every second word was a swear word. You could not speak decently with those people.

"Tommy Jacobson, the armless wonder—the first thing he did was to take a rifle and shoot, then he played the piano with his feet, then the master of ceremonies asked someone to come on the stage for a shave. He told the chap to sit down and said, 'Tommy, not as much blood as yesterday.' So the poor chap turned his head so, and Tommy took a big knife and . . . sccrrr.

"Once Tommy was standing on the platform of a London bus and a chap tried to grab hold of him to pull himself on the moving bus. He grabbed Tommy's raincoat sleeve, but there was nothing in it, so he tumbled into the street clutching a raincoat."

The Miracles of the Music Hall gave two shows a night. After doing his act for the first house, a performer was off until it was time to perform in the second show. Between shows one night, Klein dropped into a pub next door. People from the audience of the first show called him over, started buying him drinks and asking him to do calculations. By the time Klein finally went running back to the theater, the second show was almost over. Someone said to him, "Wim, be careful. The announcer is already in a bad mood."

The announcer, who was also the manager, called out, "Wim Klein, there he is, here comes Wim Klein." Klein says, "I was struggling up, you know. He still didn't notice, but then he caught a funny smell of gin. He came really close and said, 'You bloody Peruvian Chinese teapot, you. If you don't finish your act properly, I'll kick you out straightaway.' I said, 'Yeah, yeah, I've just been kidding.' So I made it, more or less, and after the show he said, 'Listen, I also like to drink, but never do it between the two houses. You promise?' 'Yes.' 'Come on, let's have a drink together.' So we both got pissed when the show was over."

After Miracles of the Music Hall, Klein returned to touring schools, first in France and then in Switzerland. But by 1957 he decided he wanted to settle down, so he returned to Amsterdam to work at the Mathematisch Centrum.

During the summer of 1958 he arranged a two-week tour of Swiss schools. The giant research complex of CERN (European Organization for Nuclear Research) is located near Geneva. Klein was mistakenly under the impression that some of the work of the Mathematisch Centrum was done for CERN, so he decided to telephone CERN while he was in Geneva. He was told to "just pop over." He was introduced to a Dutch physicist, C. J. Bakker. Klein recalled: "We talked and he said, 'Would you like to work in Geneva?' I said, 'That's for other people to say. Is there a possibility for me to get a job here?' And then Professor Bakker said, 'Listen, Wim, I cannot decide; I'm only the director general here, you see.' So I said, 'Not so bad.' Naturally, I had a feeling everything would be all right."

An arrangement was made with the Mathematisch Centrum for a three-month leave of absence. After four weeks, CERN asked Klein to stay on permanently. "These three months became eighteen years. That's the CERN story."

In the early days Klein was in considerable demand at CERN. "Computers were not very well developed, and the physicists did not yet program them themselves. From '58 to '65 it was all right for me. And then, it went down, because young physicists did their own programming, and so they did not need me as much as before. But the idea to kick me out never came, because of public relations. Very often when physicists came and they could not see the machine, someone would say, 'Hey, Wim, do something for them.'"

Jeremy Bernstein described an encounter with Klein (1963:20):

In the summer of 1961, I had an opportunity to work with Mr. William
Klein, a programmer and numerical analyst for CERN . . . , in Geneva,
who must be one of the fastest human computers who has ever lived. I was
spending the summer doing physics at CERN and had been working with
a friend on a problem. After a week or so, we produced an algebraic formula
that seemed admirable to us in many respects, and we wanted to evaluate it.
CERN has a large Ferranti Mercury computer, and since at the time neither
of us knew anything about programming, we asked for help. Enter Mr.
Klein. Mr. Klein is a short, kindly, energetic-looking man in his forties. He
is of Dutch origin. He looked at our formula for a few seconds, muttering
to himself in Dutch, and then gave us numerical estimates for several of the
more complex parts of it. Doing this, he said, helped set up the program for
the computer in the most efficient way. I had heard about Mr. Klein's almost
incredible ability, and I asked him whether he had considered evaluating our
whole expression in his head. He told me that it would involve much too
much work and that he was quite glad to turn the job over to the machine.
Watching Mr. Klein at work made a deep impression on me. . . .

By the mid-seventies, Klein was growing weary of CERN. In 1975
Amsterdam was celebrating its 700th anniversary, and Klein visited there
some eight times. The next year he again visited Amsterdam several times.
He decided to retire. "It's too monotonous—18 years. It was a golden
cage, but I prefer silver freedom. So at the end I retired one year before
I was 65."

In June 1974, shortly before his departure from CERN, Klein became
intrigued with the problem of extracting integer roots of large numbers.
The 1974 edition of the *Guinness Book of World Records* reported that
Herbert B. de Grote of Mexico City had extracted the 13th root of a
hundred-digit number in 23 minutes.

Klein says: "What is the use of extracting the 13th root of 100 digits?
'Must be a bloody idiot' you say. No. It puts you in the *Guinness Book,*
of course.

"I never came on the idea until I got this notice about this man in
Mexico. I thought, hey, how interesting. I should have thought of that.
First I had to find out how to tackle the problem. Then I needed material—I needed numbers raised to the wanted power. So they wrote a
multiprecision program on the computer. And I was practicing like hell,
like hell, like hell. Once you know the system for the first one, you have
to learn another series of numbers by heart for the next one."

By October 8, 1974, Klein succeeded in extracting the 23rd root of a 200-digit number in 18 minutes, 7 seconds, and on March 5, 1975, in Lyon, he reduced the time to 10 minutes, 32 seconds.

Later, Klein went on to extract a variety of roots: the 19th root of 133 digits (1 m. 43 sec.), the seventh root of 63 digits (8 m. 27 sec.), the 73d root of 500 digits (2 m. 9 sec.).

As explained in chapter 13, the difficulty of extracting integer roots of large numbers depends on the number of digits in the root—the size of the power is immaterial. The *Guinness Book of World Records* now accepts the extraction of the 13th root of a 100-digit number as a fair test; records now hinge upon improving the time required.

Klein has continually improved his times for extracting such roots. In Providence, Rhode Island, in September 1979, he achieved a time of 3 minutes 25 seconds; then in Paris, November 1979, 3 minutes 6 seconds; Leiden, March 1980, 2 minutes 45 seconds; London (BBC), May 1980, 2 minutes 9 seconds; Berlin, November 10, 1980, 2 minutes 8 seconds. Finally, on November 13, 1980, he got below two minutes—1 minute 56 seconds. And on April 7, 1981, at the National Laboratory for High Energy Physics, Tsukuba, Japan, he established a new record of 1 minute and 28.8 seconds. With this he is fairly well satisfied. He plans now to attempt to split up the four- or five-digit numbers as the sum of four squares within one minute.

Klein describes much of his calculating as "semimental," in that he has the problem in view while solving it (thus obviating the necessity of memorizing it) and because he often writes down parts of the answer as he calculates them, before the entire answer has been found; this means that he does not need to keep the entire answer in mind before announcing it. For example, in multiplying he uses cross multiplication, which allows him to write down the digits from right to left as they are obtained. After multiplying two eight-digit numbers for me "semimentally," Klein remarked, "Some people say to write down results as you go is not fair. You have to do it all in your head. But it takes five times as long and the audience will say, 'Forget it.'"

He asked me for two five-digit numbers and I gave him 57,825 and 13,489. In 44 seconds he multiplied these together mentally, without any intermediate results. He then repeated the experiment, writing down the answer as he calculated it—the time required was 14 seconds. "The first is more scientific, if you want. It is the real thing, but it's not what the people want."

Klein's passion, apart from numbers, is music. He is particularly fond of jazz and classical music. He says, "In New York every night I went to Jimmy Ryan's Jazz Club. I also did that when I was in New York two years ago. So when I popped in this time, they said, 'Hey, Flying Dutchman, how are you? Have a drink. What shall we play for you?' " (Here Klein gave an excellent imitation of a trombone playing *Ain't Misbehaving*.)

"I play no instruments, pity enough. I've got about 600 LPs. Not very much, but. . . ."

In spite of the justifiable pride Klein takes in his calculating ability, there is a passionate honesty in him as well. When I suggested that he may be the world's greatest mental calculator, he replied, "I'm not the world's greatest calculator. Perhaps the world's fastest calculator." In any case, Klein is surely one of the best mental calculators in history.

Chapter Thirty-five

Maurice Dagbert

MAURICE Dagbert was born June 20, 1913 in Calais, the son of a laborer. He seems to have had some difficulties in school; according to a letter he wrote me he was "a studious pupil but often punished because he would not solve his problems by the classical methods, but was inspired rather by Arabic methods of the 13th and 14th centuries."[1] He quit school at age 11, apparently for economic rather than academic or disciplinary reasons.

Just when Dagbert began serious mental calculation is not clear. He wrote of himself:

> After having quit school he became very interested in numbers and began to write his first procedures for mental calculation. Without knowledge of algebra he solved second-degree equations with the help of a method he still uses today. . . .
>
> It was after a performance given by Inaudi that Dagbert recognized his possibilities.
>
> The old calculator questioned him and predicted a brilliant future for him. It was during his captivity in Germany [as a prisoner of war in WWII] that Dagbert perfected his prodigious performance in calculation.

According to a report to the Academy of Sciences (Fayet et al. 1945), Dagbert was 14 years old at the time he first met Inaudi in Calais, but

---

[1] This apparently refers to left-to-right methods of calculation. For example, Darboux (quoted in Binet 1894:201) wrote of Inaudi's methods that "some approach, in certain respects, those which are followed by the Hindus. . . ." The Indian calculator Shyam Marathe also told me that the fifteenth-century mathematician Brahmagupta said that calculations should proceed from left to right.

Information in this chapter not otherwise attributed is from Dagbert's letter to me (my translation).

de Cressac (Barlow 1952:59), who did a study of Dagbert, gives the year as 1930, which would make Dagbert 16 or 17 years old.

According to Regnault (1952:34) in 1939 various newspapers remarked upon the 25-year-old calculator from Calais. One of his accomplishments was to extract the seventh root of 31,068,554,553,807,275, 169. (The answer, though not included by Regnault, is 609.) *Le Canard enchaîne* published a humorous note to the effect that Dagbert was having so much trouble making out his income tax forms that he had taken to bed.

After the war, Dagbert and Inaudi again met. Inaudi was then 76 years old and no longer remembered the young man he had met in Calais. He had heard of Dagbert the calculator, however, and wished to meet him. Inaudi posed some trick questions to Dagbert, and then asked: "Suppose that an hour contains 37½ minutes and a minute 96 seconds. How many seconds old would a person aged 24 years be, figuring six leap years?" Dagbert correctly responded: "757,382,400 seconds."

Dagbert reminded the old man of their previous meeting, and Inaudi said: "So it was you who questioned me that evening and asked me to calculate the cube root of 700,227,072." (It is 888.)

In 1945 Dagbert gave a two-and-one-half hour demonstration before the French Academy of Sciences (Fayet et al. 1945). Among the problems solved were the extraction of a fifth root (243) in 14 seconds; a seventh root (125) in 15 seconds; a cube root (78,517) in 2 minutes 15 seconds; and a fifth root (2,189) in 2 minutes 3 seconds. None of these problems present extraordinary difficulties for a calculating prodigy. In each case the last digit of the root can be determined instantly from the last digit of the power, and the first digit of the root can be determined from the first few digits of the power. The other digits can be got by interpolation and casting out elevens and thirteens. Logarithms can also be used if the calculator has a sufficient number of them memorized (see chapter 17.)

For example, take the answer 2,189, which is the fifth root of 50,260, 731,820,489,949. Since, in fifth roots, the last digit of the root and the power are identical, the last digit of the root must be 9. The first will be 2, as 2^5 equals 32 and 3^5 (243) exceeds 50, the digits to the left of the leftmost comma in the power. As the power ends in 49, the next to last digit in the root must be even. Since 50 is only about 8 percent of the distance between 32 and 243, the second digit of the root must be about 1. Casting out thirteens will then yield the next to the last digit, 8. (I must point out here that I am not claiming that this is the way Dagbert solved this problem, only that this is a way the problem could be solved.)

Barlow (1952:60–61) gives some other samples of Dagbert's calculations (provided by de Cressac). He is credited with "instantaneous" answers to the following problems: 3,478 times 5,685 (19,772,430), 27^3 (19,683), 34^4 (1,336,336), 31^5 (28,629,151), 72^6 (139,314,069,504), 99^7 (93,206,534,790,699).

The following problems were solved in the times indicated: the cube root of 260,917,119 (639), 4 seconds; 29^6 (594,823,321), 13 seconds; 89^6 (496,981,290,961), 10 seconds; the cube root of 49,633,171,875 (3,675), 50 seconds; and the number of seconds in 58 years (1,830,297, 600),[2] 23 seconds.

The academy states that Dagbert was ignorant of algebra. Perhaps that was true at the time (Dagbert was 32), but it is certainly not true today. In Dagbert's letter to me he gives a number of examples of methods for solving problems in mental calculation that reveal an excellent grasp of algebra.

Dagbert plays the violin, a skill he makes use of in his performances. Both Regnault (1952:34) and Tocquet (n.d.:34) refer to Dagbert's playing a fantasy from *Il Trovatore* while mentally extracting 20 three-digit cube roots and multiplying together two five-digit numbers. He completes the fantasy in seven minutes, sets aside the violin, and writes out the results.

Barlow (1952:61) also refers to Dagbert's playing the violin while calculating. In this case he extracted four cube roots of three digits each while playing a piece of unfamiliar music—32 bars of a concerto by Albert Bachmann. Dagbert gave the four roots (735, 387, 354, and 873) after a minute and 25 seconds.

Another of Dagbert's feats begins with an empty blackboard with columns labeled A B C and rows numbered from one to seven. This gives 21 spaces to be filled in. While he stands with his back to the blackboard the audience is invited to call out pairs of digits in any order until the blanks are filled in (e.g., 4C might be 04, followed by 6A as 97).

Barlow (1952:63) says: "He then repeats, by heart and without error, all the numbers that have been announced and in their normal sequence and makes the addition, figure by figure, without mistake. Finally, he repeats all the figures on the board just as though he had the board before his eyes." Apparently Barlow means that Dagbert adds together all the numbers called out.

---

[2] This includes 14 leap years.

Dagbert has done a lot of music-hall work over the years and has appeared on television in various parts of the world. He wrote me that, to his great regret, he does not speak English, which has limited his appearances.

Unlike many other calculators, Dagbert never writes any results as they are obtained (see chapter 10), but announces the entire answer after it has been calculated.

The following are methods used by Dagbert to solve some unusual problems (excerpted from a letter to the author).

(a)   What is the sum of the differences between squares equidistant from the center, the extreme squares being: 7^2 and 19^2?

Solution: Let $(19^2 - 7^2) + (18^2 - 9^2) + \ldots + (14^2 - 12^2)$
and $a = 7$ and $b = 19$.
Calculate $(b - a) + 1 = n$
There are two possible cases: n is even or odd.

For n even calculate $\dfrac{n}{2} = m$ and $S = m^2(a + b)$

For n odd calculate $\dfrac{n-1}{2} = m$ and $S = (m^2 + m)\,(a + b)$

Therefore $(19 - 7) + 1 = 13$ and $\dfrac{13 - 1}{2} = 6$

$$S = (36 + 6)(7 + 19) = 42 \times 26 = 1{,}092$$

(b)   From a perfect square of six digits, the quintuple of another square is subtracted and the difference is equal to 6,724 or 82^2. What are these squares? The solutions are of course infinite and two cases can be distinguished.

Let $x^2 - 5y^2 = a^2$ (here $a = 82$)

For a even: $x_1 = \dfrac{3a}{2}$ or 123

$y_1 = \dfrac{a}{2}$ or 41

$x_2 = 3x_1 - a$ or $(3 \times 123) - 82 = 287$
$y_2 = 3y_1$ or $3 \times 41 = 123$
$x_3 = 3x_2 - x_1$ or $(3 \times 287) - 123 = 738$
$y_3 = 3y_2 - y_1$ or $(3 \times 123) - 41 = 328$

This solution is sufficient as 738^2 gives six digits.

For a odd: $x_1 = 9a$
$y_1 = 4a$
$x_2 = 18x_1 - a$
$y_2 = 18y_1$

and continue multiplying by 18 and subtracting x_1, y_1; x_2, y_2, etc.

Remark: This shows that all perfect squares can be expressed as the difference between a perfect square, diminished by the quintuple of another square, but the converse is not true.

(c)   Find two squares of which the difference is a doubled square.

Solution: There are a number of different methods to resolve this problem. Here is the easiest.

Take the continued fractions of $\sqrt{2}$

$$\frac{3}{2}, \ \frac{7}{5}, \ \frac{17}{12}, \ \frac{41}{29}, \cdots$$

Isolate the fractions with odd denominators:

$$\frac{7}{5}, \ \frac{41}{29}, \cdots$$

Each of these fractions will give an infinity of solutions.

$\dfrac{7}{5}$: $1^2 + 7^2 = 5^2 \times 2$

$2^2 + 14^2 = 10^2 \times 2$

$3^2 + 21^2 = 15^2 \times 2$

. . . .

$\dfrac{41}{29}$: $1^2 + 41^2 = 29^2 \times 2$

$2^2 + 82^2 = 58^2 \times 2$

. . . .

(d)   Two numbers are in the ratio of a to b and the sum of their cubes is Here $a = 3$ and $b = 7$ with $S = 79{,}920$.

Solution: Calculate $a^3 + b^3$ or $27 + 343 = 370$

One quickly estimates how many times this sum is contained in S. This is very easy as the quotient is always a perfect cube. The hundreds digit of the quotient is 2 and the three-digit quotient is immediately obtained: 216 or 6^3.

Therefore: $3 \times 6 = 18$

$7 \times 6 = 42$

and $18^3 + 42^3 = 79{,}920$

(e)   A geometric progression is composed of seven terms (all odd). The sum of the first four is 1,200 and the sum of the last four is 411,600. What is this progression?

Solution: Let n be the number of terms

a the sum of the first $\dfrac{n+1}{2}$

b the sum of the last $\dfrac{n+1}{2}$

$\dfrac{b}{a}$ is an integer and a perfect power: $\dfrac{n-1}{2}$

The root gives the ratio of the progression or r.

Take then the sum: $r^0 + r^1 + r^2 + \ldots + r^{(n-1)/2}$

Divide a by this sum and obtain the first term of the progression.

Then: $\dfrac{411,600}{1,200} = \dfrac{4,116}{12} = 343$ or 7^3, therefore $r = 7$.

$1 + 7 + 49 + 343 = 400$

and $\dfrac{1,200}{400} = 3$ or the first term.

Then: 3, 21, 147, 1,029, . . .

(f)   Here is an amusing recreation of my invention which always interests the public.

Have someone write down a three-digit number (each digit different) which you cannot see. Under this number the person writes the five other permutations of the three digits and adds them up, along with one of the numbers chosen by him from the six (that is, seven three-digit numbers in all, one of which appears twice). The sum only is announced, and then one can give the added seventh permutation, along with all the others.

Solution: There are three ways to solve this problem.

This is the simplest.

Suppose, for example, 712 is chosen.

Then: $712 + 721 + 127 + 172 + 217 + 271 = 2,220$

and suppose 127 is then selected.

Then: $2,220 + 127 = 2,347$.

Take the thousands digit and add it to the units:
$$347 + 2 = 349$$
Take the remainder upon division by 9 (in this case 7), multiply it by 111 (yielding here 777), and add this to the previous total: $349 + 777 = 1,126$.

Remove the thousands digit and add it to the remaining number.

Thus: $126 + 1 = 127$, which is indeed the seventh permutation.

Chapter Thirty-six

Shakuntala Devi

S HAKUNTALA Devi's date of birth is uncertain, perhaps even to
her. It is given as November 4, 1920 in Barlow's *Mental Prodigies*
(1952:64). When I wrote to her, mentioning that I had come across a
brief description of her in that source, she immediately replied that there
was a mistake in the book—that, in fact, she was born on November 4,
1940, not 1920. And *Time* magazine for July 4, 1952 ("Numbers Game"
[1952]) gave her age as 20.

Patricia Sethi (1978), an Indian journalist working for an unspecified
American magazine, interviewed Devi in New York for an article which
appeared in the *Times* of Bombay. Sethi, too, found the question of the
date of Devi's birth puzzling:

> But even the human computer has its human failings. Devi is not *all* per-
> fect at the numbers game; she's "blown it" on figures on at least two occa-
> sions. She has great difficulty determining her age and when her baby was
> due seven years ago, her calculations were off by a whole week. That meant
> giving birth during a refuelling stop at London's Heathrow airport.

The *New York Times* of November 10, 1976 has an article about her
by Bayard Webster, which states, " 'This is my first visit to the United
States,' she told an interviewer at the bank just before her performance.
When reminded that the press had reported her previous visit in 1952
to Washington and New York, she conceded that her memory had been
faulty." By her reckoning she would have been 11 at the time of that
visit.

In her interview with Sethi her memories of her first U.S. trip were
not so vague:

> Shakuntala was in town, she explained, to introduce herself to the Amer-
> ican masses. Her tours of Germany, Japan, England and South-East Asia

have been extremely successful, but the only time she visited the United States (in the "fifties") she was broke, depressed and hungry. No one was interested in her talents—they dismissed her as a freak trying to pull a fast one on them—and she was almost totally ignored. Besides, she didn't have a dime in her pocket. Those were desperate days with meals at local cafeterias consisting of "soup" made from water mixed with the free packets of ketchup lying around on side tables.

Devi told Sethi that her parents were poverty stricken, that she never went to school, and that as a child she traveled with her father giving shows ("rather like a circus, with me standing on a table, since I was so tiny.") When Devi's father, who had married Devi's teenaged mother in his sixties, became too old to continue, Shakuntala pushed on across India, "keeping a small fee for my expenses and sending the rest home."

Devi is the author of several books—*The Perfect Murder, World of Homosexuals, Mathematical Merry-Go-Round,* and *Figuring: The Joy of Numbers.* (The last three are available in the United States.)

It is difficult to assess Devi's calculating ability on the basis of published material I have been able to find, since very little in the way of solved problems is included.

The *New York Times* (Webster 1976) gives three samples of problems solved in 20 seconds or less:

1. The addition of

$$25,842,278$$
$$111,201,721$$
$$370,247,830$$
$$55,511,315$$

with the result to be multiplied by 9,878. She correctly replied 5,559,369,456,432.

2. The cube root of 188,132,517 (573).

3. The days of the week on which the fourteenth of each month fell in 1935: (starting with January) Tuesday, Thursday, Thursday, Sunday, Tuesday, Friday, Sunday, Wednesday, Saturday, Monday, Thursday, Sunday.

Only the first of these problems could present any difficulty to a good mental calculator.

Like many other calculators, Devi extracts the roots of numbers raised to high powers, when these roots are integers. On January 24, 1977 at Southern Methodist University in Dallas, she extracted the 23rd root of a 201-digit number in 50 seconds. The size of the power in such root extraction is of no consequence—the critical factor is the number of digits in the root. In this case the root has nine digits (546,372,891); the extraction of such a root is no mean feat.

It seems that Univac 1101 at the Bureau of Standards was used to raise 546,372,891 to the 23d power, and this result was submitted to Devi. Since computers are not often called upon to raise numbers to high powers where the answers must be exact, a special program was written for the purpose. According to the *Dallas Morning News* (Smith 1977):

> SMU PROFESSORS considered themselves lucky to have a number on the chalkboard. It had taken long-distance calls to three computer centers before Dr. Myron Ginsburg located a computer that could handle such a load.
>
> Finally experts at the National Bureau of Standards agreed to program their automatous Univac. Some 13,466 instructions and 4,883 data locations were fed into the machine. Not until 3 P.M. Monday, an hour before Mrs. Devi's scheduled performance, did they arrive at an answer.

This is confusing, since only a small percentage of those instructions could represent a program especially constructed for the problem of raising numbers to high powers—the other instructions must have been part of a more general program written long before.

An editorial in the *Dallas Morning News* (Sunday, February 6, 1977) went on to pose this as a sort of woman/machine competition with the woman coming out on top: "What took the computer better than a minute to figure—the 23rd root of a 201-digit number—Mrs. Devi computed in only 50 seconds. . . . Power to Mrs. Davi . . . for boxing the ears of one of the more impudent computers."

There is some confusion in these accounts. The computer apparently did not, as did Devi, extract the 23d root of a 201-digit number where the root was known to be an integer, but rather raised a nine-digit number to the 23d power. The problems are altogether different. If the computer had been given the same 201-digit number and programmed to use methods similar to Devi's, it would have given the answer virtually instantaneously, while no one could conceivably raise an arbitrary nine-digit number to the 23d power.

If there were no restrictions on the problem except that the number whose root was to be extracted was the 23d power of a nine-digit number, however, this is a remarkable accomplishment. (For an amazing example of multiplication attributed to Devi see chapter 8.)

Chapter Thirty-seven

Hans Eberstark

He's great. He's absolutely daft, also. He does not smoke. He does not drink. He's big and fat. He's so quiet. He never gets nervous. Just the opposite from me.

—Wim Klein, describing Hans Eberstark

I am now in a wonderful nudist holiday resort in Yugoslavia. It is incredible how glorious life can become by just shedding clothes. Shopping for food, then standing in line for 10 minutes to check out your purchases is normally a dreary chore. Not so if you are surrounded by beautiful girls and women in the nude or topless. And the same holds for just about any other human activity. To think that millions of people make a living from manufacturing clothes whose only purpose seems to be to uglify women. You can see the difference in the restaurant at night or when it rains; beautiful butterflies turn back into creepy crawly caterpillars.

—Hans Eberstark in a letter to the author

H ANS Eberstark was born in Vienna on January 27, 1929.[1] He was not a childhood calculating prodigy. Though at school he was one of the best at mental arithmetic, his consuming interest was, and is, in languages. Even as a small child his first question on meeting someone was, "Are you interested in languages?" Anyone replying in the negative was "out" as far as young Hans was concerned.

Because of the *Anschluss,* the German annexation of Austria, in 1939 his family immigrated to Shanghai, where Eberstark was raised.

[1] The information in this chapter is based on personal interviews and correspondence.

After the war the family was repatriated, and Eberstark went to study at the university. His father asked him, "What are you planning to study?"

Eberstark replied, "Languages."

"Languages—you're not going to earn a lot of money with languages. It's a very interesting hobby, but why not study chemistry? Chemistry is the profession of the future. Industry is developing new substances. You're bright and you've always been interested in experiments, and it's fascinating to see a liquid turn blue and yellow and green."

"Yes, but that isn't all there is to chemistry, and while I'm interested in any kind of knowledge, I'm passionately interested in languages."

"Sure," replied his father, "but what are you going to do with it? No one is preventing you from studying languages as a sideline and reading books about languages and learning languages, but you'll never be able to earn a living and some day you'll want to marry and have children."

"I don't live for a future wife and future children that I don't even know. One-third of your life is your job, your profession, and I'd hate to have a profession that is not as interesting to me as it could be."

Eberstark now concludes: "So I insisted on studying languages and, of course, I was right. My father was wrong, and I'm glad I didn't take his advice."

Eberstark does indeed now have a family, and his profession of simultaneous translator (he is one of a relatively few people in the world capable of this most arduous form of translation) is both intellectually and financially rewarding.

Eberstark studied simultaneous translation at the University of Vienna—at that time the only place in the world where such instruction was given.

Besides German-English and English-German translations, Eberstark does translations into either language from French, Spanish, Italian, Portuguese, and Dutch. He also knows Swedish, Norwegian, Danish, Hebrew ("more or less, on the brink"), Yiddish, Albanian, Papiamento, Haitian Creole, and "above all Surinamese, or Sranantongo, which is the language on which I wrote my thesis—my favorite language.

"Surinam is ex–Dutch Guiana. It has been independent since 1975. The language is a Creolized language, which like all Creolized languages started out as a pidgin and now is a full-fledged language, but a much simpler and more functional language than the more commonly known languages that evolved in more traditional ways. And since I'm very fond of functionality, I was struck by the intrinsic beauty of this language and that is what I wrote my thesis about."

Eberstark also knows some Chinese and Japanese, "but not enough to count them as languages I really know. But I'm not lost in Japanese; I mean, I can make myself understood in Japanese."

Eberstark also speaks Catalan (closely related to Provençal), a Romance language spoken in Catalonia in Spain. "It took me four days to learn Catalan, but that was the record. On the basis of Catalan correspondences to French or Spanish, or both, I came to expect the sorts of words that would be used for any given concept, and I merely remembered divergences from my expectations."

Hans Eberstark, calculating prodigy, came into being in 1951 when Shakuntala Devi toured Europe. Eberstark read a newspaper article about her, and figured out that one of the things she did, the extraction of fifth roots, was really quite simple. He telephoned the paper and offered to tell them how it could be done in exchange for a subscription. "Do you mean to say that you can extract the fifth root?" When he replied that he could, they asked him over to the paper to show them.

As it turned out, they were not really interested in how fifth roots were extracted, they merely wanted to find an Austrian to compete against Devi. Eberstark declined, but the paper wrote a short piece exaggerating what he could do.

As a result of this Eberstark went with a reporter to the Indian Consulate. The consul was quite cool, according to Eberstark. He gave them some press notices to read and said: "Everywhere she goes there are always parasites who come up and try to cash in on her specific abilities. Now there are lots of people who know how to calculate, but this girl, I mean she doesn't calculate, she's a genius. She sees the answer flashing before her eyes. She can't even explain how she does it, and this is something entirely different. It's in a different dimension."

The reporter was miffed at this reception and wrote another article contrasting Eberstark and Devi to Eberstark's advantage. As a result, said Eberstark, "I had to catch up with my own reputation."

In order to improve his ability for root extraction, he needed a table of powers for integers. Since these were not readily available, he set out to construct his own. This work greatly improved his memory for numbers and his ability to multiply.

Like Wim Klein, Eberstark uses cross multiplication and much prefers to multiply numbers he can see, but, unlike Klein, he writes down the answers from left to right. "I write it down from left to right but I calculate from right to left. It's more spectacular writing it all down at once, rather than sort of building it up."

For my benefit he quickly and accurately mentally multiplied the following numbers which I proposed to him (in writing): 729 times 841; 6,985 times 7,832; 77,567 times 43,559. He said that he could go on to six, seven, and eight-digit numbers, if I would be willing to check the results, but that it would take more time. He also squared a four-digit number entirely mentally (that is, he did not have the problem in view), which is not something he does commonly. It was evident that the effort required was much greater than multiplying together five-digit numbers which he could see. On his first attempt to square 6,744, he gave an incorrect answer (45,465,536—45,481,536 is correct); the time required was about 20 seconds. I gave him another number, 4,687, which he correctly squared (21,967,969), but he worked much more slowly this time (about 1 minute, including 5 seconds to repeat the number), no doubt running some checks to make certain of the answer before announcing it.

Eberstark's specialty is memorizing numbers. Over lunch in a noisy crowded cafe he offered to memorize 20 digits for me if I would read them through once. He gave me the rate at which he wished to have the numbers recited; it was about one digit every 1.75 seconds. I got random digits by arbitrarily stopping the stopwatch on my wristwatch, which gives hundredths of a second. Each time I stopped the watch, I would write, on a piece of paper which Eberstark could not see, the two digits representing hundredths of a second, until I had sufficient digits. When I finished Eberstark said, "OK, add ten more digits." This I did by the same method. Then he said, "Oh, make it five more—no, ten more."

When I finished giving him the entire 40 digits, he paused and then said: "9, 7, 3, 0, 1, 6, 6, 5, 0, 7, 2, 9, 2, 2, 0, 6, 7, 1, 3, 3, 6, 9, 8, 4, 5, 2, 6, 0, 6, 3, 1, 6, 6, 7, 3, 1, 7, 9, 4, 6." Every digit was correct. I asked him whether he could repeat numbers backwards, and he immediately recited them that way, again without an error, and somewhat faster than before.

Eberstark's major memory feat involves pi. Since pi is an irrational number, the digits never repeat and it is, as Eberstark says, "the number that is most readily available and that most people have tried their brains on. At first I did 250 digits, and then it took me quite a while to get on to 500, and then to a thousand. At a thousand or a thousand five hundred I stopped for several years. Henk Wint [a mathematician at CERN, the European Organization for Nuclear Research], in order to spur me on, made a bet that I would not be able to beat the record. Our bet was six thousand digits, and I lost the bet because of a ridiculous mistake that I made. So then I had another try. By that time the record for pi was rising. It said 3,000 in the *Guinness Book of World Records,* but according to the latest information, it was five thousand; so that's why we made the bet for six thousand. But by that time somebody had already gone beyond six thousand, so then I went higher as well, and the last thing I did was 11,944 digits; but my record was beaten by Hideaki Tomoyori, and his record was beaten by Creighton Carvello. According to the latest edition of the *Guinness Book of Records,* he is the present record holder at 20,013 digits, no less!"

I asked how long it would take to memorize a hundred places of pi. He answered, "To memorize a hundred digits so as to be able to recite them doesn't take me very long—possibly five minutes or so, possibly even less. The point is that as I memorize pi, I have to keep these one hundred digits in my mind and not get them confused, and put them in the right place, so the problem is not just memorizing but linkage— linking the number to the previous 100 digits and the following 100 digits and keeping them anchored there. I haven't done any pi memorizing for several months now, which means that I've forgotten, temporarily forgotten, several of the 11,944 digits that I memorized. But I could quickly get into the swing again, and build up."

More recently Eberstark wrote me: "As for myself I must confess I have not followed through. What daunts me is the idea of starting at 7 o'clock in the morning and writing down the digits until something like 11 P.M., since every series of 100 digits must be written down twice to avoid accidental errors such as the one that made me lose my first bet against Henk. (I had to pay him a return trip to Bangkok!) The actual memorizing is not difficult at all. Incidentally one of the major difficulties is finding witnesses who are ready and willing to spend hours on the tedious nitty-gritty of checking the figures."

Chapter Thirty-eight

Shyam Marathe

If all numbers are on one side and the other things of life are on the other, then the numbers I love more, and among the numbers some are very, very close to me.

—Shyam Marathe

V. G. "SHYAM" MARATHE was born October 29, 1931 in Poona, India, where he lived until 1978.[1] As part of his arrangements for a trip to the United States in 1978, Marathe agreed to relocate to Satara. He is the Legal Officer for a divisional office of the Life Insurance Corporation of India.

In the part of India from which Marathe comes, it is common practice to name a child after a god, and then to give the child a nickname from among the other names of that god. Marathe's nickname, Shyam, is one of the names of Lord Krishna, as is his given name, Vasudeo.

Marathe's father came to Poona in 1925 to lecture at the Engineering College, from which he retired in 1946.

Marathe and his father are very close; he says: "My main gift is my father, I would say. My father always takes an interest in whatever I do. Sometimes the things I do are not liked by others, because I am not a careerist, so I let pass many chances of material progress, but it is only my father who always stands by my side."

Marathe's interest in numbers began at an early age, but he has no specific recollection of its genesis. In Indian schools children are taught,

---

[1] The information in this chapter is based on personal interviews.

by the third grade, the multiplication tables up to 30 by 30, and he recalls that he had already learned these tables before they were introduced in school.

No member of Marathe's family shares his ability for calculation, though he hopes his daughter may come to. Her name is Sankhya, the only child in Poona so named. The name is taken from a Sanskrit saying to the effect that, if there is any knowledge in this world at all, that knowledge is of numbers. Sankhya is the Sanskrit word for numbers.

Shyam was popular with his fellows as a schoolchild, but like other prodigies he spent a great deal of time alone in calculation: "In school my friends used to love me very much—I do not know why. They used to take me to their houses and they introduced me to their parents, and I used to do these feats of arithmetical calculation in their houses, and I used to get a lot of praise from the parents of my friends.

"But somehow it was always my friends coming to me, rather than myself going to any friends. Always I was at my own house working with my own hobby of numbers. Of course, whenever friends used to come to me and drag me out of the house I would go, but of my own I very rarely went to the house of a friend during school or college."

Marathe is also a skilled magician, having given performances at Magic Castle, a world-renowned academy for magicians in Los Angeles. When he was 15 he had a friend who was very interested in magic. He did various card tricks for Marathe, who was, in many cases, able to detect immediately how they were done. His friend was quite surprised, since no one before had been able to unravel them. Marathe says: "I started thinking about how the secret struck me, and I found that the majority of card tricks are based on mathematics only, and the principles involved are subtle mathematical principles. That is how I started taking more interest in the subject. I have found that mathematics and card magic are very closely related."

All Marathe's education has been at Poona (the old British spelling—now officially known as Pune). He holds three university degrees—a B.A. and degrees in commerce and law. Although he has never "been to the bar," his legal training is integral to his insurance work. He made the decision at the outset of his career to devote his life to insurance work, but he has been associated with the legal aspects—he has never done actuarial work, as one might suppose given his calculating ability. "When I got my commerce degree, I had an inclination that I should make the insurance line my career. So, without looking to what salary was offered there, I joined an insurance company, and to my satisfaction, I have found that I remained at the same job. Later my company was nationalized and I became a government servant, but I have continued in insurance so far, and I have no desire to change. Somehow I have a fascination for it."

While in the United States in 1978, Marathe gave some 15 demonstrations, including appearances at the Rand Corporation, Stanford University, the University of California at Riverside, the University of Nevada, and Northrop Institute of Technology. At Magic Castle he gave simultaneous demonstrations of calculation and magic.

At the University of California at Riverside (a typical performance) Marathe solved the following problems, prepared in advance by members of the faculty:

1. $\sqrt[3]{704,969} = 89$
2. $\sqrt[3]{491,169,069} = 789$
3. $\sqrt[3]{160,288,833,718,161} = 54,321$
4. $38^3 = 54,872$
5. $63^3 = 250,047$
6. Marathe was asked to extract the 23d root of 24,242,900,770,-553,981,941,874,678,268,486,966,725,193 = 57

This problem makes a very effective presentation, but is not at all difficult (chapter 13). It is much less difficult than finding the cube root of a 15-digit number.

7. $\{[(8^2)^2]^2\}^2$

Marathe did this problem a section at a time: $8^2 = 64$, $64^2 = 4,096$; $4,096^2 = 16,777,216$; $16,777,216^2 = 281,474,976,710,656$. He no doubt has these values memorized, particularly since they are powers of two, a favorite among calculators (the final answer is 2^{48}).

8. $\{[(5^2)^2]^2\}^2 = 152,587,890,625$

This was answered with no intervening stages.

9. $\dfrac{1}{96} = 0.010416666\ldots$ 10. $\dfrac{1}{63} = 0.015873016$

Reciprocals are another specialty of Marathe's. Problem 10 is rounded off at nine places.

11. Marathe asked for a number from the audience between 40 and 100, divisible by two but not divisible by four. The number proposed was 90. He then undertook to compose both a magic square and a magic star summing to that value. The square and star (tables 38.1 and 38.2) were quickly filled in.

In fact, Marathe's square is not a true magic square (as he acknowledged), since, although each number appears only once, not all the integers from 1 to n are included, where n is the number of boxes in the square.

But Marathe's magic square has properties beyond those imposed upon ordinary magic squares—not only do the rows, columns, and diagonals sum to 90, but the partial diagonals wrap around to sum to 90 (that is, $44 + 6 + 1 + 39$ equals 90, as do $2 + 3 + 43 + 42$ and $40 + 8 + 5 + 37$). And there are more surprises in store: any inner square composed of four adjacent smaller squares (there are nine of these), and any similar squares formed by wrapping around (there are seven) also sum to 90. The four corners sum to 90, but this is a special case of an inner square wrapped around from two directions.

The feat is particularly effective because of successive announcements of new combinations totaling the required number, but it is in reality quite simple. I will leave it to the reader to figure out just how such squares are constructed, but here are a few hints. You begin by memorizing a "canonical" magic square, having all the impressive properties of Marathe's square. This is a true magic square, containing the numbers from 1 to 16, and summing to 34. By appropriate modifications to this square, a square can be created summing to any even number above 34.

TABLE 38.1
Marathe's Magic Square

37	44	2	7
6	3	41	40
43	38	8	1
4	5	39	42

TABLE 38.2
Marathe's Magic Star

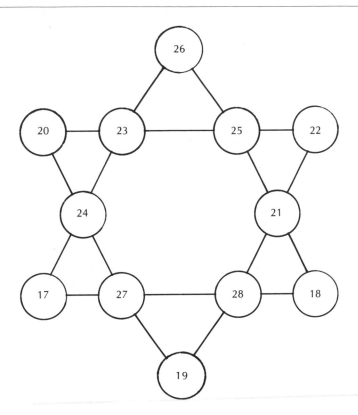

Something similar works for the magic star, but in this case the sum must be an even number equal to or greater than 26, and not divisible by four.

12. Marathe produced a calendar for the current year (1978) and had a young woman from the front row hold it so that it could be seen by the audience but not by him. He asked that a day of the week be arbitrarily selected—the day chosen was Thursday. He then rattled off the day of each month on which the first Thursday falls ("In January it falls on the first, etc.").

13. Marathe then asked the audience to give him the year, month, and day of the month, in that order, and he would supply the day of the week, for any dates for which the day of the week was known to them.

He was first given 1810, April 10, to which he quickly replied Tuesday. The man who posed the question said: "No, it was a Thursday. I know, because it is the independence day of my country." Marathe muttered a little testily that it was perhaps his wedding day. The panel of examiners, not wishing to provoke controversy, remained silent, though they knew from the perpetual calendar before them that Marathe was right and the man from the audience wrong.

The other dates, both correctly given, were: October 14, 1965 (Sunday) and February 28, 1914 (Saturday).

14. Another of Marathe's specialties is to give the years in which a particular day of the week will fall on a particular date. The question put to him was: "In what years between 1920 and 1970 does November 11 fall on a Monday?" Marathe correctly replied: "In 1928, 1935, 1940, 1946, 1957, and 1963."

15. "Give a year between 1776 and 1970 in which Friday 13 occurs in both January and July." After some pondering Marathe said: "These must be leap years," and answered correctly, 1928.

16. Raising single-digit numbers to powers up to 20 is Marathe's most remarkable feat. He told me that he also used to raise two-digit numbers to high powers in performances, but that he made occasional mistakes, and so decided to limit himself to single-digit roots in public demonstrations. The following were all correctly answered, as indicated:

$$8^{14} = 4,398,046,511,104$$
$$7^{12} = 13,841,287,201$$
$$9^{14} = 22,876,992,454,961$$

Marathe is unwilling to reveal his method for raising numbers to powers, apparently because he fears that one of his few competitors in the calculating game might attempt to emulate him. He is willing to make some general statements about it, without providing enough specifics for anyone to copy (see chapter 6).

Marathe is an interesting study while calculating. He is a visual calculator and finds it necessary to view the entire problem at once. When the numbers are large, he must sometimes clamber down from the stage, all but stumbling over those in the front row. Although some maneuvers may also give him a little extra calculating time, there is no doubt of the genuineness of his need to gain this sort of perspective on problems.

Marathe concluded his performance with a display of memory for numbers. Prior to the show he had written the numbers 1 through 70 in a seven-by-ten matrix on the back of two portable blackboards. These were now turned around, and a member of the audience crossed off numbers at random while Marathe stood with his back to the board. As each number was crossed off, it was called out. Marathe would fix a mental image of the crossing off of the number and then say "yah," after which another number would be crossed off. When about half the numbers had been crossed off in this manner, Marathe said he would call off the uncanceled numbers either forward or backward, as requested. He then correctly called the uncanceled numbers in reverse order.

Like most performers, Marathe mingles the difficult with the trivial to make a good show; and as is the case with many things, people are likely to be the most impressed by feats which are in fact the simplest. There are certain stringent requirements on problems to be solved in a performance: the problems must be intelligible and impressive to an ordinary audience; they must be such that the performer can solve them correctly without fail; they must be problems that the performer can solve quickly—in no more than a minute or two. Marathe says that there are many things that he can do if given more time than an audience could tolerate.

Since the first priority of a performer must be to entertain, there is nothing objectionable in this, but unfortunately, the fact that some of the problems are fairly easy may lead people to conclude that all the feats of a legitimate calculating prodigy are nothing more than tricks, attainable by anyone with a little diligence and a fair memory for figures. Marathe says: "Some authors on popular mathematics try to divulge a method here or there and state that this is how a lightning calculator must be calculating. For instance, I have come across a book which gives you a method to find a cube root of a six digit number, and the answer will consist of only two digits—that is, units place and tens place. The author proceeds to explain that it is easy to find the tens place if you remember a few rules. But then he only explains how to find the cube root of a six-digit number. He does not give any clue to a method for finding cube roots of numbers as such. Especially when somebody is able to extract the cube root of a 15-digit number, 18-digit number, then such authors prefer not to explain the theories, because they themselves do not know how these roots are extracted. According to me, there is nothing super-human about extracting the cube root of a 15-digit number, but not to know how to do it and to ridicule the whole process by giving a small gimmick and telling that similarly it should be done for a larger number is not really the correct approach to the thing."

Unlike most prodigies, Marathe has an outstanding memory for things other than numbers—in fact, he gives performances consisting wholly of memory feats—but in all cases there is a close connection between his number memory and his memory for things in general.

When Marathe goes about memorizing things other than numbers, such as the objects in a room or the faces and initials of a number of people, he assigns a number to each, sequentially starting from one. By recalling the number associated with the person or object, he can reel off in order the initials—or if supplied with the initials of a person or name of an object, he can give the serial number. In the case of people he can identify two of the three—initials, face, or serial number—when given the third.

Unlike most systems of memorization, which use verbal associations to retain numbers, it is the numbers for Marathe which are most easily retained, and which provide the link which allows him to recall associated information.

Cards are, like numbers, recalled directly, but, as Marathe points out, they have numerical values anyway. He tells me that in bridge he can remember all the cards that have been played, and can recall an entire deck of cards in order. As with numbers he stores a mental image of the card.

Marathe's ability to concentrate, even in the face of distractions and confusion (as, for example, in his performances) is extraordinary. He says: "I have observed that when I deal with numbers, I find that I concentrate very fast, and can concentrate for a long time. Suppose we are going to read a novel and we want then to get engrossed into the novel, we should get engrossed into the plot of the novel. But, insofar as numbers are concerned, I find when I calculate, I am able to concentrate on my work, forgetting all the noises going on around me—instantaneously; that is, no long work is required to achieve that stare of concentration. Moreover, concentration is continuous for a long time with me; there is no fatigue of mind or body involved when I deal with numbers. I can concentrate on this work for a longer time than I can concentrate on anything other than numbers.

"When I concentrate and I do the work, I always have a feeling that I am having a different existence than what I have normally. It is a different state of my being, and I enjoy those moments. They say—I don't know how far it is true, I'm not an expert on that—they call something an 'etheric double' of a person. You are a different person when you are engrossed in your work. That might be the case—I do not know. But one thing is certain—I become completely cut off from the rest of the things around me when I concentrate."

I asked him whether he ever had this feeling about another person being at work with anything other than numbers. He replied: "It's not that simple, to be expressed in that word that another person is working within me, or any such thing, because the feeling is subtle. It cannot actually be described in words. So, in a very crude way, I can say that I forget myself when I do that. And when I say I forget myself, I've got a feeling that myself is different from somebody who is concentrating on doing the work. But I'm not in a position to express exactly how that other man or other existence comes into operation. It would be a very bold statement to say that a different personality was at work there. I'm not that much different from the inner self which concentrates, but at the same time, there is a slight feeling that it is some inner power within me which is working itself—rather than the word 'power' I will use the word 'strength'—it is some inner strength which is coming out and doing that work like an automatic process. These things are very difficult to catch in exact expressions."

I asked him how long he continued in this state of intense concentration. "When I concentrate there is no mental or physical fatigue, and the thing continues until my inner self is satisfied.

"Actually it's sort of a feeling of ecstasy, I would rather say, that comes during the work; then I stop the work. It may not be the point of what I'm doing, but something I find out, some specialty of numbers, some peculiarity of numbers, and I am very happy with that. A little ecstasy comes; then my whole self is at rest, and I can go to bed."

Though Marathe does not dream of numbers, solutions to problems have occasionally come to him in his sleep. "Once or twice it has happened that I got up from my sleep with the solution to a problem. I do not remember that that day I had a dream and in that dream I solved it—no such memory is there—but definitely, distinctly I remember that at a very odd hour I got up to find the correct solution had stuck in my mind, and I immediately took a pen or pencil to jot it down.

"This actually happened when I was trying to find the relation of a digital root of a number to its powers. Similarly, one day I got the idea of basing my number system on a very large prime number. But somewhere in the background of my memory there must be the knowledge that prime numbers have some specialties, so if a number world ends in a prime then there are a lot of conveniences it can have."

I was interested to learn what he felt were the major influences on his development. "My influence is mainly the writings of our ancient Hindu mathematicians. Although my methods are my own, I have drawn inspiration from some of the things I have found in these old writings which do not resemble very much our modern methods of calculation. I found a possibility that I can evolve my own number world. For instance, we have a number we call a *lakh*. The idea of a lakh is not known here—it is five zeros on one [a hundred thousand]. Here you think immediately of a million, but we have in our ancient number system a name for all these other quantities. This method of giving names, and giving to various quantities an identity, served to me as an inspiration.

"Then there were certain maxims of old mathematicians. For instance, Brahmagupta said sometime in the fifteenth century: 'The numbers must proceed, in any calculation, from left to right.' I read that and found out it's possible to calculate every time from left to right, and so that writing did inspire me. I thought, why not make an honest effort to do it that way? And I found that I could get some success.

"So I would rather say that my interest in numbers might be natural, but this drawing of inspiration for further work, supplying me with direction, all these things, I owe to our ancient Hindu mathematicians."

I asked him whether Hindu philosophy had affected his outlook. "I can't say that there is much sense in what our Hindu philosophy pleads — perhaps it may be true, but we have been brought up from childhood with this conviction—number one is that there is definitely a rebirth for man. Now it becomes very difficult with the education that you have and with the observation of day-to-day things in life to reconcile yourself with the training that you have had since childhood, what has been impressed on your mind, that there is a rebirth for man, and that you are also a reborn man, somebody else. That has a very deep root in our minds; it's very difficult to rule out that thing. So many times when certain phenomena occur which I canot explain I try to find a solution in this old belief of mine that this must have something to do with my rebirth.

"Another impact that Indian philosophy has produced on my mind is that it's not you who does things, it's somebody else who is doing things. We call it 'aham Brahmasmi' in Sanskrit; that is, 'I am the universe.' It is a sort of preaching that is given, you are yourself a universe, and again at the same time you are what you are. So these are the things that have been very much imbibed by our minds—that whatever we do in life we should do without any attachment to it. It is some sort of kernel of something else; some other divine power which does it through you.

"Everything you do in life has an impact. The mind does not remain without the impact of all these things. So these are my influences when I do my work or try to find explanations of what has happened to me."

Chapter Thirty-nine

Arthur Benjamin

If you perform for magicians, you have to be very good or very unusual. I consider myself to be both.

—Arthur Benjamin

ARTHUR Benjamin seems to be the only American presently performing as a professional calculator. He has appeared on the *Today* show and *PM Magazine,* and he was the subject of an article in *Discover* (Schechter 1981) and an Associated Press story by Kay Bartlett (1982). He is also one of the few calculators ever to be the subject of psychological investigation (Chase and Ericsson 1982).

Benjamin was born March 19, 1961 in a suburb of Cleveland, where he spent his childhood.[1] As a child he was precocious, hyperactive, and a terrible troublemaker. He had problems with asthma, an abnormal EEG (at 3), and took medication to calm him down through the eighth grade. More than one doctor advised his father not to put him in public school, because his attention span was so short that he wouldn't be able to cope. But after he was thrown out of a couple of preschools, public school was the only place left.

His parents continued to encourage their first child's interests in the face of objections from the school. "In elementary school I was not an easy child to deal with. I couldn't sit still—I still have trouble sitting still. And I liked showing off, especially when I could correct the teacher. My parents were told to stop teaching me things, because they [the

---

[1] Except where noted, information in this chapter is based upon personal interview.

school] said, 'We are running out of things to teach him.' That is a terrible reflection on the educational system. I could have gone to a private or open school, but I was such a behavioral problem that they wouldn't accept me."

When Benjamin finally went off his medication in the eighth grade, his motor coordination improved, he went out for the track team, and got into shape. He even grew a couple of inches.

Both Benjamin's parents are college graduates, and his mother has a master's degree in special education from Kent State University. It was Benjamin's problems as a hyperactive child that first interested her in special education. "She did a lot of research on me, in a time when people were just beginning to understand what hyperactivity was all about."

Benjamin's father, brother, and sister are all involved in performing. "My dad was involved in community theater for about fifteen or twenty years and got all of us involved in performing when we were in elementary school. And I think being on the stage, being in front of a group of people, aside from being a wonderful experience, a great feeling, is very important. Not to have the fear of getting up in front of groups—I think that has helped me more ways than just about anything else, maybe including my intelligence—the ability to present myself and talk in front of a group."

Benjamin has been thinking about numbers for as long as he can remember. As a child he was fascinated by numbers, but there were many things that fascinated him—shapes, puzzles, reciting. "I learned my alphabet very young. I knew how to read before entering kindergarten. I think that had a lot to do with my parents keeping me busy. I had motivation, and they supplied me. I would ask questions and they would try to answer me."

Benjamin's earliest recollections of numbers are associated with a toy, something like a slot machine. Pressing the lever caused four arithmetic problems to appear in each of four windows—one in addition, one in subtraction, one in multiplication, and one in division. Above each of those windows were four windows which concealed the answers. He recalls: "I think I learned my multiplication tables at that point. I remember playing with that toy until I got to be really good at it."

In elementary school he began to go beyond two digits by two digits in multiplication, and to discover interesting numerical properties. "In third or fourth grade, a bunch of my classmates were all lined up in the hall ready to go to lunch, or go to the lavatory, or something like that. I can remember standing up against the wall and marveling over the fact that the number 2,520 is the smallest number that all the numbers between one and ten divide into evenly. I would amuse myself by dividing each of those numbers into 2,520. I tried smaller numbers like 1,260 and realized that eight did not divide into it. That was about as far as I went—what would be the number that the numbers one through eleven would go into—that's probably 2,520 times 11."

Later he had a small dartboard, containing the numbers from one to ten, above his bed. "Sometimes I would lay at night, staring up at my ceiling and I would see those numbers and I'd multiply them together, getting various different combinations as high as ten factorial—3,628,800."

Like most other calculating prodigies, Benjamin worked out his methods on a trial-and-error basis. It was not until much later that he gained an insight into the algebraic bases for them. The squaring formula Benjamin uses, $a^2 = (a + b)(a - b) + b^2$, is the same as that used by Alexander Craig Aitken, but Benjamin discovered it for himself.

"I can even remember figuring this one out when I was on a bus. I would take a bus downtown to Cleveland to visit my father at work and I can remember I was thinking about the numbers that added up to 20. I started with the middle and I was looking at the product of those numbers: 10 times 10 was a hundred; 9 times 11 was 99; 8 times 12 was 96. Then I said, 'Gee, these numbers are getting smaller,' and I convinced myself that as you branch out farther and farther from the center your product gets smaller, and I asked myself, 'How much smaller?'

"I noticed that 9 times 11 was one smaller than a hundred; 8 times 12 was four smaller than a hundred; 7 times 13, which is 91, was nine smaller than a hundred. So I noticed they went 1, 4, 9, and I said, 'I bet the next one is 16,' and so whatever the next one was, 6 times 14 is 84 which is 16 less than 100, and I said, 'Oh wow, I wonder if this works for other numbers,' and then I tried it for big numbers, small numbers, fractions, decimals, and I said, 'Look what I've discovered—wow, how neat.' "

This is the way Benjamin uses this formula today to square a number such as 4,273. He will take b as 273, then

$$4,273^2 = (4,273 + 273)(4,273 - 273) + 273^2 =$$
$$(4,546 \times 4,000) + 273^2.$$

The formula will be reapplied to 273, taking b as 27. Rather than doing the adding or subtracting necessary to find $a + b$ or $a - b$, Benjamin simply doubles the original number and saves the final digits.

"I double 4,273 and get 8,546. This tells me that the numbers I have to multiply are 4 [thousand] and 4,546, which gives me 18,184. So I say 18 million and I remember 184 thousand. The way I remember it is by converting 184 into the word 'dover,' using the phonetic code [chapter 6].

"Now I have to go back and square the number I went up and down [the number that he added to and subtracted from 4,273], which was 273. To square 273, the first thing I do is double it, which gives 546, which tells me that my numbers that I have to multiply are 300 and 246. Three times 246 is 738, so that gives 73,800. I add to that the square of 27, which is the difference between 273 and 300; actually it's the difference between 73 and 100—I don't have to think about the two hundreds. I add the square of 27, which I have memorized as 729, so I don't have to take really any time to do that. So I add 73,800 plus 729, which is 74,529. I have a nasty habit of forgetting the hundreds, so I put the 5 on my fingers. Now I add 74,000 to 'dover.' 'Dover' codes back uniquely into 184; 74 plus 184 is 258. So I say 258,529, with a little help from my hands."

Of his use of his fingers in calculating Benjamin says, "Every so often, if I have to remember a single digit, I use my hands to hold that one digit. It comes in handy. I'm not proud. Certainly nobody's going to see me do it. It's there. You may as well use anything that can save your memory."

Benjamin knows the squares of virtually all two-digit numbers. "There might be two or three of them I might have to think about and actually calculate, but even those take so little time."

As a child, Benjamin was intrigued by all sorts of hobbies, but he came to concentrate on magic.

"I liked showing off, entertaining people, impressing people, getting attention. So I considered just about everything to be my hobby, including acting, singing, dancing—but not for too long. I played the trombone, a lot of different things.

"I always considered magic to be one of my hobbies, but come around middle school or high school, there were the people who had been dedicating a lot of time to one or two particular areas. It turned out, though, that nobody else had gotten into magic. So, by virtue of being the only one, I was the best magician in my class. I said, 'OK, it seems that I've been outdone in singing and acting and this and that, but in magic, I'm number one.' "

Benjamin won some money in a contest and invested it in magic tricks.

He worked at a children's day camp, and while he was there his father had some business cards printed for him, saying the Great Benjamini will do magic at your next birthday party. As a result, he began to get some shows.

"I've always worked well with children—I enjoy children a lot. I put on a good show. I gave them everything I could. And eventually I grew to be a good businessman as well as a good magician. By the time I graduated from high school I was doing more children's shows than just about anybody else in the city, certainly anybody my age. I include that as one of my top accomplishments. Every kid thinks about being a magician. A lot of people even give it a try, but it's so hard, and I was lucky."

Benjamin's shows for children were purely magic, no calculations. "I was almost a clown. I was the Great Benjamini, which is almost a comical name in itself, Benjamin with an *i* at the end. I fell down and got hit over the head with wands and made the kids laugh, and that was my objective. About 90 percent of the shows I did were for children between the ages of five and seven—for their birthday parties.

"It wasn't until I started doing magic for adults that I needed some more, shall we say, sophisticated material. And there was very little that I could borrow from my children's show, because it was designed so much for young people. So, I put in a few of my card tricks, things I would do for my peers.

"I got intrigued by an area of magic called mentalism, sort of faking an ESP act. And I said, 'You know, mentalism would match my personality, because I'm intelligent, I'm articulate, and that is conveyed to the audience—except if I'm doing my kids' show.'

"I decided that a mental act would be more to my personality than an escape act or an illusion act, or even closeup. I wasn't quite the fast talker for closeup magic, and I certainly wasn't the big impressive Blackstone sort of personality for illusions. And mentalism, if anything, required that you be a thinker, or appear intelligent."

After Benjamin got into mentalism, his father suggested that he try putting some of his calculations into his act. He replied, "Yeah, but that's *real*, Dad."

But he took his father's advice, and the calculations consistently got the best response. He decided, "This must be the future of my act."

When Benjamin went away to college at Carnegie-Mellon University in Pittsburgh, he decided to put magic behind him, at least for the present.

"I was very involved in magic, so I was certainly sort of a celebrity in high school, and I don't mean entirely in a positive sense. Everybody knew me as the magician, which I brought on myself. I decided that when I went to college at Carnegie-Mellon, where there would be no students from my high school, that I was going to start over fresh. I wasn't going to bring along any magic tricks. People were going to know me as myself and maybe, like in the middle of my sophomore year, I would introduce magic tricks. I didn't want to start out being known as the magician again, like in high school."

Benjamin probably would have avoided getting involved in magic at all, except that the first month he was away at school there was a magic convention in Pittsburgh.

Benjamin went to the convention. He had no magic to bring, but he brought a pocket calculator that he used in physics class, "just in case I was in the mood to show off." He figured it couldn't hurt to show off for magicians.

Some magicians were sitting around a table showing each other card tricks and other things. Among them were one or two "big guys," renowned magicians who had been hired to appear at the convention.

"I just couldn't resist doing a little something and so I said, 'Anyone want to see an interesting mental effect?' That's the way I described it—to make it sound like a magic trick. One of the big guys said 'OK,' but they really weren't interested in seeing it at all. Mental effects are boring. They're not entertaining in general."

Benjamin gave the calculator to one of the "big guys" and said, "Somebody give me a two-digit number, and somebody else give me another two-digit number. Multiply those two together, make sure you get 5,481 or the calculator isn't working."

The magicians were taken aback. Benjamin went on to square some two-digit numbers and some three-digit numbers, and did a trick based on casting out nines.

"They were amazed. I'd never gotten a response like that before in my life, certainly not in Cleveland."

There were two men at the conference who were opening a nightclub specializing in magic, and they offered Benjamin a job. He worked there on weekends without telling his fellow students about his double life as a nightclub performer on the other side of town.

In the spring of his freshman year Benjamin was taking a course in cognitive psychology. The topic of the day was "lightning calculators." The professor started by giving simple demonstrations, such as extracting the fifth root of a perfect power, which is trivial for numbers of no more than ten digits (chapter 13).

The professor went on to say that calculators sometimes used such tricks to make it appear that they could do impressive things. Then he asked, "Does anybody else know any tricks?"

Benjamin said to himself, "Oh, Artie, you really shouldn't." But he couldn't resist. He basically went through the routine he'd been doing at the nightclub.

The last thing he did was to square a four-digit number, something he had only just begun to do in his nightclub act. While he was deep in concentration some students were whispering in the background. He said "sh," and the room went dead silent. "I've never seen a class get that quiet, fifty people in a room. I gave out the rest of the answer. It was right and there was an audible gasp."

After class Benjamin asked whether there was a professor who might want to test him on his number ability. As a result he became the experimental subject, and eventually the research assistant, of Professor William Chase, professor of psychology at Carnegie-Mellon. Not only was he a source of data, but he helped analyze the data.

One of the problems faced by Chase in analyzing Benjamin's mental calculations is that because so much happens so fast, Benjamin himself can not always be certain of what he is doing. For example, he can give the answer to a two-digit by two-digit multiplication very rapidly. Does he have such combinations memorized or does he actually calculate them? "The way Dr. Chase decided was by giving me problems with so much to remember that it slowed me down drastically. I can multiply two-digit numbers very quickly, but if I have to do it inside a six-digit multiplication, even that simple two by two is going to take me longer than it would if I didn't have all these other calculations to do. It took me longer to do a two by two inside a six by six, therefore it couldn't have been memorized."

Until the middle of college, the methods Benjamin used for calculation were "natural," that is, methods he had discovered for himself through trial and error. "Up to that point, it was all whatever felt the best or felt the easiest.

"I think the first thing I derived algebraically was I figured that since I know how to do two by twos [multiply two digits by two digits], I should be able to extend that naturally up to three by threes, and I used some algebra to figure out the best way to do that. My first unnatural calculation.

"And later on I reasoned that if I could do three by threes and I could use mnemonics effectively, then I could do six by sixes. That's the highest I have attempted at the moment."

Benjamin plans to get a Ph.D. in operations research. "If you had talked to me a week ago I would have given you a different answer. My plan would have been to graduate with my bachelor's degree, find a job, and see what happens. But I think that I'm going to be better off, career-wise, intellectually—I think I'll be more challenged with the job I get with the Ph.D. I'll be doing some more magic, but if I made a full-time profession of it, I might stop enjoying it. If I did go into magic and I then say, 'Wait a minute, I don't want to be a magician,' there's almost nowhere to go. I could become an actuary, but that is one of those well-paying slow deaths. So it seems like I keep almost all my options open by getting the Ph.D. It's all very well reasoned, but a year ago I had a good reason for becoming a magician, and I had a good reason for going into cognitive psychology."

When Benjamin performs for a private party he usually closes with a poem. "Really, it's not a magic show I'm doing, it's just an entertainment. And I'm giving them as much entertainment as I can. Some of that's math, some of that's magic, and some of that's a poem. It's really just me."

Andrè Marie Ampèr (1775–1836)

Ampère was a many-faceted genius—mathematician, scientist, biologist, poet, and psychologist.

Little is known of his talent for mental calculation, but it seems that arithmetic was the area in which his genius first became manifest. By the age of 4, knowing nothing of written figures, he had learned to calculate using pebbles. When, during a serious illness, his pebbles were removed, he used broken bits of biscuit given to him after three days on a strict diet (Scripture 1891:6).

Details of Ampère's life can be found in any encyclopedia.

Karl Friedrich Gauss (1777–1855)

Gauss has traditionally been regarded, with Archimedes and Newton, as one of the three greatest mathematicians in history. His contributions to astronomy and physics are scarcely less important. As is the case with several other geniuses who were calculating prodigies—Ampère, Euler, and von Neumann—a great deal more is known about aspects of his life other than mental calculation.

Gauss's ability for mental calculation first became known when he was 3, according to an anecdote he himself related. His father was paying off his workmen at the end of the week, but had incorrectly computed the overtime due. Little Karl, who had followed his father's calculations, called out that the amount was wrong, and gave another total. When the computation was repeated, it was found the boy was correct (Scripture 1891:9).

Though it is known that Gauss carried out some very large and complex calculations during his life,[1] little is known of his ability as a mental calculator.

For further details of Gauss's life, see any standard encyclopedia.

Richard Whately (1787–1863)

Whately was the Archbishop of Dublin from 1831 to 1863. He was the author of *Historic Doubts Relative to Napoleon Bonaparte, Elements of*

---

[1] One of his best-known feats was computing the orbit of the planetoid Ceres —extremely difficult in the days before electronic computers.

Logic, Elements of Rhetoric, and many other works, most of a religious nature. Whately was unusual in having lost his calculating power when he began school. (For discussion, see chapter 4.)

Lady Frederica Murray (about 1804–?)

She was the daughter of the Countess of Mansfield.

Zerah Colburn met her in 1812, when she was 8 (or thereabouts). He later described her (Colburn 1833:175) as possessing "a certain degree of mental quickness uncommon in her sex and years." (See chapter 5.)

Johann Casper Spurzheim, an early phrenologist, saw her in London when she was 13. He said that she could extract cube and square roots of numbers up to nine digits with great facility (Mitchell 1907:84–85).

Vito Mangiamele (1827–?)

Mangiamele was a Sicilian who, at the age of 10 years and 4 months, appeared before the French Academy of Sciences (Arago 1837:978–79). His father was a poor shepherd, unable to provide any education for his son.

Mangiamele was asked for the cube root of 3,796,416, to which he correctly replied in about one-half minute: 156. He was then asked for a number whose cube plus five times its square is equal to 42 times itself plus 40 (algebraically, $x^3 + 5x^2 = 42x + 40$). In less than a minute he replied "five," which is correct. The third problem called for the solution of $x^5 - 4x - 16,779 = 0$. (The verbal form of this problem is not indicated, but it must have been something like: What number multiplied by itself five times, and then decreased by four times itself, equals 16,779?) Vito hesitated four or five minutes and hazarded 3 as the solution. The secretary informed him that he was wrong, and shortly thereafter he found 7, the correct answer.

The last problem called for the 10th root of 282,475,249. Mangiamele quickly and correctly replied "seven."

Cauchy's (1885) report to the Academy on Mondeux complains that "Mangiamele's masters" (*maîtres,* which may also mean *teachers*) kept his methods secret.

There is nothing mysterious about how problems such as those described above are solved. Extracting three-digit cube roots is trivial for an expert calculator. The second and third problems solved by Mangia-

mele are algebraically forbidding, but not difficult for a good calculator by trial and error on the assumption that the answer is a relatively small integer.

The last problem is also very easy assuming the answer is an integer. It is instantly apparent that the root is odd and less than 10. Three is clearly too little and all powers of five end in five. Therefore the answer must be seven or nine. Even powers of nine always end in one, so seven must be the answer.

I have no information on what became of Mangiamele.

George Parker Bidder, Jr. (1837–?)

Like his father, Bidder, Jr. was a mental calculator, though far below his father's standard. He was, unlike his father, a visual calculator. He was seventh wrangler (ranked seventh in mathematics) of his year at Cambridge. He became a distinguished barrister and Queen's Counsel.

In a letter excerpted in *The Spectator* for December 28, 1878, Bidder, Jr. wrote:

> I myself can perform pretty extensive arithmetical operations mentally, but I cannot pretend to approach even distantly to the rapidity or accuracy with which my father worked. I have occasionally multiplied 15 figures by 15 figures in my head, but it takes me a long time, and I am liable to occasional errors. Last week, after speaking to Professor Elliot, I tried the following sum [multiplication] to see if I could still do it, —
>
> $$378,201,969,513,825$$
> $$199,631,057,265,413$$
>
> And I got in my head the answer, 75,576,299,427,512,145,197,597,834,-725, in which I think, if you take the trouble to work it out, you will find four figures out of the 29 are wrong.

There seems to be a misprint here—*fourteen* rather than four of the digits are wrong. The first three and the last 12 figures are correct—the digits in between are in error. Perhaps the editor of *The Spectator* lopped off the last syllable of "fourteen," figuring that Bidder, Jr. would not acknowledge so large an error. Considering what is involved, however, the calculation is quite good. The correct answer is, incidentally:

$$75,500,859,033,906,380,197,597,834,725.$$

For a description of Bidder, Jr.'s method of computing logarithms, see chapter 16.

Prolongeau (born 1838 or 1839)

The 6½-year-old Prolongeau (no first name given) was examined by a committee of the French Academy of Sciences headed by Cauchy (1845). His ability for calculation was described as "truly extraordinary." He solved a large number of arithmetic problems in his head and some problems involving first-degree equations. Unfortunately, none of the problems are specified. Again, nothing more is known of Prolongeau.

Dr. Ferrol (1864–?)

According to Mitchell (1907), neither the first name of Ferrol nor the nature of his degree are given in Möbius' *Die Anlage zur Mathematik* (1900), on which Mitchell based his account. Ferrol started calculating at an early but unspecified age. When he began the study of algebra at age 10 he developed a preference for mental algebra over mental arithmetic.

Apart from arithmetic Ferrol was a below-average student. He was an auditory calculator and in general very poor at visualization.

Mitchell (1907:85) writes: "His processes are 'intuitive'; the answer to a problem, he tells us, comes 'instantly,' and is always correct." This seems rather unlikely in the case of a man who was adept at mental algebra.

Ugo Zaneboni (1879–?)

Zaneboni, an Italian who received a "fair education" (Mitchell 1907:73), became interested in numbers rather late—at the age of 12. By 14 he was able to answer any problem in arithmetic put to him by his teacher. While serving in the army, he was stationed at a railway depot, where he amused himself by memorizing rail statistics, city populations, tariffs, etc. He later incorporated these statistics in his performances. Mitchell (1907:73) writes:

> Among his other usual feats are the repetition, either forwards or backwards, of a memorized number of 256 figures, the squaring of numbers up

to 4 figures, and the cubing of numbers up to 3 figures, finding the 5th powers of 2-figure numbers, and, conversely, extracting the 5th root of any number of 10 figures or less, the cube root of any 9-figure number, and the square root of any number of 7 figures or less, whether the given number is a perfect power or not.

Mitchell does not, however, say how square roots of nonperfect powers were calculated; such roots are irrational (that is, nonrecurring decimals). Probably Zaneboni gave the integral portion of the root plus a remainder.

(For a comparison of Zaneboni's calculating speed with that of other calculators, see chapter 8.)

Louis Fleury (1893–?)

Fleury is a most peculiar case. According to Tocquet (n.d.: 22–28) he was born blind and was abandoned by his parents at a year and a half. He was then placed with a farm family. At ten he could hardly walk and was incapable of washing or dressing himself. Sent to the school for the blind at Arras, he found arithmetic especially difficult; he was unable to learn to divide at all. When he was 15, it was decided that he could not be educated, and he was placed in an institution.

After he was there some two months, the man next to him at dinner had an epileptic attack; blind and unable to fathom what was happening, Fleury was badly shaken.

In order to put the horror from his mind, Fleury decided to concentrate on the most difficult thing he knew—arithmetic. He found that calculation, even division, came easily to him now, and soon it became a diversion to which he devoted most of his attention.

Fleury developed an interest in learning in general, and tried to get the welfare people to allow him to attend school again. To this they would not accede, and Fleury, desperate, feigned insanity simply to escape his depressing surroundings. He was sent to a mental hospital at Armentières, where his ability for mental calculation was discovered.

After he left the hospital at 21 he gave demonstrations of mental calculation, first in France and later in England and the United States.

On his return to France in 1927 he underwent tests conducted by Dr. Osty and his colleagues at the International Psychical Institute. The problems were read to Fleury at a rapid rate, and as soon as one was answered another was posed. The problems included (Tocquet n.d.:24): $553 \times 88 = 48{,}664$ (2 sec.); $649 \times 367 = 238{,}183$ (10 sec.); $5{,}364 \div 43 = 124$ remainder 32 (4 sec.); $20{,}700 \div 48 = 431$ remainder 12 (3 sec.); $5{,}287^2 = 27{,}952{,}369$ (10 sec.); $94^4 = 78{,}074{,}896$ (15 sec.); $2^{20} = 1{,}048{,}576$ (20 sec.); $2^{30} = 1{,}073{,}741{,}824$ (40 sec.); $\sqrt{13{,}250} = 115$ remainder 25 (4 sec.); $\sqrt{222{,}796} = 472$ remainder 12 (12 sec.): $\sqrt[3]{456{,}609} = 77$ remainder 76 (13 sec.); $\sqrt[5]{1{,}935{,}752{,}415} = 72$ remainder 834,783 (3 min., 10 sec.).

Fleury was asked for the values of x and y in $x^3 + y = 707{,}353{,}209$, where x and y are integers and y has four digits. In 28 seconds he found $891^3 + 5{,}238$. In a second such problem he was given 211,717,440 and came up with $596^3 + 8{,}704$ in 25 seconds.

He was asked to express 6,137 as the sum of four squares. The first answer, given in 2 minutes 10 seconds, was $74^2 + 20^2 + 15^2 + 6^2$. The second answer was given 10 seconds later: $78^2 + 6^2 + 4^2 + 1^2$. A third answer was obtained after a minute and 20 seconds: $76^2 + 15^2 + 10^2 + 6^2$.

Fleury was also adept at supplying the day of the week for dates in either the Gregorian or Julian calendars.

Fleury was most remarkable in that he was a "tactile" calculator; that is, he felt under his fingers (in his imagination) the forms of numbers used by the blind. While calculating his fingers moved very rapidly (see chapter 1).

From Tocquet's account it appears that Fleury was not at all retarded, but for physical, and possibly emotional reasons, he was unable to develop intellectually until rather late. The fact that, at the age of 10, he was barely able to walk, and could not wash or dress himself, suggests motor or psychological difficulties. Since at a later date he feigned insanity to alter his circumstances, he was very likely capable of feigning retardation.

Srinivasa Ramanujan (1887–1920)

Ramanujan occupies a curious place in the history of mathematics. He was a largely self-taught genius who pursued his own mysterious pathways. He understood little of the work of others, reinventing vast areas of mathematics for himself. His knowledge of continued fractions, however, was superior to that of any of his contemporaries.

But his knowledge was very nearly equaled by his ignorance of many matters that were common knowledge to mathematicians in his field. He did not even have a very clear idea of what constituted a mathematical proof.

Aitken (1954:296) said: "Of noted mathematicians, not many have been rapid mental calculators: John Wallis, Euler, Gauss; possibly the Indian, Srinivasa Ramanujan, though perhaps he hardly came into the really rapid class."

This is the only reference I have come across regarding Ramanujan's ability as a mental calculator, but his approach to mathematics was certainly one that required enormous calculating skills.

A story about Ramanujan told by the great British mathematician G. H. Hardy shows that he shared the typical fascination of calculating prodigies for numerical properties (Newman 1956:375).

When Ramanujan lay ill in Putney, Hardy came to visit, and remarked that the number of his cab, 1729, seemed to him "rather dull." Ramanujan replied that 1729 was very interesting, for it was the smallest number that can be expressed as the sum of two cubes in two different ways $(12^3 + 1^3$ and $10^3 + 9^3)$.

Arumogam (1896–?)

Arumogam was a native of Ceylon (now Sri Lanka). His talent for calculation was discovered when he was 12. Arumogam's only language was his native Tamil, and so calculations for English speakers had to be carried out through an interpreter. This would provide an ideal opportunity for stalling, however, particularly if he understood English better than he let on.

Arumogam was named for the god Arumukan—"the six-faced one"—because he was born with an extra finger on each hand and an extra toe on each foot. This was also true of Zerah Colburn, and is an amazing coincidence, but it is unlikely that it could be anything more than a coincidence. Although Colburn's digital peculiarity had been in his family for generations (at least), none of his predecessors were reputed to be good calculators. Similarly, in Arumogam's case, Barlow reports (1952:54): "No ancestors of talent could be traced."

Arumogam said that his talent for calculation emerged at a major festival where he had gone to beg and worship. While sleeping at night on the temple grounds he was approached in a dream by an ascetic, who wrote something on his tongue. The next day he found that he could easily do the arithmetic involved in the shopkeepers' accounts, and he was soon hired by businesses for that purpose.

Barlow (1952:54–57) includes the following problems taken from the *Ceylon Morning Leader* for September 7, 1912. The problems were given to Arumogam at the monthly meeting of the Royal Asiatic Society at Colombo on September 5, 1912. The Educational Department of Ceylon made up the problems, and the President of the Royal Asiatic Society, Sir Hugh Clifford, Colonial Secretary, said that no effort had been spared in their preparation. The problems had to be explained to Arumogam in Tamil.

They were (Barlow 1952:55–56):

Add together 8,596,497,713,826 and 96,268,593.
  Multiply 1,001,001 by 100,100.
  Multiply 45,989 by 864,726.
  If 107 is multiplied by a certain number, it is increased by 2140. find the multiplier.
  Find the factors of (a) 28,413, (b) 89,712.
  In a division sum, the divisor is twenty times the quotient and five times the remainder. What is the dividend if the remainder is 76?
  If seventeen sovereigns form a column one inch high, how many would it take to represent a height of 3451 feet?
  The diameter of a sovereign being seven-eights of an inch, how many placed in contact would it require to stretch from London to Liverpool (196 miles)?
  Find the square root of 63,409,369.
  Find the cube root of 20,570,824.
  Find the fifth root of 69,343,957.
  Multiply (a) £84 17s. 6¼d. by 24: (b) £48 14s. 5¾d. by 7694.
  A wheel has a circumference of 3¼ yards. How many times will the wheel turn in travelling 26 miles?
  If a person sells 22 articles for the same money which he paid for 36, what does he gain per cent?
  Find the simple interest on £584 for 42 days at five per cent.
  At what rate per cent, simple interest, will a sum of money double itself in thirty years?
  What weight of water is there in a room flooded two inches deep, the room being 18 ft. 9 in. by 13 ft. 4 in. and a cubic foot of water weighing 62½ lb.?
  A square field has a plantation eleven yards wide running along all four sides within the boundary of the field; this plantation contains one acre. Find the area of the field.

Unfortunately, none of the answers to the problems are supplied, but Arumogam reportedly answered each in a few seconds, any delays attributed to the necessity of translation.

The following problem was posed by a member of the audience (Barlow 1952:56): "A Chetty gave as a treat to 173 persons, a bushel of rice each. Each bushel contained 3,431,272 grains, and the Chetty stipulated that 17% should be given to the temple. How many grains did the temple get?" This was supposedly answered in three seconds, but with the necessity of translating, such times must obviously be taken with a grain of salt.

For another problem solved by Arumogam and a consideration of his method, see chapter 11.

John von Neumann (1903–1957)

Von Neumann was one of the outstanding mathematicians of the twentieth century. His obituary by S. Ulam (1958:1) calls him "a universal intellect and a unique interpreter of mathematics, who could bring the latest (and develop latent) applications of its methods to bear on problems of physics, astronomy, biology, and the new technology." He is best known popularly for his work in the development of game theory and modern electronic computers. During the second world war von Neumann was among the scientists and mathematicians working at Los Alamos on the atomic bomb, to which he made numerous contributions.

I can find no information on the origin and development of von Neumann's ability for mental calculation. His obituary has only one brief reference to it (Ulam 1958:38–39):

> Von Neumann was very adept in performing dimensional estimates and algebraical and numerical computations in his head without using a pencil and paper. This ability, perhaps somewhat akin to the talent of playing chess blindfolded, often impressed physicists. My impression was that von Neumann did not visualize the physical objects under consideration but rather treated their properties as logical consequences of the fundamental physical assumptions; but he was able to play a deductive game with these astonishingly well!

In his book on the development of the atomic bomb, *Brighter Than a Thousand Suns,* Robert Jungk (1958) describes meetings between von Neumann, Enrico Fermi, Edward Teller, and Richard Feynman, all men of unquestionable genius. Whenever a computation was needed, von Neumann, Fermi, and Feynman would begin to calculate, each after his own fashion. Fermi juggled his slide rule, Feynman pounded a desk calculator, and von Neumann calculated in his head. According to one observer, von Neumann was usually the first to finish, and the results of the three independent calculations were remarkably close.

Mlle Osaka [2]

Mlle Osaka was the stage name of a Frenchwoman born a few miles from Bagnères. According to Tocquet (n.d.:23) she was retarded, neither walking nor talking until the age of 4½. But there may be some doubt as to her retardation, since Tocquet says that she went to school very little since she was so sickly. Possibly, ignorance was mistaken for retardation.

At 26 she could barely read and write, and her knowledge of arithmetic was confined to addition. She went to a performance by a calculator and concluded that she could duplicate what she saw.

While practicing, Mlle Osaka memorized many of the calculations she carried out on paper. Her ability to carry out mental calculations and to memorize numbers grew to the point that she could give performances.

She visualized numbers, and said that they appeared to her as though on a blackboard, and were clearer than the real ones.

Some of her calculations tested by Dr. Osty of the Psychical Institute included (Tocquet n.d.:30): 97^2 (instantly); 97^{10} (instantly—obviously, this was from memory); the sixth root of $402,420,747,482,776,576$ and the square root of the same number. Tocquet reports that these were given "at once and correctly." He does not, however, include her answers.

In the course of learning to calculate Mlle Osaka had done great masses of computations in raising numbers of one and two digits to powers as high as the tenth, and three-digit numbers up to the seventh or eight powers. Apparently she was able to call to mind not merely the results of these calculations but the steps leading to these results. While she

[2] Her date of birth is not given by Tocquet, but she did not begin calculating until age 26 and he refers to her as a "girl," so that possibly she was probably no more than 30 when his description was written. There is also no date of publication in the English translation of his book, but it appears from internal evidence to have been written in the early fifties. If all this complex speculation is correct, Mlle Osaka was born in the period 1920–1925.

could hardly have memorized all such powers for these numbers, her repertoire was apparently quite large.

In spite of her colossal memory for figures, not all the feats ascribed to her could be the result of memorization. If given the date of birth she could ("at once" according to Tocquet) give the number of days, hours, minutes, and seconds a person had lived, taking leap years into account. Even though such calculations can be considerably shortened by knowing, say, the number of days in the past 62 years, a certain amount of calculation, if only addition, is nevertheless required.

Tocquet (n.d.:30–31) described a demonstration by Mlle Osaka before a small audience. Twenty people were asked to write a number on a piece of paper. The pieces of paper were then mixed together, and then drawn one by one—the numbers written in sections on the blackboard in the order drawn. The numbers ranged from millions to nonillions. Tocquet does not indicate the total number of digits, but presumably it was in the range of two to three hundred. Mlle Osaka never saw the numbers, but, after one hearing, was able to repeat them forward or backward, or call off the numbers in any given section. Meanwhile she was called upon to calculate 27^2, 27^{10}, and 55^{10} (followed by all its powers in descending order); the second, third, fourth, and fifth powers of 221; the ages of various members of the audience in days, hours, minutes, and seconds; the product of $624,987 \times 2,358$. This multiplication required seven minutes. Tocquet (n.d.:31) remarks that she produced 48 digits "without apparent effort and without error." The 48 digits appear to refer to the original problem, the answer, and the intermediate stages (except for carries).

In spite of such interruptions she was able to repeat the original number in any order desired.

Oscar Verhaeghe (born 1926)

I have no information on the current circumstances of the Belgian calculator Oscar Verhaeghe, or whether he is still alive. Verhaeghe was apparently retarded—both Barlow (1952:66) and Tocquet (n.d.:35) have statements to the effect that, at the age of 17, he spoke like a 2-year-old.

Verhaeghe appears to have been completely incapable of explaining how his calculations were performed.

Some of the problems solved by Verhaeghe at Uccle on August 10,

1946 before a committee of mathematicians were (Barlow 1952:66–67): $4,777 \times 64 = 305,728$ (15 sec.); $689^3 = 327,082,769$ (6 sec.); $1,246^4 = 2,410,305,930,256$ (10 sec.); $2^{59} = 576,460,752,303,423,488$ (30 sec.); $\sqrt[6]{24,137,585} = 17$ remainder 16 (25 sec.); $888,888,888,888,888^2 = 790,123,456,790,121,876,543,209,876,544$; $9,999,999^5$ (40 sec.; the 35-digit answer is not given).

Barlow writes (1952:67):

> It is said that this young Belgian calculator, despite his great handicap, is physically by no means unattractive and of a jovial disposition. He is very timid, awkward, and somewhat fearful. His speech is very slow, jerky, and confused. With the utmost docility, he lends himself to whatever tests are desired, however long they may be, except at meal times!

Antoon van den Hurk (born about 1930)

Van den Hurk is a Dutch calculator briefly described in Life Magazine, ("Wizard," 1952:65.) He was at that time 21, and as a result of listening to "Pascal" (Wim Klein) on the radio he was encouraged to try mental calculation for himself.

According to *Life,* he could multiply two four-digit numbers in 30 seconds and memorize 35 phone numbers in five minutes.

Van den Hurk reportedly multiplied $6,341,082,426$ by $38,254,319,074$ ($= 242,573,790,398,737,993,524$) in his head in 21 minutes flat. He explained: "It's simple. . . . You just multiply $6,341,082,426$ by $38,000,000,000$ and remember that solution. Then you multiply $6,341,082,426$ by $254,000,000$, by $319,000$ and by 74. Add them up in your head and you have the answer."

R. H. Frost (born 1931)

R. H. Frost, of York, England, was featured in the *Guinness Book of World Records* (1978) for adding a column of one hundred digits in a time of 32.57 seconds. The following is excerpted from a letter to me from Mr. Frost (March 1979).

> I was born in India in 1931, and my parents are from Suffolk, England. My father was out in India opening an Austin Agency on behalf of the owners of the then Austin Motor Car Company, Sir Herbert Austin. My

entire education was carried out in India in a Government School in the Himalayas near Darjeeling. I passed all my examinations including the last and final one which entitled me to automatic entry to Cambridge University. During my schooling my parents thought it expedient to send me for private tuition in Mathematics and Latin. This was given me by an old Oxford Blue and this I feel was what gave me a good grounding in Mathematics.

When I left school I went into a workshop for a year to get some knowledge of Engineering before I joined the Tea Industry. I took up Tea Planting at the age of nineteen and all my eleven years in the Industry was spent on gardens in North Assam, India. For the first three years I was on the agricultural side of managing a small Estate with local labour, and in my last eight years I was managing a factory producing tea mainly for the U. K. Market.

During one of my furloughs I got married, and now we have four children (three girls and a boy), the eldest was married last year and is due to start a family herself in October this year.

Unfortunately I had to leave the Tea Industry as my mother was a semi-invalid in the U. K. and it was getting worse and more difficult to export currency due to the financial restrictions. I decided to return to the U. K. at the age of 30 and looked for employment in York, as my wife is a York girl and naturally she wanted to settle down near her parents.

During 1961 I joined Rowntree of York, a big Confectionery Manufacturer, at that time second in size to Cadbury's of Bournville. I started work in the Transport Department which controlled production output through a Depot system. I first did 2½ years as Assistant Depot Manager at Nottingham and then followed this for five years as Depot Manager at Edinburgh Depot. In 1968 I was called upon to set up a Group Stock Control system for handling over 300,000 tons of products with a range of over 350 varieties of product, the most popular of which is the chocolate biscuit line 'Kit Kat'. Since that time we linked up with Mackintosh & Sons and then became the biggest Confectionery Manufacturers in the U.K. I am still in the Stock Control Department in the capacity of Assistant Stock Control Manager. All our work is now computerised but I still avoid using calculators and other aids if I can carry out the work manually.

During my life I have been a voracious reader, reading very fast at an average of a page a minute. There are times that I have read a complete novel at one session. It is this speed of reading that helps me in my mental addition.

Recognition of this skill came about by chance. In the U.K. we have a long running T.V. series called "The Recordbreakers" compered by the Entertainer Roy Castle and assisted by the McWhirter Brothers (one brother has now been killed) who publish the *Guinness Book of Records*. On one of their programmes they featured a York citizen who was claiming a record for high speed addition and he claimed a speed of 20.80 secs. for mental addition of 50 digits. The McWhirter Brothers said on the programme that this would be accepted by them for inclusion in the next edition of their book.

One of my workmates, who knew of my prowess with high speed addition, gave me several trials from which I averaged around 14.00 secs. With this knowledge I challenged the claimant record holder and we had a "shoot out" at York University a few days later. There were two other contestants, so in all there were three men and a woman. The test was run by the Science Department at York University as they have an electronic digital timer down to hundredths of a second.

The contest was held in a large hall in the presence of about 200 students and the local Press. Each contestant had four attempts at adding fifty digits picked out at random by a computer. The best time achieved by any other contestant was just over 14 secs. I got four of my runs correct, three just over 13 secs. but my last attempt came down to 12.79 secs. Although this was a lot faster than any other of the contestants, I was still of the opinion that this time could still be beaten. However, the Professor of Physiology at the University came over to congratulate me and assured me that this time would be very hard to beat. At the rate of four numerals a second, he said this time was exceedingly fast and he put this down to having the two attributes in one person, the capability of being able to read at speed and also mentally concentrate and add numerals quickly.

Armed with Press cuttings, I submitted my time to the *Guinness Book of Records* thinking that this would be automatically accepted. They wrote back and told me to do the test again, this time under clinical conditions with 100 digits. I sought help from various sources, including the local Press, but no one was interested in setting up the test, and the only timer in York was at the University.

In 1976 my Boss became Chairman of the local 'Round Table' and arranged through various contacts to set up the test on my behalf providing I assisted them with a local charity. They sold a number of tickets to the public asking them to guess my eventual accepted time in 100ths of a second. The exercise was a success as we raised nearly £400 for 'Age Concern' which enabled quite a number of elderly people to go on a week's holiday to the local seaside resort.

The test was run again at York University with five attempts at 100 digits: The computer print-out was not very distinct, in fact a few months later I had to use glasses for reading for the very first time. This must have slowed me down somewhat as I genuinely felt that I could have come below 30 secs. However, my time of 32.57 secs. was accepted by *Guinness Book of Records* and as it has been featured in two editions, I can only surmise that it is a very good time. I am eager to have another go at this record (this time with glasses) but as you are now aware it is very difficult to set up.

However, if my time is beaten at any future date, I feel sure that I can get Sponsors to set up another test.

Sheng Ke Gon (born 1969)

In October 1980 United Press International carried a story about an 11-year-old farm boy from the People's Republic of China who is nick-named "the living computer." The story says that the boy correctly re-sponded to 600 problems posed to him in 10 recent demonstrations.

The only sample problem, as reported in the Seattle *Post-Intelligencer* for October 23, 1980, is impossible to interpret with certainty. While successfully competing against three accountants with compact calcula-tors Sheng correctly answered the problem, "How much is one multi-plied by the square of 20 divided by the root of 10,000 and minus 0.25" Unfortunately, we are not told which root of 10,000, but only the square root (100) and the fourth root (10) are integers. If either of these is intended, the problem is perfectly trivial. For example, the square of 20 is 400 times 1 is 400, divided by the square root of 10,000 (100) is 4, less 0.25 is 3.75. This certainly requires no calculating prodigy.

Sheng reportedly displayed great intelligence from an early age, but does not care for talking.

These then are the great mental calculators, or rather those who have achieved sufficient fame to come to my attention. No doubt many others have lived and died in obscurity.

Even before electronic computers became commonplace, Aitken sug-gested that machines might mean the end of calculating prodigies (1954:303): "Mental calculators, then, may, like the Tasmanian . . . be doomed to extinction."

I hope that Aitken was wrong and this book may play some role in stimulating interest in mental calculation. As Wim Klein concluded in his Foreword: "Perhaps then a new calculating prodigy will be discovered."

Appendix

——

George Parker Bidder on Compound Interest

This leads me to the subject of Compound Interest, relative to which I am afraid I shall find some difficulty in making myself understood as clearly as I should desire. I am especially anxious as to this rule, because if I succeed in explaining it satisfactorily, you will comprehend the mode of reasoning by which I investigated rules and ascertained some of the properties of numbers, and more particularly of a series of numbers. I need not tell you that calculating Compound Interest, without logarithms, is a matter involving immense labour, especially if it extends over a great number of years. It is raising a fractional number to a high power, which thus becomes an expanded series and no terms can be neglected, because the ultimate value of any one term cannot be foreseen. When called upon to perform sums in Compound Interest, I found them such a source of labour and of strain upon the memory, that I was induced to seek for some means of relieving it from the pressure, and in doing this, I adopted a mode of reasoning which I will try to explain; as from it you will perceive the tentative process, by which I arrived at all the rules I adopted in arithmetic.

I will assume that I was called upon to calculate the compound interest for £100 at 5 per cent. for 14 years. In the ordinary way, without the use of logarithms, you would begin thus,—

$$£100 \times (1.05) \times (1.05) \times \&c. \ldots 14 \text{ times.}$$

Now $1.05 \times 1.05 = 1.1025$, and $1.1025 \times 1.05 = 1.57625$; which process, carried only a very little further, will involve so many figures, as to be quite impracticable for the memory.

From Bidder 1856:267–72.

Now the way in which I proceeded was this; I considered that if £100 was put out at simple interest for 14 years it would produce 14 × £5 = £70. I then regarded each £5 put out at simple interest; thus the first £5 will produce 5s. per annum, but as it commences at the end of the first year it will be for a period of 13 years instead of 14 years. In the second year the £100 gives birth to a second £5 which carries simple interest of 5s. per annum for 12 years. Similarly the third £5 carries interest for 11 years, and so on, the number of years regularly diminishing, hence the total amount of interest at 5s. per annum is expressed by a series—

$$5s. \times \{13 + 12 + 11 + 10 + 9 + 8 + 7 + 6 + 5 + 4 + 3 + 2 + 1\}$$

I had therefore presented to me the problem to sum that series.

It so happened that before I was called upon to deal with compound interest, I was asked the well-known question, "If a man pick up 100 stones a yard apart, picking them up separately and putting them in a basket, how far must he travel?" That question set my mind thinking over the series which is embodied in its solution, and the method I adopted for obtaining the summation is as follows:—Writing the series the other way we have $1 + 2 + 3 + 4 + 5 + 6 + 7 + 8 + 9 + 10 + 11 + 12 + 13$; now add the successive terms together, one after another $1 = 1$, $1 + 2 = 3$, $1 + 2 + 3 = 6$, $1 + 2 + 3 + 4 = 10$, and so on, and write them, so as to form another series, viz., 1, 3, 6, 10, 15, &c.

Divide each of these terms by the numbers representing their order as

	1st	2nd	3rd	4th	5th	&c.
viz.	$\frac{1}{1}$	$\frac{3}{2}$	$\frac{6}{3}$	$\frac{10}{4}$	$\frac{15}{5}$	&c.
or	1	1½	2	2½	3	&c.

in which it will be seen, that these quotients form a regular progression, each term of which is half an unit more than half the number expressing the position of the term in the series; for example, in the 4th term, the corresponding quotient is 2½ or ½ more than $^4/_2$ and so on; hence if 13 be the number of terms (as in the case under consideration) we obtain the sum of 13 terms =

$$13 \times \left(\frac{13}{2} + \frac{1}{2} \right) = \frac{13 \times 14^*}{2}$$

---

* Hence if n be the number of terms, we have the sum of n terms $= n(n + 1)/2$ for the general formula.

and therefore the interest =

$$\frac{13 \times 14}{2} \times 5s. = £22 \; 15s. \; 0d.$$

This added to the £70 before mentioned, gives a total of £92 15s. 0d.

The next stage of the proceeding was to consider each 5s. as put out at simple interest, namely 3d. per annum.

Now the first 5s. (the interest upon the first £5) accrues in the second year, and therefore will carry simple interest for 12 years. The second year's simple interest of 5s. arising out of the first £5 will similarly run for 11 years and so on.

Thus it appears that the calculation of the simple interest upon 5s., the interest upon the first £5, is similar to that of the 5s. the interest upon the first £5, but having one year less to run, namely, 12 instead of 13 years; hence it is expressed by the formula

$$\frac{n(n+1)}{2} \times 3d.$$

In the same way the simple interest upon the 5s.,—the interest upon the second £5,—is the result of the summation of a series like the last, except that it was for 11 years; and so of the rest.

Therefore the series expressing the total amount of interest upon all the 5s. has its terms made up of the sums of corresponding terms of the former series, or $1 + 3 + 6 + 10 + 15 + 21$, &c., giving rise to 1, 4, 10, 20, 35, &c., in which we have $1 = 1$, $1 + 3 = 4$, $1 + 3 + 6 = 10$, $1 + 3 + 6 + 10 = 20$, and so on.

Now to sum this series, divide each term by the corresponding term in the previous series thus—

$$\frac{1}{1} \quad \frac{4}{3} \quad \frac{10}{6} \quad \frac{20}{10} \quad \frac{35}{15} \quad \frac{56}{21}$$

giving quotients

$$1 \quad 1\tfrac{1}{3} \quad 1\tfrac{2}{3} \quad 2 \quad 2\tfrac{1}{3} \quad 2\tfrac{2}{3}$$

or

$$\frac{3}{3} \quad \frac{4}{3} \quad \frac{5}{3} \quad \frac{6}{3} \quad \frac{7}{3} \quad \frac{8}{3}$$

which, as in the former case, are in regular progression, and we observe that in any term, the fifth for example,

$$35 = 15 \times 2\tfrac{1}{3}$$
$$= 15 \times \frac{7}{3} = 15 \times \frac{5+2}{3}$$

or the numerator of the fractional multiplier, is the number of the term of the series $+2$, and so of the rest.

But the 15 is, as we have seen, made up of the summation of 5 terms of the previous series $(1+2+3, \&c.)$ and hence may be represented by

$$15 = \frac{5 \times (5+1)}{2},$$

and the 35 by

$$35 = \frac{5 \times (5+1) \times (5+2)}{2 \qquad 3}.$$

Now observe, this interest accrued in the second year, hence to refer the terms of the last series to the principal epoch, whence the 14 years is estimated, we have only to put $7-2$ for 5 and we obtain

$$35 = \frac{(7-2)}{3} \frac{(7-1)}{2} 7$$
$$= \frac{7 \times (7-1) \times (7-2)}{1 \qquad 2 \qquad 3}$$

and, therefore, if $a =$ number of years $= 14$, in this case we get the expression

$$\frac{a(a-1)\,(a-2)}{1 \quad 2 \quad 3} \times 3d.,$$

which put in figures gives

$$\frac{14 \times 13 \times 12}{1 \quad 2 \quad 3} \times 3d. = \text{£4 11}s.\ 0d.,$$

and this added to the previous sum of £92 15s. 0d. produces £97 6s. 0d.

I then considered each 3d. put out at simple interest, and pursuing the same mode of investigation, I found the summation of the series represented by

$$\frac{a(a-1)}{1}\frac{(a-2)}{2}\frac{(a-3)}{3}\frac{(a-3)}{4},$$

and the interest to be

$$\frac{a(a-1)}{1}\frac{(a-2)}{2}\frac{(a-3)}{3}\frac{(a-3)}{4} \times \frac{3d.}{20} = 12s.\ 6d.;$$

this added to £97 6s. 0d. gives £97 18s. 6d.

Similarly the next interest is expressed by the formula

$$\frac{a(a-1)}{1}\frac{(a-2)}{2}\frac{(a-3)}{3}\frac{(a-4)}{4}\frac{(a-4)}{5} \times \frac{3d.}{20 \times 20} = 1s.\ 3d.,$$

which added gives £97 19s. 9d., and the next

$$\frac{a(a-1)}{1}\frac{(a-2)}{2}\frac{(a-3)}{3}\frac{(a-4)}{4}\frac{(a-5)}{5}\frac{(a-5)}{6} \times \frac{3d.}{20 \times 20 \times 20} =$$

$$\frac{14 \times 13 \times 12 \times 11 \times 10 \times 9}{1 \quad 2 \quad 3 \quad 4 \quad 5 \quad 6} \times \frac{3d.}{20^3} = 1d.,$$

which added gives £97 19s. 10d.

Perceiving how rapidly the series converged, and that the remaining terms could not possibly amount to one farthing, the process was stopped and the result stated as above, £97 19s. 10d., which instead of requiring fourteen operations was arrived at in five, and these of much easier computation than may probably appear from the description just given.

Before quitting this part of the subject I will venture to express the total compound interest of any sum of money algebraically, in another more simple form.

Let P represent the principal sum,
    r the rate of interest (= $^1/_{20}$, if 5 per cent., for example),
    n the number of years.
Then compound interest =

$$P \times \left\{ nr + \frac{n(n-1)}{1 \quad 2} r^2 + \frac{n(n-1)\ (n-2)}{1 \quad 2 \quad 3} r^3 + \frac{n(n-1)\ (n-2)\ (n-3)}{1 \quad 2 \quad 3 \quad 4} r^4 + \&c. \right.$$

$$\left. + \frac{n(n-1)(n-2)\ \ldots\ (n-(n-1))}{1 \quad 2 \quad 3 \quad \ldots \quad n} r^n \right\},$$

and the amount, or interest and principal together,

$$= P \times \left\{ 1 + nr + \frac{n(n-1)}{1 \quad 2} r^2 + \&c. \ \ldots \ + \right.$$

$$\left. \frac{n(n-1)\ (n-2)\ \ldots\ (n-(n-1))}{1 \quad 2 \quad 3 \quad \ldots \quad n} r^n \right\},$$

which is the expansion, by the binomial theorem, of the expression $P(1 + r)^n$, which is the form in which the problem is presented for solution by logarithms, or by successive involution.

I do not in any way claim the discovery of a new principle; but I have endeavoured to show by what kind of process my mind, at a very early age, and when wholly unacquainted with symbolical representation and algebraic expedients, analysed the law connecting these series and rendered them available for computation.

As an example of how this was carried out mentally, I will take £100 as put out at 2 per cent. for 35 years. Then

the first term $= Pnr = \dfrac{100 \times 35}{50} \qquad = £70;$

the second $\qquad = \dfrac{70 \times 34}{2 \times 50} \qquad = $ £23 16s. 0d., which added to the foregoing gives £93 16s. 0d.;

the third $\qquad = \dfrac{£23\ 16s. \times 33}{3 \times 50} \qquad = $ £5 4s. 8½d., giving £99 0s. 8½ d.;

the fourth $\qquad = \dfrac{£5\ 4s.\ 8½d. \times 32}{4 \times 50} = $ 16s. 9d., giving £99 17s. 5½ d.;

the fifth $\qquad = \dfrac{16s.\ 9d. \times 31}{5 \times 50} \qquad = $ 2s. 1d., giving £99 19s. 6½d.;

the sixth $\qquad = \dfrac{2s.\ 1d. \times 30}{6 \times 50} \qquad = $ 2½d., giving £99 19s. 9d.;

the seventh $\qquad = \dfrac{2½d. \times 29}{7 \times 50} \qquad = $ ¼d., giving £99 19s. 9¼d.;

which of course is the last, the remaining terms obviously giving very small fractions.

Mentally, however, this would not occupy me more than a minute, so that the result is arrived at almost as quickly as by logarithms.

BIBLIOGRAPHY

Aarts, Wim. 1974. "Wereldkampioen Worteltrekken op de NOT 1974." *Teachware* (September), pp. 8–13. The Hague.

Aitken, A. C. 1954. "The Art of Mental Calculation; with Demonstrations." *Transactions of the Society of Engineers* 44:295–309. London.

Aitken, A. C. 1963. *Gallipoli to the Somme.* London: Oxford University Press.

Annual Register. 1812. Pp. 507–12 (concerns Colburn).

Appleton's Cyclopaedia. 1888. No. 5, p. 366 (concerns Safford).

Arago, François. 1837. *Comptes rendus hebdomadaires des séances de l'Académie des Sciences.* 4:978–79 (concerns Mangiamele).

Ashbrook, J. 1976. "Astronomical Scrapbook, Computers: Electronic and Human." *Sky and Telescope* (November), pp. 345–46.

Ashbrook, J. 1977. "Astronomical Scrapbook, Johann Dase and Some Other Mental Calculators." *Sky and Telescope* (November), p. 365.

Ball, W.W.R. 1956. "Calculating Prodigies." In J. R. Newman, ed., *The World of Mathematics* 1:467–87. New York: Simon and Schuster.

Ball, W.W.R. and H.S.M.C. Coxeter. 1974. "Calculating Prodigies." In *Mathematical Recreations and Essays,* ch. 13. Toronto: University of Toronto Press. (The first edition, by Ball alone, appeared in 1892; for the original version of this chapter, see Ball 1956).

Barlow, Fred. 1952. *Mental Prodigies.* New York: Philosophical Library.

Bartlett, Kay. 1982. "Carnegie-Mellon Student's Magic with Mathematics Is No Cheap Trick." *Roanoke Times and World-News* (May 16).

Bernstein, J. 1963. *The Analytical Engine.* New York: Random House.

Bidder, George Parker. 1856. "On Mental Calculation." *Minutes of Proceedings, Institution of Civil Engineers* (1855–56), 15:251–80.

Bidder, G. P., Jr. 1878. Letter to the *Spectator* (December 28), pp. 1634–35.

Binet, Alfred. 1894. *Psychologie des grands calculateurs et joueurs d'échecs.* Paris: Hachette.

Binet, Alfred. 1899. *The Psychology of Reasoning,* tr. by A. G. Whyte. Chicago: Open Court Publishing.

Bloomfield, Leonard. 1933. *Language.* New York: Holt.

Bousfield, W. A. and H. Barry. 1933. "The Visual Imagery of a Lightning Calculator." *American Journal of Psychology* 45:353–58 (concerns Finkelstein).

Bowden, B. V., ed. 1953. *Faster than Thought,* pp. 311–16. London: Sir Isaac Pitman & Sons.

Brock, Paul. 1980. "The Riddle of Human Computers." *Creative Computing* (August), pp. 54–55.

Bruce, H. A. 1912. "Lightning Calculators." *McClure's Magazine* 39:586–96.

Bryan, W. L. and E. H. Lindley. 1941. *On the Psychology of Learning a Life Occupation.* Science Series, no. 11. Bloomington: Indiana University.

Burton, D. M. 1976. *Elementary Number Theory.* Boston: Allyn and Bacon.

"Calculating Boys." 1878. *Spectator* (September 28), pp. 1208–9.

Cauchy, A. 1845. "Rapport sur la singulière aptitude d'un enfant de six ans et demi pour le calcul." In *Comptes rendus des séances de l'Académie des Sciences* 20:1629 (concerns Prolongeau).

Cauchy, A. 1885. "Rapport sur les procédés de calcul imaginés et mis en practique par un jeune pâtre de la Touraine." In *Oeuvres complètes d'Augustin Cauchy* 5:493–99; reprinted from *Comptes rendus hebdomadaires de séances de l'Académie des Sciences* 6:952–57 (concerns Mondeux).

Chase, W. G. and K. A. Ericsson. 1982. "Skill and Working Memory." Forthcoming in *The Psychology of Learning and Motivation,* vol. 16. New York: Academic Press.

Chambers's Edinburgh Journal. 1847. (July–December), 8:265–67 (concerns Safford).

Chomsky, N. 1957. *Syntactic Structures.* Hague: Mouton.

Chomsky, N. 1965. *Aspects of the Theory of Syntax.* Cambridge, Mass.: MIT Press.

Colburn, Zerah. 1833. *A Memoir of Zerah Colburn: Written by Himself.* Springfield: G. and C. Merriam.

Columbian Centinel. 1790. (December 29), vol. 14 (obituary of Thomas Fuller).

Comptes rendus hebdomadaires des séances de l'Académie des Sciences. 1852. 34:37 (concerns Grandmange).

Concise Dictionary of American Biography. 1964. P. 903 (concerns Safford).

Crelle: Journal für die reine und angewandte Mathematik. 1844. 27:198 (concerns Dase).

Critchley, M. 1953. *The Parietal Lobes.* London: Arnold.

Crockett, D. B. 1972. "More on Conjunction Reduction." *Papers from the Eighth Regional Meeting,* Chicago Linguistic Society, Chicago, Ill., pp. 52–61.

Dase, Z. 1849. "Dase (Johann Martin Zacharias)." In *Lexicon der hamburgischen Schriftsteller,* comp. by Hans Schröder, p. 637.

Dase, Z. 1862. *Factoren-Tafeln.* Vol. 1. Hamburg (the preface contains a letter from Gauss regarding Dase's calculating skill).

" 'De Flesh' and 'De Steel'." 1977. *The Dallas Morning News,* February 6; editorial page (concerns Devi).

"De handel en wandel van Willie Wortel!" 1975. *Teachware* (July), p. 1318. The Hague (concerns Klein).

Devi, Shakuntala. 1977. *The World of Homosexuals.* New York: Advent Books.

Devi, Shakuntala. 1978a. *Figuring: The Joy of Numbers.* New York: Harper and Row.

Devi, Shakuntala. 1978b. *Mathematical Merry-Go-Round.* New York: Plenum Press.

Dimond, S. J. and J. G. Beaumont. 1972. "A Right Hemisphere Basis for Calculation in the Human Brain." *Psychonomic Science* 26:137–38.

Dimond, S. J. and J. G. Beaumont. 1974. "Experimental Studies of Hemisphere Function in the Human Brain." In S. J. Dimond and J. G. Beaumont, eds., *Hemisphere Function in the Human Brain.* New York: Halsted Press.

Dudgeon, H. W. and H. E. Hurst. 1934. "Arithmetical Prodigy in Egypt." *Nature* 133:578–79.

Elliot, J. 1878. "Letters to the Editor." *The Spectator* (December 28), pp. 1634.

Erdös, P. 1970. "Child Prodigies." Paper presented at the Third CSMP International Conference of the Teaching of Algebra at the Pre-college Level, November 21–27.

"An Explanation of Arithmetical Precocity." 1908. *Scientific American Supplement* (July), 66:27.

Fayet, G., J. Chazy, and J. Pérès. 1945. "Le calculateur mental Maurice Dagbert." *Comptes rendus hebdomadaires des séances de l'Académie des Sciences* (April 25), 220:37–38.

Frege, G. 1884. (English trans. 1968.) *The Foundations of Arithmetic.* Evanston, Ill.: Northwestern University Press.

Gardner, Martin. 1975. *Mathematical Carnival.* New York: Alfred A. Knopf.

Gauss, K. F. and H. C. Schumacher, 1861. *Briefwechsel zwischen Gauss und Schumacher.* Altona, Germany.

Gödel, Kurt. 1931. (English trans. 1962.) *On Formally Undecidable Propositions of Principia Mathematica and Related Systems.* Edinburgh: Oliver and Boyd.

Gradenwitz, A. 1907. "A Remarkable Arithmetician." *Scientific American Supplement* (August), 64:93.

Guicciardi, G. and G. C. Ferrari. 1897. "Il Calcolatore Mentale 'Zaneboni'." *Rivista sperimentale di Freniatria* 23:407–29.

Guinness Book of World Records. Various eds. New York: Sterling, Bantam Books (see "Human Calculation").

Hamblin, D. J. 1966. "They are 'Idiot Savants'—Wizards of the Calendar." *Life* (March 18), 60:106–8.

Hoffman, A. 1978. "Visitor to UCR Proves That as a Figger Filbert, He's Number 1." *The Enterprise,* October 27. Riverside, Calif. (concerns Marathe).

Hofstadter, Douglas R. 1979. *Gödel, Escher, Bach: An Eternal Golden Braid.* New York: Basic Books.

Holliday, T. 1751. "Account of Jedediah Buxton." *Gentlemen's Magazine* 21:347–49.

Holliday, T. 1753. "Instances of a Surprising Memory." *Gentlemen's Magazine* 23:557 (concerns Buxton).

Horwitz, W. A., C. Kestenbaum, E. Person, and L. Jarvik. 1965. "Identical Twin—'Idiot Savants'—Calendar Calculators." *American Journal of Psychiatry* 121:1075–79.

Hunter, I. M. L. 1962. "An Exceptional Talent for Calculative Thinking." *British Journal of Psychology* 53:243–580 (concerns Aitken).

Hunter, I. M. L. 1968. "Mental Calculation." In P. C. Wason and P. N. Johnson-Laird, eds., *Thinking and Reasoning,* pp. 341–51. Middlesex, Eng.: Penguin Books (concerns Aitken). This is an excerpt from the original English version of "Kopfrechnen und Kopfrechner," *Bild der Wissenschaft* (April 1966), pp. 296–303.

ICE. 1878–79. "Memoirs of Deceased Members." *Minutes of Proceedings, Institution of Civil Engineers,* vol. 42, part 3, pp. 294–317 (obituary of George Parker Bidder).

Jacoby, E. 1853. *Caractères de divisibilité des nombres par des valeurs donn'es de 1 a 50.* Paris.

Jacoby, E. 1860. *La Clé de l'arithmétique.* Paris.

Jacoby, E. n.d. *Vie de Henri Mondeux.* Paris.

Jakobsson, Stig. 1944. "Report on Two Prodigy Mental Arithmeticians." *Acta Medica Scandinavica* 119:180–91.

Jungk, R. 1959. *Brighter Than a Thousand Suns.* New York: Harcourt Brace.

Katz, J. K. and J. A. Fodor. 1963. "The Structure of a Semantic Theory." *Language* 39:170–210.

Kidson, H. P. 1968. "Alexander Craig Aitken, 1895–1967." *Comment—A New Zealand Quarterly Review* (April), no. 34. pp. 12–19.

Kidson, H. P. 1973. "New Zealand's Greatest Mathematician." *The New Zealand Mathematics Magazine* (November), 10:129–33.

Lenneberg, E. H. 1971. "Of Language Knowledge, Apes, and Brains." *Journal of Psycholinguistic Research* 1:1–29.

"The Life of Jedediah Buxton." 1754. *Gentlemen's Magazine* 24:251–52.

MacNeven. 1811. "An Account of Zerah Colburn, the Wonderful Calculator." *The New-York Medical and Philosophical Journal.* New York: T. & J. Swords.

Menninger, K. 1964. *Calculator's Cunning.* New York: Basic Books.

Miller, J. C. P. 1968. "A. C. Aitken's Work in Numerical Analysis." *Proceedings of the Edinburgh Mathematical Society* (December), pp. 158–62.

Mitchell, F. D. 1907. "Mathematical Prodigies." *American Journal of Psychology* 18:61–143.

Müller, G. E. 1911. *Zur Analyse der Gedächtnistätigkeit und des Vorstellungsverlaufes.* Leipzig: Johann Ambrosius Barth (concerns Rückle).

Myers, F. W. H. 1913. *Human Personality.* London: Longmans, Green.

"A Negro Mathematical Genius." 1913. *The Literary Digest* (April 26), 46:971–72.

Newman, J. R. 1956. "Srinivasa Ramanujan." *The World of Mathematics,* pp. 368–76. New York: Simon and Schuster.

The New Yorker. 1979. (October 1), pp. 28–29 (concerns Klein).

Nouvelle biographie général. 1865. Paris: Firmin Didot Frères (entry for Mondeux).

"Numbers Game." 1952. *Time* (July 14), 60:49 (concerns Devi).

Osmond, C. M. 1879. Letter to the *Spectator* (January 25), 52:111–12 (concerns Bidder).

People Weekly. 1976. (September 27), pp. 29–30 (concerns Klein).

Peters, S. P. and R. W. Ritchie. 1971. "On Restricting the Base of Transformational Grammars." *Information and Control* 18:483–501.

Peters, S. P. and R. W. Ritchie. 1973. "On the Generative Power of Transformational Grammars." *Information Sciences* 6:49–83.

Pole, W. 1890–91. "Mental Calculation. A Reminiscence of the late Mr. G. P. Bidder, Past-President." *Minutes of Proceedings, Institution of Civil Engineers* 103:250–56. London.

Preyer, W. 1886. "Counting Unconsciously." *Popular Science Monthly* 39:221–26.

Prime, S. I. 1875. *Life of S. B. Morse.* New York: Appleton.

Proceedings of the Edinburgh Mathematical Society. 1968. (December) vol. 16, ser. 2, pt. 2, pp. 151–62 (obituary of Alexander Craig Aitken).

Proctor, R. A. 1875. "On Some Strange Mental Feats." *The Cornhill Magazine,* vol. 32. London.

Proctor, R. A. 1879. "Calculating Boys." *Belgravia* 38:450–70.

Regnault, J. 1952. *Les calculateurs prodiges.* Paris: Payot.

Rimland, B. 1978. "Inside the Mind of the Autistic Savant." *Psychology Today* (August) 12(3):68–80.

Robertson, F. 1951. "Super Quiz Kids of Math." *Science Digest* (June), 29:55–58.

Rush. 1789. *American Museum* 5:62–63. Philadelphia (concerns Fuller).

Saxe, George. 1751. "Jedediah Buxton, a Surprising Arithmetician." *Gentleman's Magazine* 21:61–62.

Schechter, Bruce, 1981. "The Fine Art of Calculating." *Discover* (October), pp. 34–38.

Schreiner, Samuel, Jr. 1976. "Meet the Human Computer," *Reader's Digest* (November) pp. 133–38. European English-language ed. (concerns Klein).

Scripture, E. W. 1891. "Arithmetical Prodigies." *American Journal of Psychology* 4:1–59.

Seidenberg, A. 1960. *The Diffusion of Counting Practices.* Berkeley and Los Angeles: University of California Press.

Sethi, P. 1978. "The Human Computer." *The Times of India,* February 4. Bombay (concerns Devi).

Smith, C. S. 1969. "Ambiguous Sentences with *And.*" In D. A. Reibel and S. A. Schane, eds., *Modern Studies in English*. Englewood Cliffs, N.J.: Prentice-Hall.

Smith, L. A. 1954. "Number Wizards Baffle Science." *Science Digest* (May), pp. 13–16.

Smith, Nancy. 1977. "Woman's Math Sets World Record." *The Dallas Morning News*, January 26 (concerns Devi).

Smith, W. G. 1914. "Notes on the Special Development of Calculating Ability." In E. M. Horsburgh, ed., *Handbook of the Exhibition of Napier Relics and of Books, Instruments, and Devices for Facilitating Calculation*, pp. 60–68. Edinburgh: Royal Society of Edinburgh.

Sperry, R. W. 1968. "Mental Unity Following Surgical Disconnection of the Cerebral Hemispheres." *The Harvey Lecture Series* 62:293–323.

Stockwell, R. P., P. Schacter, and B. H. Partee. 1973. *The Major Syntactic Structures of English*. New York: Holt, Rinehart, and Winston.

Stokvis, B. 1949. "A Medico-Psychological Account, Followed by a Demonstration of a Case of Supernormal Aptitude." In I. C. van Houte and B. Stokvis, eds., *Proceedings of the Second International Congress on Orthopedagogics*. Amsterdam: Systemen Keesing.

"Story of a Wonderful Boy Mathematician." 1871. *Every Saturday* (June – December), 9:118 (concerns Mondeux).

Tee, Garry J. 1979. "Alexander Aitken: Master Mathematician." *New Zealand Listener* (January 6), pp. 14–15.

Tee, Garry J. 1981. "Two New Zealand Mathematicians." In John N. Crossley, ed., *First Australian Conference on the History of Mathematics*. Clayton, Aust.: Monash University.

Tocquet, R. n.d. *The Magic of Numbers*, tr. by Denis Weaver. New York: A. S. Barnes.

Turing, A. M. 1936. "On Computable Numbers, with an Application to the Entscheidungsproblem." *Proceedings of the London Mathematical Society* (November), vol. 42, ser. 2, pt. 4, pp. 230–65.

Ulam, S. 1958. "John von Neumann 1903–1957." *Bulletin of the American Mathematical Society* (May), vol. 64, no. 3, pt. 2 (whole no. 654).

Webster, Bayard. 1976. "She Does Cube Roots in Her Head." *The New York Times*, November 10 (concerns Devi).

Weinland, J. D. 1948. "Memory of Salo Finkelstein," *Journal of General Psychology* 39:243–57.

Weinland, J. D. and W. S. Schlauch. 1937. "Examination of the Computing Ability of Mr. Salo Finkelstein." *Journal of Experimental Psychology* (October), 21:382–402.

Whately, E. J. 1866. *Life and Correspondence of Richard Whately, D. D.* London: Longmans, Green.

"Wizard of 0000s." 1952. *Life* (February 18), 32:65.

Wizel, A. 1904. "Ein Fall von phanomenalem Rechentalent bei einem Imbecillen," *Archiv fur Psychiatrie und Nervenkrankheiten* 38:122–55.

INDEX

First names were unavailable for some of the nineteenth-century figures in this book.